Praise for *Effective REST Services via .NET*

"The World Wide Web was probably designed in a lab, but to become the Web we know and use today it followed a number of routes, went over decisional crossroads, and zigzagged according to architects' inspiration and users' demand. At some point, SOAP seemed to be the way to go for implementing data remote operations. More recently, the community of architects and developers is shifting back toward its origins symbolized by the REST approach. As this book clearly explains, it is not a matter of SOAP versus REST. It is, instead, a matter of making the right architectural decisions timely and effectively for your application. This book is an excellent resource to see where REST does fit and where it doesn't. This book helps to understand the REST approach to services and applications in the context of a number of technologies and products such as WCF and ASP.NET MVC. The book excels in the guidance it provides to architects and support for decisions. As expected, it is not a cookbook. The rest about REST is up to you."

—*Dino Esposito, Senior Architect, IDesign Inc.*

"Kenn and Scott teach the principles of REST in a very interesting and engaging way. The book takes the reader through the principles of REST as originally described by Dr. Fielding and shows how Microsoft technologies can and should be used to embrace these core principles. (They even point out where Microsoft took things in some not-so-RESTful directions and offer their helpful knowledge and advice.) As a developer who frequently writes SOAP-based WCF solutions, I learned a great deal from this book about the REST perspective. Kenn and Scott wrap things up with an introduction and sample application using Azure, Microsoft's entry into Cloud Computing. The last chapter alone is worth the price of the book for any developer interested in service-oriented architectures, or who might dare to imagine a future Internet as an operating system."

—*Paul Mehner, Senior Consultant & Trainer WCF, WF, ASP.Net; Wintellect, LLC.*

"Effective REST Services via .NET provides a great overview of building RESTful services and clients for the .NET developer. Kenn and Scott do a nice job of balancing detailed examples showing the various Microsoft technologies available for building these services today, along with information about how IIS, ASP.NET, WCF and Azure Services work. If you are building services on the Microsoft platform and overwhelmed by all of the choices, this book will help you see how each toolkit can be leveraged. As a reader, I liked that the authors did not take a hard line on their approach and at several points indicated why they made certain design choices, inviting the reader to make different choices based on their own experiences and preferences."

—*Matt Milner, Independent .NET Consultant and Speaker*

"There is a lot be said for simple software architectures and implementations, and because of this REST services is gaining a lot of industry support. *Effective REST Services via .NET* will help you understand proper design principles and the code examples and discussions give you a great start in producing your own REST services. I have known Kenn and Scott for several years, and I'm glad to see their knowledge and experience encapsulated in this book."

—*Jeffrey Richter http://Wintellect.com*

"Kenn and Scott have done a fantastic job by blending their in-depth knowledge in HTTP protocol and various developers tools/technologies to give a nice experience to the readers on building RESTful services. The content of this book is targeted nicely for developers creating RESTful services as well as those consuming them."

—*Buddhike de Silva, Lead Engineer, Readify*

Effective REST Services via .NET

Microsoft .NET Development Series

John Montgomery, *Series Advisor*
Don Box, *Series Advisor*
Brad Abrams, *Series Advisor*

The award-winning Microsoft .NET Development Series was established in 2002 to provide professional developers with the most comprehensive and practical coverage of the latest .NET technologies. It is supported and developed by the leaders and experts of Microsoft development technologies, including Microsoft architects, MVPs, and leading industry luminaries. Books in this series provide a core resource of information and understanding every developer needs to write effective applications.

Titles in the Series

Brad Abrams, *.NET Framework Standard Library Annotated Reference Volume 1: Base Class Library and Extended Numerics Library*, 978-0-321-15489-7

Brad Abrams and Tamara Abrams, *.NET Framework Standard Library Annotated Reference, Volume 2: Networking Library, Reflection Library, and XML Library*, 978-0-321-19445-9

Chris Anderson, *Essential Windows Presentation Foundation (WPF)*, 978-0-321-37447-9

Bob Beauchemin and Dan Sullivan, *A Developer's Guide to SQL Server 2005*, 978-0-321-38218-4

Adam Calderon, Joel Rumerman, *Advanced ASP.NET AJAX Server Controls: For .NET Framework 3.5*, 978-0-321-51444-8

Eric Carter and Eric Lippert, *Visual Studio Tools for Office: Using C# with Excel, Word, Outlook, and InfoPath*, 978-0-321-33488-6

Eric Carter and Eric Lippert, *Visual Studio Tools for Office: Using Visual Basic 2005 with Excel, Word, Outlook, and InfoPath*, 978-0-321-41175-4

Steve Cook, Gareth Jones, Stuart Kent, Alan Cameron Wills, *Domain-Specific Development with Visual Studio DSL Tools*, 978-0-321-39820-8

Krzysztof Cwalina and Brad Abrams, *Framework Design Guidelines: Conventions, Idioms, and Patterns for Reusable .NET Libraries*, Second Edition, 978-0-321-54561-9

Joe Duffy, *Concurrent Programming on Windows*, 978-0-321-43482-1

Sam Guckenheimer and Juan J. Perez, *Software Engineering with Microsoft Visual Studio Team System*, 978-0-321-27872-2

Anders Hejlsberg, Mads Torgersen, Scott Wiltamuth, Peter Golde, *The C# Programming Language*, Third Edition, 978-0-321-56299-9

Alex Homer and Dave Sussman, *ASP.NET 2.0 Illustrated*, 978-0-321-41834-0

Joe Kaplan and Ryan Dunn, *The .NET Developer's Guide to Directory Services Programming*, 978-0-321-35017-6

Mark Michaelis, *Essential C# 3.0: For .NET Framework 3.5*, 978-0-321-53392-0

James S. Miller and Susann Ragsdale, *The Common Language Infrastructure Annotated Standard*, 978-0-321-15493-4

Christian Nagel, *Enterprise Services with the .NET Framework: Developing Distributed Business Solutions with .NET Enterprise Services*, 978-0-321-24673-8

Brian Noyes, *Data Binding with Windows Forms 2.0: Programming Smart Client Data Applications with .NET*, 978-0-321-26892-1

Brian Noyes, *Smart Client Deployment with ClickOnce: Deploying Windows Forms Applications with ClickOnce*, 978-0-321-19769-6

Fritz Onion with Keith Brown, *Essential ASP.NET 2.0*, 978-0-321-23770-5

Steve Resnick, Richard Crane, Chris Bowen, *Essential Windows Communication Foundation: For .NET Framework 3.5*, 978-0-321-44006-8

Scott Roberts and Hagen Green, *Designing Forms for Microsoft Office InfoPath and Forms Services 2007*, 978-0-321-41059-7

Neil Roodyn, *eXtreme .NET: Introducing eXtreme Programming Techniques to .NET Developers*, 978-0-321-30363-9

Chris Sells and Michael Weinhardt, *Windows Forms 2.0 Programming*, 978-0-321-26796-2

Dharma Shukla and Bob Schmidt, *Essential Windows Workflow Foundation*, 978-0-321-39983-0

Guy Smith-Ferrier, *.NET Internationalization: The Developer's Guide to Building Global Windows and Web Applications*, 978-0-321-34138-9

Will Stott and James Newkirk, *Visual Studio Team System: Better Software Development for Agile Teams*, 978-0-321-41850-0

Paul Yao and David Durant, *.NET Compact Framework Programming with C#*, 978-0-321-17403-1

Paul Yao and David Durant, *.NET Compact Framework Programming with Visual Basic .NET*, 978-0-321-17404-8

For more information go to informit.com/msdotnetseries/

Effective REST Services via .NET

For .NET Framework 3.5

- Kenn Scribner
- Scott Seely

✦✦ Addison-Wesley

Upper Saddle River, NJ • Boston • Indianapolis • San Francisco
New York • Toronto • Montreal • London • Munich • Paris • Madrid
Capetown • Sydney • Tokyo • Singapore • Mexico City

The publisher offers excellent discounts on this book when ordered in quantity for bulk purchases or special sales, which may include electronic versions and/or custom covers and content particular to your business, training goals, marketing focus, and branding interests. For more information, please contact:

> U.S. Corporate and Government Sales
> (800) 382-3419
> corpsales@pearsontechgroup.com

For sales outside the United States please contact:

> International Sales
> international@pearson.com

Visit us on the Web: informit.com/aw

Library of Congress Cataloging-in-Publication Data:

Scribner, Kenn.
  Effective REST services via .NET : for .NET Framework 3.5 / Kenn Scribner, Scott Seely.
     p. cm.
   ISBN-13: 978-0-321-61325-7 (pbk. : alk. paper)
   ISBN-10: 0-321-61325-2 (pbk. : alk. paper) 1. Web services. 2. Representational state transfer (Software architecture) 3. Web site development. 4. Internet programming. 5. Microsoft .NET Framework. I. Seely, Scott, 1972- II. Title.
   TK5105.88813.S32 2009
   006.7'882—dc22

                                        2009002859

ISBN-13: 978-0-321-61325-7
ISBN-10: 0-321-61325-2

Text printed in the United States on recycled paper at Courier in Westford, Massachusetts.
First printing April 2009

To my daughter Katie, my son Aaron, and my lovely wife Judi,
who make it all worthwhile.
—Kenn Scribner

To my children Vince, Angeline, and Phillip—thanks for pulling me out
of the book for swimming and video games every so often.

To my wife Jean, thanks for being so supportive and loving.
I could not have done this without you.
—Scott Seely

Contents at a Glance

Contents

Foreword

SOAP has been with us for the better part of ten years now, but few would argue that it has lived up to its promise. It works, and it has been used to tie together thousands of services and service consumers. But if you believe simpler is better, SOAP falls short. XML is verbose, WS-* is complex, and interoperability is elusive. SOAP may be the right tool for the job when it comes to composing an SOA symphony from disparate enterprise servers, but for the vast majority of today's consumer-oriented applications, SOAP is not only overkill, it's too slow and too complex to merit honest consideration.

Enter REST. Fast becoming the most important Web service protocol on the planet, REST is everything SOAP isn't. Want to dress up an application with real-time weather data? How about firing off an HTTP request to http://www.contoso.com/weather/98052 and parsing a few bytes of XML returned in the response? You don't need elaborate tooling support to consume WSDL contracts and generate Web Service proxies, nor do you need SOAP libraries to generate and digest hundreds of lines of message headers. A few lines of code and an XML parser will do. Moreover, you might not even need the parser; REST services can return data in any format they want. With REST, the wire format is driven by the requirements of the application, not by the protocol that the application uses.

This is why the world seems to have settled on REST as the simplest and most effective means for publishing data and services to consumer-oriented applications. Flickr exposes a REST API for searching its massive store of photographs; Amazon offers a REST API for searching its product catalog; Google and Yahoo provide REST APIs for search, traffic data, geographical data, and more; and Digg makes news stories, videos, and more available via REST. The list could go on and on, but the upshot is that REST is the language spoken by the most "interesting" public-facing services today and is likely to be used to expose even more interesting stuff in the future. When you publish data the REST way, you're in good company. And understanding REST is the key to building content-rich applications that draw from resources outside your own application domain. You probably don't have access to your own Doppler weather radar, but somebody else does—and if they're willing to share that information through REST, then you, too, can incorporate real-time weather data into your UI.

Microsoft's Web stack offers a number of ways for developers to build RESTful services. You can implement them using IIS, ASP.NET, ASP.NET's MVC framework, WCF, and even Azure and .NET Services. Understanding the programming models is a key first step in architecting and implementing REST services and clients. Should you author services using WCF or ASP.NET? Should data be encoded as XML or JSON? Which model delivers the best balance of performance and ease of implementation, which one provides the best support for unit testing, and what should I know about best practices before I start?

I can't think of anyone better or more qualified to answer these questions than Kenn Scribner and Scott Seely. I've had the privilege of working with both of them in recent years, and besides being passionate about the subject, both are world-class presenters with a knack for breaking down complex information and presenting it in understandable, bite-sized chunks. Both have real-world experience building Web Services and Web Service clients on Microsoft platforms. And both possess the perspective needed to present a fair and balanced view of REST development, sharing with you not only the hows but the whys—and in some cases, the why-nots.

I can't promise you that REST won't be displaced in a year or two by something sexier. In fact, I can guarantee that it *will* be replaced someday, perhaps sooner rather than later; such is the nature of our industry. But for the time being, REST is where the action is, and becoming REST-literate is one of the smartest things a developer can do to sharpen his or her skill set. Join Kenn and Scott as they take you on a RESTful journey through the Microsoft technology stack; and most of all, sit back and enjoy the ride!

Jeff Prosise
Knoxville, TN
February 2009

Preface

Kenn's Thoughts: The Road to REST, an Engineer's Tale

It was the spring of 2008, and I had just completed some work for Justin Smith, a senior engineer and connected systems expert at Microsoft. The work involved developing two related Web sites that would consume services offered by a third Web application that would be hosted in something known as the "cloud." After six weeks of iterative development, we had a set of Web applications that were designed to demonstrate nearly all the ways Web applications can communicate using .NET technologies.

I'd heard about REST, of course, having been fortunate enough to work with Dino Esposito on several of his ASP.NET and AJAX books. Dino is a huge REST proponent. But I admit my background was more along the lines of the SOAP protocol, and I looked at Web services more as remote method calls than creatures of the Internet ecosystem. It didn't bother me that I needed fancy proxies to communicate with XML-based (and not JSON-based) Web services. I truly hadn't consciously considered the notion that remote procedure call (RPC) style messaging wasn't quite architecturally in harmony with the Internet itself.

But I'd had this nagging concern for some time. SOAP and XML-RPC services were becoming very complex, and it seemed that at every turn we were trying to solve some problem that the basic architecture of the Internet presented. Security, streaming large binary objects, browser-based proxies (for AJAX), and so forth were leading to an ever-increasing number of new specifications, each designed to layer more complexity on to what had started as a simple concept. And in most cases, we were trying to bypass the basic workings of the Internet rather than using them to our advantage.

After working with Justin, and after building a very detailed and fully functional set of Web applications that were primarily based on RESTful principles, I found I had drunk from the RESTful Kool-Aid pitcher, and I was stunned by what I had overlooked all of these years. I can remember the epiphany...I literally sat up in my chair, stunned by what I had realized.

What I had overlooked was the simplicity and elegance of the Web's architecture and design. I had been overcome by the glamour of XML and serializing binary information for transmission in response to requests for actions. I had lost sight of the Internet's most basic capability of asking for and receiving a resource's representation. The simplicity and elegance of the Internet struck a new chord with me that day. Even though I had been working with Internet-based technologies for nearly ten years, I found I'd suddenly rediscovered programming for the Internet.

And the simple truth is this is not a bad thing, nor is it uncommon. REST as an architectural concept is precisely in line with the architecture of the Web itself. Any tool you have that can build Web applications can be used to build RESTful services. If you have access to the HTTP method—GET, POST, and so forth—and if you have access to the HTTP headers and entity body, you have all you need to create a RESTful service. Anything else is there only to make creating RESTful services easier by hiding some of the detail. I haven't had the pleasure of meeting Dr. Roy Fielding, but based on his doctoral dissertation that introduces us all to the concept of REST, I'd hazard a guess that he'd prefer you understand REST at its lowest level before using frameworks that mask the underpinnings. When you do, REST makes perfect sense and things become very clear. Or at least I felt so.

Scott's Thoughts: REST Is Best

From 2000 until the middle of 2006, I worked at Microsoft on Web services. For four of those years, I worked on Windows Communication

Foundation (WCF)—that amazing, transport-agnostic, messaging-unification machine. When WCF finally came out, it supported WS-* and some very basic REST/POX messaging. A few folks on the team were hard at work adding first-class REST support in the form of URI templates and extra functionality for HTTP-hosted services that were later released in .NET 3.5. Why this focus on REST? REST was starting to get very popular, thanks to Roy Fielding's dissertation. Like many in the Web service community, I read his dissertation many times, trying to really understand what made the Web scale as well as it did. When the WCF 3.5 bits started coming out as previews, I checked out the greatly improved REST support. I was getting excited by what I was seeing and learning. In the broader community and at work, I was finding that people were getting more and more comfortable using HTTP as a communication medium to create, retrieve, update, and delete resources.

I also started seeing the value in easy-to-type URLs. Furthermore, I found that the architecture and code just makes sense to developers. During 2006, I taught several multiday classes on WCF and gave presentations on WCF at a few conferences across the country. My talks on REST were well received. My talks on WCF internals weren't. People appreciated the elegance of what WCF can do. They just did not see the value in the steep learning curve one had to traverse to master the technology. The thing that pushed me over to REST was the realization of why people were flocking to REST over WS-*. In general, developers used Web browsers and built Web applications long before they ever had to add a service of any kind. REST development builds on what Web developers already know, so there is less to learn. WS-* might be elegant and cover many scenarios, but it does not build on what most developers in most shops across the globe already know.

In the summer of 2008, I joined the development team at MySpace as an architect. Guess what architectural style one of the world's largest .NET sites uses to handle access to Friends, photo albums, and other resources. Yes, it's REST. The platform is, first and foremost, a Web platform. REST holds more value for HTTP base endpoints than a WS-* one ever will. REST integrates well with so many other platforms without a whole lot of effort. It doesn't impose structure on the payload contents—only on the payload metadata. REST is a model that novice developers understand and that expert-level developers can easily manipulate. I love the fact that it is penetrating so much of service development. My day job involves working on OpenSocial—already one of the most successful REST APIs ever developed. Through my work with OpenSocial, I have seen that HTTP and REST compose well with many different security mechanisms. I find it interesting that WS-* protocols compose well with other XML mechanisms. REST composes with other HTTP mechanisms. After spending so many years working with SOAP and other RPC mechanisms, I like what REST has to offer.

How This Book Approaches REST

Today, we use this stuff. We build solutions based on this stuff. We like this stuff. And we're truly glad to have this book in our hands as architects and developers. Both authors and the entire team behind this book hope you will find it informative and useful as well.

One thing we didn't want was a 1,000-page monster. When you understand REST, the concept is actually simple, and applying .NET technologies to create RESTful solutions becomes a relatively easy task. If it can't be explained in a few pages, something's not right.

The first couple of chapters introduce you to the concepts involved with REST. In a sense, you're taken back to the earliest days of the Internet to rediscover how the Internet works and how the architectural concept known as REST fits into the Internet ecosystem so well. The first chapter, "RESTful Systems: Back to the Future," addresses REST itself, and you learn what it means to be RESTful and how to identify behaviors that are *not* RESTful. Chapter 2, "The HyperText Transfer Protocol and the Universal Resource Identifier," is devoted to HTTP and the URI. These are the two fundamental tools you'll work with when developing .NET-based solutions.

Chapters 3 and 4 dig into the client side of the equation. RESTful services are there to serve a client's needs, and there is no better way to begin to use REST than to consume RESTful services from a client's perspective. There you learn what works and what doesn't, with the lessons you learn translating to design principles when you create RESTful services your-self. Chapter 3, "Desktop Client Operations," shows you how to access RESTful services from desktop applications (both authors believe that the desktop is not a dead platform but is instead enhanced by Internet data and service access), and Chapter 4, "Web Client Operations," shows you how to access RESTful services from Web-based applications, including Silverlight 2.0. For consistency, both chapters access a single REST service. Later chapters build individual services unique to each chapter to increase the breadth of exposure to different RESTful service implementations.

After you have a feel for how a client might use your service, it's time to dive into server-side programming. Here the book starts with the basics: what Internet Information Services (IIS) is, how it is put together, and how you use it to implement RESTful services. Chapter 5, "IIS and ASP.NET Internals and Instrumentation," leads you through the most foundational server-side technology: Microsoft's premier Web server. Clearly this is one technology that supports nearly all the other .NET Web-based technolo-gies, RESTful or otherwise, and understanding how it works is crucial to building effective REST services.

Chapters 6 though 8 then use higher-order .NET technologies to imple-ment RESTful services. Chapter 6, "Building REST Services Using IIS and ASP.NET," uses what you learned in Chapter 5 to create a Web blog serv-ice using only traditional ASP.NET constructs. Chapter 7, "Building REST Services Using ASP.NET MVC Framework," introduces you to the ASP.NET MVC framework and shows how implementing a RESTful serv-ice might differ from traditional ASP.NET when you have the MVC frame-work to rely on. Of course, no .NET book discussing RESTful technologies would be complete without digging into the nuts and bolts of WCF, and Chapter 8, "Building REST Services Using WCF," does just that.

The final chapter, Chapter 9, "Building REST Services Using Azure and.NET Services," shows how you would combine cloud computing with RESTful services to accomplish tasks that otherwise would be nearly impossible. In this case the sample application demonstrates a comment service you can execute from behind your firewall on your private net-work. Your service will reach out and allow other people over the Internet who are working behind their firewalls to work with your service.

We then provide three appendixes we hope you'll find helpful. The first, Appendix A, ".NET REST Architectural Considerations and Decisions," discusses some of the architectural aspects and why you might choose a particular .NET technology over another. Appendix B, "HTTP Response Codes," discusses each of the possible HTTP response codes and in particular what they mean to RESTful services and clients. And, finally, Appendix C, "REST Best Practices," tries to provide some concise guidance for creating RESTful services.

Let's face it. When it comes to writing effective software, the more you know, the more effective your software will be. Although we don't assume that you're the world's foremost expert on writing ASP.NET applications, we do believe you'll have some real-world .NET experience before reading this book. We're going to be working at some of the lowest levels of HTTP, IIS, and even ASP.NET, so some familiarity with each of these is a plus. But neither is this book a 1,000-page monster, so if there are bits and pieces you're not so familiar with, there should be plenty here to introduce you to concepts and techniques you'll find useful in your daily work.

Finally, we've set up a Web page in addition to the publisher's page where you can send comments and questions directly to us. If anyone (gasp!) finds...inconsistencies...in our sample software, we'll post updated code there for you to download. Interesting and informative tidbits might find their way there as well, time permitting. Both authors earn their living writing software just as you do, and we're every bit as busy as you are making ends meet with the world economy the way it has been in the latter part of 2008. But both authors love this architectural concept and are committed to helping you understand and use it as well. So if interesting and informative things come up, we'll put them on the book's Web page:

www.endurasoft.com/rest.aspx

Acknowledgments

Kenn

When I was asked to create an initial table of contents for this book, Scott was one of the reviewers Addison-Wesley requested to provide feedback. For each book I'd written previously, I'd created a meticulous table of contents that I literally pasted into each chapter when it started as a blank page. This time, however, I thought I'd be a touch more free-wheeling and use the Force, so the table of contents was more a collection of ideas and concepts I felt should be covered. Scott, also typically of a meticulous nature, had...interesting comments as feedback, not the least of which was to the effect of "I couldn't write this if Kenn were hit by a beer truck." (Scott and I both partake of the golden beverage as often as we can.) I had to laugh when Scott accepted my fervent request to help with this book. You couldn't have a finer author. Scott not only worked on the Windows Communication Foundation team but also finds himself today an architect for MySpace, assisting with their RESTful services offerings. To my great delight, Scott not only completed his chapters, but also brought more to the table than I could have hoped for. I'm specifically delighted with his work surrounding ADO.NET Data Services. When he says developers shouldn't write off that technology, he is referring specifically to me! I'm also awed by the tremendous depth of information he introduced, and most particularly his guidance regarding WCF diagnostics. This book is far better because of his work, and I wholeheartedly thank him for the time and effort he put into this project. He has young children, and from experience I can personally vouch for how hard it is to write books when your children ask you to play with them. (The book loses every time, by the way.)

I'd also like to thank Justin Smith and Don Box. I'd worked with Justin on a RESTful project in early 2008, and (to my great delight) Justin suggested this book to me at that time. On a trip to Redmond, I stopped by and talked with Justin and Don at length about this project. I've known Don a long time, but I was surprised by his enthusiasm regarding my possible authorship; and it inspired me to work long and hard, to research each detail, and to try to craft sentences and paragraphs that convey the ideas and impetus behind .NET RESTful services without being overly verbose (something Dino Esposito will tell you I can be from time to time). Hopefully my thanks and gratitude toward these fine gentlemen is a solid effort and a fine book, one that you'll both learn from and refer to as you explore the inner workings of .NET and REST. Thank you, guys.

I'd also like to thank Dino Esposito. He'll wonder why, but my reasons are simple. I'm fortunate enough to have edited Dino's books for years, and I've learned (at least) two things from Dino. First, for an Italian whose English is a second language, he writes better than most Americans. That lights a fire. And second, he teaches me far more than I help him when it comes to technical matters. He introduced me to REST long before it was a twinkling in the WCF team's eye, and naturally I started digging into REST after he introduced the concept. I'll send him a copy of this book, and I hope he'll enjoy reading it as much as I enjoy reading his works. It's fun to trade books, come to think of it.

If you've ever had the pleasure of editing a book, you'll know what I mean when I say each chapter is a "diamond in the rough." Actually, sometimes rough drafts are more like coal than diamonds. They're both based on carbon, but that's where the similarities end. It's the often-thankless job of the editors to take the garbage I turn in and remake it into the shining brilliance it appears to be. Believe me, they don't all start out that way. And it's thanks to Steve Maine, Buddhike de Silva, and Paul Mehner, your hardworking technical reviewers, who were hit with the worst Scott and I could offer. We threw all kinds of horrible things at them! But they each persevered and turned lumps of coal into shining pieces of RESTful technical brilliance. Any of the black coal dust that remains belongs entirely to Scott and me. The not-so-brilliant parts, same thing.

And speaking of thankless jobs, Joan Murray and Olivia Basegio have been champs. They acted more like a cheering section than publishers, editors, and project managers, and not a day went by while I worked on this that I was not thankful for their tireless support. Scott and I worked hard to maintain communications, to get our work in on time, and to generally keep them informed regarding our progress. And although it might sound odd to say it, I'll bet they'd tell you that's the best "thanks" we could give them. Even so, I'd like to offer my thanks to them here too. Thank you, Joan and Olivia!

It takes an army to actually produce a book, though. It's one thing to write it, but it's another to actually edit, print, and bind the written words. If you're familiar with the 80/20 rule, it applies here. Scott and I did 20% of the job—the remaining 80% is left to the hardworking crew at Addison-Wesley, and all of you there should know that I'm deeply appreciative of your efforts on my behalf. I'd especially like to thank Cheri Clark, the book's copy editor, and Lori Lyons, the production side project manager. Unfortunately I'm not Dino Esposito, so you both had your hands full. Along with my apology for your blistered fingertips, I'd like to offer my deepest thanks for your diligent work. I'm still not sure how you read all of this and didn't fall asleep...caffeine?

And last but most certainly not least, I would like to thank my family for not only helping me with this book, but also helping me get through each and every day feeling blessed and thankful for their company and love. My once-empty heart is filled with laughter and joy just thinking about my crazy bunch. You guys make it all worth it, and I love you all. Thank you!

Scott

Kenn and I "met" when he wrote *Applied SOAP* back in 2001 and I acted as technical editor. I left that project with a desire to work with him on something, eventually. Over the years, we regularly corresponded, helping each other with various development items. Over time, I got to know Kenn and grew to think of him as a friend. During the summer of 2008, he asked if I'd be interested in writing this book with him, and I had to say yes. It's been great writing this with him. He has kept things moving throughout the process and has done an excellent job acting as the lead author on this book. Kenn, thanks for asking me to collaborate!

Much thanks and praise is also due to our reviewers: Steve Maine, Buddhike de Silva, and Paul Mehner. All three have done a wonderful job in finding mistakes and pointing out where various sections could be changed to add clarity. Although all mistakes are owned by Kenn and me, it was great to have them watching everything. Having these three as reviewers was very gratifying. Steve owned the project manager role at Microsoft for the REST enhancements added to Windows Communication Foundation. After being teammates on WCF 3.0 with Steve, I was happy to be able to work with him again on this project. Buddhike has been active in the Web and WCF communities for several years. We've corresponded in the past about other .NET topics. Finally, there is Paul, who is an amazing developer, the proud founder of the oldest, still functioning .NET User Group, and a great person to present a talk with. Paul also teaches Wintellect's Windows Workflow Foundation and Windows Communication Foundation classes. And no, just because we have all this WCF talent does not mean that this is a WCF book. Far from it; this is a book about developing RESTful services using the different technologies that Microsoft brings to the table.

My family has been incredibly supportive while this book was being written. My wife, Jean, and my children all were very understanding when I had to spend a few more hours getting another chapter written or more code working. My parents helped out whenever they could as well. It's important to have family and friends to support you when you're taking on a something like writing a book, which easily consumes more hours in a week than a typical job can.

Thanks to my co-workers at MySpace. You have allowed me to work on this book as well as some of the largest scale REST and Web services on the planet.

This book represents the fourth book I've worked on for Pearson Education and the second I have written for the Addison-Wesley imprint. I have always enjoyed writing for this group thanks to the excellent teams they put together to help authors create great books. Thanks to Joan Murray and Olivia Basegio, who guided us through the whole process and never once yelled at me when I turned in a chapter late. It is true—book publishers hate it more when you "go dark" than when you let them know that you are going to be late. (Kenn was *always* on time, which kind of explains why he was the lead author and I was not.) I'd also like to thank the rest of the production team: Lori Lyons and Cheri Clark. Special thanks go out to Lisa Stumpf, who put together the Index at the back of the book, and Nonie Ratcliff, for laying out text. I had to do this for my first book and it was *tough!* There is an art to building a good index, and I am not that kind of artist.

About the Authors

Kenn Scribner is a software developer who happens to write books as an excuse to learn new technologies. There is nothing quite like a deadline to get those creative neurons firing. He's been working with computers since he built a breadboarded Z-80 in college a few too many years ago. (Happily, the Z-80 survived the encounter.) Although he fondly remembers writing 6502 assembly language on his Apple][, he's quite happy writing complex C# applications today, both for the Web and for the desktop. This is his seventh computer book, and he truly hopes you'll enjoy reading it and learning how to apply .NET to your RESTful application needs. His personal Web site is http://www.endurasoft.com.

Scott Seely is an architect at MySpace working on OpenSocial, which has been criticized by Roy Fielding as not being pure REST (it's okay, Roy is a critical guy, REST is his baby, and we know that the OpenSocial RESTful API isn't pure). Prior to his life in social networking, Scott spent several years writing about Web services and several more as part of the Microsoft team that created the first version of Windows Communication Foundation. He co-founded the Lake County .NET Users' Group (lcnug.org) with Tim Stall. In his free time, he loves to read Batman comics, go golfing, and play board games with his family. He blogs at www.scottseely.com/blog.aspx.

1.

RESTful Systems: Back to the Future

T ODAY, REST IS A hot topic. Its often ardent followers argue strongly in its favor over RPC-based Web services. Why? What makes REST such a powerful architecture and concept? In this chapter you'll explore REST as an architecture and begin to learn what makes REST tick. The next chapter dives into even more detail. Given an understanding of these first two chapters, you should be well prepared to work through the concepts and examples throughout the remainder of the book.

What is Representational State Transfer (REST)? Why is everyone talking about it now? How do I make use of RESTful services in my own systems? Can the .NET Framework help me produce RESTful services my clients might use? These are excellent questions many people are asking, and they're some of the topics we'll cover in this book, starting with this chapter. Since these are probably burning questions, here are some quick answers: REST is a design philosophy that encourages us to use existing protocols and features of the Web to map requests for resources to various representations for manipulation over the Internet. REST isn't a specific architecture or toolkit, so to use it we need to understand RESTful design philosophy and use the tools we have to create architectures that exhibit RESTful qualities. And the .NET Framework can absolutely help us write RESTful systems!

But often more important than "What are RESTful services?" or "How are they implemented and used?" is "*When* should we use RESTful techniques?" Where does using them make the most sense? We'll also examine those questions throughout the book. Sometimes the built-in tools .NET provides are perfectly suited for your architectural needs. Other times REST concepts would be better applied even if you need to write a bit more code at times. The goal is to understand the concepts behind Web data communication so you make an appropriate, informed design decision.

This chapter examines the "what." Chapter 2, "The HyperText Transfer Protocol and the Universal Resource Identifier," digs more deeply into the mechanisms that make REST work. The chapters that follow provide working examples of RESTful systems and discuss the architectural merits (or demerits) of each. Our goal is to show you how the various .NET technologies work when used to implement RESTful services and give you the knowledge you need in order to select the right .NET technology for the job. In many cases more than one will work, but some mitigating circumstance or requirement will normally draw your attention to a clear preference.

In any case, let's begin. Sometimes it's best to learn a new technology from the bottom up. But in this case, I think it's a better idea to take a step back and look at a bigger picture. When we dive into the nuts and bolts of REST, having a wider view is helpful when putting the pieces together. Let's start with a brief discussion of where Web services have been going in recent years, services in general, and how services have historically been built. Knowing that, and taking a look at how the Internet was architected, should lead you to designing architectures that support RESTful services with relative ease.

> ### ■ NOTE
>
> It is not my intention in this chapter to say one technology is "better" than another. Rather, I want to provide an understanding of why REST has become so popular. I also want to show that REST is an architectural style that can be used with great success in many situations. However, as with any tool, you need to understand its strengths and weaknesses. This is exactly why you'll find the brief discussion of SOAP in the following section. SOAP and its related technologies are also tools. The more you understand, the better armed you'll be to make the most appropriate architectural choice for your particular application's needs.

The Shift (Back) to REST

When Tim Berners-Lee and a talented group of engineers and scientists designed the World Wide Web as we know it today, they had several design principles in mind, including the transfer of documents using *hypermedia* principles (markup, linking to other documents, and so forth), scalability, and statelessness. Their initial idea was to be able to share marked-up documents quickly and simply.

It wasn't long before people realized that, though sharing documents is good, sharing data outside the context of a Web page is also good. Early in the Internet's history, circa 1995, the Common Gateway Interface (CGI) was created to handle computational and data-centric requests that didn't necessarily always fit into the hypertext-based document model. Payment processing, for example. CGI, however, had many issues, not the least of which was the constraints of the early CGI implementations that created a new process to handle each request. Since process creation is expensive in terms of processing and memory, the resulting lack of scalability and higher cost were factors that drove people to look for alternatives.

> **NOTE**
>
> In the spirit of providing interesting examples, CGI is still used for data transfer today. See http://penobscot.loboviz.com/cgidoc/ for a working CGI-based data service.

Another famous approach to handling data-centric Web requests came about in late 1999—the Simple Object Access Protocol, now just known as SOAP. (There were others, such as XML-RPC, but we'll concentrate on SOAP for this discussion.) SOAP defined a *wire protocol* that standardized how binary information within the computer's memory could be serialized to the Extensible Markup Language, or XML. At the time SOAP was invented, XML was also in its infancy (even before XML schemas were standardized). Initially there were no discovery and description mechanisms either, but eventually the Web Service Description Language (WSDL) was settled on. WSDL enabled SOAP-based service designers to more fully describe the XML their service would accept as well as an extensibility mechanism. The SOAP specification didn't describe the policies that dictate how your service should be used (whether the messages should be encrypted, for example). But using WSDL, this sort of "meta" information *could* be described, making SOAP-based services more interoperable and widely accepted.

For example, the Web service community came up with a collection of extensional specifications that together are referred to as the *WS-** ("WS-star") specifications. These include WS-Security, WS-Reliable Messaging, WS-Addressing, and WS-Policy, to name just a few. These specifications all essentially added layered metadata to the SOAP payload by modifying the header while keeping the message body intact.

But there is a pattern here we should more closely examine. In the beginning we had simple hypermedia documents. However, as soon as we added the capability to access server-based application data processes, the basic architecture of our applications began moving away from the pure hypermedia model. CGI introduced a "gateway" where none had existed. SOAP introduced a novel use of XML, but this then required servers to accept and handle SOAP requests with arbitrarily complex payloads or negotiate lowest common denominators. Then came WSDL. Before WSDL, you had to precisely match the SOAP-based service's XML payload format requirements by hand, rather than using automated tools as we do today that consume WSDL, or the service request would fail. With WSDL it became easier to modify the client's SOAP request to match what the service provider required, but then the server needed to formulate the WSDL, adding more processing requirements and moving the data communication architecture even further away from a pure hypermedia basis. And when the incredible complexity of the WS-* specifications is added, the entire data communication process incorporates processing and metadata transfer completely unforeseen only a few years ago.

There are several good reasons to question the data transfer process as it has evolved, however. To begin, the architecture of the data services migrated away from the original intent of the Internet designers. This in and of itself isn't so bad. Technologies change and transform all the time, so who's to say the data service architecture is somehow bad? Actually, it isn't that it's "bad." It's just that the data services now represent remote procedure calls (RPC), and as such, require additional overhead to formulate the wire protocol—serialization and deserialization of the in-memory binary information to be transmitted back and forth—as well as communicate the serialized information to the single server endpoint.

By simply using this wire protocol and single endpoint, Web services forced a huge architectural change on the Internet (see Figure 1.1). Instead of a server examining the HyperText Transfer Protocol (HTTP) HTTP method—GET, POST, and so forth—and shuttling that request to a resource handler, the server now needs to crack open the HTTP payload and decipher the contents to decide what to do. There is a special HTTP SOAP header that's designed to assist with method routing, but the point is that the payload will need to be examined and handled much differently than requests for, say, a Web page. Moreover, other Web systems designed to increase scalability and throughput, like caching, are hindered. Since there is one endpoint for the Web service, all possible service invocations can't be cached, and you lose the performance boost that caching often provides high-throughput systems.

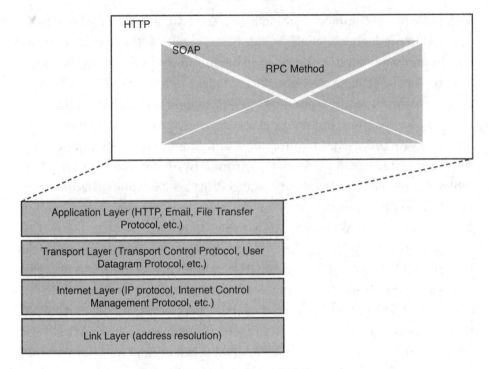

FIGURE 1.1: The TCP-IP protocol stack hosting SOAP RPC data

The RPC method serialization also adds a tremendous amount of complexity on the client. For example, if you're writing a .NET Windows application, life is good since the tools Microsoft has provided will accept WSDL and can produce a *proxy* that rather faithfully mimics the method on the server. The proxy handles all the data serialization and deserialization for you. Your application executes compiled code, has access to nearly unlimited memory from the application's perspective, and isn't subject to the same security restrictions as, say, a Web site whose pages are rendered in a Web browser (although perhaps in some cases it should be).

But applications today are moving toward Web-based, hosted scenarios. Take that same data service your Windows application uses and consume it in a Web browser, and things get much more interesting—and not necessarily interesting in a good way. Over time several alternatives have surfaced that manage the proxy task, but they all suffer from some of the same limitations. Security, for example, must necessarily be quite stringent. Security that protects your users from malicious virus software also often interferes with beneficial data services. Another issue commonly faced is the varying ways different browser manufacturers support the basic tool these proxies use, the `XmlHttpRequest` object. Activating and using the `Xml-HttpRequest` object is different for Firefox than for Internet Explorer, and your client code must be robust enough to take this fact into account. If you also consider the performance penalty usually associated with parsing and working with XML using JavaScript in a browser, you can quickly see why the RPC-style data service is so hard to work with in a generic sense. When the overhead associated with the WS-* specifications is applied, it's very possible the service couldn't be used in a browser at all. It depends on how much metadata the service mandates, how many parameters are present in the remote method's signature, and so forth.

The gist of all of this is that somewhere along the way, all of us associated with designing and developing RPC-based Web services diverted from the basic architecture of the Internet. SOAP and WS-* started from examining various platform-specific solutions like DCOM (Distributed Component Object Model) and CORBA (Common Object Request Broker Architecture), and their ultimate goal was to build those same types of systems in a platform-neutral way. To accomplish this goal, they built on the substrate of some of the emerging Internet protocols of the time. HTTP was chosen as a framing protocol mostly because it was entrenched enough so that people already had port 80 open in the firewall. XML was chosen because the bet was that XML was going to be *the* platform-neutral meta-schema for data. All the advanced WS-* specifications (Security/Reliability/Transactions) were taking application server features du jour and incorporating those protocols into this platform-neutral protocol substrate.

From an architectural perspective, is all of this necessary? That depends....

In 2000, which is about the time the SOAP protocol started to take root, Roy Fielding, a co-designer of the HTTP specification, finished his doctoral dissertation, titled "Architectural Styles and the Design of Network-based Software Architectures" (www.ics.uci.edu/~fielding/pubs/dissertation/top.htm). His dissertation revolves around the evaluation of network-based architectures, but his final two chapters introduce the concepts of *Representational State Transfer*, or REST. His intent was to show how network architectures could be evaluated, the reasons for which he explains here:

Design-by-buzzword is a common occurrence. At least some of this behavior within the software industry is due to a lack of understanding of why a given set of architectural constraints is useful. In other words, the reasoning behind good software architectures is not apparent to designers when those architectures are selected for reuse.

Dr. Fielding didn't invent the way the Internet works. But he did sit down and rigorously articulate the underlying principles that drive it. In that light, if you peel away the wrapper, REST essentially formalizes data services using concepts inherent in the Internet. Why? Simplicity is one reason, or as Dr. Fielding might argue, why reinvent the wheel when it's better to understand and use the wheel you already have? Why create complex data service architectures when the Internet as it was originally conceived is perfectly suited for transferring both hypermedia-based documents *and* data? And to prove his point, as well as earn his doctorate, he describes the principles that guide architectures that should be considered RESTful. More to the point, he mentions that those principles have been in effect since 1994, which is nearly a year before CGI came to the fore.

Put another way, REST describes for us, or perhaps reminds us, that the protocols we use over the Internet are already capable of mapping information and resources. We don't need to overlay complex protocols—we just need to create architectures that correctly apply existing protocols.

■ NOTE

If you scan contemporary blogs and articles, you'll probably find strong proponents of REST arguing against the SOAP RPC model, while strong proponents of SOAP argue that it can nicely manage situations in which REST is not as architecturally appropriate. I personally don't see the question as being "Is REST right and SOAP wrong?" Rather, I think it is much better to understand both and then evaluate your architectural implementation choices in light of your application's requirements rather than attempting to blindly adhere to one or the other. Appendix A, ".NET REST Architectural Considerations and Decisions," has some guidance here.

So what does it mean to be RESTful? Do we need massive specifications and layered metadata? How is data to be communicated without all the trappings of the RPC systems we've been building since about the time Dr. Fielding wrote his dissertation? To begin to answer this question, let's look at some real-world services and pick up some experience along the way. It's important to understand the contrasting points of view—RPC-based services versus RESTful services—to fully comprehend how a RESTful architecture works, or how it avoids some of the complexities RPC-style architectures rely on.

What Are Web Services?

So let's go back and formalize things a bit. When we design services, we're really designing mechanisms to allow external access to our internal application resources. Perhaps we have a computational engine that external clients need to use for financial calculations. Or maybe we have information our clients need to query to support their business processes. We might even have services that invoke actions on behalf of some client activity.

Web services are services that allow machine-to-machine communication using interoperable protocols over a network, and given that definition, both RPC and RESTful services qualify. We'll look at an example of an RPC-based service first. Let's say you want your application to include current weather forecast information. This isn't something you can most likely generate yourself, so you look for a service on the Internet that you can use (ideally for free). As it happens, at least for consumers in the United States, there is a free service available through the National Weather Service described here: www.weather.gov/xml/.

The National Digital Forecast Database (NDFD) is accessible through a SOAP-based Web service. Figure 1.2 shows a small sample Windows Presentation Foundation (WPF) application, which allows you to type in your United States postal code (your Zone Improvement Plan code, or ZIP Code) and receive some basic weather forecast information.

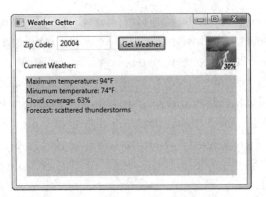

FIGURE 1.2: The Weather Getter National Digital Forecast Database Web service test application

The NDFD service exposes several Web-based methods you can invoke to request forecast information. However, the forecast is indexed by latitude and longitude. Unless you happen to have a Global Positioning Satellite (GPS) receiver with you, chances are good you don't know your current global position. Luckily, the NDFD service offers several methods for converting more-obtainable location information into global position coordinates. In this case you can provide a ZIP Code and the service will transform that into the appropriate latitude and longitude.

The response to any of the NDFD methods requires deserialization to extract the payload from the SOAP envelope. In this case, each method returns a SOAP response containing another XML document (as a string), and it's up to you to parse the response XML for the data of interest. As an example, the HTTP response to a ZIP Code conversion request (ZIP Code: 20004, or Washington, D.C.) is shown in Listing 1.1. The latitude and longitude are 38.895 and -77.0373 respectively, as shown toward the end of Listing 1.1.

LISTING 1.1: HTTP Response to ZIP Code conversion for code 20004

```
HTTP/1.1 200 OK
Date: Sat, 09 Aug 2008 22:30:22 GMT
Content-Length: 966
Content-Type: text/xml; charset=ISO-8859-1
Expires: Sun, 10 Aug 2008 00:30:22 GMT
Cache-Control: max-age=7200
Server: Apache
X-SOAP-Server: NuSOAP/0.7.2 (1.107)
```

```
Vary: Accept-Encoding,User-Agent
Via: 1.1 nws-hq-cache02 (NetCache NetApp/6.0.6)

<?xml version="1.0" encoding="ISO-8859-1"?>
 <SOAP-ENV:Envelope SOAP-
   ENV:encodingStyle=http://schemas.xmlsoap.org/soap/encoding/
   xmlns:SOAP-ENV=http://schemas.xmlsoap.org/soap/envelope/
   xmlns:xsd=http://www.w3.org/2001/XMLSchema
   xmlns:xsi=http://www.w3.org/2001/XMLSchema-instance
   xmlns:SOAP-ENC="http://schemas.xmlsoap.org/soap/encoding/">
 <SOAP-ENV:Body>
  <ns1:LatLonListZipCodeResponse xmlns:ns1=
    "http://www.weather.gov/forecasts/xml/DWMLgen/wsdl/ndfdXML.wsdl">
    <listLatLonOut xsi:type="xsd:string">
      &lt;?xml version=&apos;1.0&apos; ?&gt;
      &lt;dwml version=&apos;1.0&apos;
      xmlns:xsd=&quot;http://www.w3.org/2001/XMLSchema&quot;
      xmlns:xsi=&quot;http://www.w3.org/2001/XMLSchema-
      instance&quot;
      xsi:noNamespaceSchemaLocation=
      &quot;http://www.nws.noaa.gov/mdl/survey/
➥pgb_survey/dev/DWMLgen/schema/DWML.xsd&quot;&gt;
      &lt;latLonList&gt;38.895,-77.0373&lt;/latLonList&gt;
      &lt;/dwml&gt;
    </listLatLonOut>
   </ns1:LatLonListZipCodeResponse>
  </SOAP-ENV:Body>
 </SOAP-ENV:Envelope>
```

The response for the actual weather forecast itself is very much more complex and requires quite a bit of processing to present it in a reasonable user interface (and the sample application that calls this service is admittedly weak in that respect). The routines for converting SOAP XML into binary, in-memory objects can be resource intensive, especially if arrays and structures are used. The time it takes and the processor utilization levels can be significant, especially if you're concerned about high throughput and high scalability (something to keep in mind).

Here's the point: Traditional Web services are invoked just as you would invoke methods on any locally instanced object you had access to. Because the methods are actually hosted on another server, the methods are known as remote procedure calls, or RPC methods. You as a consumer invoke a method provided by a producer (the remote server) and process the results to suit your needs.

The methods themselves could be thought of as verbs, or perhaps as commands: "Convert my ZIP Code." "Give me the weather forecast." Moreover, often the remote methods involve the storage of client state on the server. Processes that invoke methods in a specific order, such as with remote workflow, usually need to keep track of internal state on the server between client method invocations. Windows Workflow Foundation (WF) and Windows Communication Foundation (WCF) since version 3.5 have extensive support for just this purpose. And although the Weather Getter application shown in Figure 1.2 is invoking methods using the HTTP protocol, there is no requirement to do so; this is just how the NDFD implemented their service. You could just as easily invoke methods using the Simple Mail Transfer Protocol (SMTP), Microsoft Message Queue (MSMQ), or even raw network sockets. All that's necessary is that the SOAP-based packet reaches the destination, assuming you both agree on which transport protocol to use.

There are some issues with this model, however. First, the RPC-based method you're invoking is embedded in the SOAP protocol, so the server must necessarily be capable of interpreting and reacting to the SOAP request. In production environments, where the SOAP messages can be quite complex, this is a nontrivial task. Second, the basic premise of the HTTP protocol is one of statelessness. Ideally, when the server fields one request and then another from the same client, it has no knowledge of the relationship between the requests. RPC programming methods often encourage the opposite, in which the server must maintain internal state for the duration of the client interaction. Third, although some caching scenarios are possible, in general RPC Web service method invocations return client-specific results and therefore preclude cache support for all possible responses to all possible client requests. RPC requests typically are issued to a single endpoint Uniform Resource Identifier (URI), and knowing this, which method result for which client do you cache? Finally, the methods and their underlying wire protocols can grow in complexity nearly beyond imagination when you apply the WS-* specifications. Not only do you need some serious horsepower on the server to field remote method calls that involve encrypted contents with reliable messaging to be issued to several different intermediaries, but you also need similar capabilities on the client. Something I've noted in my various studies is that critics argue that REST requires equivalent processing horsepower for the same levels of confidentiality and verifiability provided by SOAP and its associated specifications. But it also seems that these levels can often be more than many business scenarios necessarily require, kind of like using a sledgehammer to nail a picture to the wall.

Another issue is that it's hard to change behavior. That is, if you add, remove, or modify your service methods, two things are guaranteed. First, you'll need to recompile and redeploy your service. And second, your existing service clients will very likely need to revise their code, both their proxies and their internal application processing, and based on the changes you deploy, those changes could be extensive. (Keep this thought in mind…I'll return to it when I discuss the RESTful example to follow.)

It's also illuminating to look at a bit of code. When I created the Weather Getter application, I accessed the WSDL document the NDFD service offered to describe the remote methods and data structures I would be required to use. The WSDL document was translated and converted into C# source code using tools provided with the .NET Windows Software Development Kit. When I make NDFD remote method requests in my code, I access the service using the C# proxy the tools created. The proxy hides the complexity of the service invocation, but make no mistake—there is tremendous support in the .NET Framework for servicing RPC-based remote methods, and that software is anything but simple. However, my own software does appear rather simple, as shown in Listing 1.2.

LISTING 1.2: Calling the NDFD ZIP Code conversion service

```
ndfdXMLPortTypeClient ws = null;
string latlonXml = String.Empty;
try
{
    // Call Web service with the ZIP Code
    // to determine latitude/longitude values.
    ws = new ndfdXMLPortTypeClient();
    latlonXml = ws.LatLonListZipCode("20004");
    // Interpret the XML and retrieve the return values.
    ...
}
catch
{
    // Handle error...
    ...
}
```

You do not see the code in Listing 1.2 accessing information over the Internet using direct access, such as might be done with .NET's `WebRequest` or `HttpWebRequest` objects. The proxy `ndfdXMLPortTypeClient` is used instead, and the reason is probably obvious. The SOAP wire protocol must be serialized and deserialized by the proxy for use in the application. "Must" is a strong word, since you could theoretically do the serialization and deserialization yourself, but it makes little sense to do so. The .NET Framework code supporting the proxy is exceptionally complex, well tested, and freely available.

What you also do not see is the management of the service's endpoint. Using the development tools Microsoft provides, the WSDL conversion not only creates C# code for my application's use, but also stores the service's endpoint in the application's XML-based configuration file. If you open the configuration file, you'll find only *one* endpoint mentioned (http://www.weather.gov/forecasts/xml/SOAP_server/ndfdXMLserver.php). That is, even though the NDFD service currently exposes a dozen remote methods, they all are processed by a single service endpoint. This is a direct result of storing the SOAP envelope in the HTTP packet and sending all possible SOAP envelopes to the single service endpoint for processing.

REST—The RPC Web Service Alternative

This discussion of RPC-based Web services was intentionally short. The reason for this is, of course, that this book deals with a different kind of Web service, the RESTful service. Although the RPC style of Web service undoubtedly has a place in our application toolbox, it isn't a good fit for all usage scenarios we can envision.

To understand what makes a RESTful service tick, it's important to understand how the Internet (TCP-IP) protocol stack differs as compared to RPC-based Web services (see Figure 1.3). The basic levels are unchanged, but look at the contents of the application layer. This content is no different than it would be for a request issued by your Web browser. (In fact, you'll use your Web browser to access a RESTful service in a few paragraphs.)

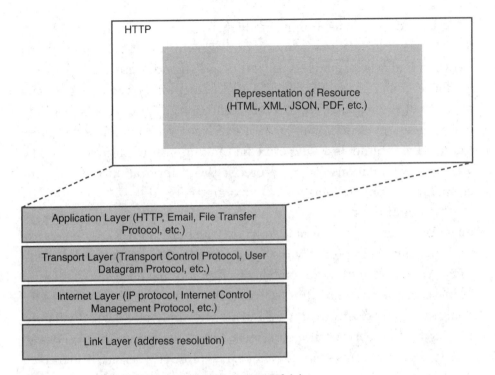

FIGURE 1.3: The TCP-IP protocol stack hosting RESTful data

Although you'll look at the HTTP protocol in more depth in Chapter 2, in HTTP protocol terms, items of information you request over the Internet are called *resources*. Resources are *addressable*. That is, each resource has an Internet address, identified by its URI.

> **■ NOTE**
>
> I should make something very clear at this point. REST as an architectural and design concept is *not* tied to the HTTP protocol. However, in this book we're talking about implementing RESTful architectures for the Internet using the .NET Framework. Using that more pragmatic outlook, I *will* discuss REST in terms of HTTP and other Internet specifications. But you should be aware of the distinction and why I seemingly equate REST and HTTP in this and the next chapter.

So let's consider what this means. First, when we work with .NET-based RESTful services, we'll be working directly with the HTTP protocol, the design of which is for stateless behavior. And second, since we'll be accessing those services using the "http:" URI scheme, we'll be accessing a *representation* of the resource by the very definition of URI. This is precisely where the "representational" part of REST comes from. Since the entire focus of the Internet is on hypermedia (linking)—after all, we call it "the Web"—representations (or more precisely the application state of your client application) are *transferred* as links are accessed.

This might not at first sound like a big deal, but the implications are huge. Whether we're accessing an HTML resource or a RESTful service, we'll access each in precisely the same way. Want to use a Web browser? REST works. Want to write some JavaScript and make a resource request from a client application? REST works well there too. The mechanisms for doing so already exist, are proven, and are well understood. We don't need a proxy, and the service endpoint doesn't need to dig into the HTTP payload to decide which service to invoke. Each RESTful service is identified by a URL. The server returns resource representations to the caller as it always has, whether the client asked for a Web page or for the local area weather forecast.

But this also relates to changing behavior versus updating a resource. In the preceding section I mentioned reasons why changing behavior is difficult, but when clients update a resource in your RESTful service, it isn't behavior that changes but the resource. Adding new resources is a simple matter—just add a new URI. This doesn't harm existing clients and doesn't force inadvertent changes to any client code.

To see REST in action, let's look at a RESTful service, *MusicBrainz*. MusicBrainz, or the organization behind the service (www.musicbrainz. org), has compiled a database of musicians, albums, and musical track metadata that you can search. They don't provide the songs in digital format. Rather, they can tell you which group recorded a particular song, how many songs by the same title have been recorded, how long a particular song track takes to play, and so forth.

RESTful services offer their services directly through URIs, and MusicBrainz is no exception. No SOAP. No service-specific proxies. Just good old direct Internet access. Because of this, your Web browser is as good a consumer of the RESTful service as anything else, at least for demonstration purposes. If you open your browser and type in the following URI, you should see results similar to those shown in Figure 1.4: www.musicbrainz.org/ws/1/artist/?type=xml&name=puddle+of+mudd.

FIGURE 1.4: Accessing MusicBrainz using a Web browser

By simply looking at the URI, you can tell a lot about the service. Its endpoint is hosted by www.musicbrainz.org. You'll be performing an artist search. The returned information comes in XML form, which happens to be the only result format MusicBrainz supports at the moment. And you're searching for information for a group named "Puddle of Mudd." Each of the services MusicBrainz offers follows this pattern, the details for which are found at the MusicBrainz Web site (http://wiki.musicbrainz.org/WebService). All you need to do is compose a valid URI for the service you're using and submit that service to the MusicBrainz host. Assuming that all goes well, MusicBrainz will return to you an XML document you can access to extract the search results.

In fact, this is exactly what the Music Searcher sample application does, as shown in Figure 1.5. The document you receive is representative of the data in the MusicBrainz internal data store. Maybe they're using XML, but it's more likely they're using a database. As external users of their system, we don't (and shouldn't) have access to their internal implementation. Instead, MusicBrainz provides us with a representation of the requested data. At present, MusicBrainz issues only "plain old XML" (POX), which is XML formatted using their proprietary schema. But other RESTful services are a bit more sophisticated and can export XML in the Atom Syndication Format (ATOM), JavaScript Object Notation (JSON), or even simple HTML. Something else to notice is that you receive a document, which is an object. Objects are nouns. RESTful services deliver representations of data and are considered to be based on nouns rather than on verbs as with RPC-based services. Any changes we would make to the document can be forwarded to the server and its internal resource updated.

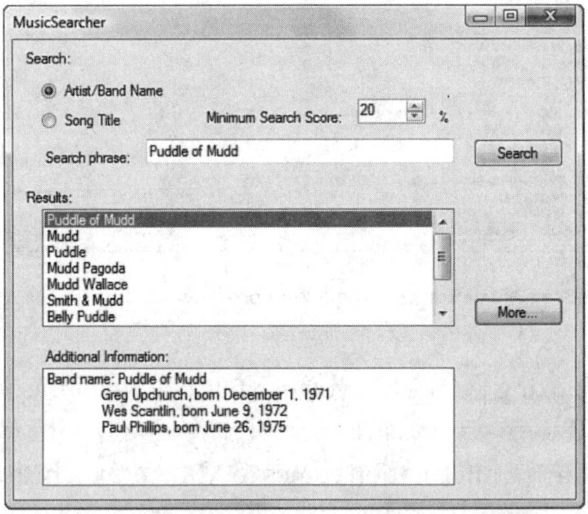

FIGURE 1.5: The Music Searcher MusicBrainz RESTful service test application

The first service request, which is for a list of artists that match the search criteria provided by the user interface, returns a collection of XML elements. Each element represents a single group along with a "search score," which is akin to a search result confidence level. The higher the confidence level, the more likely the results represent the group you're searching for based on the criteria you specified. The Music Searcher lists the groups in descending search score order.

Making the service call is rather simple, as shown in Listing 1.3. The code in Listing 1.3 composes a URI with the search criteria embedded as URI query parameters in typical Internet fashion (i.e., spaces are removed in lieu of plus signs, multiple parameters are separated by an ampersand, and so forth, which is known as *URL encoding*). The URI is then accessed using .NET's HttpWebRequest object. The results are returned in XML form, so the code creates an instance of XmlDocument, reads the response stream, and then processes the service's representation-specific information.

LISTING 1.3: Calling the MusicBrainz service

```
// Make Web request
string url = "http://musicbrainz.org/ws/1/artist/" +
             "?type=xml&name=puddle+of+mudd"
HttpWebRequest request = (HttpWebRequest)WebRequest.Create(url);
WebResponse response = request.GetResponse();

// Retrieve service response
XmlDocument xdoc = new XmlDocument();
xdoc.Load(response.GetResponseStream());

// Process returned XML information
...
```

From the code in Listing 1.3, it's evident that no proxy is being used—the information is requested directly from the server and consumed in the native response format. Moreover, we could send the server an infinite number of URI-formatted requests. Not all of them might be valid, in which case the server would return an error. But the server isn't tying the services to a single endpoint as with RPC. (The server *could* do that but probably isn't...you can't discern the server implementation based solely on the URI content and formatting.) The server instead can process service requests just as it processes other Web-based requests that are handled by its resource handling architecture.

RESTful Details

If at this point you have an intuitive feeling that RPC-based Web services are different from RESTful ones, your understanding is taking shape. Let's look at the mechanics of RESTful services in a bit more detail. The goal here is to begin to understand how to evaluate architectures as either RESTful or not and to understand enough to begin to design new architectures to be RESTful.

Generally speaking, RESTful architectures are simpler to implement because you're using protocols, techniques, and tools you've used to develop Web applications from the beginning. HTTP is the protocol RESTful services use, and it defines boundaries your RESTful services will work within. Put another way, HTTP defines the system your architecture will fit into. When you've learned how to work with the system, your RESTful architectures fit within the Web ecosystem better than other architectures do. RPC-based services can work over HTTP, but RPC semantics go against the natural flow of the Internet. For example, as mentioned, RESTful architectures inherently dovetail with caching techniques while RPC-based architectures fight it. RESTful architectures marry one resource to one or many URIs, while RPC architectures marry many methods to a single URI.

Four Guiding Principles

If you wanted look at how SOAP-based RPC Web services are composed, you would need to read, comprehend, and implement the requirements set forth in the SOAP specification (www.w3.org/TR/2001/WD-soap12-20010709/). This huge specification describes such things as how individual data types are converted to and from XML, how arrays are stored, and how single messages can be conveyed to multiple recipients with information unique to each recipient contained in the single message.

On the other hand, Dr. Fielding tells us what RESTful systems must abide by to be considered RESTful in his doctoral dissertation. If you were to read his dissertation, you would find that REST, in stark contrast to RPC-based services, is guided by four simple principles:

- Resources maintained by the server are separate from the representations returned to the client.
- Resources on the server are manipulated via the representations issued to the clients.
- The messages used to convey representations to the client are self-describing.
- Application state is transferred using hypermedia techniques.

The sections that follow go into these principles a bit more deeply. But they essentially say that however the server maintains its internal information and processing capabilities, the consumers of the resources are provided only representations of those resources, not the resources themselves. MusicBrainz doesn't send us their database. Instead, they send us XML representing the returned search information. When a client obtains a representation of a resource, it can modify or delete the resource on the server using the representation it has obtained. If you're a member, MusicBrainz will allow you to update information in their database, but you do so by returning XML to the server.

Messages issued between client and server do not require complex description standards. Just by looking at a RESTful message, we know the host, the requested resource, the requested representation (the "content type"), and the transport protocol and version being used (HTTP 1.0 or 1.1). And if we want to look for related resources, we should find links to those resources contained in the response we receive when requesting a current resource's representation. This notion has the unfortunate moniker Hypermedia as the Engine of Application State, or HATEOAS. But it essentially boils down to using hyperlinks to move from URI to URI, allowing you to examine logically related resource representations. The server doesn't keep track of where your client application is any more than it does my client application. Individual requests for resource representations are unrelated, even with the same client. The only tie you have to other resource representations is through hyperlinks provided to you by the current server response.

Resources

At the heart of REST is the concept of a resource. After all, it's the representation of the resource that drives us to build RESTful systems. But what is a resource?

We find a somewhat formal definition of *resource* in the architectural document for the Internet itself ("Architecture of the World Wide Web, Volume One, W3C Recommendation 15 December 2004," found at www.w3.org/TR/2004/REC-webarch-20041215). There, a resource is defined as such:

> The term "resource" is used in a general sense for whatever might be identified by a URI. It is conventional on the hypertext Web to describe Web pages, images, product catalogs, etc. as "resources." The distinguishing characteristic of these resources is that all of their essential characteristics can be conveyed in a message. We identify this set as "information resources."

The architectural document further states:

> However, our use of the term resource is intentionally more broad. Other things, such as cars and dogs (and, if you've printed this document on physical sheets of paper, the artifact that you are holding in your hand), are resources too. They are not information resources, however, because their essence is not information. Although it is possible to describe a great many things about a car or a dog in a sequence of bits, the sum of those things will invariably be an approximation of the essential character of the resource.

What is all of this saying? It says that nearly anything can be a resource. Some resources are more readily handled in electronic form, such as Web pages, product catalogs, and weather forecasts. But you can have other resources that are not electronic, like cars and dogs, and those types of resources will necessarily be approximated when converted to electronic form. In other words, I can't physically place my car on the Internet, but I can easily place metadata describing my car on the Internet. That metadata forms the electronic resource, the representation for which you would access using a RESTful service. MusicBrainz and its services are a good example. They don't store the actual artists or albums at their location; instead, they store metadata regarding artists and albums and provide that information to us in XML form. The quality of those resources is directly related to the quality of the metadata, but at least you can make the metadata available, as devotees of eBay can attest to when they try to sell items over the Internet (see www.ebay.com).

Addressability and the URI

I intentionally sidestepped a bit of the definition of a resource as identified by W3C in the preceding section. Looking again at the Internet's architectural document, the definition of a resource has this specific statement:

> The term "resource" is used in a general sense for whatever might be identified by a URI.

Resources are identified by URIs. And though it might sound like an oversimplification, without a URI you cannot have a resource. That is, if you have something you'd like to place on the Web, unless there is a URI associated with it, it's *not* on the Web. I'll have more to say about this in the next chapter when I get into more detail surrounding URIs.

Types of State

RPC-based Web services are not tied to a specific transport protocol. Given enough time, you could write a SOAP-based service that worked equally well over HTTP and SMTP without changing the encoded SOAP messages themselves. (Note that as of .NET 3.5, you can handle SOAP messages using both Microsoft Exchange Server and Internet Information Services.) SOAP has a definite affinity for HTTP, but HTTP use isn't required.

REST, on the other hand, is indelibly linked with HTTP when talking about implementing RESTful services using .NET-based technologies. And as you probably know, one of the foundational concepts of the HTTP protocol is that it is a stateless protocol. One HTTP request is completely unrelated to another, and in a pure HTTP world, the server is under no obligation to associate any two or more HTTP requests.

In today's electronic commerce world, however, we know that Web sites do, in fact, keep track of previous encounters. An obvious example is the Internet shopping cart. If I browse Acme's Web site and order half a dozen of the famous Eludium Q-36 Explosive Space modulators, I expect to later be able to advance to the "checkout" page, provide my payment information, and complete my purchase transaction. If the checkout page had no idea that I'd wanted to purchase six modulators, there wouldn't be much point to having a checkout page.

I used that example intentionally, by the way. I slipped in the use of *two* different kinds of state, one you're probably familiar with if you've ever designed interactive Web sites, and one you might not have thought of as "state." The first kind of state is *session state,* and the shopping cart is an example of that kind of stateful behavior. For any given session in which I'm interacting with a Web application, the maintenance of information regarding previous page access represents session state. Another form of session state involves "logging in" to a Web application. We expect to authenticate only once and then access any of the secured resources at will until we log out or are otherwise kicked out (timeout, for example).

The other type of state is *application state.* The fact that I could maneuver my browser, or any service client for that matter, from the product order page to the checkout page using a button or hyperlink is an example of application state. My "view" into the application is at first a product-centric view and then later a transactional-completion view. Although the two views are obviously related, they're clearly also different. The Web application I'm working with is presenting me with the parts of the application that apply to the specific tasks I'm trying to accomplish. When I want to select a product, the application presents me with product selection logic. When I later need to pay for the products, the application presents me with the product payment logic.

RESTful systems embrace application state. In fact, application state is so important that I mentioned it as part of the fourth principle of RESTful systems, and we'll revisit the concept later in the chapter in the section titled "Linking and Connecting."

RESTful systems eschew session state when it's hosted on the server, however, and by that I mean any form of server-based session state. (Cookies pose a special problem, which we'll look at in the "If You Give a Client a Cookie" section later in the chapter.) The concept of a product order page and a checkout page having knowledge of the products to be purchased is a fabrication Web site developers have developed over the years, and admittedly it works. However, strictly speaking, linking the two pages using server-based constructs violates the RESTful architectural style.

This violation has a cost. The session state information must be stored somewhere. It must age and eventually be timed out and destroyed if not explicitly terminated by the client. Although the client initiates and terminates sessions, it's the server that nearly always bears the responsibility for keeping track of users and their session state. Imagine the mayhem that would ensue if people who purchased goods through Amazon were asked to pay for someone else's order. The Amazon server must stringently keep track of users and their specific session state.

What's more, this information often must be made available across a Web farm where multiple servers are active. If you force a piece of equipment to keep track of the *specific* server a user has been accessing, usually a load balancer, the problem is by far *worse*. Using server-based session state at all reduces your Web application's scalability, but this is often a restriction Web site designers are willing to sacrifice to maintain proper application and transactional logic for their particular case. Very, very few experienced Web application designers, however, would force a given user's session information to remain with a specific server machine for the duration of their session. The effort to do that far exceeds any conceivable value, so alternatives like a "session state server" (a shared database) or a "distributed session cache" are typically used to allow multiple servers to share a single session structure. The cost of maintaining session state is therefore both financial and in terms of performance and system complexity.

This is not to say that maintaining such state is to be avoided at all costs when designing RESTful systems. Far from it. If the client browser generates a URI that moves them between pages while sending those pages session-based information, that's fine. You probably wouldn't want to do this with financial information, or even a shopping cart. But other applications we can envision can work perfectly well maintaining session state in this manner. Most Internet search services work in this manner as well.

Therefore, to be considered RESTful, the aspect of session state to avoid involves maintaining the session state *on the server*. It's not uncommon for Web site toolkits to implement server-based session state and ask the client to remember a "session key." Each request made to the server forces this session key to be sent so that the server can tie accesses to resources together.

The reasons for avoiding server-based session state management involve the interplay between client and server. If the server doesn't maintain session state, the user's session will never age and require timing out or forced removal. The client controls where it moves within the application, and the server is relieved of maintaining awareness of where in the application the client is currently working. Servers can then more easily cache resource representations, greatly increasing their availability and scalability.

> **■ NOTE**
>
> Actually, completely avoiding server-based session state is something RESTful systems do in an ideal world. In the real world, some resource access is limited and accomplished only after successful authentication and authorization, in which "roles" or "permissions" are granted based on authenticated credentials. In those situations in which authentication and authorization are required, REST tends to "look the other way," although we can imagine solutions that are more RESTful than others if not completely RESTful by nature. The "Security, Authentication, and Authorization" section has more to say on this matter. Other forms of server-based session state must be avoided at all times.

If You Give a Client a Cookie

If your service gives a client a cookie, it's entirely likely your service would be considered not RESTful. Dr. Fielding has this to say in Section 6.3.4.2 of his dissertation:

> An example of where an inappropriate extension has been made to the protocol to support features that contradict the desired properties of the generic interface is the introduction of site-wide state information in the form of HTTP cookies. Cookie interaction fails to match REST's model of application state, often resulting in confusion for the typical browser application.

General cookie use is considered not RESTful except in the specific case in which the client controls what cookie to send (by consuming and using the HTTP Set-Cookie header). The more common use for cookies is to maintain some measure of application or session state. In that case, the client no longer has total control over how it progresses through the application. Accessing the same resource through different hyperlinks could easily result in the creation and storage of different cookies. The mere fact that we have different cookies means we have different state. If we have different state when accessing the same resource, the system is not RESTful, as Dr. Fielding explains:

> The problem is that a cookie is defined as being attached to any future requests for a given set of resource identifiers, usually encompassing an entire site, rather than being associated with the particular application state (the set of currently rendered representations) on the browser.... [The] next request sent to the same server will contain a cookie that misrepresents the current application context, leading to confusion on both sides.

In general real-world scenarios, this usually isn't a huge restriction. Web sites as accessed by humans don't usually suffer greatly when cookies are employed. They often benefit. If you access an Internet search page and it "remembers" your last search because that information was stored in a cookie, the added user interface feature might be considered a good thing. It just depends on your personal preferences. RESTful services, however, are generally designed for electronic access and don't require such user interface trappings. For them, cookies are simply not used, again as discussed by Dr. Fielding:

> Cookies also violate REST because they allow data to be passed without sufficiently identifying its semantics, thus becoming a concern for both security and privacy.

Representations of Resources

Earlier, I mentioned that RESTful services return representations of resources to clients, and that the representations might be HTML, XML, JSON, or whatever other encoding the service is able to produce. How is this accomplished?

The choice of what representations to produce is up to the service designer. MusicBrainz, for example, produces only XML. Other RESTful services are capable of returning information in various representational formats, and there are a couple of ways the client can inform the server which representation it desires. The first technique is known as *content negotiation*. The second technique is to provide individual URIs for different representational formats.

Content Negotiation

Let's return to using a RESTful service to ferret out information for Eludium Q-36 Explosive Space modulators. Imagine this URI:
http://www.acme.com/Products/Eludium/Q/36

Given only this URI, the service has no idea in what format the client wants the representation. And yet, RESTful services quite often expose URIs that look just like this. So how will the service "know" what representation is desired?

The answer is formally known as *content negotiation*, but the term makes it sound more complex than it really is. The concept of content negotiation comes from the HTTP Request for Comment (RFC), Section 12, found at www.w3.org/Protocols/rfc2616/rfc2616.html. When HTTP requests are created, the protocol specifies headers that are used to convey information (as you'll see in Chapter 2). A few of those headers are most often used to determine what representation to return.

The first header, `Accept-Language`, tells the server what language you desire, whether it's English, French, or what have you. If the representation involves language-specific interpretation, this header conveys the desired language to the server. If the header is omitted from the HTTP request, the server is free to issue a default representation, with the server (and the designer) deciding what "default" means.

The other header is the `Accept` header. The `Accept` header tells the server specifically what content type to return, whether it's XML, JSON, XHTML, HTML, ATOM, or whatever. Some typical `Accept` header values are shown in Table 1.1. If the `Accept` header is missing or has the value */*, then as with a missing `Accept-Language` header, the server issues a default representational content type.

Table 1.1: Common HTTP content type header values

Accept/Content-Type Header Value	Representation
text/html	HTML
application/x-www-urlencoded	URL query string parameters encoded as name-value pairs in the HTTP entity body (more commonly used by the client to issue representational information to the server rather than as a returned representational type)
application/xhtml+xml	XML using the XHTML vocabulary
text/xml	Plain old XML (POX)
application/atom+xml	XML using the ATOM vocabulary
application/json	JavaScript Object Notation

If the client provides information to the service, such as a representation to create or modify, the client indicates the content type using the HTTP Content-Type header. The returned content type, whether default or not, will also be identified using the Content-Type header. Something to consider for a RESTful service is that the client might not be, and in all likelihood will not be, a Web browser. In other words, patently returning HTML might not be the best choice for a default representation. You'll have to decide based on your individual service needs.

URI Design

Content negotiation is completely RESTful because it uses HTTP constructs to issue information. However, the HTTP headers are really just text-based metadata. As such, it isn't necessarily obvious which representation is to be requested. An alternative is to design your resource URIs with content in mind.

For example, returning to the Eludium Q-36 Explosive Space modulator URI, if we wanted the returned information as English encoded in JSON, the service could expose the URI like so:

http://www.acme.com/Products/EN/JSON/Eludium/Q/36

The URI clearly tells us that we will be looking at English (the "EN") as encoded in JSON. This might appear a bit frightening if you take it to the obvious extent. If we support eight languages and five encodings, we have $8 * 5 = 40$ different URIs to support. Does this mean our server needs to route 40 different requests?

In reality, no. We would handle this via *URL rerouting*. In this case, the "Products" resource at www.acme.com would interpret the URI and return to the client the appropriate representation. We'll look into URL rerouting more in the next chapter when we examine `UriTemplate`.

Given the two different schools of thought, content negotiation and URI design, which is the more appropriate? This is a matter of opinion. Although it's a simple task to examine the HTTP headers on the server and route the request to the appropriate handler based on the content of the header, it also masks the client's desired return content type. It's a bit more difficult to parse and interpret the URI string in your application logic, but it's very much apparent which content type is desired just by examining the URI. Dr. Fielding tells us this:

> The protocols are specific about the intent of an application action, *but the mechanism behind the interface must decide* how that intention affects the underlying implementation of the resource mapping to representations. (emphasis added)

He also says this:

> Because a client is restricted to the manipulation of representations rather than directly accessing the implementation of a resource, the implementation can be constructed in whatever form is desired by the naming authority without impacting the clients that may use its representations. In addition, if multiple representations of the resource exist at the time it is accessed, a content selection algorithm can be used to dynamically select a representation that best fits the capabilities of that client.

Essentially, Dr. Fielding is leaving it up to you. And so will I.

Linking and Connecting

The final principle of RESTful systems is the concept of maintaining application state through the use of links, otherwise referred to as Hypermedia as the Engine of Application State (HATEOAS). As I've mentioned before in this chapter, the Web application you access in your Web browser allows you to traverse both its internal links and any external links that might be present. By navigating any of these links, your "view" into the Web application changes. In other words, the application state, as maintained by the browser, changes. The existence of the links in the HTML documents you're viewing allows you (and the browser) to move through the application at will. This is what makes the Web the Web. The best part is that this costs your server little to nothing—the additional bytes of the URI as stored on disk and issued via the network. The client makes the choice to navigate and change application state.

RESTful services can exhibit this behavior as well. Representational responses to requests might provide related additional links or linking mechanisms that could be used to traverse the application space. Perhaps the link is represented by another URI as directly embedded in the representation, or a link could be suggested in the HTTP `Location` header (in some cases). This isn't to say *all* representations *must* return links to other resource representations. However, if other representations exist that are indeed related, you have a mechanism in place to make those resources more readily identifiable.

Security, Authentication, and Authorization

If there is a single area within the REST sphere of influence that is least well defined, it would be how RESTful systems handle authentication and authorization. Things change quickly, so it's entirely likely that by the time you read this, opinions and options will have changed; but what you see here is how things shape up at the time this was written.

First, let's get the easy stuff out of the way. If your RESTful service is important enough to require authentication, it's important enough to merit transport encryption, whether that's Secure Sockets Layer (SSL), Transport Security Layer (TSL), or even IP Security (IPSec) or a Virtual Private Network (VPN). Authentication issues aside, encrypt your important data using one of these means.

Authorization is also something we can dismiss rather quickly. How your application manages authorization is specific to your application and any framework you use to build your application. Authorization is the process of determining what a validated user can do within your system. Some users might only retrieve resource representations, whereas others have greater system access and can perhaps add or delete resources. ASP.NET, for example, has significant built-in support for authorization, although whether you can use ASP.NET's implementation without adding your own code is doubtful (see Chapter 6, "Building REST Services Using IIS and ASP.NET," for more detail). In the end your application merely requires a way to segregate users into those who can perform an activity with your service, or even invoke it at all, and those who cannot. The logic for this isn't usually very difficult, although admittedly it's unfortunate that at the present time we must write a lot of it ourselves rather than using reliable frameworks to do the heavy lifting. We can expect this to change over time as frameworks and toolkits grow to embrace RESTful principles.

The toughest nut to crack is authentication. Authentication is the process whereby an anonymous user requests credential validation and is granted access to the application, or in some cases is not granted access. But it's more than the simple act of logging in—after login, the service must maintain the knowledge that the validated client can now access protected resources. Logging in can be as simple as sending credentials, essentially the username and password, to the server and requesting validation. But what happens then? HTTP is supposed to be stateless. If the request to validate my credentials is forgotten the very next time I make a service request, what good is the system? I will never be allowed to access the service.

Clearly this involves some form of client session state. ASP.NET, if left to its own devices, would create an authentication cookie for you, the default name for which would be .ASPNETAUTH. An ASP.NET `HttpHandler`, the `FormsAuthenticationHandler`, then opens and validates the cookie each time the user accesses a secured Web page. And if in the end you decide to force this on your RESTful clients, it wouldn't be the end of the world. It's not entirely RESTful, of course, but the cookie contents don't represent something truly not RESTful like personalization information or a true session key. But even though it's an option, if possible you should stick to a more fundamental authentication scheme that's supported directly by HTTP and the Internet in general.

This scheme is of course *HTTP Basic Authentication*, which is described in RFC 2617 (www.ietf.org/rfc/rfc2617.txt). By itself, HTTP Basic Authentication is considered a very weak form of authentication. But when coupled with secured transport (SSL or TLS), HTTP Basic Authentication's weaknesses are for all practical purposes mitigated. The power of HTTP Basic Authentication is that it is implemented using the HTTP `Authorization` header. Since your RESTful service is most likely interpreting HTTP headers anyway, even if using designed URIs for content requests, this represents only one more header to examine. You'll look more closely at this header in Chapter 2.

Here's the problem. If your service caches the authentication information in any way, your server is maintaining client session state. The appropriate thing to do is to mandate that the client issue the `Authorization` header for each and every RESTful service call it makes. This places the added burden on your service to check for and validate every secured service request, but it's the only true way to be sure that the client is who they claim to be for any given RESTful resource representation request.

> ### ■ NOTE
>
> When using transport-level security, such as SSL, the HTTP headers are encrypted with the HTTP packet payload. Therefore, the contents of the HTTP `Authorization` header cannot be discerned by anyone but the client and the server under nominal conditions (i.e., the cipher isn't compromised).

.NET Tools for Building RESTful Services

If you're reading this book, your focus will probably be developing RESTful services using Microsoft technologies. Other technologies exist, such as Rails, but it's more likely you're familiar with .NET and want to leverage your existing skills and experience. This final section takes a quick look at the basic tools you have to work with.

http.sys and Internet Information Services (IIS)

Although there is a rudimentary development Web server available for use with Microsoft Visual Studio, the production-quality Web server you'll use is IIS. Early versions of IIS worked entirely in the Windows user mode, which is to say, in traditional application address space. But network drivers work in the kernel, so network information was required to be passed through the kernel/user mode boundary at high rates. This posed a significant performance bottleneck.

To alleviate this bottleneck, as of IIS version 6.0 Microsoft moved much of the IIS functionality into the kernel, the result of which was the creation of `http.sys`, the kernel-mode HTTP packet processor. In this way, network traffic and raw Web server processing both occur in the kernel, eliminating the kernel/user processor mode switch.

■ NOTE

Interestingly, the performance issue wasn't the driving factor behind the modification to IIS and the release of `http.sys`. Developer demand to have independent access to port 80 drove the change to IIS. However it happened, it's a tremendous benefit to Windows Web application developers.

As it happens, what remains of IIS in the user application address space is, in a sense, just another consumer of `http.sys`. Your own applications can also directly access `http.sys` and benefit from the architectural benefits that result, not the least of which is that you can directly control Web requests and responses. The performance benefits are significant.

That's not to suggest that working with IIS results in poor performance. Far from it. Today's IIS is very performance-minded, and what's more, ASP.NET constructs are now directly integrated into IIS processing space. You can augment processing by introducing ASP.NET modules directly into the IIS packet processing stream, and offload processing of specific request types to specialized ASP.NET handlers. These techniques can provide a significant increase in performance. We'll work with both IIS and `http.sys` in much more detail in Chapter 5, "IIS and ASP.NET Internals and Instrumentation."

HttpListener

When working with `http.sys`, you're working directly with Windows internal components. .NET provides a wrapper class for `http.sys` called `HttpListener`. By using `HttpListener`, you can create managed code that accepts HTTP packets directly from the network protocol stack, and you can work with those packets in a synchronous or asynchronous manner. `HttpListener` employs the familiar .NET eventing model to make your application aware of incoming packets, and you have total control over the packet processing and response creation and disposition. In effect, your application *becomes* a Web server itself. We'll work with `HttpListener` in Chapter 2.

ASP.NET

Without a doubt, ASP.NET offers a huge boost to producing RESTful services. It's packed with tools you can use, and what's more, if you're an experienced ASP.NET developer, writing RESTful services using ASP.NET will be easy and familiar to you.

ASP.NET now comes in two different varieties, or, more precisely, provides two different user interface models. The first is the traditional ASP.NET page mode in which HTTP responses are generated based on Web Forms. Web Forms model Web user interaction using programming techniques similar to traditional Windows applications—clicking buttons on the client results in events on the server you can handle, for example. You also have full access to the current request's context object, and through that you can decipher incoming HTTP headers and create an appropriate response.

The second user interface model is the model-view-controller, or MVC. Although the traditional ASP.NET page model is useful and allows for rapid Web development, it tends to couple the user interface components with logic that drives them. This makes integrated testing more difficult and mars the distinction between business logic and user interface. The ASP.NET MVC framework was developed to alleviate this problem. With MVC, there is a clear distinction between how the data to be presented is stored (the model), processed (the controller), and displayed (the view). Test-driven development is now possible, and there is a clear "separation of concerns" (the MVC mantra). Moreover, the MVC framework relies on a powerful URL mapping component that greatly assists you when designing URIs for your system. No more reason to design your systems to support ugly URLs!

We'll look deeply into ASP.NET's traditional page handling model in Chapter 6 and its new MVC model in Chapter 7, "Building REST Services using ASP.NET MVC Framework." The .NET tools that support MVC's URL mapping are things we'll cover in detail in Chapter 2.

Windows Communication Foundation

No discussion of REST and .NET would be complete without looking at the Windows Communication Foundation (WCF). WCF was created to unify the programming models for a variety of very different communication mechanisms, such as .NET Remoting, Web technologies, and message queuing. Because of this, it's an ideal candidate for creating RESTful services, and indeed you'll find such support in WCF today. Chapter 8, "Building REST Services using WCF," gets you working with WCF in general and introduces you to the ADO.NET Data Services framework, which is built atop WCF. You'll then take your WCF-based RESTful services into the cloud using Microsoft's Azure platform in Chapter 9, "Building REST Services Using Azure and .NET Services."

Where Are We?

In this chapter we looked at both RPC and RESTful services—their strengths as well as possible architectural detractions. RPC services map many methods to one URI, and because of this by their very nature they're different architecturally than traditional Web systems. The server must dig into the payload to process the methods, and because of that, things like caching and discovery are not typically possible. REST, on the other hand, maps resources to URIs. Each resource has at least one URI but can have several URIs. REST URIs are discoverable, and REST requests themselves are self-describing.

REST is based on the notion that requests for resources are provided representations of those resources, and if the underlying resources should require modification, the resource is manipulated via the representation. RESTful service consumers can navigate through the service application space using URIs just as human users would do using hyperlinks to navigate to different Web pages.

Both RPC and REST have their place in today's Web application. RPC services, though complex, offer architectural options that REST services do not, such as message-based encryption and digital signatures, multiple intermediate recipients, and federation. REST offers simplification and a return to fundamental Internet concepts when providing for data communication and service processing.

The next chapter takes you deep into the HTTP protocol, which is the engine that drives REST. There you'll see how the protocol works and what you need to understand to properly handle RESTful service requests. You'll also look at .NET support for processing and interpreting URIs, because the URI is central to RESTful architectures and concepts.

2

The HyperText Transfer Protocol and the Universal Resource Identifier

C HAPTER 1 DISCUSSED REST and what being RESTful means. This chapter takes us into how REST works. What makes it go? How does it work under the covers? Of course, the foundational technologies are the HTTP protocol and the URI. To understand these technologies is to understand REST to a great degree. Conversely, failing to understand these technologies often leads to non-RESTful implementations. So the chapter also discusses what not to do by exploring a set of HTTP and RESTful anti-patterns and why implementing services using one or more of these anti-patterns makes your service non-RESTful. Then you'll get into your first RESTful service as you look at the `HttpListener` and how to simulate RESTful services and clients.

When you are working with REST and RESTful systems using the .NET Framework, there are two areas you need to be quite familiar with. The first area is the transport protocol the .NET RESTful system will use to send information to you, which is the HyperText Transfer Protocol (HTTP). The second is the concept of the Universal Resource Identifier (URI) and some of the .NET technologies surrounding it.

HTTP has been around for quite some time, but how many of us give it a second thought? We happily type something into the address control for our Web browser, and the browser dutifully retrieves the information and displays it for us. However, the simple truth is that without a way to identify resources on the Internet and a way to transfer them from the remote system to your browser, there would be no Internet. That's how important these two technologies really are. And, as you might discover (as I have), their brilliance is in their simplicity. Just like intricate and beautiful compositions come from simple notes on a staff, so can complex and valuable services flow from proper applications of HTTP and well-designed URIs. The URI is your map and HTTP is your limousine. Well, maybe a jeep. Anyway, let's see how these technologies fit into the RESTful service space.

HTTP 101

The HTTP protocol was born from the need to transmit hypermedia documents between computers. As such, it is a request/response protocol. The client creates a request for a resource and the server provides a representation or an error in the response. The definitive source for information regarding HTTP is, of course, the HTTP "request for comment" document, or RFC, found at www.ietf.org/rfc/rfc2616.txt.

Requests and responses are called messages. Messages contain encoded text. Part of the text represents metadata intended for the server or for the client application. This metadata exists in headers. The payload of the message, also in encoded text and known as the entity-body, can be nearly anything. Separating the headers from the entity-body is a blank line (a carriage return/linefeed pair). Figure 2.1 shows sample HTTP request and response messages.

How the entity-body text should be interpreted is usually dictated by a header. Even binary attachments, like compressed application executable files, are sent as encoded text. The binary information is converted to a narrow range of acceptable characters in a scheme known as Base64 encoding. As it happens, this is done to protect various server technologies as some respond to textual commands (SMTP e-mail servers being a prime example).

The request message conveys a desired action using one of a small group of HTTP methods, which are shown in Table 2.1. With the methods themselves, Table 2.1 shows you the associated RESTful action. By inserting one of these methods into the HTTP request message, the server will be instructed to perform the RESTful activity using data encoded in the payload, if any.

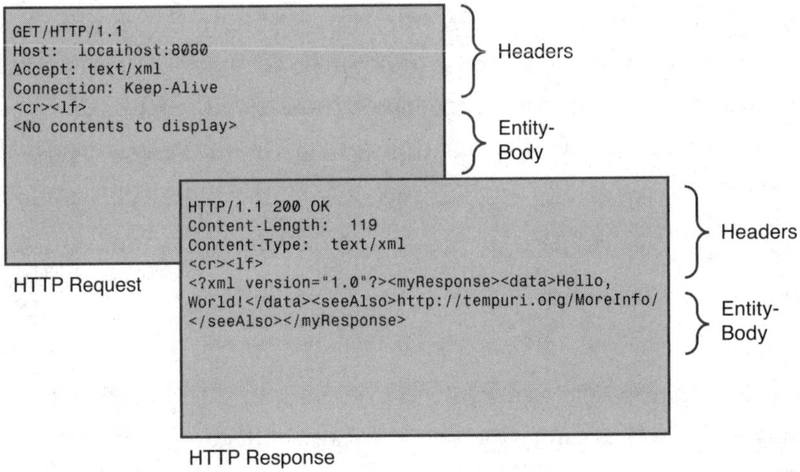

```
GET/HTTP/1.1
Host:  localhost:8080
Accept: text/xml
Connection: Keep-Alive
<cr><lf>
<No contents to display>
```
Headers

Entity-Body

HTTP Request

```
HTTP/1.1 200 OK
Content-Length:  119
Content-Type:  text/xml
<cr><lf>
<?xml version="1.0"?><myResponse><data>Hello,
World!</data><seeAlso>http://tempuri.org/MoreInfo/
</seeAlso></myResponse>
```
Headers

Entity-Body

HTTP Response

FIGURE 2.1: The basic HTTP message layout

TABLE 2.1: HTTP methods and RESTful interpretations

HTTP Method	RESTful Purpose
OPTIONS	Request HTTP methods the resource supports
GET	Retrieve a resource's representation but do not alter the resource in any way
HEAD	Retrieve the resource's associated HTTP headers (metadata) only
POST	Create a subordinate resource (server creates URI)
PUT	Create or modify the resource (client dictates URI)
DELETE	Delete the resource
TRACE	None (used to trace packet routing)
CONNECT	None (reserved)

Although it might be hard to believe at times, nearly all Internet activity requiring the HTTP protocol uses one of the HTTP methods shown in Table 2.1. The table identifies all there are, at least for HTTP version 1.1. (I'm discounting WebDAV, for example.) These methods form your programmer's "HTTP toolkit," or your application programming interface. Let's look at each in turn to see how each affects RESTful service operations, with the exception of the last two, which have no specific RESTful use. Although you'll see these covered in order (the order you see is specified by RFC 2616), I'll reserve the POST method for last. POST can be confusing and is often misunderstood when applied to RESTful systems, so I'll spend a bit more time there. We'll start with an easy one.

OPTIONS

The OPTIONS method isn't guaranteed to be supported, but when it is, it can be handy. It's used to query the server for the collection of HTTP methods the server will allow you to use. Wondering if you can delete a resource? How about create a new one? You can find out by issuing an HTTP request with the OPTIONS method and deciphering the results, which will be represented by a comma-separated value list identified by the HTTP Allow header.

Which HTTP methods the server supports might differ depending on specific conditions. For example, the server might respond with HEAD and GET for unauthenticated users, whereas it might respond with HEAD, GET, PUT, and DELETE for requests containing valid credentials (when using HTTP Basic Authentication, this would be the Authorization header).

GET

Probably not too surprisingly, the purpose of the HTTP GET method is to retrieve a resource's representation. If the representation exists and is otherwise authorized to be disseminated, the server will return the representation as encoded text in the entity-body. The client must then extract the encoded text and perform whatever conversions are required. An image, for example, might be encoded in Base64. The client must extract the Base64 text; decode it, which turns it back into binary information; and then process the image according to its needs.

GET request messages by specification must be both safe and idempotent. This is an important point, and one worth spending some time discussing.

HTTP Methods and Safety

Simply stated, safety refers to the state of the resource, or to be more precise, asking for a representation doesn't alter the resource's state simply because a request was made. That is, if you issue a request for a given representation using GET, or its related cousin HEAD, the resource remains as it was before, during, and after the request, at least as far as the client is concerned. Asking for the representation dozens of times has no more effect than asking for the resource once, or even not at all.

Practically speaking, many resources keep track of numbers of hits or keep tabs on which client makes a request. These things clearly do change the resource's state, but the key is that the client didn't impose a change, such as when using PUT to create a resource, or DELETE to remove a resource. To the client-facing world, the resource is essentially the same. Merely making the request for a representation didn't cause the resource to be deleted, moved, or otherwise mishandled.

Therefore, GET and HEAD are defined to be safe and must be implemented as such, the reasons for which will become clear in a few pages.

HTTP Methods and Idempotency

Idempotency is a concept that has its roots in mathematics, but the same principle applies to several HTTP methods, including GET. Idempotency states that performing an action many times yields the same result as performing the action once. Anything multiplied by zero yields zero. If I multiply by zero once or a thousand times, the result is still zero. You have the same situation multiplying by one. Multiplying a number by one yields the original number. Multiply the number by one a thousand times and you still are left with the original number.

How does this apply to HTTP? If you request a resource's representation once or a thousand times, assuming that the underlying resource wasn't otherwise modified or deleted, you'll get the same representation. It's a little more interesting with some of the other HTTP methods, and at the risk of repeating myself later, idempotency as related to PUT means you can create the resource over and over again, and in the end you have...the resource. An error is not supposed to be returned saying that the resource already exists. If you DELETE the resource once or a thousand times, the resource is deleted. In this case, an error is not supposed to be returned saying that the resource is already deleted. Idempotency as it relates to PUT has some implications regarding correct resource behavior, and I'll mention those when I discuss PUT in a bit more detail.

In the final analysis, GET, HEAD, PUT, and DELETE are defined to be idempotent and should be carefully implemented to truly be so.

Why Safety and Idempotency Matter

There are actually several reasons why safety and idempotency matter. Safety is *the* reason you know it is okay to receive GET responses from a cache instead of forwarding the request to the origin server for fulfillment. Since GET is safe, it can't have detrimental side effects, and thus it doesn't matter if the origin server actually processes the request or it's served by someone else on its behalf. You know by definition that you're not potentially breaking things by introducing caches.

Idempotency is similarly important when it comes to reliability. For example, deleting a previously deleted resource isn't an error since idempotency tells you that the side effects you sustain from performing the operation once are the same as those you get by doing the operation many times. POST (which is neither safe nor idempotent, as I'll discuss shortly) is the only operation in which each individual message is really important, and sending the same message twice might actually achieve different things. This is why you sometimes see browser prompts when you click the browser's Back button that say, "This was the result of a POST; do you want to resubmit?" You don't need to worry about resubmission issues for GET because GET is idempotent.

HEAD

The HEAD method represents an abbreviated request for HTTP headers, which in effect is a request for metadata. If the client issues the HEAD method, the server should respond with a valid message containing only the HTTP headers, but the very same headers it would have provided with an entirely valid response message. In other words, HEAD returns the same information in the HTTP headers that a GET request would have returned. The reason this is useful is that the client can determine whether a representation for a selected resource exists, how large the representation will be, and other useful information without actually retrieving the representation.

PUT

HTTP's PUT method is used with a known URI to both create a resource and update a resource, depending on whether the resource exists when the request message is processed. The new representation is typically conveyed in the request message's entity-body. How the new representation is interpreted by the server, and what information is represented, is specific to the service. But after the server accepts the PUT message, if the representation can be interpreted and is otherwise valid, the resource is created or updated. The resource's state has now changed.

Idempotency plays a role, and it's important to understand how idempotency relates to PUT. If a client issues a valid PUT message, the resource is updated (or created). Whatever the resource had been, after the PUT message is processed, the resource is updated (or created) in its entirety. What you cannot do is something like increment or decrement a resource. Imagine a resource as a simple integer. If I assign that resource to be 1024 once or a thousand times, the resource is still 1024. This is idempotent behavior. But if I tell the resource to decrement by 1 each time I make a PUT request, the first request yields 1023. The second yields 1022, and so forth. This is not idempotent behavior. If the behavior is not idempotent, the service does not abide by the HTTP specification. This is all too easy to overlook when implementing RESTful services, the result of which provides services that are well-intentioned but not RESTful.

DELETE

The HTTP DELETE method does pretty much as you'd expect—it deletes a resource. Because DELETE is idempotent, deleting the resource once or a thousand times yields the same result, which is the deletion of the resource. Your service can return an error on the first deletion request—perhaps the client wasn't authorized to delete the resource. But after the resource is deleted, it is not considered an error condition if another valid deletion request is received. The server might return some sort of status message in the entity-body, but typically an empty entity-body is returned to the client.

POST

HTTP POST is probably the most easily misunderstood of the HTTP methods because it can be used in several ways. Some of those uses are RESTful by nature, and some are not.

Let's start with the very definition of POST, which is provided by RFC 2616:

> The POST method is used to request that the origin server accept the entity enclosed in the request as a new subordinate of the resource identified by the Request-URI in the Request-Line.

The key phrases here are "accept the entity" and "as a new subordinate." When a server accepts a new entity, what RFC 2616 is really saying is that the client is trying to tell the server to create or update a resource, which sounds a lot like the PUT method. What differentiates it from PUT is the second phrase. The resource being created or updated is in some ways subordinate to or is a child of another resource.

Let's return to RFC 2616 and see what else it has to say:

> POST is designed to allow a uniform method to cover the following functions:
>
> – Annotation of existing resources;
> – Posting a message to a bulletin board, newsgroup, mailing list, or similar group of articles;
> – Providing a block of data, such as the result of submitting a form, to a data-handling process;
> – Extending a database through an append operation.

Here the RFC gives us some examples. The third example is one nearly all Web developers are familiar with, and it's a variation of this that the

RPC-style Web services rely on. (The variation is part of what makes the RPC-style services non-RESTful, by the way, as discussed in the preceding chapter.) The nature of the rest of these examples is essentially the same—they all speak to extending an existing resource.

How about an example? Imagine you have a RESTful service that stores photographs. Your service clients can create virtual photo albums, upload photos to those albums, and share them with the world. Your service allows the world to view the photos and leave kind comments. When your clients create new photo albums with your service, that action requires the PUT method. However, when they upload photographs, those photographs are subordinate to the album, so a POST method should be used. Similarly, when other clients provide comments, those comments are subordinate to the individual photograph and should also use the POST method.

There are two other ways to look at this. The first way is provided by RFC 2616 itself:

> The posted entity is subordinate to that URI in the same way that a file is subordinate to a directory containing it, a news article is subordinate to a newsgroup to which it is posted, or a record is subordinate to a database.

In a sense, you can think of this as master-detail information if you're familiar with that concept from database programming. You would use PUT to record the master record, but you use POST to record the detail records as they're associated with the master record.

The second way is to realize that when as a client you use PUT, you are essentially telling the server the URI to use to access the resource since URIs and resources are related. When you use POST, the server will assign the URI for you based on the parent resource's URI.

POST *Responses*

Although we'll discuss response codes for various HTTP methods and scenarios in the next section, I wanted to add what RFC 2616 states here since it has explicit guidance:

The action performed by the POST method might not result in a resource that can be identified by a URI. In this case, either 200 (OK) or 204 (No Content) is the appropriate response status, depending on whether or not the response includes an entity that describes the result.

If a resource has been created on the origin server, the response SHOULD be 201 (Created) and contain an entity which describes the status of the request and refers to the new resource, and a Location header

The first paragraph says that if the information that is posted has no associated URI, such as might be the case with comments to photographs, the appropriate response codes are OK or No Content. If you return OK, then you would also return some information in the entity-body. Such as? Nothing more is required than a textual message stating that the input was received and processed, but you could get fancier if you like. If you return no information, No Content is the proper response code.

The second paragraph says that if a URI is created, you should return the Created response code, as well as some sort of information in the entity-body that includes the new URI, and provide the URI in the Location header. Both are required.

POST *and Idempotency*

If you refer to "HTTP Methods and Idempotency," you'll notice that POST is conspicuously absent. If PUT is idempotent, why not POST? The reason is found in the underlying meaning of the method itself, which, if you refer to the RFC functions to which POST can be used, break down into two major categories: append actions and process actions.

PUT is idempotent because the resource is entirely replaced when the PUT method is accepted and processed. POST, on the other hand, could mean "append this resource to a parent resource," or it could mean "take this information and process it." To be idempotent, POST would require the server to identify all possible appended resources and ignore a POST request if it matches any existing appended resource information.

Let's return to the photo album example. To be idempotent, if a client used the POST method to provide the comment "Cool picture!" the server would need to ignore the request to append the comment if a comment that said "Cool picture!" already existed. This is the very essence of idempotency.

However, for the RFC to place such a restriction on all servers for all time is clearly too limiting, so POST is simply not idempotent when appending resources. In the case of the online photo album, you *want* each comment appended, even if the comment repeats previous comments.

It's far worse when considering the second use of POST, which means "process this." This use of POST is precisely how the RFC-based Web services use the POST method. Not only is this use not idempotent, but it's actually not even RESTful since the server must crack open the entity-body to decide what processing is required. A RESTful solution would have discerned that information from the URI as coupled with the HTTP method. There is no guesswork in that case.

To summarize, HTTP provides a limited set of methods we use to implement our RESTful services: OPTIONS, GET, HEAD, POST, PUT, and DELETE. It's important to recognize and properly implement the safe methods, GET and HEAD, as well as the idempotent methods, GET, HEAD, PUT, and DELETE. There is nothing inherently wrong with using POST, but use with caution because it's easy to misuse POST.

Of equal importance, however, is a fundamental understanding of the HTTP response codes. Let's look at those next.

HTTP Response Codes

Appendix B, "HTTP Response Codes," provides more details surrounding each of the HTTP status codes, of which there are only 40 (and one of those is marked as unused). The specific conditions under which the response codes are used are specified in RFC 2616, and you should consult RFC 2616 when developing your RESTful services to be sure you are returning proper codes for the given conditions.

That said, you'll undoubtedly become quite familiar (if you aren't already) with some of the more common ones. 200 (OK) indicates that the request was accepted and no errors were encountered. Other 200-level codes indicate varying degrees of success. The 300-level codes all involve a redirect of some kind, whether temporary or permanent. You return one of these codes when a client asks for resources that have moved.

The 400-level codes wrap client errors and generally indicate that the request will never succeed unless the client modifies the request and resends it. We're all probably familiar with 404 (Not Found). But other codes are important, such as 401 (Unauthorized). When you return a response code of 401 to your client, you're telling them that they need to provide authentication credentials. You express credential demands through the WWW-Authenticate HTTP header. The client will respond with a corresponding HTTP Authorization header. Other 400-level codes you'll encounter are 403 (Forbidden), which means the client can't access the resource even if they authenticate, and, at least with RESTful services, 409 (Conflict), which means there was a problem accepting the client's input, such as using the HTTP PUT method to update a resource with an older version.

Finally, there are both 100-level and 500-level response codes. The 100-level codes are informational, and you might see 100 (Continue), which means only that the server is still processing your request. This is generally used to preclude connection timeouts. Also common would be 500 (Internal Server Error), which you might issue if an error prevented you from returning information to your client, such as the loss of a database or another internal system, and perhaps 501 (Not Implemented) when designing or versioning your services. If a client issues a request using an older version of HTTP, say 1.0 or 0.9, you might want to return 505 (HTTP Version Not Supported). Unlike 400-level errors, 500-level errors generally indicate that the client has a reasonable expectation that resending the request unchanged will succeed at some later time. It might be a *long* time, however. There is no guarantee as to when an unavailable application resource such as a database connection might become available, for example.

HTTP Headers

Just as there is a wide variety of HTTP response codes, there is also a wide variety of HTTP headers. This section covers a few of the more common ones you'll use with RESTful services. RFC 2616 has the complete set of headers identified and is the source of all standard HTTP header definitions and usage scenarios.

Accept, Accept-Encoding, Accept-Language

Each of these headers specifies the content format the client would like. Accept specifies the content type (plain text, XML, image types, and so forth). The Accept-Encoding header dictates the desired encoding type, such as UTF-8, UTF-16, ASCII, or compressed. And of course the Accept-Language header value would be the language the client desires, such as English, Spanish, German, and a host of other languages.

Authorization

If a client attempts to consume a RESTful service and the service responds with a 401 (Unauthorized) code, the client can respond by providing this header and the appropriate credentials for the service. This header can be used in other situations, of course; and keep in mind that, at least for HTTP Basic Authentication, because the information is not encrypted, using a form of transport encryption is also appropriate.

Cache-Control

The Cache-Control HTTP header conveys cache information that all layers of caching must obey. For example, if the Cache-Control header contains the value no-cache, the message should not be cached in any way. RESTful services, however, try to take maximum advantage of cache.

Content-Encoding

When an HTTP message is issued with information contained in the entity-body, the Content-Encoding header tells the recipient how the information is encoded.

Content-Language

The converse of Accept-Language, the Content-Language header tells the recipient in what language the entity-body information is returned. Ideally it matches the Accept-Language, but if the server cannot return information in that language, a suitable default can be used.

Content-Length

Content-Length provides the number of octets (think: bytes) that follow the blank line separating the headers from the entity-body.

Content-Type

Content-Type is the converse of Accept in that it identifies the content type of the response. As with the desired language, ideally the returned content type matches the type that was requested, but this is not guaranteed. The server may, if necessary, return another content type if it cannot otherwise meet the request, or it might return one of several HTTP response codes with no returned representation. For example, the server might return 303 (See other), 400 (Bad Request), 404 (Not Found), 415 (Unsupported Media Type), or even 500 (Internal Server Error), depending on the specific service implementation.

ETag

The HTTP entity tag header, ETag, is used for comparison with other versions of the same resource or to manage concurrency. The value of the header is resource-specific.

Host

The Host header simply specifies the host (and optional port) to which the message is directed.

If-*

Several HTTP headers control content requests based on cache information, including If-Match, If-Modified-Since, If-None-Match, If-Range, and If-Unmodified-Since. A related header, Last-Modified, conveys the date the resource was last updated (or created).

Location

When resources are created, or when suggesting a URI to be redirected to, the HTTP Location header contains the URI of interest.

User-Agent

This HTTP header contains information about the client requesting the resource's representation. Servers can use this information to better provide appropriate response messages, use it for statistical purposes, or ignore the header completely.

WWW-Authenticate

The WWW-Authenticate header must be included in any message your service issues for which the HTTP response code is 401 (Unauthorized). It contains a comma-separated list of challenges that indicate the authentication schemes the service will accept.

There are many more HTTP headers I didn't mention. If they're not included here, it does not mean you won't need them—Pragma, User-Agent, and Expires, to name a few. The few shown here were simply my selection for the more common headers you would encounter. Be sure to see RFC 2616 for the complete list.

ETag, *Caching, and Conditional* GET

I mentioned ETag and some of the If-* HTTP headers, but as in RFC 2616, I've mentioned them in the context of "they exist." But how are they used? Why are they really there? The answers to those questions aren't necessarily obvious.

The purpose of these HTTP headers is to support a *conditional GET*, which is defined as the following by RFC 2616:

> The semantics of the GET method change to a "conditional GET" if the request message includes an If-Modified-Since, If-Unmodified-Since, If-Match, If-None-Match, or If-Range header field. A conditional GET method requests that the entity be transferred only under the circumstances described by the conditional header field(s). The conditional GET method is intended to reduce unnecessary network usage by allowing cached entities to be refreshed without requiring multiple requests or transferring data already held by the client.

In a nutshell, RFC 2616 is telling you that you can reduce your server's overall workload and create more efficient RESTful services by using a combination of `If-*` headers. `ETag`, which is new for HTTP 1.1, is typically used to identify the current version of the resource being requested. By combining `ETag` and `If-*` headers, you can examine the client request, and if the resource is unchanged, your service can immediately issue an HTTP 304 (`Not Modified`) response code and skip any further processing.

Here's how it works, and (by design) the algorithm is rather simple:

1. If the client requests a resource and includes the `If-None-Match` HTTP header, continue. If not, return the current representation to the client. Without `If-None-Match` you can't take advantage of this efficiency and must always return the latest version (note most browsers include this for you, as should your custom RESTful service consumer applications).

2. Generate or look up the `ETag` value you would assign to the requested resource. It might be a date, a `Guid`, or another unique value for that resource.

3. Compare the `ETag` value you generated against the value the client issued in the `If-None-Match` header.

4. If the values match, return an HTTP 304 (`Not Modified`) response code. The version the client already has is current. If the values do not match, return the current representation to the client. In that case, return the `ETag` value you created in the second step using the `ETag` header and return the date and time the resource was last modified (or created) in the `Last-Modified` header.

In code, the algorithm would be implemented much like what is shown here:

```
void ProcessResponse()
{
    ...

    // Step 1: look for If-None-Match
    string ifNoneMatchHeader = request.Headers["If-None-Match"];
    if (!String.IsNullOrEmpty(ifNoneMatchHeader))
    {
```

```
        // Step 2: generate appropriate ETag key
        string etag = GenerateETagKey();

        // Step 3: compare incoming header to our ETag
        // Note the precise comparison...the values must
        // match exactly.
        if (ifNoneMatchHeader == etag)
        {
            // Step 4: matched, so return Not Modified
            response.StatusCode = (Int32)HttpStatusCode.NotModified;
            response.StatusDescription = "Not Modified";
            return;
        }
        else
        {
            // Step 4: not matched, so create headers
            response.Headers.Add("ETag", etag);
            response.Headers.Add("Last-Modified",
              GenerateLastModified());
        }
    }

    // Return appropriate (current) representation
    ...
}

static string GenerateETagKey()
{
    return "\"appropriate ETag key, with double quotes\"";
}

static string GenerateLastModified()
{
    DateTime lastModified = ...; // appropriate date, in UTC
    string lastModifiedHeader = lastModified.ToString("r",
      DateTimeFormatInfo.InvariantInfo);
    return lastModifiedHeader;
}
```

The `GenerateETagValue` and `GenerateLastModified` methods are there as placeholders for this example, but their use is hopefully clear. `GenerateETagValue` will need to examine the resource and determine what the appropriate `ETag` value should be. If the resource is a file, you could use the file's last modified date. If the resource is represented by a row in a database, you could use a `Guid` (perhaps the unique identifier primary key or the row version). The only requirements are that you should make the value unique for the resource so that it will be easy to determine whether the client is requesting the representation with an older version in hand. Of course, syntactically the header value must be enclosed in double quotes.

GenerateLastModified is somewhat related in that it generates the last modified date for the resource. Note the string formatting, however. In GenerateETagValue if you returned a date for the ETag, you would probably use the DateTime "universal sortable date time pattern":

```
eTag.ToString("u", DateTimeFormatInfo.InvariantInfo);
```

The Last-Modified header, however, must have a date formatted according to RFC 1123, section 5.2.14. To do this, use the DateTime "RFC1123 pattern":

```
lastModified.ToString("r", DateTimeFormatInfo.InvariantInfo);
```

The date formatting is a subtle distinction between the two headers, but an important one. You're not required to use the sortable date time pattern in the ETag header, and in fact you're not required to use a date at all. But the universal sortable date time pattern is the pattern for a date identified by XML schema and is very compact. The RFC 1123 format is more verbose but was identified before XML schema had been created.

Finally, you probably noticed that I set the ETag header directly in the previous code snippet. I did this because there is a bug in ASP.NET that survives yet today. If you set the response's cacheability to private and then use the SetETag method, the ETag header will actually not be set. That is, if you wrote code like

```
response.Cache.SetCacheability(HttpCacheability.Private);
response.Cache.SetETag(key);
```

the ETag header won't be issued to the client. You might think that simply not setting the cacheability will fail to trigger the bug, but unfortunately private cacheability is the default setting. You can read more about this particular bug here: http://connect.microsoft.com/VisualStudio/feedback/ViewFeedback. aspx?FeedbackID=289274

HTTP Basic Authentication

Now that we've discussed the HTTP headers and response codes, it is probably a good time to talk about how you authenticate a client using HTTP

Basic Authentication. HTTP Basic Authentication is one of the two primary challenge-response schemes supported by the WWW-Authenticate header and is far more common than the other, which is HTTP Digest Authentication. The Basic Authentication scheme is more common simply because it is easier to implement. However, it is also less secure. It is completely unsecure if not coupled with some form of transport encryption, such as secure sockets or a virtual private network. RFC 2617 will provide you with more information (www.ietf.org/rfc/rfc2617.txt).

The Basic Authentication process is as follows:

1. The client requests a secured resource but lacks credentials.
2. The server responds with a 401 (Unauthorized) response code and informs the client that HTTP Basic (or Digest) authentication is accepted using the WWW-Authenticate header. Note that returning a 401 response code requires you to include the WWW-Authenticate header.
3. The client issues a follow-on request using the Authorization HTTP header.
4. If the credentials are acceptable to the server, the desired resource representation is returned. If not, an error is returned (which might include a reissuance of 401).

WWW-Authenticate works in terms of *realms*. As originally conceived, a realm is essentially a branch in the given Web site's page storage structure. The realm might be the entire Web site, or it might be one page or several pages hosted by the site. After the client authenticates for a given realm, the client is authorized to access all child folders and resources as well, unless additional authentication is implemented for more secure items. In the case of most RESTful services, the realm is simply the service itself.

The format for the WWW-Authenticate header is this:

```
WWW-Authenticate = "WWW-Authenticate" ":" 1#challenge
```

What this is really saying is probably easier to see by example:

```
WWW-Authenticate: Basic realm="www.contoso.com"
```

The WWW-Authenticate header text itself is followed by the authentication scheme, which includes but might not be limited to Basic and Digest. Following the authentication scheme is the realm. You might have more than one WWW-Authenticate header in your service's response, as would be the case if you supported both HTTP Basic and Digest authentication. The client is then free to select the method they choose.

When the client receives the 401 response containing the WWW-Authenticate header, they can either dismiss access to the site (perhaps because they are indeed not authorized), or prepare credentials to be included in the HTTP Authorization header, which is defined as such:

```
Authorization = "Authorization" ":" credentials
```

The credentials are also probably better understood by example.

```
Authorization: Basic a2VubjpteXBhc3N3b3Jk
```

The Authorization header contains the selected authentication scheme and the information necessary to authenticate using that scheme. In the specific case of HTTP Basic Authentication, the information is in the following form:

```
username:password
```

The strange mix of characters you saw in the previous example are simply the *username* kenn and the *password* mypassword concatenated with a colon and converted to Base64:

```
string decoded = "kenn:mypassword";
string encoded =
    Convert.ToBase64String(Encoding.ASCII.GetBytes(decoded));
```

The value kenn:mypassword is then a2VubjpteXBhc3N3b3Jk in Base64-encoded form.

Finally, RESTful services are supposed to be stateless from a session point of view. Just because a client authenticates through one RESTful method doesn't mean that the client is authenticated for other methods. Normally, Web sites issue a cookie and the client forwards the cookie with each page request as proof of authentication. But RESTful services should avoid requiring these types of cookies if at all possible and instead allow clients to authenticate with each request. For example, RESTful services that form part of a larger ASP.NET application could use the standard ASP.NET authentication cookie with each request to the REST service. However, a stand-alone RESTful service should prefer instead to use other authentication mechanisms—such as with the `WWW-Authenticate` and `Authorization` headers shown here—or perhaps even X.509 certificates. This latter approach more closely follows RESTful principles.

I should also mention that the client is free to issue the `Authorization` header at any time and need not wait for a `401` response from the server. Because of this, the challenge-response round trip isn't strictly necessary.

HTTP and REST Anti-Patterns

Now that we've seen enough of the HTTP protocol to understand how it works and how it relates to RESTful solutions, let's describe some REST anti-patterns. As you might already know, an "anti-pattern" is a way not to do something. We could have placed these in the first chapter where we described REST itself, but doing so without understanding HTTP has less meaning and impact.

GET Tunneling

It might seem odd to say this, but HTTP `GET` is used for retrieving representations of resources, and only for that purpose. Why would I state something so obvious? The specific reason has to do with application form URL encoding, but the concept is true in general. `GET` means `GET`, nothing more.

Application form URL encoding simply refers to the concatenation of form query parameters to the resource URI, as with this example:
www.acme.com/Products.php?Family=Eludium&Model=Q&Type=36

The values following the question mark (?) are the "form encoded" parameters the server would use to refine the request for the representation.

If that's all your RESTful service did—decipher query string parameters to refine the representation to be returned to the client—then your service is RESTful even if using ugly URLs.

However, consider this URL:

www.acme.com/CustomerMailing.php?method=remove&email=kenn@tempuri.org

In this case, the client's intention isn't to request a resource's representation but instead to cause the service to interpret the query string for the action to take. The desired action is now "tunneled," or masked, in the URI for the GET request and the request is no longer safe. As a result the action is not following RFC 2616 and is therefore improperly implemented.

POST Tunneling

If you've written many applications for the Web, you know that the very same query parameters shown with GET tunneling can be moved to the entity-body and interpreted identically on the server if the POST method is used. That is, we could POST the query parameters to the URL and the server would interpret them the same as it would having the parameters in the query string using GET.

For example, consider what happens when POST is used with this URL:

www.acme.com/CustomerMailing.php

The server would expect this information in the entity-body:

```
method=remove
email=kenn@tempuri.org
```

In effect, all we've done is moved the query parameters from the URL in the earlier example to the entity-body in this example. In this case we're using POST, so we don't have to worry about safety or idempotency, but the issue here is that there is another more appropriate HTTP method: DELETE. By using POST in this way, we're breaking the universal HTTP interface defined in RFC 2616.

Misused Content Types

The content types we use with RESTful services often dictate the particular representation of the resource we desire. If we ask for a representation using text/html, clearly we are asking for an HTML version of the resource to be returned to us. If we receive text/xml in response, we know to process the response entity-body as XML.

The anti-pattern here comes in two flavors: content types incorrectly applied and proprietary content types. Content types as specified in HTTP messages should reflect the most precise representation of the information. That is, `text/plain` is a perfectly valid content type, and it covers a wide range of possible representations, including both HTML and XML. However, it doesn't give the client much to work with. The client knows that the returned information is text, but it would then need to discover whether the text was HTML, XML, or indeed simply just text. It is not appropriate to return representations using general content types if a more specific (and accurate) content type exists.

The other flavor, that of creating proprietary content types, has to do with the ability of any client anywhere to access your service. If you use one of the standard content types, a list of which you'll find at

www.iana.org/assignments/media-types/

then your clients have a reasonable expectation as to the representation format they'll receive and how they can utilize it. If you create your own content types, the client cannot process the representation without a detailed understanding regarding what the representation means or how it is to be used. Without that knowledge, the client can't later update the resource if desired and authorized. Unless you have a very good reason for doing so, using one of the standard content types is always a better design choice.

Misusing Status Codes

As the section titled "HTTP Response Codes" explains, the HTTP protocol has a wide range of standard return values. Each of those values has a specific meaning. Even the given range of values has a specific connotation—the `100` range is informational, the `200` range indicates success, the `300` range indicates redirection, the `400` range indicates a client error, and the `500` range indicates a server error. With no other logic than to examine the leading digit, client applications know the basic outcome of the previous request even if they cannot interpret the specific response code.

When writing general Web applications, you probably don't need to worry about specific error codes in many cases. The codes `200` (OK), `403` (Forbidden), `404` (Not Found), and `500` (Internal Server Error) are what most applications use, and for the most part these suffice.

RESTful services, however, should be more expressive. Do not patently return a 200-level error code with an embedded error message if the REST-ful request indeed failed. Instead, return the most appropriate HTTP response code to give your service clients more information regarding the error and what might be done to correct for it. Appendix B provides more guidance regarding status codes, their meanings, and when you might return them from your RESTful services.

Misusing Cache

One of the reasons the Internet is so scalable is the fact that many representations are cacheable. If for every resource request a new representation had to be generated, today's servers would be far more busy generating content than they need to be. Many representations simply don't change often, and for those that don't, caching makes good sense. REST embraces caching as well, if only because REST is so closely aligned with the design and intent of the Web itself.

Therefore, two conclusions arise. First, cache as much as you can, both on the server and on the client. Enable your platform's cache mechanisms—if ASP.NET, enable output caching there; if hardware-based, put the cache tools in place there. Second, make sure that the infrastructure you're using doesn't automatically inject the HTTP Cache-Control header set to no-cache unless your specific intent was to disable cache.

Cookies

Cookies are an HTTP construct and are conveyed in the message along with everything else. The Set-Cookie (or Set-Cookie2) HTTP header conveys name-value pairs that represent the name of the cookie and the textual value to be stored with the cookie on the local file system. The original intent of the cookie was to manage user session state (see RFC 2109, www.w3.org/Protocols/rfc2109/rfc2109, and RFC 2965, www.ietf.org/rfc/rfc2965.txt), although contemporary cookies are used for more than strictly session state.

Because of their stateful nature, cookies are generally considered not RESTful. There are some limited instances in which cookies are accepted, such as for authentication or where nonsession information is maintained, but cookies should never be the only authentication mechanism if a more

RESTful means is available (Basic HTTP authentication, for example). Cookies are to be avoided if they contain session-based information, as described in the preceding chapter.

Lack of Hypermedia Support

One of the four main tenets of RESTful systems described in Chapter 1, "RESTful Systems: Back to the Future," is "Hypermedia as the Engine of Application State," or HATEOAS. The purpose of HATEOAS, admittedly an unfortunate acronym but one REST uses nonetheless, is to use the Web to maintain application state for you. Hypermedia links enable your client application to traverse the Web, URI to URI, in a way most meaningful to the client. If a service along the way doesn't provide links to other related resources, the client remains at a standstill.

Here's an example from MusicBrainz. Figure 1.5 from the preceding chapter showed you a nice user interface in response to the following XML:

```
<track id="3cab369b-c9be-41ad-b3b6-54258af0c765" ext:score="99">
  <title>Drift & Die</title>
  <duration>217573</duration>
  <artist id="ff460a70-fdf4-4aa2-b021-8a04da76d88e">
    <name>Puddle of Mudd</name>
  </artist>
  <release-list>
    <release id="af4f3859-4d53-4ccc-95e1-b1b00c0b24cf">
      <title>Come Clean</title>
      <track-list offset="1" count="11" />
    </release>
  </release-list>
</track>
```

When I searched for the song "Drift & Die," my application was given this bit of XML. Since the score was above the threshold the application was given by the user interface, the sample application then used the Guid shown in the artist node to query MusicBrainz about the band "Puddle of Mudd." With the band's identifier Guid, the application retrieved data regarding the individual band members, which it then displayed in the "additional information" list in the lower half of the sample's user interface.

My application's ability to query for more information based on a current RESTful response is the very essence of HATEOAS. MusicBrainz assumed that once I had track (song) information, I probably would want to know more about the band that created the track. MusicBrainz also provided information about the album (or albums) that contain the track if I wanted to find out more about those.

Just as MusicBrainz has done, your RESTful services should endeavor to not only return the prescribed resource representation but also incorporate related URIs into representations for client consumption. This then uses the hypermedia capabilities of the Web as intended and reduces server overhead for maintaining application state. The client applications traverse the URIs of interest to them rather than having the server maintain any particular state on their behalf (such as session state).

Lack of Self-Description

Another of the four main tenets of RESTful systems identified in Chapter 1 is the notion that they are self-describing. Whenever you create an artificial protocol, invent a new, custom HTTP header, or otherwise don't follow the HTTP protocol precisely, clients that assume your service is RESTful can't properly assimilate the messages coming from your service (or, conversely, you can't process incoming messages because the client didn't issue something you expected to be in the message).

RESTful services should follow the HTTP protocol, to include properly handling the HTTP methods and returning appropriate response codes. Clients then don't have to somehow satisfy your service's unique (non-RESTful) needs, and your service gains a wider audience.

Uniform Resource Identifier 101

At first it might seem simple-minded to talk about URIs. After all, we're all used to typing them into our browser and accessing the information they indicate. But when you're designing RESTful services, the URI is significant because it is tantamount to your service's interface, less the HTTP methods you allow. Good URI design can make for easier service consumption. Moreover, the terms I'll identify are used by tools in the .NET Framework, so they're terms and concepts you should be familiar with.

Historically, the URI was considered to be of two main subspaces: the Uniform Resource Locator (URL) and the Universal Resource Name

(URN). Over time, however, the distinction became less relevant as individual schemes simply didn't need to be broken into separate distinct categories. That is, the HTTP scheme, http:, clearly differs from the FTP scheme, ftp:. The URI scheme, urn:, is today simply a URI scheme that identifies namespaces. URL is now considered to associate a resource with a network location, according to "W3C Note 21, September 2001" (www.w3.org/TR/uri-clarification/):

> URL is a useful but informal concept: *a URL is a type of URI that identifies a resource via a representation* of its primary access mechanism (e.g., its network 'location').... (emphasis added)

Over time, the Internet community has come to realize that in reality, resource names and locations are really subsets of the resource identifier. This has come to be an important realization, because the URI is a central concept in Internet programming and use, whether your intention is to create RESTful services or not. Without the URI, there is no Web.

Addressability and the URI Revisited

In the first chapter, I touched on URIs and addressability. Every resource on the Internet must have a URI or it cannot be accessed via the Web. However, it is *not* the case that every resource must have one and only one URI. You must have *at least one,* but you *could* have more than one. If I placed vehicle metadata for all the cars I've owned on the Internet, I would have a URI for each car's metadata. But I might also have a URI for my favorite car, my current car, or the car I was most glad to be rid of:

http://www.endurasoft.com/Cars/Favorite
http://www.endurasoft.com/Cars/Current
http://www.endurasoft.com/Cars/Clunker

These URIs could be tied to individual copies of the metadata for my cars in general, but it's more likely the case that I would store car metadata once and my server implementation would provide multiple links to the existing metadata for the various cars of interest (my favorite, my current, and so on). This way I make more effective use of my limited server disk space and processing capabilities. The data maintenance costs are also reduced. For example, if I added the car's value, maintenance records, and so forth to my car resources, it's much easier to do so and the URIs don't necessarily change.

The reverse is not true, though. Two resources cannot share the same URI or you could not distinguish between them. URIs uniquely identify resources, and intuitively that makes sense. How would your browser react if you typed in a URL and the Internet somehow decided that *two* pages existed for that single URL?

The notion that resources are tied to URIs also leads to the concept of *tunneling*. This is a more formal term for the situation we face when using RPC-based services. RPC-based services use a single endpoint, and all requests for service are funneled though that one entry point. URIs allow us to layer access to representations of resources because we can have as many URIs as we need. We don't need to arbitrarily limit our service to a single entry URI. And in fact we truly don't want to route all of our requests through a single endpoint when designing RESTful architectures.

Why? For discoverability. That is, Internet search services crawl the Web looking for information to index. If you have URIs associated with your services, your services are discoverable by the algorithms the crawlers use. RPC-service endpoints are not discoverable in this sense. For them to be found and be searchable (by humans, mind you, not machines), the RPC-service must also provide a Web page with the germane keywords necessary for you to locate the services they provide. RESTful architectures, however, embrace discoverability. One can easily envision a resource having an HTML representation for discovery and general information while supporting other representations in more electronically digestible formats.

> **▪ NOTE**
>
> RPC-based services formerly used a protocol for discoverability known as Universal Description Discovery and Integration (UDDI). The idea was that there would be an Internet-wide central clearinghouse for service information, supported by Microsoft, IBM, and Ariba, that would provide you with service identity and capability in electronic form. However, although the protocol certainly still exists and is used within the firewall, the Internet-wide service failed to catch on and is now extinct. To find RPC-based services, you are relegated to using traditional Internet search engines.

To this point, what you've read is the "official word" on resources and URIs as interpreted and presented by yours truly. If you have a resource, you have a URI. No URI, no resource. But there is a cultural side to the URI as well that doesn't show up in the "official" Internet architectural document. I'm referring to the "ugly URL."

Although there is no requirement for you to do so, many designers architecting RESTful systems strive to use URIs that are both expressive and easily remembered (by you, not your software). Let's again imagine you were interested in looking for product information regarding Acme's Eludium Q-36 Explosive Space modulator. One possible URI is the following:

```
http://www.acme.com/Products.php?Family=Eludium&Model=Q&Type=36.
```

Just by inspection, you can ascertain that the product the URI refers to is Eludium Q-36, but try closing the book, taking a break (perhaps grabbing a cold Diet Dew), and then sitting down and typing that URI into your browser from memory. Were you successful? Could you recall it after a week? Even if you could, Internet search engines can't do more than search for available information contained within the Products.php page. Unless the entire URI was stored as a hyperlink somewhere, the query string parameters are undiscoverable. That is, the Eludium Q-36 hyperlink would need to look like so:

```
<a href="http://www.acme.com/Products.php?Family=Eludium&
Model=Q&Type=36">Eludium Q-36</a>
```

If all you knew was "Products.php," you would have no idea what query string parameters were necessary for finding information regarding Eludium Q-36 Explosive Space modulators. You couldn't *synthesize* the URI. This is the very essence of an ugly URL. You can't search for it and you can't create it out of thin air.

Now let's contrast the ugly Eludium Q-36 URL to one that is more intuitive. Consider this sample URI:

```
http://www.acme.com/Products/Eludium/Q/36
```

This URI is clearly easier to remember, and what's more apparent is that it's easier to search for and synthesize. Even if I was wrong synthesizing the URI, I'd probably be close, and Internet search engines can easily find this information, assuming that the RESTful system behind the URI exposes the resource information as (at least) HTML (which while violating principles of presentation versus data seems to be the most often-selected default content type). To make it a more complete RESTful service, the server would expose the product information as HTML and something else that's more electronically friendly, like XML or JSON.

And as you might expect, .NET provides you with some superior tools to work with URIs, far more than simple things like `String.Format`. (However, some of these tools didn't appear until .NET version 3.5, so if you've never heard of them, don't worry too much.) Before we dive into the tools, though, let's look at the URI to see why it's such a simple yet powerful concept.

The Power Behind the Concept

The formal definition of the URI has gone through many iterations, but the latest RFC is RFC 3986 (www.ietf.org/rfc/rfc3986.txt). Contained within the RFC is a section that talks about the design considerations for the URI itself: transcription, separating identification from interaction, and hierarchy. It also addresses syntax, which we'll look at shortly. But because the URI is so central to RESTful systems, and because of its simplicity we often overlook the thought that went into it. I'll reiterate the design considerations here.

Transcription

Obviously the URI is critical to the Internet from a parsing and electronic use standpoint. Without it, our browsers and service clients have no means to address resources and their representations on the Web.

But the URI is also something you and I can talk about. I can tell you to "check out the latest version of Unity at CodePlex.com," and though you might not know what Unity is, you can still access CodePlex.com and find it. (Unity, by the way, is a toolset to inject aspect-oriented programming into your own applications, and my apology for the pun…see www.codeplex.com/unity/.) The classic scenario is writing a URI on a napkin and handing the napkin to a colleague.

The idea is simply that we can transcribe (write down) the URI and work with it in non-electronic means as easily as with electronic tools. The alphabet the URI must consist of is the Latin alphabet, digits, and a small handful of special characters such as %, &, and ?, although there are suggestions in the works to include other character sets. The reason for this is primarily that people will need to remember URIs and the keyboards we use don't necessarily have other special characters that otherwise might have been included. When the URI was designed, it was designed with the specific intent of making it readable over using other more electronically optimized encodings.

Why mention this? I mention it because RESTful services strive to use meaningful URIs. And if you strive to use meaningful URIs, you're working in concert with the explicit intent of the Internet design community. That and you can still jot down your service's URI and hand it to a friend to try.

Separating Identification from Interaction

As its name suggests, the URI is an identification mechanism. The URI in no way guarantees you'll have access to the resource (or its representation). It only provides a way to identify the resource. Accessing the resource is the responsibility of the protocol or system context in which the URI is used. There is a distinct separation between identifying something, say potato chips, and accessing them by driving to the grocery and buying a bag.

The RFC does identify two actions to be taken with URIs: resolving and dereferencing. Resolving a URI means to determine the access mechanism to be used to dereference the resource, and the RFC notes that this can be iterative. Dereferencing refers to the actual access mechanism determined by resolution. Access is not guaranteed, however.

Dereferencing is designed to be late-bound, which is to say how the resource is accessed is determined at the point in time the request for access is made. This allows for things to change over time. The RFC also states that even though protocols are often specified in the URI, access to the resource isn't necessarily accomplished using the specified protocol. HTTP GET is a good example of dereferencing.

As applied to RESTful systems, we know that a single URI can be used for a number of different interactions, which is to say a single URI can be used for insertion, update, and deletion, as well as simple reads. We don't need one URI to insert a resource and another to read it back. We also know that clients of our services should expect to bind to our services at the time they are accessed, which allows us to change underlying implementations and physical locations without harm to the client.

Hierarchical Identification

If you were to look at a URI closely, you would undoubtedly notice that it's hierarchical by nature with more-significant (least specialized) components toward the left and less-significant (most specialized) components to the right.

For example, a URI that begins with http: could be referring to any resource available on the Internet. That's a pretty large group of resources, so more specialization is needed. Next you typically see some sort of domain name, like contoso.com. This is a bit more specialized—we know we're going to access resource representations hosted by Contoso. As more pieces are added, we get more and more specialized.

RFC 3986 provides us with the syntax for a URI, which is shown in Figure 2.2.

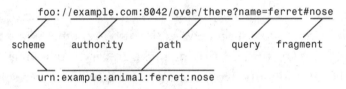

FIGURE 2.2: URI syntax

What you're probably used to calling the protocol is actually known as the *scheme*. The host piece, including an optional port identifier, is called the *authority*. Everything following the authority up to an optional question mark is the *path*. The query string parameters following the question mark are collectively known as the *query*. And if there is a hash (the #), that's called a *fragment*.

From a RESTful perspective, this is important for a couple of reasons. First, URIs are becoming useful for more than napkin-passing fodder. Applications in addition to browsers use them, a great example being the Help system included with Visual Studio 2008. Presumably these same applications should be able to also access a RESTful service with little to no change depending on the nature of the service. Therefore, understanding the composition of the URI is of more than passing interest to RESTful system architects. And second, the terms in particular are used by the .NET Framework, so understanding what they mean and to which part of the URI they refer is necessary when using the tools.

.NET Tools of the Trade—`UriTemplate`, `UriTemplateMatch`, `UriTemplateTable`, and `UriBuilder`

URIs are used for a great many things today, and because of this, it's a wise idea to consider designing URIs for your services in nearly the same way you'd design a C# interface class. But as good as that sounds, in practical terms it tends to be difficult. For each URI you produce, you have to provide a resource, so the implied contract is one URI, one resource. More than one URI can identify the same resource, but you shouldn't have URIs that map to no resources. Right?

Looking at `UriTemplate` *and* `UriTemplateMatch`

Well, let's think about that. In the end the client is asking for a particular representation. If I have the following two URIs, do they have to identify the same resource, two resources, or any resource I care to return?

```
www.acme.com/Products.php?Family=Eludium&Model=Q&Type=36

www.acme.com/Products/Eludium/Q/36
```

RFC 3986 tells us that we can do just about anything we like, and that the preceding two URIs might or might not be equivalent. Which brings me to the point: In pragmatic terms, our server logic needs to be able to break apart URIs handed to us to decide how to handle the request. Naïve implementations certainly do place a resource for every URI, and the servers that serve the resource's representation dutifully return whatever it is they're asked to return.

However, since we have no requirement to physically tie a resource to a given URI, wouldn't it be great to be able to easily design URIs, and when our application is actually running, take incoming URIs and parse them into the designs we established? If an incoming request matches a URI we designed, we serve the request. If not, we return an HTTP error code, probably `404` (`Not Found`). With this mechanism in place, we don't need to statically bind resources to URIs. We can instead process incoming requests and dole them out based on thoughtful application logic. Put another way, imagine being a certain online merchant that provides millions of products, or another online auctioning service. Would they bind each product to a specific resource within their application stack? More pragmatically, RESTful applications often have to deal with a large number of URIs. Do you want to write one `if` statement for every single URI your service must process? Of course not, and here's how to tackle this problem.

It just so happens that version 3.5 of the .NET Framework provides a tool we can use to do just this—`UriTemplate`. `UriTemplate` allows you to establish patterns in URIs in the same way `String.Format` allows you to establish substitution patterns in templatized format strings. (However, note that `UriTemplate` properly handles the escaping of input values for you, unlike `String.Format`.) Let's look at an example.

Here is our Eludium Q-36 URI again:

```
www.acme.com/Products/Eludium/Q/36
```

If we take a wider view of this, we might break the path down into three parts: the product family, the product model, and the product number. If we were to put those concepts into a template, it might look like this:

```
www.acme.com/Products/{family}/{model}/{number}
```

The values in the curly braces are variable, and with this template we shift from a single product (Eludium Q-36) to the capability to handle an infinite number of products using this structurally equivalent URI.

This is precisely what `UriTemplate` does. `UriTemplate`, in the `System` namespace, provides two inverse methods, `Bind` and `Match`, that accept a templatized string, as in the earlier example, and allow you to create a full URI from the template using variable information you provide, or you can determine whether a URI you have been provided matches any pattern you support (at which time the variable components are handed to you for processing). The latter method, `Match`, which returns an instance of `UriTemplateMatch`, is particularly interesting from a RESTful perspective since we now have a tool to break incoming requests into manageable pieces we can shuttle to the appropriate processing logic. Note that even though `UriTemplate` resides in the `System` namespace, you'll need to add a reference to the `System.ServiceModel.Web` assembly to use it.

■ **NOTE**

In Chapter 7, "Building REST Services Using ASP.NET MVC Framework," you'll learn how to use the ASP.NET model-view-controller (MVC) framework to build RESTful services. It shouldn't be a surprise when you find yourself building URI templates the framework will accept, and when your services are invoked, the bound parameters are returned to you. The MVC framework is using `UriTemplate` under the covers.

Let's see this in code. Listing 2.1 shows the most basic use of `UriTemplate`, but you could easily use it in a more substantial application.

LISTING 2.1: Simplified `UriTemplate` use

```
// Establish our scheme/authority for later matching.
Uri authority = new Uri("http://www.acme.com");

// Create our template.
UriTemplate templateUri =
    new UriTemplate("Products/{family}/{model}/{number}");

// Create (simulate) the incoming URI.
Uri incomingUri =
    new Uri("http://localhost/Products/Eludium/Q/36");

// Match the incoming URI to the template.
UriTemplateMatch matchResults =
    templateUri.Match(authority, incomingUri);

// Report to user.
string report =
    String.Format("UriTemplate: Matching {0} to {1}\n",
    incomingUri.ToString(), templateUri.ToString())
Console.WriteLine(report);

// See if we matched.
if (null != matchResults)
{
    // We matched, so show results.
    foreach (string key in matchResults.BoundVariables.Keys)
    {
        string match = String.Format(" {0}: {1}",
```

continues

LISTING 2.1: Continued

```
            key, matchResults.BoundVariables[key]);
        Console.WriteLine(match);
    }
}
else
{
    // We did not match.
    Console.WriteLine("The incoming URI did not match.");
}

Console.Write("\nPress <enter> to exit.");
Console.ReadLine();
```

When you execute the application, the output appears as shown in Figure 2.3.

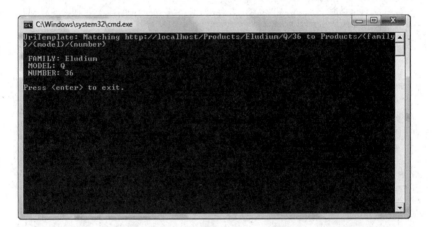

FIGURE 2.3: UriTemplate sample application output

UriTemplate is such a handy tool that you'll see its use here in this book many times over, but you'll find it embedded within its closely related cousin, UriTemplateTable.

Looking at UriTemplateTable

A common use for UriTemplate is to combine one template with many and effectively build a group of related URIs. And a typical way to group items in a collection is as a table, and this is precisely what `UriTemplateTable` does for you. The truly useful thing about `UriTemplateTable`, however, is that when it finds a match for a given URI, it returns a piece of associated data. If that data happens to be a delegate that handles that given URI match, you can invoke the delegate. The logic for selecting a method to handle a particular incoming request is then managed for you.

For example, look back at the URI used for the earlier example:

```
www.acme.com/Products/{family}/{model}/{number}
```

The parameterized values, {family}, {model}, and {number}, are optional from the client's point of view. But your service would need to handle one of many possible cases:

www.acme.com/Products/

www.acme.com/Products/{family}

www.acme.com/Products/{family}/{model}

www.acme.com/Products/{family}/{model}/{number}

Each of these instances represents a different nuance of service. The first URI would yield a representation of all products, like a product catalog. The second narrows the representation to a family of products, and similarly the third limits the returned information to a specific model. Finally, the last URI returns information about a particular product instance. If you needed to add logic to determine what to return, you would have to look at various possible URI matches. The code for this tends to be brittle and harder to maintain than it could be.

This is where `UriTemplateTable` is so very useful. If you create an instance of `UriTemplate` for each URI pattern you intend to support, and add that to an instance of `UriTemplateTable`, then `UriTemplateTable` will tell you whether an incoming URI matched. By judiciously choosing the data to be returned by the match—a delegate—you can easily invoke a method of your choosing for the given match. Let's work through an example. Imagine you want to return a full product catalog, information about a specific product, and information about a product family, but you didn't want to return model information. The code in Listing 2.2 does just this for you.

LISTING 2.2: Simplified UriTemplateTable use

```
class Program
{
    // The base address we'd determine from the first request (which
    // is when we'd create the template table). Since this isn't a
    // Web application, we'll simply assign the base URI.
    const string BaseUri = "http://www.acme.com";

    // The address path comes from the request, but we'll also
    // simply assign that for this example.
    const string ApplicationPath = "";

    // Normally the "context" would be an instance of HttpContext,
    // but since this isn't a Web application, we'll fake it.
    delegate void HandleRequest(object context,
                                UriTemplateMatch template);

    // The UriTemplateTable is created in this manner because
    // it will be created in a very similar manner in the
    // multithreaded IIS environment. This is the pattern
    // you will see in the remainder of the book where
    // UriTemplateTable is used.
    UriTemplateTable _templateTable = null;
    UriTemplateTable TemplateTable
    {
        get
        {
            if (_templateTable == null)
            {
                _templateTable = new UriTemplateTable();
                _templateTable.BaseAddress = new Uri(BaseUri);
                _templateTable.KeyValuePairs.Add(
                    new KeyValuePair<UriTemplate, object>(
                      new UriTemplate(
                        ApplicationPath + "/Products"),
                        new HandleRequest(HandleAllProducts)));
                _templateTable.KeyValuePairs.Add(
                    new KeyValuePair<UriTemplate, object>(
                        new UriTemplate(
                            ApplicationPath + "/Products/{family}"),
                            new HandleRequest(HandleFamily)));
                _templateTable.KeyValuePairs.Add(
                    new KeyValuePair<UriTemplate, object>(
                        new UriTemplate(
                            ApplicationPath +
                            "/Products/{family}/{model}/{number}"),
                            new HandleRequest(HandleProduct)));
            }
```

```
            return _templateTable;
        }
    }

    static void Main(string[] args)
    {
        Program pgm = new Program();
        pgm.Run();
    }

    void Run()
    {
        // Build a set of test URIs. Normally these come into IIS
        // as separate requests, but we'll simulate that by asking
        // for a match all four times.
        string[] testUriSet = {
          "http://www.acme.com/Products/Eludium/Q/36",
          "http://www.acme.com/Products",
          "http://www.acme.com/Products/Eludium/Q",
          "http://www.acme.com/Products/Eludium"};
        foreach (string uri in testUriSet)
        {
            UriTemplateMatch match =
              TemplateTable.MatchSingle(new Uri(uri));
            if (match == null)
            {
                Console.WriteLine("{0} has no match, not found.", uri);
            }
            else
            {
                HandleRequest handleRequest = (HandleRequest)match.Data;
                handleRequest(uri, match);
            }
        }

        Console.Write("\nPress <enter> to exit.");
        Console.ReadLine();
    }

    void HandleAllProducts(object context, UriTemplateMatch template)
    {
        // Return product catalog
        Console.WriteLine("{0} matched all products catalog",
          context.ToString());
    }

    void HandleFamily(object context, UriTemplateMatch template)
    {
```

continues

LISTING 2.2: Continued

```
        // Return product family information
        Console.WriteLine("{0} matched the family {1}",
          context.ToString(), template.BoundVariables["family"]);
    }

    void HandleProduct(object context, UriTemplateMatch template)
    {
        // Return product item information
        Console.WriteLine("{0} matched a specific product:",
          context.ToString());
        foreach (string key in template.BoundVariables.Keys)
        {
            string match = String.Format(" {0}: {1}", key,
              template.BoundVariables[key]);
            Console.WriteLine(match);
        }
    }
}
```

The result of this is shown in Figure 2.4.

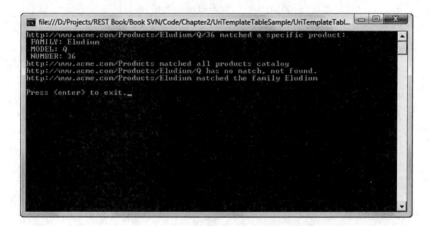

FIGURE 2.4: UriTemplateTable **sample application output**

The magic in Listing 2.2 comes from code like this:

```
templateTable.KeyValuePairs.Add(
  new KeyValuePair<UriTemplate, object>(
    new UriTemplate(
        ApplicationPath +
        "/Products/{family}/{model}/{number}"),
        new HandleRequest(HandleProduct)));
```

Here you're adding a single instance of `UriTemplate` to the URI template table. When a URI match is requested, `UriTemplateTable` will match the incoming URI against all the table's templates, and if a match is returned, you have access to the bound values (`family`, `model`, and so forth for this example), as well as the associated data you provided when you created the table. The data in this case is a delegate that is appropriate for that given match. Simply invoke the delegate and the appropriate method for handling the URI is called.

Looking at `UriBuilder`

`UriBuilder` has been around a lot longer than `UriTemplate`, and in a sense isn't nearly as useful. After all, you could use the `Bind` methods `UriTemplate` offers to achieve the same thing, or even `String.Format`. So why mention it?

Well, completeness is certainly one reason. But it can be handy for creating URIs nonetheless. `UriTemplate` will create URIs based on a template, but keeping HATEOAS in mind, you might need to build URIs given other information than merely a template. If you know the host, port, and path of another related resource representation and want to create the URI for that hypermedia link, `UriBuilder` is a nice tool to have. Listing 2.3 demonstrates `UriBuilder` in action. Like `UriTemplate`, `UriBuilder` is found in the `System` namespace and is found in System.dll, which all .NET assemblies use.

LISTING 2.3: Using `UriBuilder`

```
// Set up our URI components.
string scheme = "http";
string host = "www.acme.com";
Int32 port = 8080; // set to -1 to use default port
string path = "Products/Info/Eludium/Q/36";

// Create a builder object.
UriBuilder builder = new UriBuilder(scheme, host, port, path);

// Ask the builder for the URI.
string uri = builder.ToString();
Console.WriteLine(uri);

Console.Write("\nPress <enter> to exit.");
Console.ReadLine();
```

Of course, the output for UriBuilder is simply a string, which is obtained using its ToString method. The output of the UriBuilder sample application is shown in Figure 2.5.

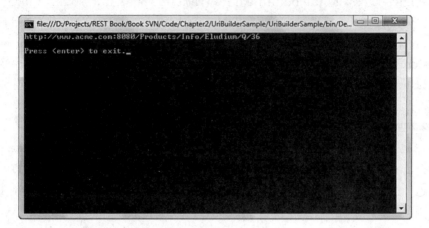

FIGURE 2.5: UriBuilder sample application output

Introducing HttpListener

The final sections in this chapter deal with HttpListener. Before writing the chapter, I wanted to produce a sample application you could use to view raw HTTP messages. The application quickly grew into a full-fledged RESTful service simulation tool, and I'll discuss the tool briefly. The point here is that in order to display HTTP packets, I had to capture HTTP packets from the network. To do that, I needed to find some way to hook the network protocol stack. I could have used raw sockets programming, used some socket driver (like a Web server), or even (gasp) dipped into the kernel and written some driver code. I don't think any of us wants to see that!

Actually, the perfect solution in this case is to use .NET's HttpListener. HttpListener is a tool you can use to hook into a specific port (socket) and intercept HTTP message traffic in much the same way a client HTTP proxy does. When you start HttpListener, you tell it what port to listen to, and any HTTP traffic coming into or going out from that port results in an event your application can handle. If you choose to record the messages, as the sample application does, that's fine. What you do with the event is application-specific.

`HttpListener` is essentially a .NET wrapper for access to `http.sys`, which you'll read about in far more detail in Chapter 5, "IIS and ASP.NET Internals and Instrumentation." `HttpListener` will listen synchronously or asynchronously. If used synchronously, `HttpListener` will block the current thread indefinitely, waiting for input HTTP traffic via the port it was told to monitor. The asynchronous wait follows the typical .NET pattern in which you tell `HttpListener` to begin listening but you also provide it with a delegate it can use to return the available HTTP information.

An example of synchronous HTTP listening operations is shown here (the asynchronous use is similar):

```
// Create a listener.
HttpListener listener = new HttpListener();

// Add prefixes to listen for over port 8080.
listener.Prefixes.Add("http://*:8080/");

// Start the listener.
listener.Start();

// Wait for input. Note thread blocks here...
HttpListenerContext context = listener.GetContext();
```

When `HttpListener` receives input, the `GetContext` method returns an instance of `HttpListenerContext`. Through `HttpListenerContext`, you have access to the request message and can formulate your response.

■ NOTE

`HttpListener` allows you to access the HTTP headers for both the request and the response messages. However, the `WWW-Authenticate` header is a notable exception—`HttpListener` won't allow you to access this header directly. Instead, you have to set the `HttpListener`'s `AuthenticationSchemes` property. To use HTTP Basic Authentication, use `AuthenticationSchemes.Basic`. Note also that in this case `HttpListener` will issue the `401` (Unauthorized) response for you.

The HttpExerciser Sample Application

As mentioned, before I started writing this chapter, I knew I would want to provide real-world HTTP packet examples. To do that, I knew I'd need to capture HTTP packets, but I didn't want to use a commercially available package (the legal arrangements are easier if I don't). So I began to write my own, using HttpListener.

I didn't get too far in my development when I realized I'd need a client application capable of sending various HTTP methods and a flexible way to tweak the HTTP headers so I could demonstrate content negotiation. But where would I find such a client? No Web browser would let me do this.

So the sample application quickly grew into a full-fledged RESTful service simulator, which I named HttpExerciser. It's a multithreaded Windows Presentation Foundation (WPF) application, complete with all manner of data binding, user settings, and all the latent bugs you'd expect from a sample application. (Well, I hope not, but it is only a sample.)

The application is complex enough that I thought I'd spend a page or two describing how the tool is used. There is a lot of capability for examining RESTful scenarios here. The primary user is shown in Figure 2.6.

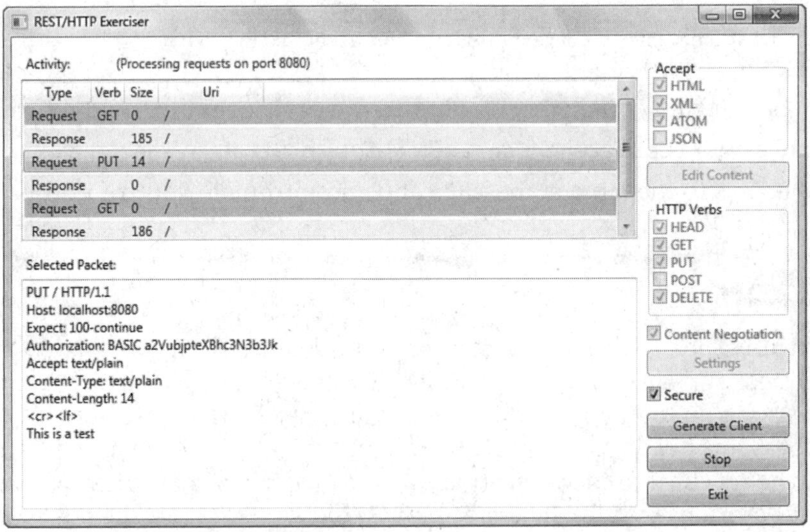

FIGURE 2.6: HttpExerciser primary user interface

When the internal instance of HttpListener is active, several controls are disabled (as shown in Figure 2.6). But when the HttpListener is stopped, you can choose to provide representations in HTML, XML, ATOM, and JSON. You can also choose the HTTP methods you want to support, including HEAD, GET, PUT, POST, and DELETE. Deselecting any of these effectively means your RESTful service won't support them. In the figure, we're not supporting JSON or POST. If the client asks for JSON or uses the POST method, they'll receive 404 (Not Found) and 405 (Method Not Allowed), respectively. To reenable either of these, select the appropriate check box.

You can choose to support content negotiation by selecting the Content Negotiation check box. If you don't support content negotiation, the URIs you want to use for the various representations you desire can be established using the Settings button. Clicking Settings allows you to choose the URIs just mentioned, the port you want to use, the resource value the representations will represent (a string), and the username and password that you'll accept for authentication.

The Secure check box dictates whether you want authentication to be in effect. Selecting Secure causes HttpListener to issue the WWW-Authenticate HTTP header and internal HttpExerciser logic to look for and process the returned HTTP Authorization header.

The Stop button toggles its text to Start depending on the state of the internal HttpListener object. Figure 2.6 shows that the HttpListener is active because the button indicates that it will stop listening operations when clicked. While the service is running, HTTP packets are recorded and are available for you to examine in the Activity list. Selecting one of the packets in the Activity list causes the cached packet contents to be displayed in the Selected Packet window. From Figure 2.6 we know that the client changed the resource value to This is a test. Here you see the HTTP headers, their values, and the packet entity-body contents.

When the application is actively listening, the Generate Client button is enabled. Clicking Generate Client brings up the client application shown in Figure 2.7.

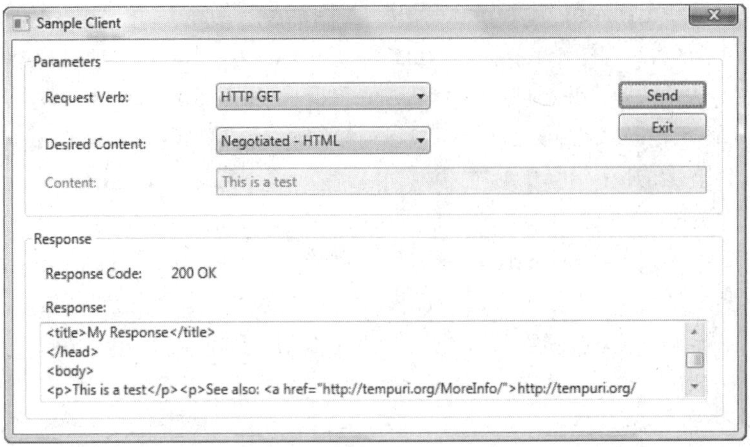

FIGURE 2.7: HttpExerciser client user interface

Using the client, you can communicate with the primary RESTful service simulation. You can select the HTTP method you would like to use, including HEAD, GET, PUT, POST, and DELETE. You also can experiment with content negotiation using the Desired Content list. If the RESTful service supports content negotiation, using one of the negotiated content types will return the content you request (assuming that the service supports that content type). If you use the URI-based content selection and the RESTful service is supporting content negotiation, you'll receive a 404 response. The converse is also true.

If you select the PUT or POST methods, you can declare the new resource value using the Content text box. The client application will send the resource value (as a representation) to the RESTful service, and the service will accept the new value and persist it.

If the RESTful service requires authentication, the client will pop up the dialog box shown in Figure 2.8. Here you type in the username and password, and if you don't want the dialog box popping up for the duration of the client's execution, simply select the Remember Me check box.

HttpExerciser allows you to experiment with nearly all the concepts you've read about in this and the preceding chapter. It also provides code you can explore to see a fully operational (or nearly so) RESTful service, and, if you're interested, allows you to see how multithreaded tasks can be accomplished in a WPF application (not a trivial task in itself).

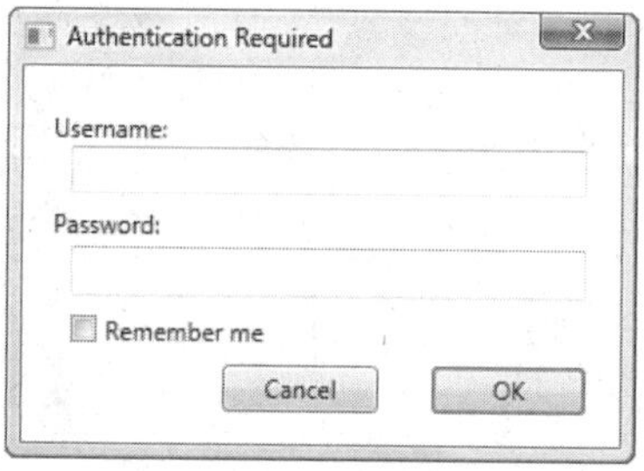

FIGURE 2.8: HttpExerciser credential request

Where Are We?

If you've waded your way through these first two chapters, you should have a good idea of what makes RESTful services tick. In this chapter, you looked in greater detail at the HTTP Protocol, including its messaging structure, its headers, and how it conveys information in the entity-body. You also saw how HTTP Basic Authentication works and even have a sample application you can use to experiment with not only authentication but also a great variety of HTTP-related concepts discussed here. The application provides you with the contents of HTTP packets.

You also took a brief look at `UriTemplate`, `UriTemplateTable`, and `UriBuilder`. `UriTemplate` is used to match URIs by pattern, allowing a single pattern to evaluate to nearly an infinite variety of actual URI values. `UriTemplateTable` uses instances of `UriTemplate` grouped in a table fashion to match more than a single URI. `UriBuilder` allows you to easily create URIs given the basic constituent parts.

Finally, you took a brief look at `HttpListener` and a sample application that uses `HttpListener` to simulate a RESTful service. `HttpListener` binds to a port and intercepts HTTP packets in much the same way a proxy does, allowing you to manipulate the packet contents as required.

Chapter 3, "Desktop Client Operations," takes you into the client's world where RESTful services are consumed. That chapter sets up the remainder of the book, where you learn to build RESTful services using tools that both .NET and Windows provide.

■ 3 ■

Desktop Client Operations

E VERY DAY, MORE RESOURCES are made available on private intranets
and the Internet at large. .NET has many different tools that allow you
to consume these services from any application environment: Web, desktop, and mobile. In this chapter, we will examine the classes and tools you
need to use in order to build applications for both of the .NET desktop class
libraries: Windows Forms (WinForms) and Windows Presentation Foundation (WPF).

We Still Write Desktop Applications

The desktop application has all sorts of benefits that, today, trump anything
you can do on the Web. Desktop applications have access to storage
devices, arbitrary network resources, and network hardware. They can
make application demands that their Web brethren cannot. For example,
you can write a desktop application that will install only to a Windows
machine that has .NET 3.5 or greater installed. Finally, these applications
can do something useful even when they are disconnected from the network. Outlook will still let you read e-mail and create new messages when
you are disconnected from your Exchange server. Outlook's fraternal twin,
Outlook Web Access, needs a network connection to work. Because of the
capability to do so much more when having access to inexpensive yet

powerful hardware resources (memory, CPU, storage, and so forth), desktop applications are not going away any time soon.

These desktop applications frequently become more useful, however, when they can connect to network-based resources. E-mail can be sent and received. Games get updates, communicate high scores, and, most important, allow for players to meet and play interactively. Individuals at your company update, modify, and delete documents through WebDAV and Windows Explorer. As a desktop application developer, you have one question you have to answer: "How do I get that data?" This chapter shows you how to obtain information from RESTful services.

Everything in this chapter can be applied to any executable you might write. Accessing RESTful data does not change whether you use a command-line application, a Windows service, a Windows Forms (WinForms) application, or even a Windows Presentation Foundation (WPF) application. The chapter concentrates on applications created using WinForms and WPF because those two environments have a requirement you do not necessarily have in other environments. Such as? The user interface (UI) has to stay responsive while the Web request is executing.

An Introduction to our Web Service

This chapter and the next focus on consuming RESTful services. The later parts of this book focus on implementing RESTful architectures. In Chapter 8, "Building REST Services Using WCF," we talk about building RESTful services using Windows Communication Foundation (WCF). This chapter utilizes one of the WCF services from Chapter 8. At this point, you do not need to know how the service is built, but you do need to know what the service does. A copy of the service is provided in this chapter's sample project in order to keep things easier to build and navigate as you work with this chapter's sample client applications.

The service itself demonstrates a few basic capabilities that pretty much every consumer/producer needs to understand:

- Exchanging binary data
- Exchanging simple data types

- Exchanging structured data
- Exchanging arrays of structured data

Understanding these simple building blocks enables you to build or consume any RESTful service. When I was looking at scenarios that demonstrate the previous capabilities without needing to implement an overly sophisticated solution, one scenario popped out as simple to understand and small enough to fit within the chapter of a book: sharing photos. Photos are binary and have extra, interesting attributes, such as an owner and a caption. In our case, photos have these pieces of metadata:

- Is the photo public or private?
- Who is the photo owner?
- Does the photo have a caption, and if so, what is it?
- Does the photo have an extended description?
- What is the photo's unique identifier?

The REST service allows users to do all sorts of things with photos. For photos you own, you can update the caption and description, and state whether the photo is public. Regardless of who you are, you can ask for a list of photos from a particular user. If you are that user, the list contains all photos. If you ask for someone else's list, only public photos are returned. To do all this work, the service supports URLs of the following forms:

- Add an image: POST to [base service address]/AddImage
- Update an image: PUT to [base service address]/Image/{imageId}
- Delete an image: DELETE to [base service address]/Image/{imageId}
- Get images for a user: GET to [base service address]/Images/{username}
- Get a single image for a user: GET to [base service address]/Image/{imageId}

For this chapter, we will be using the XML-based endpoint for this service. The POST, PUT, and GET verbs all manipulate an ImageItem, which in serialized XML form appears as shown in Listing 3.1.

LISTING 3.1: `ImageItem` serialized as XML

```xml
<ImageItem xmlns="http://www.scottseely.com/RESTBook/2008"
    xmlns:i="http://www.w3.org/2001/XMLSchema-instance">
    <Caption>Some caption</Caption>
    <Description>Some description</Description>
    <ImageBytes>AQIDBAUGAQIDBAU[...]</ImageBytes>
    <ImageId>33f741ae-934a-4c77-b7f8-0f316000ab53</ImageId>
    <ImageUrl>[path to ashx that will yield a valid
              image/jpeg]</ImageUrl>
    <PublicImage>true</PublicImage>
    <UserName>restuser</UserName>
</ImageItem>
```

Chapter 4, "Web Client Operations," shows the same object in JavaScript Object Notation (JSON) format. Just to show the difference here, the JSON representation of the object is given in Listing 3.2.

LISTING 3.2: `ImageItem` serialized as JSON

```json
{
    "Caption":"Some caption",
    "Description":"Some description",
    "ImageBytes":[1,2,3,4,5,6 ...],
    "ImageId":"4bfa5653-be2b-4198-8c21-bdbf5d2f7bc6",
    "ImageUrl":>[path to ashx that will yield a valid image/jpeg],
    "PublicImage":true,
    "UserName":"restuser"
}
```

It's important to note that the only time `ImageBytes` will contain data is for an HTTP POST request. The only time that `ImageUrl` will be populated is in response to an HTTP GET request. (You'd use the URI contained within `ImageUrl` to request the actual image.) Lastly, the RESTful service validates users based on a username and password.

Reading Data

We have lots of options for dealing with XML markup. Because reading and writing data is a big part, maybe even the biggest part, of consuming RESTful services, the first code examples in this chapter detail how we would read the `ImageItem` as XML. A complete description of every possible mechanism to read and write data is far beyond the scope of this book. Instead, this section introduces you to the .NET namespaces and tools most often used—those you need to be familiar with. With knowledge of the basics, you should be able to implement special cases and go as deep as you need to go. As a goal, we want to read the XML and transform it into an object that is more useful to a .NET developer, a process known as *deserialization*. Let's start with an object that can hold the data, which I've named ImageItem. ImageItem needs seven fields: one for each element in the XML representation shown in Listing 3.1. Given the XML from Listing 3.1, the ImageItem class should have the structure shown in Listing 3.3.

LISTING 3.3: The ImageItem class

```
public class ImageItem
{
    public string Caption { get; set; }
    public string Description { get; set; }
    public byte[] ImageBytes { get; set; }
    public Guid ImageId { get; set; }
    public Uri ImageUrl { get; set; }
    public bool PublicImage { get; set; }
    public string UserName { get; set; }
}
```

> **■ NOTE**
>
> Something to keep in mind is that you do not always need to populate a class to make use of the data. You could keep the data in an XML document, a database, or another storage medium. Populating the ImageItem class is simply for the convenience of the application's C#-based code. Populating a form, placing data in a database, or something else are also possible goals that similarly rely on the capability to extract information from an XML stream.

With .NET, we have lots of options for dealing with XML markup. We can parse the XML manually using System.Xml.XmlDocument and System.Xml.Linq.XDocument. We can also create special classes and use the serialization mechanisms offered by System.Runtime.Serialization.DataContractSerializer and System.Xml.Serialization.XmlSerializer.

To demonstrate the various techniques for working with XML data, I've created a sample application called SerializationSampler and placed it in this chapter's demonstration solution. All the XML deserialization techniques just mentioned are illustrated using a static method that returns a single ImageItem object, which is hard-coded as an XML string for simplicity. The code offers access to the XML-based representation via a System.IO.Stream named DataStream, which is shown in Listing 3.4.

LISTING 3.4: The preserialized ImageItem resource

```
const string Data =
    "<ImageItem xmlns=\"http://www.scottseely.com/RESTBook/2008\" "
        + "xmlns:i=\"http://www.w3.org/2001/XMLSchema-instance\">"
        + "<Caption>Some caption</Caption>"
        + "<Description>Some description</Description>"
        + "<ImageBytes>AQIDBAUGAQIDBAUGAQIDBAUGAQIDBAUGAQIDBAUGAQIDBAUG"
        + "</ImageBytes>"
        + "<ImageId>33f741ae-934a-4c77-b7f8-0f316000ab53</ImageId>"
        + "<ImageUrl>"
        +    "http://www.scottseely.com/PhotoWeb/Image.ashx"
        +    "/33f741ae-934a-4c77-b7f8-0f316000ab53</ImageUrl>"
        + "<PublicImage>true</PublicImage>"
        + "<UserName>restuser</UserName>"
    + "</ImageItem> ";

static Stream DataStream
{
    get { return new MemoryStream(Encoding.UTF8.GetBytes(Data)); }
}
```

The sample code demonstrates deserializing XML data using XmlDocument, XDocument, XML serialization, and data contract serialization, as well as a modified technique I call XDocumentAlternate. Each of these techniques is executed using a simple loop that iterates a list of delegates, as shown in Listing 3.5.

LISTING 3.5: SerializationSampler Main method

```
delegate ImageItem DemoXml();

static void Main(string[] args)
{
    List<DemoXml> examples = new List<DemoXml>()
      { UseXmlDocument,
        UseXDocument,
```

```
        UseXDocumentAlternate,
        UseXmlSerialization,
        UseDataContractSerialization};
    foreach (DemoXml demo in examples)
    {
        Console.WriteLine("{0}: {1}{2}",
            demo.Method.Name,
            Environment.NewLine,
            demo());
    }
}
```

XmlDocument

XmlDocument has a long history with the .NET Framework—it has been part of the framework since the beginning. To use XmlDocument, you load the document with XML that might come from a number of sources: a file, a URL, a string, or a stream. You can also populate an XmlDocument from scratch using code, creating each element by hand.

To load XML data into an XmlDocument instance, you would use its LoadXml to load an XML string or its Load method to use XML data encoded within one of the other sources (file, stream, and so on). After the document is loaded, you can extract the data; a number of mechanisms exist to help extract data to be placed in objects for code manipulation. An obvious approach is to iterate over the contents of the document, looking for nodes with known element names. Unfortunately, this technique can be fairly code heavy. Another technique involves writing code that knows where the element should be located within the document and then using indexers to grab the text of that node. This technique winds up being very fragile because the layout of the document might change over time. Adding or deleting items from the document can cause specific indexes to change and code to malfunction accordingly.

My preferred technique to extract data from an XmlDocument involves using XPath expressions and System.Xml.XmlReader. XmlDocument has a method named SelectSingleNode that accepts an XPath expression and an optional XmlNamespaceManager. XPath is a rich language for querying XML. The most common queries involve looking for elements or attributes with known names. Each element and attribute in the XML has an XML *qualified name* (QName). To choose a specific element or attribute, you need to know the item's QName. The QName is consistent no matter the XML namespace being used.

`ImageItem` has a namespace of http://www.scottseely.com/REST-Book/2008. The `ImageItem` XML shown in Listing 3.4 establishes the default namespace with this markup:

```
xmlns="http://www.scottseely.com/RESTBook/2008"
```

This allows us to identify `ImageItem` content without any prefixes for our convenience. The declaration could have just as easily been

```
xmlns:restbook="http://www.scottseely.com/RESTBook/2008"
```

If this was the case, the `ImageItem` XML would have to be changed to prefix all element tags with `restbook:`. The resulting XML, regardless of how the namespace was declared, would be considered equivalent between the two documents. What does this digression have to do with anything? Well, if we want to ask for the caption, description, or other elements contained within the XML document, we have to present a name that is meaningful via the XPath expression. These prefixes do not have to match what is in the actual XML document because XPath expressions operate against the *infoset* representation of the document, not the string representation.

■ NOTE

One cannot talk about XML without talking about the infoset. In a nutshell, the infoset representation concentrates on the tree-based structure of the XML document rather than what data the tree structure contains. Everything in an infoset is some type of XML node: attribute, text, element, whitespace, comment, processing instruction, and so on. Elements and attributes have QNames. Using this, specification authors found it easier to write specifications because they were no longer worrying about XML representation. Developers have since used this to introduce new serialization schemes beyond XML 1.0 (text). Today, many binary serializers have been created to reduce the bulkiness issues associated with XML.

To read more about infosets, consider going to the source specification at www.w3.org/TR/xml-infoset/. O'Reilly also has a great site with articles and information about XML in general at www.xml.com.

Knowing what we do about infosets, we need a crash course in XPath. XPath expressions can get complicated. However, most queries are fairly straightforward: Select all nodes with this name, select the first node with this name, only select nodes at this location relative to the root, and so forth. Here is some of the basic XPath syntax:

- `//`: Used at the start of an expression to select any node with a given name. Example: `//id` selects all nodes named `id`.

- `/`: When used as a single character, denotes that the expression starts at the node being queried. Example: `/ImageItem/Caption` selects all nodes named `Caption` that are children of a node named `ImageItem`.

- `text()`: An element may contain a text node. The expression `text()` allows the query to select the child text nodes. Example: `/ImageItem/Caption/text()` selects all text contents within nodes named `Caption`.

- `@attribute name`: Elements may contain attribute tags. The @ syntax says that the name that follows in the XPath expression is an attribute. Example: If we have XML such as `<foo @bar="some value" />` and the XPath expression `//foo/@bar/text()`, then the result of the expression is `some value`.

XPath allows for other options too. You can perform logical tests such as =, !=, <, >, and more. You can also check for string contents and other things to filter the results to a finer degree. The articles at xml.com provide a rich source of information for how to handle most of these deeper issues.

For our example, we will want to parse all nodes with the following QName:

```
http://www.scottseely.com/RESTBook/2008:ImageItem
```

To identify the prefix we will map to the namespace, we use a class called `System.Xml.XmlNamespaceManager`. By setting up the name correctly, we can now ask for all `ImageItem` elements:

```
XmlNamespaceManager nsMgr = new XmlNamespaceManager(doc.NameTable);
nsMgr.AddNamespace("item", "http://www.scottseely.com/RESTBook/2008");
XmlNode node = doc.DocumentElement.SelectSingleNode(
    "/item:ImageItem", nsMgr);
```

At this point, we can use additional XPath expressions to iteratively select child nodes, or we can use a `System.Xml.XmlReader` to read the remaining data directly. The choice is up to you. The `XmlReader` approach has the benefit of being able to spin through the node data fairly quickly, whereas the XPath approach is more deliberate. The `XmlReader` approach is presented only for completeness because both approaches are useful. An `XmlReader` tends to require more testing effort as changes to document structure can introduce bugs fairly easily, which is something to keep in mind.

Using an `XmlNodeReader`, we can then look at each element individually. Each element has two name properties: `Name` and `LocalName`. The `Name` represents the QName for the element. The `LocalName` represents the simple form of the element tag name—essentially a non-namespace version. If your expectation is that the names within a given node will not vary, and that name collisions will not occur, you can safely use `LocalName`. Otherwise, if names in a node might be reused across XML namespaces (for example, *address* could mean *memory address* or *street address*), use the `Name` property instead. The `XmlNodeReader` then has helper methods to read common data types: strings, numbers, and Boolean values. Using this knowledge, we can now read the XML using an `XmlDocument`. The code I've provided introduces a helper method, `ReadToText(XmlReader)`, that advances the reader to the (child) text node. This particular function exists to make sure that we don't skip over other elements by advancing the reader too far using functions like `ReadElementContentAsString`. `ReadElementContentAsString` will advance the reader to the next `Element` node. A call to `XmlReader.Read()`, as in the `while` loop shown in Listing 3.6, would march past too many elements without `ReadToText` to slow it down.

LISTING 3.6: Reading and consuming XML using XMLDocument **and XPath**

```
static void ReadToText(XmlReader reader)
{
    while (reader.Read())
    {
        if (reader.NodeType == XmlNodeType.Text)
        {
            // Break when we hit a Text node.
            break;
        }
    }
}

private static ImageItem UseXmlDocument()
{
    ImageItem retval = new ImageItem();

    XmlDocument doc = new XmlDocument();
    doc.Load(DataStream);

    // Set up the Infoset mapping information.
    XmlNamespaceManager nsMgr = new XmlNamespaceManager(doc.NameTable);
    nsMgr.AddNamespace("item",
        "http://www.scottseely.com/RESTBook/2008");

    // Only pick the first node named ImageItem.
    // Use SelectNodes to pick ALL.
    XmlNode node = doc.DocumentElement.SelectSingleNode(
        "/item:ImageItem", nsMgr);

    // Look at each node in the document.
    XmlNodeReader reader = new XmlNodeReader(node);
    while (reader.Read())
    {
        // Ignore anything that isn't a start element.
        if (reader.NodeType == XmlNodeType.Element)
        {
            try
            {
                switch (reader.LocalName)
                {
                    case "Caption":
                        ReadToText(reader);
                        retval.Caption = reader.ReadContentAsString();
                        break;
                    case "Description":
                        ReadToText(reader);
```

continues

LISTING 3.6: Continued

```
                            retval.Description =
                                reader.ReadContentAsString();
                            break;
                        case "ImageBytes":
                            ReadToText(reader);
                            retval.ImageBytes = Convert.FromBase64String(
                                reader.ReadContentAsString());
                            break;
                        case "ImageId":
                            ReadToText(reader);
                            retval.ImageId = new
                                Guid(reader.ReadContentAsString());
                            break;
                        case "ImageUrl":
                            ReadToText(reader);
                            string tempUri = reader.ReadContentAsString();
                            if (Uri.IsWellFormedUriString(tempUri,
                                UriKind.Absolute))
                            {
                                retval.ImageUrl = new Uri(tempUri);
                            }
                            break;
                        case "PublicImage":
                            ReadToText(reader);
                            retval.PublicImage =
                                reader.ReadContentAsBoolean();
                            break;
                        case "UserName":
                            ReadToText(reader);
                            retval.UserName = reader.ReadContentAsString();
                            break;
                    }
                }
                catch
                {
                    // Parse failure—do nothing
                }
            }
        }
        return retval;
    }
```

As you can see from Listing 3.6, that is an awful lot of code to translate the XML into something readable. If this RESTful services thing is ever going to take off, there needs to be a simpler solution. There is, and we will get to it. For this very reason, we will be skipping how to serialize data back out. If you are writing the object, you have more control and better options than manipulating XML documents directly for most situations, so it doesn't make sense to even describe how that's done here. We'll save that topic for later in the chapter when we look at the XML serializers.

XDocument

If you are using .NET 3.5 or later, you have something truly wonderful at your disposal. You have Language Integrated Query (LINQ). LINQ is mostly syntactic sugar when represented in a .NET language like C# or VB.NET. The actual generated code is very procedural. But, from a developer point of view, the expressions are declarative. Fortunately, the technology has been written about enough that it is unnecessary to promote its use here. If you do any work with LINQ, you have to go out and buy the `LINQ Pocket Reference` by Joseph and Ben Albahari, ISBN 978-0-596-51924-7, from O'Reilly. It's a tiny 160-page book that will literally fit into the back pocket of your jeans.

Within LINQ, there are all sorts of variants. LINQ to objects lets you execute nifty queries over collections. LINQ to SQL generates SQL queries. And perhaps not surprisingly, LINQ to XML operates over XML documents. Specifically, LINQ to XML (XLINQ) operates on types known as `System.Linq.Xml.XDocument`. XDocument knows how to read and write using `System.Xml` data types: `XmlReader` and `XmlWriter`. As a result, you can use the `XmlReader` code from the preceding section to do your parsing. So we will skip that and move on to other concepts, like queries.

With XLINQ, we still need to think in terms of infosets. When we ask for an element with a particular name, we ask for the element by QName. The XLINQ type representing the QName is named `System.Linq.Xml.XName`. You create an `XName` by concatenating a `System.Linq.Xml.XNamespace` with a string representing the element name. To create the `XNamespace` for `ImageItem` and then create the appropriate `XName`, use the following bit of code:

```
XNamespace ns = "http://www.scottseely.com/RESTBook/2008";
XName imageItemName = ns + "ImageItem";
```

Most of the types we deal with in LINQ are IEnumerable types. In our case, we will normally want only the first item in that list (and, in fact, the XML document we're working with contains only one element). .NET 3.5 implements an extension method for IEnumerable<T> called First that provides this capability quite handily. Using all this basic knowledge, the code to parse the XDocument into an ImageItem becomes simpler. To select a named node within the current node, you pass the XName of the target node to the current node's Elements(XName) method. You can then select the first element from that list and pick off the Value of that item, as demonstrated in Listing 3.7.

LISTING 3.7: Reading and consuming XML using XDocument **and XLINQ**

```
static ImageItem UseXDocument()
{
    XDocument doc = XDocument.Load(new XmlTextReader(DataStream));
    XNamespace ns = "http://www.scottseely.com/RESTBook/2008";
    var items = from imageItemNode in doc.Elements(ns + "ImageItem")
        select new ImageItem()
        {
            Caption = imageItemNode.Elements(ns +
                "Caption").First().Value,
            Description = imageItemNode.Elements(ns +
                "Description").First().Value,
            ImageBytes = Convert.FromBase64String(
                imageItemNode.Elements(ns + "ImageBytes").
                    First().Value),
            ImageId = new Guid(imageItemNode.Elements(ns +
                "ImageId").First().Value),
            ImageUrl = new Uri(imageItemNode.Elements(ns +
                "ImageUrl").First().Value),
            PublicImage = bool.Parse(imageItemNode.Elements(ns +
                "PublicImage").First().Value),
            UserName = imageItemNode.Elements(ns +
                "UserName").First().Value
        };
    return items.First();
}
```

The XDocument code has some advantages over the XmlDocument version. First and foremost, it is a lot shorter. Shorter code typically leads to fewer bugs since most developers implement code with a consistent ratio of bugs to lines of code. This ratio is not intentional—as humans we just tend to make mistakes at a steady pace. An issue with the code in Listing 3.7 is that it has very little in the way of error handling. If the `ImageUrl`, `ImageId`, `ImageBytes`, or `PublicImage` items fail to parse, the code fails for all items. If we would rather load the `ImageItem` and leave fields blank on failure, the code could be rewritten as shown in Listing 3.8 to provide for deserialization failover.

LISTING 3.8: Reading and consuming XML using XDocument and XLINQ with failover

```
static ImageItem UseXDocumentAlternate()
{
    XDocument doc = XDocument.Load(new XmlTextReader(DataStream));
    XNamespace ns = "http://www.scottseely.com/RESTBook/2008";
    var items = from imageItemNode in doc.Elements(ns + "ImageItem")
        select new
        {
            Caption = imageItemNode.Elements(ns +
                "Caption").First().Value,
            Description = imageItemNode.Elements(ns +
                "Description").First().Value,
            ImageBytes = imageItemNode.Elements(ns +
                "ImageBytes").First().Value,
            ImageId = imageItemNode.Elements(ns +
                "ImageId").First().Value,
            ImageUrl = imageItemNode.Elements(ns +
                "ImageUrl").First().Value,
            PublicImage = imageItemNode.Elements(ns +
                "PublicImage").First().Value,
            UserName = imageItemNode.Elements(ns +
                "UserName").First().Value
        };
    ImageItem retval = new ImageItem();
    foreach (var item in items)
    {
        retval.Caption = item.Caption;
        retval.Description = item.Description;
        retval.UserName = item.UserName;
        bool publicImage;
        if (bool.TryParse(item.PublicImage, out publicImage))
            retval.PublicImage = publicImage;

        if (Uri.IsWellFormedUriString(item.ImageUrl, UriKind.Absolute))
            retval.ImageUrl = new Uri(item.ImageUrl);
```

continues

LISTING 3.8: Continued

```
            try
            {
                retval.ImageId = new Guid(item.ImageId);
            }
            catch { }
            try
            {
                retval.ImageBytes =
                    Convert.FromBase64String(item.ImageBytes);
            }
            catch { }
            break;
        }
        return retval;
    }
```

Again, this all depends on whether you want things to fail whenever bad input data is encountered. Most of the time, invalid data that appears anywhere in the object implies that you do not want to continue deserializing that XML stream. When that is the case, the short version of this code is completely appropriate. When failover is called for, however, you need the extra code shown in Listing 3.8.

XmlSerializer

Wouldn't it be great if you could just tell the runtime what your object looked like and then it could figure out how to read the XML and populate that object for you? As it happens, this is possible. To do this, we can go to one of my favorite .NET namespaces: `System.Xml.Serialization`. In the .NET world, it is the king of XML reading and writing within the bits shipped with the framework. It handles attributes, special serialization, and schema generation. Most of this work is directed with simple attributes placed on public classes, fields, and properties. And it implements the parts of the XML Schema specification that map into .NET.

> **▪ NOTE**
>
> As it happens, .NET doesn't implement the full suite of schema constructs identified in the XML Schema specification. If you create a schema using a tool outside of .NET, you could be asking for trouble if you later try to incorporate those schemas into .NET code. For example, Altova has tools with XML Spy that implement all far corners of the XML Schema Document specification and provide features not found in .NET. If you need to support facets and other fancy features of XSD, you need to go beyond what Microsoft ships with the framework. In practice, this kind of specialization is needed only for sophisticated XML processing in a small set of scenarios.

The most common attributes used in the System.Xml.Serialization are listed here:

- XmlElementAttribute: Declares the XML element name and namespace for a given property when that property appears in an XSD or XML document.
- XmlAttributeAttribute: Declares the XML attribute name and namespace for a given property when that property appears in an XSD or XML document.
- XmlTypeAttribute: Declares the name and namespace for a given class or enum within an XSD.
- XmlRootAttribute: Declares the name and namespace for a given class or enum when that data type is used as the root of an XML document.
- XmlEnumAttribute: Declares the name of an enumeration value when that enum appears in an XSD or XML document.
- XmlIgnoreAttribute: Prevents serialization of this member. By default, all public members are serialized.

- `XmlArrayAttribute`: Allows the developer to control the names used when serializing arrays of items.
- `XmlArrayItemAttribute`: Collaborates with `XmlArrayAttribute`. `XmlArrayItemAttribute` allows for a given collection to contain more than one type of object.

This information is consumed by another class named `System.Xml.XmlSerializer`. `XmlSerializer` learns how to convert between XML and .NET types by reading these attributes via reflection. The initial instance of an `XmlSerializer` for a given type is expensive to build in terms of time, so quite often an instance is created early and held for the duration of the application's lifetime. After you have the serializer in hand, however, you can read XML into objects and write objects as XML into a stream or file with a single method call.

Using this knowledge, we need to decorate the `ImageItem` class with the right set of attributes to drastically reduce the amount of code we have to write to eventually serialize and deserialize it. The class should be decorated with an `XmlRootAttribute` and all properties with `XmlElementAttribute`. The code in Listing 3.9 demonstrates these attributes in action. I could have written even less code by not filling in the `ElementName` information as the XML element name defaults to the property name, but I wanted to demonstrate how you establish the tie between the property name and the corresponding XML element. If you want to reduce the size of the serialized XML stream, one way to do it is to provide very short XML element names, and `XmlElementAttribute` is the tool you'd use for this. We do run into one snag, though: `ImageItem.ImageUrl` is of type `System.Uri`. `Uri` does not have a parameterless constructor, which is a requirement for `XmlSerializer`. Because of this, `XmlSerializer` cannot automatically read and write `Uri` values. There is a workaround: We create a new `String` property, `ImageUrlString`. Within that property, we read and write the `ImageUrl` for everyone else to use. It's a small change to the class but results in simpler code overall than any mechanism seen so far.

LISTING 3.9: ImageItem **with XML serialization attributes applied**

```
[XmlRoot(Namespace="http://www.scottseely.com/RESTBook/2008")]
public class ImageItem
{
    [XmlElement(ElementName = "Caption")]
    public string Caption { get; set; }

    [XmlElement(ElementName = "Description")]
    public string Description { get; set; }

    [XmlElement(ElementName = "ImageBytes")]
    public byte[] ImageBytes { get; set; }

    [XmlElement(ElementName = "ImageId")]
    public Guid ImageId { get; set; }

    [XmlIgnore]
    public Uri ImageUrl { get; set; }

    [XmlElement(ElementName = "ImageUrl")]
    public string ImageUrlString
    {
        get { return ImageUrl == null ? null : ImageUrl.ToString(); }
        set
        {
            Uri tempUri = null;
            if (Uri.TryCreate(value, UriKind.Absolute, out tempUri))
                ImageUrl = tempUri;
            else
                ImageUrl = null;
        }
    }
}
```

With the data type decorated with all these different attributes, what code do we implement to read an ImageItem now? Happily, deserialization distills down to two lines of code:

```
static ImageItem UseXmlSerialization()
{
    XmlSerializer ser = new XmlSerializer(typeof(ImageItem));
    return (ImageItem)ser.Deserialize(DataStream);
}
```

As you can see, we are no longer parsing the XML ourselves. This means that potential bugs in the code we write become less likely—less code means fewer defects. The great thing about XmlSerializer is that it handles elements being out of order, missing elements, and so on. There is one more serialization mechanism that has an extra benefit if you can use this mechanism: blindingly fast speed. Let's look at that topic next.

DataContractSerializer

System.Runtime.Serialization.DataContractSerializer is part of a family of serializers introduced with .NET 3.0 that all inherit from System.Runtime.Serialization.XmlObjectSerializer. These serializers specialize in reading and writing objects to XML, JSON, and other formats. In general, these serializers read and write XML faster than anything else on the .NET platform. When looking specifically at DataContractSerializer, however, understand that the speed comes at a price: DataContractSerializer does not handle XML attributes and it does not handle arbitrarily ordered elements. DataContractSerializer handles serialization of the following types of data:

- Classes that implement System.Runtime.Serialization.ISerializable.
- Types marked with the System.SerializableAttribute.
- Primitive types and enumerations. These types are implicitly serializable.
- Types marked with System.Runtime.Serialization.DataContractAttribute.
- Undecorated objects. This feature, new in .NET 3.5 SP1, allows for serializing objects that have no special attribution. In this case, only types with public, default constructors can be serialized. The DataContractSerializer will serialize only public fields and properties.

Like XmlSerializer, DataContractSerializer's explicit serialization model relies on attributes.

- `DataContractAttribute`: Indicates that the data type has explicit serialization rules. Using this attribute, one can set the way the data type is represented in XML with a name and namespace. Note that the namespace information might be ignored by other serializers, such as the `System.Runtime.Serialization.Json.DataContract JsonSerializer`, because JSON has no equivalent of XML namespaces.

- `DataMemberAttribute`: Indicates that the field or property is read/write. Besides the usual name and namespace settings, this attribute lets the developer express the requested relative order of the element within any serialization scheme.

- `CollectionDataContractAttribute`: Used to indicate how a collection should be serialized. You can set the name of the collection, the name of elements within the collection, and the XML namespace associated with the collection.

- `EnumMemberAttribute`: Allows you to set the names and values of elements within an enumeration.

We are primarily interested in properties and related fields that use the explicit serialization rules, which is to say have serialization attributes applied. The rest of this section focuses on the explicit aspects alone. Elements are ordered following these rules:

1. All elements within a type are ranked according to the value of the `DataMemberAttribute.Order` property.

2. Within an `Order` value, members are serialized and deserialzed in alphabetical, ascending order. By default, the value of `Order` is 0. Members are always sorted first by `Order`, then by alphabetical order within a given `Order` value. Upon deserialization, if a member is out of order, it will appear with its default value (typically a 0 or null) within the deserialized object.

> **■ NOTE**
>
> If you need to use DataContract and must accept out-of-order param-
> eters, consider using the DataContractJsonSerializer and the JSON
> format instead. You can also support both XmlSerializer and Data-
> ContractJsonSerializer on the same data type if you need to handle
> unordered XML.

Assuming that you are guaranteed the order of the elements, you can
use the code shown in Listing 3.10 to read the XML information. You'll
probably notice that this looks very similar to what we did for XmlSerializer. However, a benefit of DataContractSerializer is that it doesn't need
a public, default constructor to create an object. As a result, it can instantiate System.Uri without the workaround needed for XmlSerializer.

LISTING 3.10: ImageItem with data contract attributes applied

```
[DataContract(Namespace = "http://www.scottseely.com/RESTBook/2008")]
public class ImageItem
{
    [DataMember(Name = "Caption")]
    public string Caption { get; set; }

    [DataMember(Name = "Description")]
    public string Description { get; set; }

    [DataMember(Name="ImageBytes")]
    public byte[] ImageBytes { get; set; }

    [DataMember(Name = "ImageId")]
    public Guid ImageId { get; set; }

    [DataMember]
    public Uri ImageUrl { get; set; }

    [DataMember(Name = "PublicImage")]
    public bool PublicImage { get; set; }

    [DataMember(Name = "UserName")]
    public string UserName { get; set; }
}
```

As with XmlSerializer, we wind up with a fairly short code snippet to
deserialize an ImageItem object:

```
static ImageItem UseDataContractSerialization()
{
    DataContractSerializer dcs = new
        DataContractSerializer(typeof(ImageItem));
    return (ImageItem)dcs.ReadObject(DataStream);
}
```

Writing the object is a matter of calling `DataContractSerializer`'s `WriteObject` method. With all this information in place, we are ready to start talking about building actual applications.

Working with WinForms

There are a lot of WinForms applications out there. These applications will be improved, extended, and maintained for a long time. Some of those enhancements and changes might need to make use of RESTful services. If they do, you will need to familiarize yourself with the following concepts:

- **Using `System.Net.WebRequest/WebResponse`**: This pair of classes provides the best overall developer tools for communicating with other HTTP-based services, although you can use the derived classes `HttpWebRequest` and `HttpWebResponse` as well. You also have at your disposal `System.Net.WebClient`, but I find I prefer `WebRequest` and `WebResponse`. I like the greater control I have over the request/response process when using `WebRequest` and `WebResponse`. For example: Credentials frequently need to be passed between the service and the client. The normal `WebClient` behavior issues a challenge/response pair of HTTP messages for any secured resource. `WebRequest`, on the other hand, allows you to set its `PreAuthenticate` property and save a round trip.

- **Sharing the UI thread**: .NET (actually, Windows itself) gives you only one thread for the UI. If you use that single thread for synchronously accessing a RESTful service, the user will feel the application is unresponsive.

- **Using asynchronous programming techniques**: Learn to use `System.Threading.ThreadPool`, the `BeginInvoke` method implemented by many data types, and what `System.IAsyncResult` is used for. Something to keep in mind is that it's the client that implements asynchronous request processing. To the service, a synchronous client request is no different than an asynchronous one. But your application users will definitely notice the difference.

Our example here revolves around a simple WinForms application that interacts with the Photo Service described at the beginning of this chapter. This application does not include mechanisms for storing information to be synchronized later. It only shows how to connect with the Photo Service. The code for this example can be found in the `WinFormPhotoClient` project included with this chapter's sample solution.

This chapter also comes with a copy of the Photo Service presented later, in Chapter 8. To install the service, please do the following:

1. Open the Chapter 3 Solution file.
2. Right-click on PhotoWeb and select Publish. Publish the Web application to http://localhost/PhotoWeb.
3. Create the PhotoWeb database using the scripts found in the PhotoWebDb database project. You'll find one script for creating the database and another for creating all the associated tables. The database creation script, `CreatePhotoWebDb.sql`, assumes you're using SQL Express and creates the `.mdb` file accordingly. If you're not using SQL Express, simply edit the script and store the resulting `.mdb` file in an authorized location or create the database using the graphical tools found in SQL Server Management Studio, giving the new database the name PhotoWebDb.

Let's take a quick look at *Photo Client*, the WinForms sample application that demonstrates RESTful service access. When the Photo Client application executes, the user can either log in or create a new user account. Figure 3.1 shows the initial application user interface.

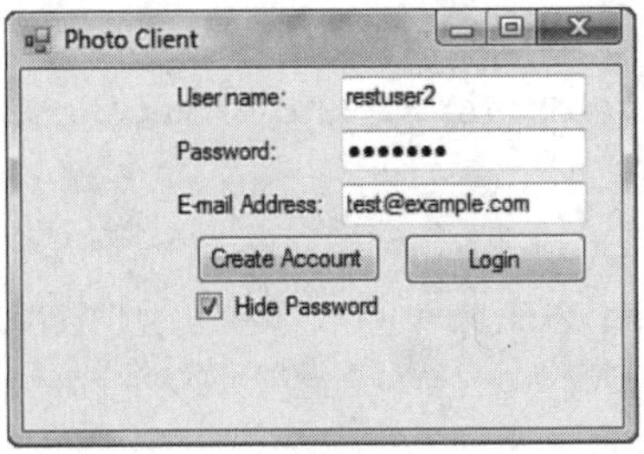

FIGURE 3.1: WinForms startup screen

Because users might want to see the password as they type it in, the application allows them to show or mask the text in the password input TextBox with a password-hiding feature they can turn on or off. If the login information is new, which is to say unknown to the service, users can create a new service account from the Photo Client application. Pressing the Login button only caches the credentials within the application. The credentials are not actually submitted until the user begins to interact with the Photo Service. If the user clicks Create Account, the following tasks need to take place:

- The application needs to ask the Photo Service for a new user account, providing the username, password, and e-mail address the user provided. The e-mail address might seem like an odd piece of information, but the service can use this to help the user reset the password in the event that the user forgets the password.

- The application waits for a response indicating that the new username was accepted and the password met the password strength requirements. If the username is already in use, or if the password does not meet password strength requirements, the user is notified and can resubmit new information.

These tasks are implemented in the sample's LoginControl.cs file. The code first constructs a new URI. Because the application knows exactly what user to create, the code uses a PUT request (versus a POST request). As service application developers, we know that these are the service's rules for creating a new user:

- HTTP request verb: PUT
- URI template:

  `http://localhost/PhotoWeb/UserManager.svc/CreateUser/`
  `➥{username}?email={emailAddress}`
- Request body: XML-serialized password. Because the password is issued in the HTTP entity body as clear text, you should use transport-level security, such as secure sockets (HTTPS), to protect it.

Although not a requirement, most services provide some form of documentation that tell you, the application developer, how to interact with the service. In this case, you would be given the URI template, the XML schema (or format) for the new account request, and so forth. If you're writing a service, you should provide this information.

Anyway, to call the RESTful service and create the new service user account, you use the System.Net.WebRequest class. You never create an instance of WebRequest directly, however. Instead, you use WebRequest.Create, providing an instance of System.Uri that represents the URI of the request. Create looks up the right type of request to create based on the URI scheme. In our case, the scheme is http: or https: (versus ftp: or gopher:). After the request object is returned, we can change existing HTTP header values, add new HTTP headers, establish the HTTP method, and assign other values necessary to issue the request over the network. If we do nothing special, the UI thread will be using the request object, but requests and associated responses over the network take time. To allow the UI to remain responsive while the user waits for the service response, the application should use asynchronous service request techniques for any RESTful service calls it makes. The asynchronous request for creating a new user is shown in Listing 3.11. You can tell that the request is made asynchronously because BeginGetResponse is used (its cousin GetResponse is its synchronous counterpart).

LISTING 3.11: Photo Client asynchronous user account creation

```
private void btnCreateAccount_Click(object sender, EventArgs e)
{
    // Construct the call.
    Uri callUri = Utility.CreateUri(ServiceType.Manager,
        string.Format("CreateUser/{0}?email={1}",
        HttpUtility.UrlEncode(txtUserName.Text),
        HttpUtility.UrlEncode(txtEmailAddress.Text)));

    // Create the WebRequest
    WebRequest request = WebRequest.Create(callUri);
    request.Method = "PUT";
    Stream stream = request.GetRequestStream();
    request.ContentType = "application/xml";
    DataContractSerializer stringSer = new
        DataContractSerializer(typeof(string));
    stringSer.WriteObject(stream, txtPassword.Text);
    stream.Close();
    // Asynchronously wait for the response.
    request.BeginGetResponse(new AsyncCallback(CreateAccountResponse),
        request);

    // Disable the UI while waiting.
    this.Enabled = false;
}
```

Sometime later, the Photo Service responds, letting us know of any issues or if the account creation was successful. For any issues, we need to notify the user. If the account creation was successful, we let the user know that as well and ask if the user would like to log in.

A successful response will have an associated 200-level status code. But how will we know if there were issues with the request? As it happens, 300-level or higher response status codes will cause WebRequest to throw a WebException. WebException contains information about which HTTP response code was returned, as well as any information present in the response stream. We can use these pieces of information to find out what the server told us went wrong.

But hold on a minute...we're using an asynchronous request pattern (we initiated the request using BeginGetResponse). Whenever we receive responses via these asynchronous calling patterns, we have no knowledge about which application thread is being used for the response. It is almost always a safe bet to assume that we aren't on the original UI thread. However, any code that updates the user interface *must* be invoked using the UI thread. This model is strictly enforced by the framework (as well as Windows) and serves to prevent race conditions while updating the UI.

This necessarily means we have to have some way to switch thread contexts and gain access to the UI thread. How is this accomplished? To execute code on the UI thread, one technique is to invoke a parameterless delegate. In these cases, I frequently prefer to pass along an anonymous delegate: The code is frequently short and easier to understand when viewed in the context of when the delegate is actually called. You can call this delegate method via the `System.Windows.Forms.Control.Invoke` or `BeginInvoke/EndInvoke` pair. Either mechanism will make sure that your code runs on the UI thread, allowing your application to update the screen. For short functions, I typically call `Invoke` since it involves less code and I'm generally not too concerned about a short pause on the background (asynchronous) thread. The callback for account creation, using `Control. Invoke` and an anonymous delegate, is shown in Listing 3.12.

> **■ NOTE**
>
> Failing to modify the state of the window controls via the original creating UI thread usually results in an `AsyncCallbackException` (or in some cases a `COMException`). This is by design and has been so since the first version of Windows. It's not something we can pick and choose to deal with—we must deal with it when creating multithreaded Windows applications, whether .NET-based or not.

LISTING 3.12: Asynchronous response handling

```
void CreateAccountResponse(IAsyncResult result)
{
    // Capture the request from the state.
    WebRequest request = (WebRequest)result.AsyncState;
    try
    {
        // Ask for the response. Any exceptions will get thrown here.
        WebResponse response = request.EndGetResponse(result);
        this.Invoke((MethodInvoker)delegate
```

```
            {
                // Lack of exceptions means that we got a 2xx back.
                if (DialogResult.Yes == MessageBox.Show(this,
                    "Account created. Do you want to log in?",
                    "Success", MessageBoxButtons.YesNo,
                    MessageBoxIcon.Information))
                {
                    btnLogin_Click(null, EventArgs.Empty);
                }
            });
        }
        catch (WebException we)
        {
            // Let the user know what happened.
            HttpWebResponse httpResponse = (HttpWebResponse)we.Response;
            if (httpResponse.StatusCode == HttpStatusCode.Conflict)
            {
                // Conflict means the name was in use.
                this.BeginInvoke((MethodInvoker)delegate
                {
                    MessageBox.Show(this,
        "This username is already in use. Cannot create a new account.",
        "Username in use", MessageBoxButtons.OK,
        MessageBoxIcon.Exclamation);
                });
            }
            else
            {
                // Something else happened.
                this.Invoke((MethodInvoker)delegate
                {
                    MessageBox.Show(this, string.Format(
                        "Code: {0}\r\nDescription: {1}.",
                        httpResponse.StatusCode.ToString(),
                        httpResponse.StatusDescription),
                        "Failed to create a new user.",
                        MessageBoxButtons.OK, MessageBoxIcon.Exclamation);
                });
            }
            Debug.WriteLine(we.ToString());
        }
        this.Invoke((MethodInvoker)delegate
        {
            // Re-enable the UI.
            this.Enabled = true;
        });
    }
```

After we have a valid account, we can log in. The application simply caches the username and password values in memory for use when contacting the Photo Service. Once authenticated, and if we have used the service before, we are greeted with the form shown in Figure 3.2. Note that the mechanisms used to pass authentication credentials use HTTP Basic Authentication for this service, which passes the username/password in clear text (as with account creation, which placed the password in the HTTP entity body). If your service uses HTTP Basic Authentication to authenticate users, make sure that this is done over a secure, HTTPS channel. Otherwise, the credentials can be viewed by any router, proxy server, or machine between the source and destination of the HTTP request.

FIGURE 3.2: The Photo Client details view

To display images coming from the service, a couple of things have to happen. First, the user needs to authenticate with the service using HTTP Basic Authentication (this will be the case for each and every RESTful service invocation). Normally this involves one or more trips to the server, but in our case we'll preload the credentials in `WebRequest` by setting its `PreAuthenticate` property to `true`. You'll learn much more about HTTP Basic Authentication and its relationship to RESTful services in Chapter 6, "Building REST Services Using IIS and ASP.NET."

Then we make a request for images. This request asks for all the images associated with a particular user. If the authenticated user and the user whose images are being requested are the same, the returned list of images includes all images, both public and private. If the users differ, the returned list includes only public images associated with the requested user. (Actually, the list includes only the URLs that the application will use to fetch the images. The application needs to send out another batch of requests to actually retrieve the image bytes.) Because we are using a RESTful service, we treat each interaction as a brand-new request. This means that each request for secured information, as for the list of pictures, needs to include authentication information.

How does authentication work for us? WebRequest has a property named Credentials of type System.Net.ICredentials. This interface defines a lookup table of endpoints, authentication mechanisms, and username/password combinations. Fortunately, System.Net.CredentialCache implements the interface and handles our needs quite well. Our code makes use of a helper class, PhotoShared.Utility, in the PhotoShared project. This class holds a common CredentialCache and a shared method to handle setting up our WebRequest in a uniform way. When we click the Login button (refer to Figure 3.1), the small amount of code shown in Listing 3.13 (contained within LoginControl.cs) executes.

LISTING 3.13: Photo Client Login button click handler

```
private void btnLogin_Click(object sender, EventArgs e)
{
    // Clear any stored credentials and store the new ones.
    Utility.ClearCredentialCache();
    NetworkCredential credential = new
            NetworkCredential(txtUserName.Text,
            txtPassword.Text);
    Utility.CredentialCache.Add(new
        Uri(Properties.Settings.Default.PhotoService),
        "Basic", credential);
    if (this.LoggedIn != null)
    {
        // Raise the LoggedIn event
        this.LoggedIn(this, EventArgs.Empty);
    }
}
```

Whenever the application needs to send an authenticated request, it can use the `Utility` class's `CreateRequest` method, shown in Listing 3.14. This utility method encapsulates and standardizes the code necessary for setting the credentials. It also makes sure that any outgoing requests send credentials on the first request—alleviating a possible challenge/response pair of messages between the server and the client as previously mentioned.

> **■ NOTE**
>
> Some examples later in the book, such as the client application for Chapter 6, don't use the credential cache as implemented here but rather insert the credentials directly into the HTTP request. This is done for illustrative purposes, and practically speaking is functionally equivalent to the technique used in this chapter. Feel free to use whichever technique you prefer.

Listing 3.14: The `CreateRequest` method

```
public static WebRequest CreateRequest(Uri uri)
{
    WebRequest retval = WebRequest.Create(uri);
    retval.Credentials = CredentialCache;
    retval.PreAuthenticate = true;
    return retval;
}
```

To add an image to the collection on the server, we use the HTTP POST method. Why POST? In our case, the server controls the issuance of new photo identifiers. Clients have no idea what identifier the server will assign to the new image. The new identifier might be a string, an integer, or something else—to service consumers it is just an opaque identifier. When this situation arises, from Chapter 2, "The HyperText Transfer Protocol and the Universal Resource Identifier," we know that RFC 2616 tells us the HTTP POST method is appropriate. After the data is posted, the client waits for the response so that it can discover the identifier for the newly added image.

Our user interface allows the user to select files using the `System.Windows.Forms.OpenFileDialog`. When the user clicks Open, the list of selected files is returned to the application. This list is then passed to a function named `AddImages`. `AddImages` is executed in a background thread obtained from the .NET thread pool:

```
ThreadPool.QueueUserWorkItem(new WaitCallback(AddImages),
    ofdOpenFile.FileNames);
```

As I mentioned earlier, the `ThreadPool` is a class you often use with asynchronous programming. It allows you to spin up a thread, execute a task, and return the thread to the system with little effort on your part. Unlike spinning up your own threads, the `ThreadPool` automatically increases and decreases the number of threads in an application depending on needs and available resources. Threads in the pool come into being, are used, and are reused using patterns that are efficient for the operating system. For us as application developers, the good part is that all of this behavior is free. The `WaitCallback` accepted by the worker item takes a method that has a signature of `void (System.Object)`, and the `AddImages` implementation of this is shown in Listing 3.15.

LISTING 3.15: The `AddImages` method

```
void AddImages(object data)
{
    // Cast the data to a list of filenames.
    string[] filenames = (string[])data;

    // Create a serializer.
    DataContractSerializer itemSerializer =
        new DataContractSerializer(typeof(ImageItem));
    foreach (string filename in filenames)
    {
        // If the string doesn't map to an existing filename,
        // go the next string in the list.
        if (!File.Exists(filename))
        {
            continue;
        }

        // Create the URI for the service via the helper
        Uri callUri = Utility.CreateUri(ServiceType.Image, "AddImage/");


        WebRequest request = Utility.CreateRequest(callUri);
        request.ContentType = "application/xml";
        request.Method = "POST";
```
continues

LISTING 3.15: Continued

```
        Stream requestStream = request.GetRequestStream();
        ImageItem imageItem = new ImageItem()
        {
            PublicImage = false,
            ImageBytes = File.ReadAllBytes(filename),
            UserName = LoggedInUserId
        };
        itemSerializer.WriteObject(requestStream, imageItem);
        requestStream.Close();
        IAsyncResult result =
            request.BeginGetResponse(ReadResponse, new object[]
                {request, imageItem});
    }
    this.Invoke((MethodInvoker)delegate
    {
        // Enable the control.
        this.Enabled = true;
    });
}
```

AddImages works in concert with the application's ReadResponse
method to retrieve the new image identifier from the response stream, to set
the identifier to an accessible location, and then to signal MessagingEvent,
a ManualResetEvent object, which allows the blocked AddImages to continue, as shown in Listing 3.16.

LISTING 3.16: Photo Client's ReadResponse method

```
void ReadResponse(IAsyncResult result)
{
    DataContractSerializer guidSerializer = new
        DataContractSerializer(typeof(Guid));
    object[] values = (object[])result.AsyncState;
    WebRequest request = (WebRequest)values[0];
    ImageItem imageItem = (ImageItem)values[1];

    try
    {
        WebResponse response = request.EndGetResponse(result);
        Guid lastImageId = (Guid)guidSerializer.ReadObject(
            response.GetResponseStream());
        response.Close();
        // Set the ID
        if (lastImageId != Guid.Empty)
        {
            imageItem.ImageId = lastImageId;
```

```
            ImageDocument.Add(imageItem);
            this.Invoke((MethodInvoker)delegate
            {
                lstImages.Items.Add(new ListViewItem(imageItem.Caption,
                    AddImageToList(imageItem.Image)) {
                        Tag = imageItem });
            });
        }
    }
    catch (WebException we)
    {
        Debug.WriteLine(we.Message);
    }
}
```

The only HTTP method we haven't looked at yet is DELETE. Like the other HTTP methods Photo Client deals with, it is a matter of setting the WebRequest.Method property to DELETE and then sending a request to the right resource. When the Delete button is clicked (refer to Figure 3.2), this line sets things into motion:

```
ThreadPool.QueueUserWorkItem(new WaitCallback(DeleteImage),
    lstImages.SelectedItems[i].Tag);
```

The ThreadPool then calls DeleteImage, which asynchronously executes the WebRequest. Since this is a DELETE, we aren't too worried about the response. We just need to make sure that EndGetResponse is called so that no operating system resources are left hanging and so that the WebResponse is closed, as shown in Listing 3.17.

LISTING 3.17: Photo Client's DeleteImage and DeleteResponse methods

```
void DeleteImage(object data)
{
    ImageItem imageItem = (ImageItem)data;
    if (data == null)
    {
        return;
    }

    // Set the URI
    Uri callUri = Utility.CreateUri(ServiceType.Image,
        string.Format("Image/{0}", imageItem.ImageId));

    // Execute the request.
```

continues

LISTING 3.17: Continued

```
        WebRequest request = Utility.CreateRequest(callUri);
        request.ContentType = "application/xml";
        request.Method = "DELETE";
        request.BeginGetResponse(DeleteResponse, request);
    }

    void DeleteResponse(IAsyncResult result)
    {
        try
        {
            WebRequest request = (WebRequest)result.AsyncState;
            // nothing to read, so just complete the request.
            request.EndGetResponse(result).Close();
        }
        catch (WebException)
        {
            Invoke((MethodInvoker)delegate
            {
                MessageBox.Show(this,
                  "Failed to delete an image. Try logging back in again.",
                  "Delete Failed", MessageBoxButtons.OK,
                  MessageBoxIcon.Error);
            });
        }
    }
}
```

As you read through the sample code, you'll probably notice that the code always calls WebResponse.Close(). You must do this so that connections to the server can be returned to the server's connection pool. This allows the server to serve more clients and is simply good programming practice. Failure to do so can generate sluggish performance for your client application and others that consume the RESTful service.

Working with Windows Presentation Foundation

Thankfully, the RESTful service communication tools you use with Win-Forms and WPF are identical. The only difference when creating WPF client applications is that the data binding mechanisms change and the mechanisms to apply updates to the user interface using the single UI thread change. If you are a WPF developer, read the WinForms section to understand the RESTful communications tools introduced there if you're not already familiar with them.

As mentioned, the only real difference in these two sample applications is the mechanism by which you update the user interface when a RESTful response comes back. As with WinForms, you can execute the update tasks on a background thread using an asynchronous request or by making the request on a background thread via `QueueUserWorkItem`. When the response is returned, you still need to be sure to process updates on the main user interface thread. WPF user interface objects have a property named `Dispatcher` of type `System.Windows.Threading.Dispatcher`. Through the `Dispatcher` property, we can make sure that our code executes on the main UI thread just as we used `Invoke` with the WinForms application logic.

For much of the application code in the WPF version of the Photo Sharing application, we use a simple delegate of the form:

```
delegate void PlainMethod();
```

This delegate is used to cast the anonymous delegates used by our code to a known type when we need to update the user interface in some way. After the list of images is known, for example, the code needs to retrieve the images and place them into the list for viewing. Each image might take a bit of time to load. Because of this, `ShowImages` is executed using a background thread obtained from the thread pool, which is shown in Listing 3.18.

LISTING 3.18: Photo Client's `ShowImages` method (WPF version)

```
private void ShowImages()
{
    foreach (ImageItem imageItem in ImageDocument)
    {
        // This is executing on a background thread, so we block
        // and wait for each image to load.
        BitmapImage image = new BitmapImage(new
            Uri(imageItem.ImageUrl));

        // Add the image to the screen.
        this.Dispatcher.Invoke((PlainMethod)delegate
        {
            StackPanel sp = new StackPanel();
            sp.Children.Add(new Image() { Source = image, Height=100,
                Width=100 });
            sp.Children.Add(new Label() {
```

continues

LISTING 3.18: Continued

```
                    Content = imageItem.Caption });
                lstImages.Items.Add(new ListViewItem() {
                    Content = sp, Tag = imageItem });
            });
        }
    }
```

Although we bind to data using normal WPF mechanisms for most of this example application, the images themselves are bound a bit differently, as you see in Listing 3.18. Otherwise, the application logic is nearly identical to that in the WinForms version, including the mechanisms for service authentication and invocation.

Where Are We?

In this chapter we looked at techniques to read and write RESTful service data. RESTful Web services frequently use a neutral data format like XML or JSON, but our application code uses classes and objects to represent the data. Client applications need to know how to translate between those representations. You also need to be able to send and receive representational data between your application and the RESTful service. Fortunately, System.Net includes plenty of classes and makes this easy. For the most part, you will use WebRequest/WebResponse, or their HTTP-based derivatives, to send and receive information from RESTful services. Because you'll want to keep your application responsive to user inputs when making long-running network requests, you should become familiar with the various mechanisms to call remote methods asynchronously (in the background). When service invocations return information to be presented to the user, be sure to update the user interface via the application's UI thread.

This chapter focused on desktop applications, although Windows services and console applications would use the same techniques to invoke RESTful services as well. But how are RESTful services consumed when the client application is Web-based? In the next chapter we'll look at both browser-based and Silverlight clients and see how this is accomplished.

▛ 4 ▪

Web Client Operations

W EB-BASED APPLICATIONS offer many things that their desktop brethren lack. For the user interface component, which is all that most of your users care about, you can make beautiful, highly responsive applications that "install" in a heartbeat—installation of a Web application is the same thing as using "Add to Favorites" or bookmarking the page. These days, with Asynchronous JavaScript and XML (AJAX) being the rage, how does REST fit into the Web programming picture? Can you make AJAX-like RESTful service calls from your Web-based client applications? As it happens, you can.

So You Want to Write a Web Client

In the preceding chapter, "Desktop Client Operations," I talked about all sorts of things that the .NET libraries provide for you to make it easier to interact with RESTful Web services. They provide you with simplified XML serialization and deserialization tools through the `System.Xml` and `System. Runtime.Serialization` namespaces. `System.Net` gave you ways to invoke the services and receive responses over the network. You had XLINQ and XPath.

For applications running in the browser, however, the desktop tools aren't available. Those applications have to do something else to obtain and use RESTful data. What that "something else" is depends on your target application goals. Do you want the broadest possible range of browsers and devices to be able to view your page? Do you need functionality that is normally on the desktop? You also have to think about the set of skills you and your co-workers have. Are they comfortable with JavaScript programming? How about AJAX (Asynchronous JavaScript and XML)? If you want to provide an enhanced user interface using Silverlight, do they understand how to write Silverlight clients? Where do you and your co-workers want to grow as developers? All of these things need to be factored into your decisions. With so many questions to answer, your first decision will normally be to decide where to start.

In this chapter, we will continue to use the photo service introduced in the preceding chapter. If you need a refresher regarding service functionality, look through that chapter and read the section "An Introduction to our Web Service."

Here, I modify the service a bit to focus on the most common scenario for consuming REST services: consuming the services your website provides to allow for AJAX-style interactions. The only change I made to the photo service is to refactor its security infrastructure to use typical ASP.NET forms authentication (the reason for which I'll explain later in the chapter). The goal here is to show how you will normally use REST-based AJAX services in your Web applications. To facilitate this task, I'll present a short section showing how to pass client credentials using `XMLHttpRequest`, which is the engine that drives AJAX. This chapter does *not* teach you to program in JavaScript or all the details surrounding AJAX. If your JavaScript is a bit rusty, I recommend grabbing a copy of *JavaScript: The Good Parts*, by Douglas Crockford. For AJAX in ASP.NET applications, I recommend *Introducing Microsoft ASP.NET AJAX*, by Dino Esposito.

To understand all the client options for Web applications and RESTful services, we will work through the three mechanisms a .NET developer can use: custom scripts written using `XMLHttpRequest`, service-generated JavaScript, and Silverlight. Obviously, you can also use non-Microsoft technologies like *ActionScript* (which drives Adobe *Flash*). Even in non-Microsoft technologies, you will be able to apply the concepts you learn here. In your own applications, you will frequently use some combination of these options, depending on what services you need to consume and your ability to enhance those services.

The sample for this chapter is a single Web application that essentially builds the same user interface using the three RESTful service access technologies at our disposal. The user interface of the application allows a user to log in and then to pick a technological "view" to see the resulting images. Figure 4.1 shows the initial login screen.

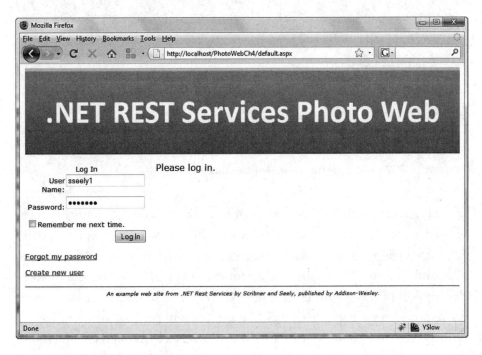

FIGURE 4.1: Photo Web login page

After logging in, the user is presented with the page shown in Figure 4.2.

From here, the user can choose to update his own images using one of several technologies: through XMLHttpRequest (XHR), Microsoft AJAX (MS-AJAX), or Silverlight. Options exist for viewing images of friends or your own images. You will note that the Silverlight option does not have a "friends" option. This part of the application combines the two notions, providing you with a user interface and application logic that is very similar to the Windows Presentation Foundation desktop application shown in the preceding chapter.

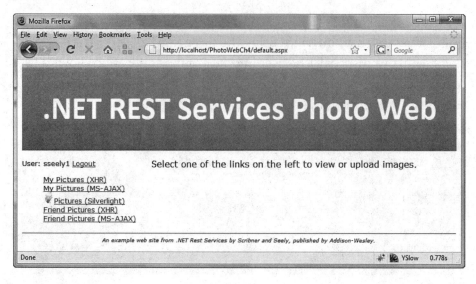

FIGURE 4.2: Photo Web page for an authenticated user

In the sections that follow, we will develop the code that supports the various technological views. The goal is to show how to accomplish the different tasks depending on what resources you might be given. We start with a custom solution, having been given only a set of URI endpoints and some description of how to access those URIs. Next, assuming that the service we're accessing is capable of this, the service will provide our application with a JavaScript proxy we can use to call the service from our client. Finally, we will use Silverlight and demonstrate the flexibility it provides as we interact with the RESTful Web service through .NET as well as JavaScript code.

Working at the Metal: XMLHttpRequest

For any browser introduced since 2002, JavaScript has access to a very special object: XMLHttpRequest, also known as XHR. Introduced in Internet Explorer 5.0 to support Outlook Web Access, XHR became a de facto standard and allows browsers to send requests to a Web server in the background without clicking a submit button to send a full-fledged postback to the server. As of Internet Explorer 7.0, all major browsers support XHR as a native object type. When talking about AJAX, people are really talking about XHR. This class serves the same roles as System.Net.WebRequest and

`Sytem.Net.WebResponse` serve for .NET desktop-based clients. But there are a few important things to know about this class before we use it.

To begin, many people will still be using Internet Explorer 5.x or 6.x, as well as Mozilla or WebKit-based browsers. Due to the differences in JavaScript implementations in these various browsers, when people access your Web pages, you need to know how to get access to a proper instance of XHR, which will depend on the browser type they're using. In Internet Explorer 5.x and 6.x, the browser supports XHR through an ActiveX object. In all other browsers, XHR appears as a native JavaScript object, just like `window` and `document`. Over time, people have come up with several (very similar) algorithms to correctly instantiate an XHR independent of the browser manufacturer. The algorithm is simple; if the object is not available natively, JavaScript tries loading the ActiveX version of the object. I typically use the JavaScript shown in Listing 4.1 to create an instance of XHR regardless of the browser my page is running within.

LISTING 4.1: **Browser-independent XHR instantiation**

```
var XHRCreator = {
    // List of functions to try when creating an XHR.
    // Order is important, these are ranked from the most preferred
    // mechanism to least preferred.
    _factories: [function() { return new XMLHttpRequest(); },
        function() { return new ActiveXObject("Msxml2.XMLHTTP"); },
        function() { return new ActiveXObject("Microsoft.XMLHTTP"); }
    ],

    // Remembers which function to use when creating a new XHR.
    _factory: null,

    // Creates an XHR referencing the 'right' logic.
    CreateRequest: function() {
        var retval = null;
        if (this._factory == null) {
            for (var i = 0; i < this._factories.length; ++i) {
                try {
                    retval = this._factories[i]();
                    if (retval != null) {
                        this._factory = this._factories[i];
                        break;
                    }
                } catch (e) {
```

continues

LISTING 4.1: Continued

```
                continue;
            }
        }
    }

    if (retval == null) {
        retval = this._factory();
    }
    return retval;
    }
};
```

Creating a request becomes a simple matter of using JavaScript code similar to the following:

```
var xhr = XHRCreator.CreateRequest();
```

After we have an instance of XHR, we can use it to do some work. When I write any XHR-based code, I always provide for these application capabilities:

1. Tell XHR which HTTP method and which URI to access using `XMLHttpRequest.open(httpMethod, destinationUrl, async, username, password)`. The last three parameters are optional. By default, all requests are asynchronous. Username and password can be sent as necessary. XHR supports the five most common HTTP methods: `GET`, `POST`, `PUT`, `DELETE`, and `HEAD`. XHR does not support custom HTTP methods.

2. If using a `PUT` or `POST` HTTP method, construct the body of the message, normally using a simple string.

3. Tell XHR to send the message. This means calling `XMLHttpRequest.send(data)`. When you have no data to send, always use `null` for the data argument. Passing nothing at all tends to cause non-Microsoft browsers to fail on the call to `send`.

4. Provide the code to handle the XHR response by implementing a function for `XMLHttpRequest.onreadystatechange`.

   a. Handle a success response.

   b. Handle a failure response.

Although I do provide for these capabilities, I actually rarely ever arrange the lines of code in the order I presented them. Reading the sample code I've provided from top to bottom, you will see I prefer to implement the capabilities in this alternate order:

1. If using a PUT or POST HTTP method, construct the body of the message. If the code fails to read the expected values from the Web page or elsewhere, there is no need to issue a network request, so cease processing the script at this point.

2. Provide the instance of XHR the code will use to handle the response. This is the first thing I do with a valid instance of XHR. I like to make sure that the event handler is declared long before it will be needed, just in case the response comes back before the script has a chance to declare how responses should be handled.

   a. Handle a failure response. I like to think about how the code will handle a failure before I worry about the success case. Typically, I will create the error handling code and then enhance it as the success code is constructed.

   b. Handle a success response.

3. Tell XHR which HTTP method and which URL to send data to. This is generally easy to implement.

4. Tell XHR to send the message. This is also typically easy to implement.

Let's write some application code and try this out. If we obtain the list of images for the user, we can place them in a list and allow the user to select one for viewing. By sending a GET request to [ApplicationBase]/Images/{username}, we can obtain that list. The response is (currently) XML, which needs to be parsed to extract image URLs, captions, and other photo-specific data.

Therefore, the client user interface provides a mechanism for the user to select from a set of public images to view. The application then needs to retrieve each image identified by the image list and display those images within the browser. The simplest example of all this is the Friend Pictures (XHR) page, FriendPicturesXHR.aspx. Shown in Figure 4.3, this page allows the user to select a friend from an HTML `select` control and then view that user's photos.

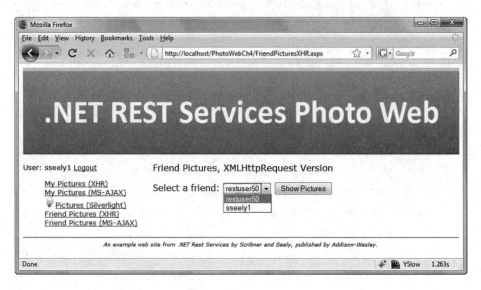

FIGURE 4.3: Selecting a friend to view their photos

Not pictured in Figure 4.3 is an HTML `div` tag whose element identifier is `divImages`. When a user clicks the Show Pictures button, the button's `onclick` event invokes this small JavaScript snippet:

```
PhotoWebXHR.LookupImages('<%=lstFriends.ClientID %>', 'divImages');
```

What is `PhotoWebXHR` and what do the parameters to `LookupImages` mean? `PhotoWebXHR` is a JavaScript class I created to contain all JavaScript code related to using plain old XHR to access the Web service. `Lookup Images` is a class method associated with `PhotoWebXHR` that takes the element identifier of an HTML `select` tag and `div` tag. `LookupImages` extracts the friend's user identifier from the `select` control and uses that information to dynamically populate the `div` tag with the appropriate content. When the function is complete, the `div` will be populated with the selected user's photos. Figure 4.4 shows the result.

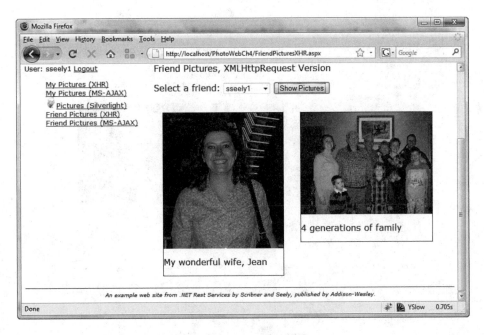

FIGURE 4.4: Result of retrieving "friend" images using XHR

The current user's images are loaded through the My Pictures (XHR) link by ViewMyPicturesXHR.aspx. Figure 4.5 shows this alternative view of the user's images. The differences in the user interface are subtle, but those differences represent very different application capabilities. Figure 4.4 shows the HTML select control that allows you to choose someone's images to view. But Figure 4.5 shows a file upload control that allows you to add images to your own collection. Naturally you would be able to upload images to your account only. In addition, the images themselves differ. In Figure 4.5 the images have the addition of a "delete bar" across the top of the image. The delete bar allows you to delete an image by clicking on the X within the bar. Both views use the same LookupImages method to obtain images.

So how did the images load into the user interface? Let's go through LookupImages, step by step, and see how things were constructed. This method is designed to retrieve both someone else's images and the current user's images. The method also has extra capabilities for adding, deleting, and updating an image.

FIGURE 4.5: Result of retrieving "my" images using XHR

The first thing `LookupImages` does is determine the user's identifier. That code is fairly straightforward, as shown in the following snippet. If the `select` control's identifier cannot be found (because it is nonexistent, which is the case for "my" photos), the code knows to use the `@self` identifier instead:

```
LookupImages: function(lstId, divId) {
    var userId = document.getElementById(lstId);
    var showDeleteBar = true;
    if (userId == undefined) {
        userId = "@self";
    }
    else {
        showDeleteBar = false;
        userId = userId.value;
    }
```

With the user identifier now determined, we have enough information to create the URL for the request. We create an instance of the XHR object and send the request:

```
var xhr = XHRCreator.CreateRequest();
xhr.open("GET", "/PhotoWebCh4/ImageManager.svc/Images/" + userId);
xhr.send(null);
```

We don't send any data in the body of the request, so null is provided to send. The request URL contains all the information we need in order to retrieve a user's image list. At this point the code has issued a RESTful service request for photo information.

With the request issued, we now handle XHR state changes by assigning a function to xhr.onreadystatechange. This event is fired whenever the XHR changes internal state. The current state of the XHR can be discovered by inspection of the readyState property. The valid values for readyState are integer-based:

- 0, *Uninitialized:* The XHR has been created but open has not been called.
- 1, *Open:* The object has been created and open has been called.
- 2, *Sent:* The send method was called.
- 3, *Receiving:* Data has begun to arrive.
- 4, *Loaded:* The response is complete. The XHR properties response-Text, responseXML, responseBody, and status are all available when this state is achieved. Note that responseXML is available only on Gecko/Mozilla and WebKit-based browsers. Internet Explorer 7.0 and earlier do not have this property.

Most of the time, the JavaScript method processing this event will not need to do anything until the readyState reaches Loaded (4). All the other states indicate that valid response information is unavailable and are reporting request status only. However, after the readyState reaches Loaded, you check the status property. The status reports the HTTP response's status code. In our case, we can do something productive only if the service returns a status code of 200 (OK). Given that our response comes back as XML, we need to extract the XML data and do something with it. If responseXML is defined on xhr, we use what we find there. Otherwise, we create an ActiveX XML object and use that object instead. Fortunately, the code for using responseXML and the ActiveX object are very similar. The code in Listing 4.2 shows how all of this is accomplished.

LISTING 4.2: **XHR** OnReadyStateChange **event handing**

```javascript
xhr.onreadystatechange = function() {
    var xmlDoc = null;
    if (xhr.readyState == 4 && xhr.status == 200) {
        if (xhr.responseXML == undefined) {
            if (window.ActiveXObject) {
                xmlDoc = new ActiveXObject("Microsoft.XMLDOM");
                xmlDoc.loadXML(xhr.responseText);
            }
        }
        else {
            xmlDoc = xhr.responseXML;
        }
        if (xmlDoc == null) {
            alert("XML not supported by this browser. Failed to " +
                "get a useable response: " + xhr.responseText);
            return;
        }
    ...
```

With the response in hand, we just need to parse the XML. Because this is JavaScript, we do not have access to different types of serializers to get the job done. You are limited to using the XML Document Object Model. When processing the inner content of various nodes, happily the code is very similar for the ActiveX and the native XML document type. The ActiveX variant calls the inner text `text`, whereas the native version uses `textContent`, but that's the only major difference. When asking for the list of images, we will be provided an XML document that contains a number of child nodes named `ImageItem`. Each `ImageItem` looks something like this (which is the same as it was in the preceding chapter since we're using the same service):

```xml
<ImageItem xmlns="http://www.scottseely.com/RESTBook/2008"
    xmlns:i="http://www.w3.org/2001/XMLSchema-instance">
    <Caption>Some caption</Caption>
    <Description>Some description</Description>
    <ImageBytes>AQIDBAUGAQAQIDBAU[...]</ImageBytes>
    <ImageId>33f741ae-934a-4c77-b7f8-0f316000ab53</ImageId>
    <ImageUrl>[path to ashx that will yield a valid
                image/jpeg]</ImageUrl>
    <PublicImage>true</PublicImage>
    <UserName>restuser</UserName>
</ImageItem>
```

The code is going to ask for all the child nodes named ImageItem. For each node, we will ask it whether any child nodes have a particular name: Caption, Description, ImageId, PublicImage, and UserName. Each of those child nodes is used to create a div element containing markup for the associated image, hidden fields for the image identifier and the image description, and an HTML paragraph tag (<p></p>) to display a caption under the image. The code to do this is provided in Listing 4.3.

Listing 4.3: XHR OnReadyStateChange **event handing, continued**

```
...
var imageItems = xmlDoc.getElementsByTagName("ImageItem");
var imageUrl;
var imageCaption;
var htmlText = "";
for (var i = 0; i < imageItems.length; ++i) {
    var imageNode = imageItems[i];
    var captionNode = imageNode.getElementsByTagName("Caption");
    var urlNode = imageNode.getElementsByTagName("ImageUrl");
    var descriptionNode = imageNode.getElementsByTagName("Description");
    var idNode = imageNode.getElementsByTagName("ImageId");
    var publicNode = imageNode.getElementsByTagName("PublicImage");
    if (captionNode.length == 1 && urlNode.length == 1) {
        var imgSrc;
        var caption;
        var description;
        var imageId;
        var publicImage;
        if (urlNode[0].textContent == undefined) {
            imgSrc = urlNode[0].text;
            caption = captionNode[0].text;
            description = descriptionNode[0].text;
            imageId = idNode[0].text;
            publicImage = publicNode[0].text;
        } else {
            imgSrc = urlNode[0].textContent;
            caption = captionNode[0].textContent;
            description = descriptionNode[0].textContent;
            imageId = idNode[0].textContent;
            publicImage = publicNode[0].textContent;
        }
        var deleteBar = showDeleteBar ?
            "<div class='Delete' onclick=\"PhotoWebXHR.Delete('" +
            imageId + "');\" >X</div>" : "";
        htmlText += "<div class='imageItem' id='" + imageId + "'>" +
```

continues

Listing 4.3: Continued

```
                deleteBar + "<div onclick='PhotoWebXHR.ShowDialog(\"" +
                imageId + "\");' ><img class='actualImage' src='" +
                imgSrc + "' alt='" +
                caption + "' /><input type='hidden' value='" +
                description + "'/>" + "<input type='hidden' value='" +
                publicImage + "'/><p>" + caption + "</p></div></div>";
        }
    }
    var divElement = document.getElementById(divId);
    divElement.innerHTML = htmlText;
    }
```

The last two lines of the preceding listing take all the concatenated text and apply those tags to the content of the div element passed into LookupImages. This provides images for viewing, but how are images provided to the service?

If you look at Figure 4.5, you will see that the Web page has what looks like (and in fact is) a file upload control. The ImageManager service does have a mechanism to add images. That particular mechanism relies on the ability to open a file, convert the bytes to a Base64 encoded byte array, and assign that byte array into an ImageItem object for upload. JavaScript does not give us access to the bytes in a file upload HTML control. To get around this problem, we need another mechanism. So we simply POST the image to the server. The service executing on the server simply adds the image to the list of images owned by the current user. Sometimes the best way to implement a RESTful service request is to issue a simple browser form POST.

Toward the end of the LookupImages method shown in Listing 4.3, the JavaScript code is writing some markup to call two other methods implemented by PhotoWebXHR: Delete and ShowDialog. As you might recall, a photo deletion request is issued whenever someone clicks on the delete bar at the top of an image. When deleting an image, we need to do two things:

1. Send an HTTP DELETE message to the service at /PhotoWebCh4/ ImageManager.svc/Image/{ImageID}.

2. Remove the div containing the image from the browser window.

This is the simplest request we send to our service, as evidenced by the code shown in Listing 4.4.

LISTING 4.4: PhotoWebXHR Delete **method**

```
Delete: function(divId) {
    var xhr = XHRCreator.CreateRequest();
    if (xhr != undefined) {
        xhr.onreadystatechange = function() {
            if (xhr.readyState == 4 && xhr.status == 200) {
            }
        };
        xhr.open("DELETE", "/PhotoWebCh4/ImageManager.svc/Image/" +
            divId);
        xhr.send(null);
        var theDiv = document.getElementById(divId);
        if (theDiv != undefined) {
            theDiv.parentNode.removeChild(theDiv);
            theDiv.outerHTML = "";
        }
    }
}
```

Finally, we need to implement the capability to update image details. When a user clicks on one of her images, the user interface causes a pop-up to appear. This pop-up allows the user to change the image caption, change the image description, and indicate whether the image should be considered public or private. The pop-up itself makes use of *JQuery* and some of the *JQuery UI* JavaScript library (see http://jquery.com). Figure 4.6 shows the details pop-up in action.

When the user clicks OK, we want to capture the changes back into the page as well. After the changes are captured, the update XML message needs to be created and sent on its way to the service. When posting the data back to the server, we need to state the type of resource being posted: application/xml. We set the Content-Type request header by calling the XMLHttpRequest.setRequestHeader method. When we receive a response, we close the pop-up. If there was a failure of any kind, we alert the user that the update failed and show them the response code and reason for failure, as implemented by the code shown in Listing 4.5.

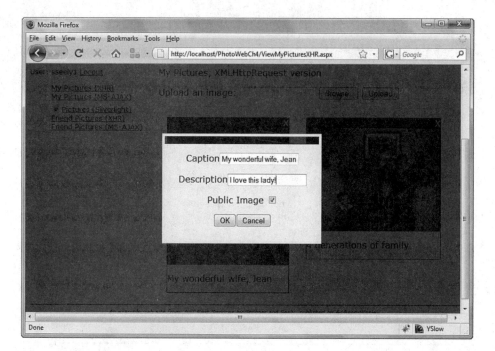

FIGURE 4.6: Image details pop-up

LISTING 4.5: PhotoWebXHR SaveData **method**

```
SaveData: function() {
    // Capture edits.
    var txtId = document.getElementById("txtId").value;
    var txtCaption = document.getElementById("txtCaption").value;
    var txtDescription =
        document.getElementById("txtDescription").value;
    var chkPublicImage =
        document.getElementById("chkPublicImage").checked;

    // Save the edits back to the page.
    var theDiv = document.getElementById(txtId);
    theDiv.getElementsByTagName("p")[0].innerHTML = txtCaption;
    var img = theDiv.getElementsByTagName("img");
    img[0].alt = txtCaption;
    theDiv.getElementsByTagName("input")[0].value = txtDescription;
    theDiv.getElementsByTagName("input")[1].value = chkPublicImage;

    // Create the XHR
    var xhr = XHRCreator.CreateRequest();
    if (xhr != undefined) {
        xhr.onreadystatechange = function() {
```

```
        if (xhr.readyState == 4) {
            $('#dialog').dialog('close');
            if (xhr.status != 200) {
                alert('Update failed. Returned status was: ' +
                    xhr.status);
            }
        }
    };
    xhr.open("PUT", "/PhotoWebCh4/ImageManager.svc/Image/" + txtId);
    xhr.setRequestHeader("Content-Type", "application/xml")
    var upload = "<ImageItem xmlns=" +
        "\"http://www.scottseely.com/RESTBook/2008\">" +
        "<Caption>" + txtCaption + "</Caption>" +
        "<Description>" + txtDescription + "</Description>" +
        "<PublicImage>" + chkPublicImage + "</PublicImage>" +
        "</ImageItem>";
    xhr.send(upload);
    }
}
```

Security with XMLHttpRequest

Before exiting the section, I want to say a word about XHR and security. So far, I have avoided talking about security with XHR because (at least presently) XHR can be used to get or post data only to the current website and not to a third party. JavaScript attempting to contact a server outside the domain of the originating server is known as cross-side scripting (XSS), and contemporary browsers deny this due to the negative security implications. As such, the service authentication is already baked into the cookies or other headers that will automatically be sent to the same-domain service by the browser. Since this happens automatically, I didn't mention it previously.

> **■ NOTE**
>
> This is also why I modified the photo service to use traditional ASP.NET Forms Authentication. Forms Authentication involves a security cookie that is automatically transmitted to the server via the XHR request.

When an external service needs to be involved, it is recommended that the same-domain server proxy the cross-site service access for the user, a process known as *tunneling*. To provide an example, imagine you've written a Web application that displays weather information. The browser will communicate using XHR only with your domain; however, if you don't produce the weather data yourself but rather request it from a third-party source, the service in your domain must request weather data on behalf of your user. The user won't be able to access it directly, at least via XHR.

Other far less secure mechanisms do exist. For a real-world example of token-based authentication, look at the REST architecture for MySpace's *OpenSocial* framework. OpenSocial uses *OAuth* tokens to handle security requests from browser applications. However, OpenSocial and its use of OAuth do not meet stringent security standards. It is good enough for simpler things such as playing online games or delivering weather information, but is in no way secure enough for financial or personal information. This is most often the case when "homegrown" security mechanisms are devised.

For that reason, your application is usually better off using tried-and-true security techniques and frameworks rather than those you create yourself. Moreover, if your application maintains highly valuable or sensitive information, you should have a recognized security expert review your application to make sure it meets all contemporary security standards and protects against known security threats and hacks.

Moving Up a Level: WCF Provided JavaScript/AJAX

In the preceding section, we looked at what it takes to write code using XHR. You will notice that there is a fair amount of code that depends on the parameter values the interface expects to receive. When consuming services, I prefer that the service creator provide me with a library or some other mechanism that reduces the work and number of mistakes I might make when trying to utilize the Web service. To allow Web clients to correctly contact REST services, the two Web services frameworks from Microsoft, ASP.NET XML Web Services (`.asmx`) and Windows Communication

Foundation (WCF), do provide special URLs that automatically generate JavaScript proxies for you to download. Chapter 8, "Building REST Services Using WCF," covers the code needed to automatically provide these files. On the client side, we just want to consume the JavaScript. To look into how all of this works, we use two other Photo Client Web page files: `FriendPictures.aspx` and `ViewMyPictures.aspx`. In the end, the user experience will be identical to the fully custom XHR solution. The difference is in the details.

Our server-side page code makes use of `System.Web.UI.ScriptManager` and its related class, `System.Web.UI.ScriptManagerProxy`. `ScriptManager` and `ScriptManagerProxy` are two classes that work together. Typically, a `ScriptManager` appears on an ASP.NET master page, and pages derived from the master page use `ScriptManagerProxy`.

The reason for this is that ASP.NET has a rule that only one `ScriptManager` can exist per master/derived page combination. To allow you to add `Scripts` and `Services` to child pages, your child page must do so through `ScriptManagerProxy`. `ScriptManagerProxy` merges those extra child page scripts and services into the scripts and services registered with the master page.

`ScriptManager` maintains two collections we are interested in: `Scripts` and `Services`. Both of these ultimately contain JavaScript. `Scripts` contains references to JavaScript that will be provided to the page as it renders (which might result in inline scripts or scripts to be downloaded as `.js` files). `Services` contains the URLs of any `.asmx` or WCF (`.svc`) services that the page needs to access.

The `Services` list works exclusively with .NET-based services because those services are designed to provide custom JavaScript proxy code that makes accessing the service easier. Services registered with the `ScriptManager` are written such that for release builds each service will concatenate `/js` to the URL and debug builds will concatenate `/jsdebug`. If you access the service URI with either `/js` or `/jsdebug`, the service will provide your page with JavaScript proxy code you can use to easily invoke the service. `/js` provides your code with optimized JavaScript, while the `/jsdebug` JavaScript is easier to trace through on the client when debugging.

For this example, the master page declares the `ScriptManager` using the simplest possible syntax:

```
<asp:ScriptManager ID="ScriptManager1" runat="server">
</asp:ScriptManager>
```

This way, when we are ready to actually add service scripts as well as JavaScript resources to generate fancier menus and support common features, each page in the application will have access to those scripts.

The `ScriptManagerProxy` for `ViewMyPictures.aspx` contains a reference to the `JsonImageManager.svc` file as well as a few general-use JavaScript files the page uses:

```
<asp:ScriptManagerProxy ID="ScriptManagerProxy1" runat="server">
    <Services>
        <asp:ServiceReference Path="~/JsonImageManager.svc" />
    </Services>
    <Scripts>
        <asp:ScriptReference Path="~/Scripts/PhotoWebAjax.js" />
        <asp:ScriptReference Path="~/Scripts/jquery.js" />
        <asp:ScriptReference
            Path="~/Scripts/jquery-ui-personalized-1.6rc2.min.js" />
    </Scripts>
</asp:ScriptManagerProxy>
```

The `Services` link fetches the JavaScript used to contact the RESTful service hosted by `JsonImageManager.svc`. Plugging in http://localhost/PhotoWebCh4/JsonImageManager.svc/jsdebug into my browser's address bar shows me the actual JavaScript proxy. The script itself is fairly lengthy and a little hard to read. Here is the definition of www.scottseely.com. RESTBook._2008.IImageManager.GetImagesForUser (with some modest editing):

```
GetImagesForUser:function(username, succeededCallback, failedCallback,
    userContext) {
/// <param name="username" type="String">System.String</param>
/// <param name="succeededCallback" type="Function"></param>
/// <param name="failedCallback" type="Function"></param>
/// <param name="userContext"></param>
return this._invoke(this._get_path(),
                    'GetImagesForUser',
                    false,
                    {username:username},
```

```
succeededCallback,
failedCallback,
userContext);
```

From the code snippet you can see that this method takes four parameters. One parameter is familiar: the name of the user. The next two parameters are functions to be invoked upon the success or failure of the service invocation. The final parameter represents user-defined context that will be provided to the success and failure functions when they are called. For example, you might pass the div to be filled with photo markup when the callback executes. Note the names of the functions: succeededCallback and failedCallback. Under the covers, GetImagesForUser will call XHR and then return. In general, these calls will be asynchronous. When XHR finally reports that it is in readyState Loaded (4), the implementation will decide whether the call is a success or a failure. If the response status is 2xx, the call was successful and the function associated with succeededCallback is invoked. This method can have the following signature:

```
function succeededCallback(result, userContext, methodName)
```

For GetImagesForUser, the result is an array of ImageItem JavaScript objects. If the response status is 4xx or 5xx, the call failed. In that case, the method signature looks like the following, where the first parameter is a JavaScript exception indicating what went wrong:

```
function failedCallback(exception, userContext, methodName)
```

You can also set page level handlers for success and failure via two generated methods named xxx.set_defaultSucceededCallback and xxx.set_defaultFailedCallback. In these cases, knowing the name of the method comes in handy. A method even exists for passing in the default user context: xxx.set_defaultUserContext. We will not use any of these mechanisms since every response is unique enough to warrant special handling. The xxx represents the "namespace" associated with the generated JavaScript. I placed "namespace" in quotes because JavaScript has no concept of a namespace as we understand it with C# or Visual Basic. Instead, xxx is a concatenation of the service's namespace and contract interface (WCF) or the namespace of the class supporting your ASP.NET XML Web

Service and its type if using .asmx. This simply provides a unique string value that, in effect, disambiguates the JavaScript functions in very nearly the same way a true namespace would. A clever trick.

This whole mechanism winds up being fairly pleasant to work with. You can avoid parsing XML, worrying about browser incompatibilities, and even being concerned about how the service is invoked. There is an unfortunate side effect to this technique: It isn't as RESTful as one might like. The reason for this is that using the HTTP GET verb opens security holes: The service method can be invoked through a cross-site scripting attack that attaches external script to the <script> (or even <img>) HTML tags (see http://en.wikipedia.org/wiki/Cross-site_scripting). These HTML elements are the *only* elements allowed to access resources from outside the originating server's domain, and they always retrieve data using the HTTP GET method. This means that disabling the HTTP GET verb for the Web service method prevents any possible cross-site scripting attacks. The effect of this, however, is that all of our service invocations use HTTP POST in much the same way RPC-style Web services do. However, you might decide that the ease of programming and configuration more than make up for the digression from "pure" RESTful mechanics in this specific instance. I'll leave that choice to you.

In any case, the implementation for LookupImages is shown in Listing 4.6.

LISTING 4.6: Photo Client's WCF-based LookupImages method

```
LookupImages: function(lstId, divId) {
    var userId = document.getElementById(lstId);
    var showDeleteBar = true;
    if (userId == undefined) {
        userId = "@self";
    }
    else {
        userId = userId.value;
        showDeleteBar = false;
    }
    www.scottseely.com.RESTBook._2008.IImageManager.
        GetImagesForUser(userId,
            function(result, context) {
                var div = document.getElementById(context);
                var htmlText = "";
```

```
            for (var i = 0; i < result.length; ++i) {
                var imgSrc = result[i].ImageUrl;
                var caption = result[i].Caption || "";
                var description = result[i].Description || "";
                var imageId = result[i].ImageId || "";
                var publicImage = result[i].PublicImage || "false";
                var deleteBar = showDeleteBar ?
                    "<div class='Delete' onclick=" +
                    "\"PhotoWebAjax.Delete('" + imageId +
                    "');\" >X</div>" : "";
                htmlText += "<div class='imageItem' id='" +
                    imageId + "'>" + deleteBar +
                    "<div onclick='PhotoWebAjax.ShowDialog(\"" +
                    imageId + "\");' ><img class='actualImage' src='" +
                    imgSrc + "' alt='" +
                    caption + "' /><input type='hidden' value='" +
                    description + "'/>" +
                    "<input type='hidden' value='" + publicImage +
                    "'/><p>" + caption + "</p></div></div>";
            }

            div.innerHTML = htmlText;
        },
        function(response, context) {
            var div = document.getElementById(context);
            div.innerHTML = "Failed to get images for " + userId +
                ". <p>Reason: " + response.get_message() + "</p>";
        },
        divId);
    }
```

Writing the code to update the `ImageItem` is also a bit easier. In this case,
instead of formatting the XML, we just instantiate a new `ImageItem`, set its
properties, and fire it off to the server, as shown in Listing 4.7.

LISTING 4.7: Photo Client's WCF-based `SaveData` **method**

```
SaveData: function() {
    var txtId = document.getElementById("txtId").value;
    var imageItem = new www.scottseely.com.RESTBook._2008.ImageItem();
    imageItem.Caption = document.getElementById("txtCaption").value;
    imageItem.Description =
        document.getElementById("txtDescription").value;
    imageItem.PublicImage =
        document.getElementById("chkPublicImage").checked;
    var dialogContainer = document.getElementById("dialogContainer");
    var theDiv = document.getElementById(txtId);
```

continues

LISTING 4.7: Continued

```
    var imgMgr = new www.scottseely.com.RESTBook._2008.IImageManager();
    theDiv.getElementsByTagName("p")[0].innerHTML = imageItem.Caption;
    var img = theDiv.getElementsByTagName("img");
    img[0].alt = imageItem.Caption;
    var hiddenFields = theDiv.getElementsByTagName("input");
    if (hiddenFields.length == 2) {
        hiddenFields[0].value = imageItem.Description;
        hiddenFields[1].value = imageItem.PublicImage;
    }
    if (imgMgr != undefined) {
        imgMgr.UpdateImage(imageItem, txtId,
            function() {
                $('#dialog').dialog('close');
            },
            function(response, context) {
                alert("Failed to update image ID " + divId +
                    ".\r\n Reason: " + response.get_message());
            });
    }
}
```

All the script shown here is contained in the sample file Scripts\
PhotoWebAjax.js. The main idea you should remember is that the service-
generated scripts handle much of the XHR related code for you, allowing
you to write much more focused application code. This option might bring
in more JavaScript on page load than a custom solution, but the extra code
in most instances won't matter a great deal. The code itself normally does
not get executed in a tight loop, and the code is relatively small and
efficient.

Programming the Web in C#: Silverlight 2.0

Up until this point, we have covered the two traditional ways to handle
AJAX interactions with the Web client: XHR and through generated proxy
script files. One of the downsides to AJAX- and JavaScript-based user interfaces is that it remains difficult to provide the rich user interfaces users have
come to expect. Essentially, you have to find developers who are also great
Web interface designers, which is a challenging task. Fortunately,
Silverlight brings Windows Presentation Foundation and the related
designer tools to the browser. If you run a Safari, Firefox, or Internet

Explorer browser on Windows, or Mac OS 10.4.8, you can view a Silverlight application, and this combination covers almost every computer user on the planet. The remainder are covered by Moonlight—the Mono project's implementation of Silverlight. As a result, you can now develop Web applications using .NET programming languages that execute in the context of the Web browser. In this chapter, you will see how to send requests using System.Net as well as through JavaScript and XHR when needed.

One thing that I have found incredibly interesting with Silverlight and its related libraries is that Silverlight is very well suited to using asynchronous data retrieval patterns. It gravitates to them so much that the miniature version of the .NET Common Language Runtime (CLR) that runs Silverlight does not contain ports of the synchronous mechanisms from the original desktop-based framework class libraries.

When I first started learning how Silverlight worked, I questioned the level of commitment to this model. Silverlight is *very* committed. Consider the following scenario, which is possible on the desktop: You want to call an asynchronous method in a synchronous fashion. The typical asynchronous method takes a few parameters, a callback function, and an object used for state management. Let's focus on a pair of methods that we will be using in this section that are implemented by System.Net.WebRequest:

```
System.IAsyncResult
  BeginGetRequestStream(System.AsyncCallback, System.Object)
```

and

```
System.IO.Stream
  EndGetRequestStream(System.IAsyncResult)
```

The synchronous method, GetRequestStream, simply doesn't exist in the Silverlight libraries. If you are crafty, or like to think you are, you might be tempted to write code like this to achieve the same effect:

```
Stream stream = request.
    EndGetRequestStream(request.BeginGetRequestStream(null, null));
```

This will compile, but what happens when you try to run this code? The Silverlight "mini" CLR throws a NullReferenceException and you lose your application's display in the browser. Why? Silverlight trusts you to call asynchronous methods with non-null parameters. When you violate that trust and the assumptions Silverlight makes on your behalf, the mini CLR does not throw `System.ArgumentException` with helpful warnings. That would make the libraries and other related code much larger. Instead, it simply throws a `NullReferenceException` when it tries to access the null-valued parameters.

You will see this design philosophy throughout the mini CLR. Enumerations have been stripped of helpful values. If synchronous and asynchronous options exist, the synchronous version was removed. (And for us, this last one is important to keep in mind.)

Silverlight is designed to lead us down a path of responsive application creation. And naturally this means avoiding blocking calls that might take a while to complete, such as when invoking RESTful Web services. With general REST applications, any call from the browser to a server might take time and could potentially lock the browser. Silverlight, however, is designed to avoid this and promote responsive applications even during lengthy data requests or other long-running processes.

Interestingly, for the Web version of the WPF interface, we can largely take the existing UI from the preceding chapter's WPF sample application and tweak it a bit, and the application is essentially complete. The Silverlight UI is shown in Figure 4.7, running in Safari.

For demonstration purposes only, this version of the photo application uses three different mechanisms to interact with the REST service: JSON, XML, and bridging through to JavaScript in the browser. We will finish by looking at how to get files from the browser to the server using Silverlight.

The first thing we want to do is calculate the URL for the JSON and XML versions of the service. We know that they are located in the same folder as the current Web page (because we developed the services with the intention of using the services from our Silverlight client). The constructor for the `Page` class we'll use to support our application establishes the URI values with these lines:

```
XmlImageService = new Uri(App.Current.Host.Source,
    "../ImageManager.svc");
JsonImageService = new Uri(App.Current.Host.Source,
    "../JsonImageManager.svc");
```

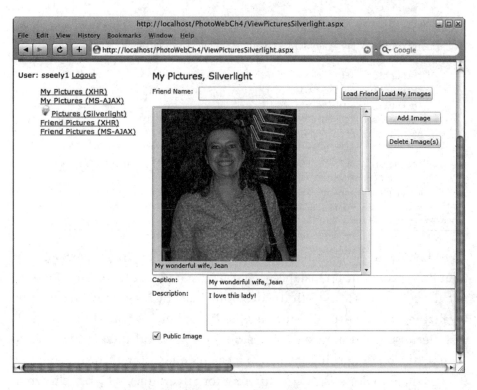

FIGURE 4.7: The Silverlight user interface, running in Safari

XmlImageService and JsonImageService are just private class properties. As with the data returned in the preceding chapter, we will receive a
collection of ImageItem objects that we will bind to the image list. When the
image selection changes, the Caption label, Description label, and Public
Image check box all change as well, and any modifications to the state of
those controls is posted back to the server to be persisted. As you can see,
the user interface/service interaction model did not change from the preceding chapter, so there is no need to revisit that topic. Instead, let's concentrate on the differences between retrieving the list of images as XML
versus JSON.

When the user provides the application with an identifier for a friend
and clicks the Load Friend button, the LoadFriend_Click method is
invoked. The code disables many of the user interface's controls and then
fires a GET request to the XML-based service, as shown in Listing 4.8.

LISTING 4.8: The Silverlight application's Load Friend button click handler

```
private void LoadFriend_Click(object sender, RoutedEventArgs e)
{
    txtCaption.IsEnabled = false;
    txtDescription.IsEnabled = false;
    chkPublic.IsEnabled = false;
    btnAddImage.IsEnabled = false;
    btnDeleteImage.IsEnabled = false;

    string imageUri = string.Format("{0}/Images/{1}", XmlImageService,
        txtFriendName.Text);
    WebRequest request = WebRequest.Create(new Uri(imageUri));
    request.BeginGetResponse(ImagesResponse, request);
}
```

When the response is ready, the mini CLR invokes `ImagesResponse`. At that time, we create an instance of `DataContractSerializer` and deserialize the returned XML. With the deserialize list of `ImageItem` objects now available, `ImagesResponse` updates the list of images bound to the image list. Because the response executes on a background thread, we have to update the binding using the `Dispatcher` member of the XAML page (the requirement to do so isn't any different for Silverlight), which is shown in Listing 4.9.

LISTING 4.9: The Silverlight application's `ImagesResponse` method

```
void ImagesResponse(IAsyncResult result)
{
    WebRequest request = (WebRequest)result.AsyncState;
    try
    {
        WebResponse response = request.EndGetResponse(result);
        DataContractSerializer serializer =
            new DataContractSerializer(typeof(ImageItem[]));
        ImageDocument = new ObservableCollection<ImageItem>();
        foreach (ImageItem item in
            (ImageItem[])serializer.ReadObject(
                response.GetResponseStream()))
        {
            ImageDocument.Add(item);
        }
        response.Close();
        Dispatcher.BeginInvoke(delegate
        {
            lstImages.DataContext= ImageDocument;
        });
```

```
    }
    catch (WebException we)
    {
        HttpWebResponse response = (HttpWebResponse)we.Response;
        Debug.WriteLine(we.ToString());
        response.Close();
    }
}
```

Just to try this, when we load the current user's images ("my" images), we will use the JSON-based service interface instead of the XML-based one. If I were building this application for production, I would use the same mechanism for fetching images for the current user and any other users on the system. But in this case I thought demonstrating JSON was appropriate, so the JSON-based service is used here.

As it happens there are a few minor differences. We still have to write to the request stream, set the `Method`, and establish the `WebRequest`'s `ContentType` (application/json). The difference is we need to get comfortable with a new, Silverlight-specific library: `System.Json`.

"But what about `DataContractJsonSerializer`?" you might (rightfully) ask. After all, with `DataContractJsonSerializer`, we should be able to construct appropriate `DataContract`-based objects and never have the need to learn how `System.Json` works. Although on the surface that might appear to be true, the simple fact is that though it is possible to get `DataContract` to work with types executing in the mini CLR, doing so is not necessarily easy. Often, it is easier to just parse and generate the JSON by hand. I have found that I can generate the JSON I need for transmission much faster by just knowing how the JSON is constructed. To support this, `System.Json` contains five basic data types:

- `JsonValue`: Base class for the types in the namespace. It handles basic things like parsing JSON strings and writing JSON to a `System.IO.TextWriter` or `System.IO.Stream`.
- `JsonObject`: A collection of `KeyValuePair<string, JsonValue>`.
- `JsonArray`: A collection of `JsonValue`.
- `JsonPrimitive`: Converts between the basic CLR primitives and JSON primitives.

- JsonType: JavaScript only recognizes a small set of basic types. All other JavaScript objects build on these basic types. The JsonType enumeration maps to that set of basic types: Array, Boolean, Number, Object, and String. The only type not in this list is Function. Functions are not normally passed using JSON, so this isn't necessarily surprising.

We will use this knowledge to interact with the JSON-based service. As with the XML-based service earlier, this service is supported by WCF. Because of this, you will need to POST the user identifier using a JSON formatted request, which is shown in Listing 4.10.

LISTING 4.10: The Silverlight application's Load My Images button click handler

```csharp
private void LoadMyImages_Click(object sender, RoutedEventArgs e)
{
    txtCaption.IsEnabled = true;
    txtDescription.IsEnabled = true;
    chkPublic.IsEnabled = true;
    btnAddImage.IsEnabled = true;
    btnDeleteImage.IsEnabled = true;
    try
    {
        // Use the JSON service to show how to read JSON data
        string imageUri = string.Format("{0}/GetImagesForUser",
            JsonImageService);
        WebRequest request = WebRequest.Create(new Uri(imageUri));
        request.Method = "POST";
        request.ContentType = "application/json";
        request.BeginGetRequestStream(GetMyImagesRequestStreamCallback,
            request);
    }
    catch (Exception ex)
    {
        Debug.WriteLine(ex.ToString());
    }
}
```

Invoking BeginGetRequestStream naturally leads to an invocation of EndGetRequestStream. With the request stream in hand, we write the data to the stream.

> ## ■ CAUTION
>
> Remember to `Close` the `Stream`. Forgetting this is probably the most frequent bug I see. It manifests itself as a mysterious situation in which the response never seems to come back. It has become a habit for me to look for a call to `Close` whenever I see strange behavior.

The code in Listing 4.11 creates the simple request. The exact JSON format can be discovered in a couple of ways. One technique is by knowing how the parameters the Web service expects would map into JSON. The other mechanism is to fire up something that watches the traffic between the browser and the Web server. I chose the latter technique. Recall that we had already written some code that retrieves the current user's list of images using the JSON-based service. To determine what was actually sent, I use my favorite Web-based diagnostic tool: Firebug. This tool is the reason most of the figures in this chapter show the Firefox browser instead of any other choice. Figure 4.8 shows the Firebug plug-in revealing the exact information posted to the server.

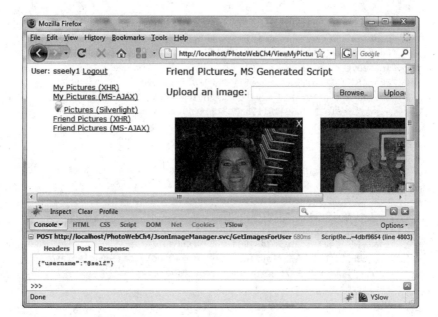

FIGURE 4.8: Firebug showing the JSON content posted to the server

As you can see, the posted information is very basic. This is a simple JSON object with one property, username, that has a string value, @self. We then save that object to the request Stream and send the request on its way (see Listing 4.11).

LISTING 4.11: Initiating the JSON-based "my images" service request

```
void GetMyImagesRequestStreamCallback(IAsyncResult result)
{
    WebRequest request = (WebRequest)(result.AsyncState);
    Stream stream = request.EndGetRequestStream(result);
    JsonObject json = new JsonObject(new KeyValuePair<string, JsonValue>
        ("username", "@self"));
    json.Save(stream);
    stream.Close();
    request.BeginGetResponse(JsonImagesResponse, request);
}
```

As you can see from Figure 4.8, you can also examine the HTTP headers sent to the server as well as the complete response from the server. If you were to click the Response tab for this request, you would see that the response looks like the following:

```
{"d":[
    {"__type":"ImageItem:http:\/\/www.scottseely.com\/RESTBook\/2008",
     "Caption":"My wonderful wife, Jean",
     "Description":"I love this lady!",
     "ImageBytes":null,
     "ImageId":"16e81e22-9c9e-451f-b804-83ff59c22d3",
     "ImageUrl":"http:\/\/localhost\/PhotoWebCh4\/ImageHandler.ashx
        ➥\/16e81e22-9c9e-451f-b804-283ff59c22d3",
     "PublicImage":true,
     "UserName":"sseely1"},

    {"__type":"ImageItem:http:\/\/www.scottseely.com\/RESTBook\/2008",
     "Caption":"4 generations of family",
     "Description":"Jean, Dzadza, Grandpa, Grandma, Aunt Laurie,
        ➥Dad, Phil, Angie, Vince",
     "ImageBytes":null,
     "ImageId":"4a4aff8b-967d-488e-90e7-fcb6e0f73fef",
     "ImageUrl":"http:\/\/localhost\/PhotoWebCh4\/ImageHandler.ashx
        ➥\/4a4aff8b-967d-488e-90e7-fcb6e0f73fef",
     "PublicImage":true,
     "UserName":"sseely1"}
    ]
};
```

The top level of the response contains one object with a single value named d. d maps to an array of ImageItem. A basic DataContractJson Serializer set up to deserialize ImageItem[] will quietly fail when encountering that top-level d object. (This is a known limitation in Data-ContractJsonSerializer.) That's okay, though. The code we need to write to read the JSON is not too complicated. We know that all JSON objects are just key/value pairs. The custom code we'll provide to read the response makes sure that the top level of the JSON contains only one object and that this object contains a single JsonArray. From there it is a simple matter of executing some code to iterate over the collection to extract the ImageItem objects and bind the list of ImageItem objects to the display. This is shown in Listing 4.12.

LISTING 4.12: Interpreting the JSON-based service response

```
void JsonImagesResponse(IAsyncResult result)
{
    WebRequest request = (WebRequest)result.AsyncState;
    try
    {
        WebResponse response = request.EndGetResponse(result);
        Stream responseStream = response.GetResponseStream();
        JsonObject value = (JsonObject)JsonObject.Load(responseStream);
        ImageDocument = new ObservableCollection<ImageItem>();
        if (value.Count == 1)
        {
            JsonArray valueArray = (JsonArray)value.Values.ElementAt(0);

            var imageItems = from JsonObject obj in valueArray
                        select new ImageItem()
                        {
                            Caption = obj["Caption"],
                            Description = obj["Description"],
                            ImageId = obj["ImageId"],
                            ImageUrl = obj["ImageUrl"],
                            PublicImage = obj["PublicImage"],
                            UserName = obj["UserName"]
                        };
            foreach (ImageItem item in imageItems)
            {
                ImageDocument.Add(item);
            }
            Dispatcher.BeginInvoke(delegate
```

continues

```
                {
                    lstImages.DataContext = ImageDocument;
                });
            }
        }
        catch (WebException we)
        {
            HttpWebResponse response = (HttpWebResponse)we.Response;
            Debug.WriteLine(we.ToString());
            response.Close();
        }
        catch (Exception e)
        {
            Dispatcher.BeginInvoke(delegate
            {
                MessageBox.Show(e.ToString());
            });
        }
    }
```

We have looked at how to retrieve the lists of images and examined the differences in requesting the list using the XML and JSON-based services. The next bit of functionality we need requires access to the client file system.

As you might know, HTML has a mechanism to transfer files from the client to the server:

```
<input type="file" />
```

Silverlight applications need to have an equivalent mechanism. The Silverlight team could have recommended some sort of interoperability with HTML markup. Instead, they created something that is a viable alternative to HTML. Silverlight does support `System.IO.File` and its related types. Even if it did, most uses of these classes would result in access-denied exceptions simply because of the reduced access rights any Web-based application would be subject to.

However, Silverlight does support its own version of the HTML input file functionality via a very old and dear friend: `OpenFileDialog`. If a user selects a file from his or her computer using `OpenFileDialog`, that file and all of its contents are made available to the Silverlight application. That is one feature that JavaScript developers do not have (outside of some old hooks allowed by the Netscape browser that are, today, deemed too risky due to implementation decisions surrounding those settings). Silverlight can access the file *only* via the OpenFileDialog instance—no other mechanism will work. Moreover, the Silverlight application cannot pick other files on the computer not selected via OpenFileDialog. The code shown in Listing 4.13 loads that image into an ImageItem in preparation for transmission to the service.

LISTING 4.13: **Preparing image files for transmission to the photo service**

```
private void AddImages_Click(object sender, RoutedEventArgs e)
{
    OpenFileDialog ofd = new OpenFileDialog();
    ofd.Multiselect = false;
    ofd.Filter = "JPEG Files|*.jpeg;*.jpg|PNG Files|*.png" +
        "|GIF Files|*.gif|All|*.*";
    bool? result = ofd.ShowDialog();
    if (result.HasValue && result.Value)
    {
        ImageItem item = new ImageItem();
        Stream stream = ofd.File.OpenRead();
        item.ImageBytes = new byte[ofd.File.Length];
        stream.Read(item.ImageBytes, 0, item.ImageBytes.Length);
        stream.Close();
        string imageUri = string.Format("{0}/AddImage/",
            XmlImageService);
        WebRequest request = WebRequest.Create(new Uri(imageUri));
        request.Method = "POST";
        request.ContentType = "application/xml";
        request.BeginGetRequestStream(GetAddImageRequestStreamCallback,
            new object[] { request, item });
    }
}
```

Once again we use BeginGetRequestStream to obtain the request stream, and with the stream we write the ImageItem data using an instance of DataContractSerializer. Again, note that we close that request stream immediately after writing the object. This makes sure that the data is actually sent to the Web server. If a WebException is thrown, we record it to the debugger as shown in Listing 4.14.

LISTING 4.14: Initiating the JSON-based "upload photo" service request

```
void GetAddImageRequestStreamCallback(IAsyncResult result)
{
    object[] stateVariables = (object[])result.AsyncState;
    WebRequest request = (WebRequest)stateVariables[0];
    ImageItem imageItem = (ImageItem)stateVariables[1];
    try
    {
        Stream stream = request.EndGetRequestStream(result);
        DataContractSerializer dcs = new
            DataContractSerializer(typeof(ImageItem));
        dcs.WriteObject(stream, imageItem);
        stream.Close();
        request.BeginGetResponse(AddResponse, request);
    }
    catch (WebException we)
    {
        HttpWebResponse response = (HttpWebResponse)we.Response;
        Debug.WriteLine(we.ToString());
        response.Close();
    }
}
```

Finally, the application reads the response to retrieve the identifier of the newly added image. Then we retrieve the individual `ImageItem` from the server by using the single item photo request URI. This is shown in Listing 4.15.

LISTING 4.15: Retrieving a single photo instance

```
void AddResponse(IAsyncResult result)
{
    WebRequest request = (WebRequest)result.AsyncState;
    try
    {
        WebResponse response = request.EndGetResponse(result);
        DataContractSerializer dcs = new
            DataContractSerializer(typeof(Guid));
        Guid imageId =
            (Guid)dcs.ReadObject(response.GetResponseStream());
        response.Close();
        string imageUri = string.Format("{0}/Image/{1}",
            XmlImageService, imageId.ToString("D"));

        request= WebRequest.Create(new Uri(imageUri));
        request.BeginGetResponse(GetIndividualImageResponse, request);
    }
    catch (WebException we)
```

```
    {
        HttpWebResponse response = (HttpWebResponse)we.Response;
        Debug.WriteLine(we.ToString());
        response.Close();
    }
}
```

The last scenario I want to cover with Silverlight involves interaction with existing JavaScript that calls REST methods. In this case, the Silverlight application is simply calling existing JavaScript. But sometimes you will have existing code that works well, is well debugged, or is otherwise suitable for use if only it could be accessed by Silverlight code. Instead of rewriting the JavaScript in C#, you can just call the JavaScript method directly. For this sample, we have a small JavaScript method on the host page:

```
<script type="text/javascript">
    function DeleteImage(imageId) {
        PhotoWebXHR.Delete(imageId);
    }
</script>
```

To access the `DeleteImage` method, we take advantage of the `System.Windows.Browser.HtmlPage.Window.Invoke` method. This method takes a method name and an array of objects that represent parameters. When the method completes its task, the method returns a `null`, some primitive type, or a `System.Windows.Browser.ScriptObject`. In our case, we are asking to delete a photo, which naturally means we are not looking for any return values. The JavaScript invocation is shown in Listing 4.16.

LISTING 4.16: Invoking a JavaScript method from Silverlight

```
private void DeleteImages_Click(object sender, RoutedEventArgs e)
{
    if (grdDetails.DataContext != null)
    {
        ImageItem item = (ImageItem)grdDetails.DataContext;
        HtmlPage.Window.Invoke("DeleteImage",
            item.ImageId.ToString("D"));

        ImageDocument.RemoveAt(lstImages.SelectedIndex);
        grdDetails.DataContext = null;
    }
}
```

Before leaving this section, we need to take a moment and talk about sending requests across domains. By default, a Silverlight application hosted by www.scottseely.com can invoke services hosted within the same domain. To protect against the application maliciously calling services from another domain, that other domain has to explicitly state which domains can talk to it.

Let us assume that we have a service hosted at www.endurasoft.com and a Silverlight application at www.scottseely.com. For the application to successfully talk to the service, www.endurasoft.com has to provide a special file authorizing scottseely.com to make cross-domain service invocations. To do this, endurasoft.com must deploy a file at a very specific URI: www.endurasoft.com/clientaccesspolicy.xml. If endurasoft.com is willing to allow anyone to contact the service, the file will indicate that it accepts requests from anywhere with the following file syntax:

```xml
<?xml version="1.0" encoding="utf-8"?>
<access-policy>
  <cross-domain-access>
    <policy>
      <allow-from http-request-headers="*">
        <domain uri="*"/>
      </allow-from>
      <grant-to>
        <resource path="/" include-subpaths="true"/>
      </grant-to>
    </policy>
  </cross-domain-access>
</access-policy>
```

To constrain access to scottseely.com, the domain line would be changed to the following:

```xml
<domain uri="http://scottseely.com"/>
```

Note that this special file will have no effect on a malicious application. clientaccesspolicy.xml only protects against mistaken but otherwise well-behaved applications. If you create a service that needs to be accessible from Silverlight applications executing in other domains, you need to explicitly tell the Silverlight runtime that it is acceptable for applications running in those different domains to issue service requests using this mechanism.

> **■ NOTE**
>
> Silverlight also honors most Flash x-domain policy files. Appendix C, "REST Best Practices," discusses this in a bit more detail.

Where Are We?

We have taken a look at the different ways we might be asked to develop client code for a Web application. If the service we connect to does not provide a client library, we will find ourselves writing rather low-level code using XHR directly. If we are lucky, the service might provide us with a JavaScript proxy we can use to invoke service methods. If the service endpoint is supported by a `.asmx` or `.svc` service, the JavaScript proxy is obtained by passing `/js` or `/jsdebug` to the endpoint. When developing richer applications, Silverlight allows us to work with XML, JSON, and any client-provided JavaScript. The choice depends on where the application will need to run.

This chapter finishes our discussion of client-side development. The remainder of the book covers how to build REST services using the various Microsoft server-side .NET technologies, starting with the lowest level, the Web server.

■ 5 ■

IIS and ASP.NET Internals and Instrumentation

To UNDERSTAND HOW an HTTP request is processed by Microsoft Windows, we need to understand the big picture. Who are the actors? How do they relate? What do they do? In this chapter, I'm going to assume that you are already familiar with ASP.NET and some of the more common classes. For example, I assume that you are familiar with `System.Web.HttpContext` and how that class works. Instead, I'm going to concentrate on how Windows shuttles an incoming client HTTP request to your Web application for response processing and how you can track that process after your application has been deployed. This chapter covers how the software nearest the wire works and how you can use that software to enhance your own applications.

The Big Picture

Internet Information Server 7.0, or simply IIS, is the latest iteration in the evolution of Microsoft's first line production Web server. What we think of as IIS (as of version 7.0 anyway) is really made up of four components: `http.sys`, the *Windows Process Activation Service*, worker process components (which I'll often refer to as the "application" part of IIS since they have no specific name), and ASP.NET. Each of these components serves a different role in processing a request. `http.sys` listens for incoming HTTP requests. When a request arrives, `http.sys` looks up the URI (or a base portion of it) to ensure that the caller has appropriate permission (called a *reservation*) for that URI. Assuming that the caller has permission, `http.sys` forwards the request to the Windows Process Activation Service (WAS) through the World Wide Web Publishing Service (W3SVC). WAS then looks at the request URI and compares that request URI to the list of URIs registered to various applications on the computer, forwarding the request to the longest matching URI. If a match is found, WAS passes the request on to the IIS worker process components.

To illustrate what happens when a request arrives at a computer, let's work through a small example. Imagine we have an application named Foo. The Foo application lies dormant until called on for action. At some point, an HTTP request arrives. The `http.sys` driver receives the request and passes that request to the W3SVC, which then forwards it to WAS. WAS takes a look at the URL to see whether it knows what to do with the request (because the URL might or might not be registered with WAS). Because the request went to a machine that had IIS installed and the request came through `http.sys`, the request will get dispatched to IIS. From there, IIS maps the request to an application, fires up the application, and assists the application as it handles the request. Figure 5.1 illustrates this process.

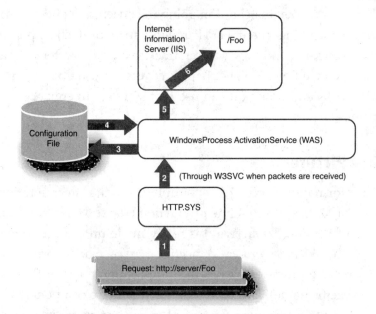

FIGURE 5.1: WAS activation

As developers of RESTful services, we want to understand the details of how each actor behaves so that we can make the right architectural, design, and coding decisions. The remainder of this chapter explains how these actors behave.

http.sys

The TCP/IP communication protocol stack specifies how all implementations of the Transmission Control Protocol (TCP) and Internet Protocol (IP) protocols behave so that all implementations behave similarly. Each network card, whether it's wired or wireless, is assigned one IP address. That IP address allows for connection multiplexing by using TCP port numbers. Web servers like IIS and Apache will use TCP port 80 for HTTP traffic and TCP port 443 for HTTPS traffic.

From the first release of IIS and continuing through Windows XP Service Pack 3, if you ran IIS on a Windows machine with default options selected, no other application could run on port 80. This happened because IIS took exclusive control of port 80 and, when SSL is enabled, port 443. When IIS was first introduced, this was perfectly acceptable. Over time, however, people asked for the ability to write other applications that also used port 80. They wanted to multiplex port 80 by using the HTTP application layer protocol to determine which application should receive the request message. This desire leads to the development of http.sys, which allows for any TCP port hosting HTTP applications to share that port.

When a TCP/IP packet is issued from a source machine, that packet contains a lot of information in addition to the payload. These are generically known as the *framing* bits. Different parts of the packet target different protocols, which in turn specify different arrangements of framing bits.

The first set of bytes in the packet identifies the intended recipient of the packet as well as the size of the packet. This IP information ensures that devices on the network route the packet to the intended recipient. After the packet arrives at a computer, the TCP protocol kicks in and looks at which port receives the message. Individual applications on a computer will normally take exclusive ownership of a given TCP port. (You can see the standard TCP port assignments at www.iana.org/assignments/port-numbers.)

In Windows XP Service Pack 1 and earlier, IIS took exclusive control of port 80. In Windows XP Service Pack 2 and Windows Server 2003, another option became available: a driver-level service named `http.sys`. `http.sys` uses the HTTP application protocol and URLs to multiplex a TCP port in the same way TCP uses port numbers to multiplex an IP address.

> **■ NOTE**
>
> Windows XP SP1 and earlier still ships with IIS 5.1. IIS 5.1 does not use `http.sys`, which makes sharing of ports 80 (HTTP) and 443 (HTTPS) impossible on a Windows XP machine with IIS enabled.

`http.sys` maintains a list of HTTP URLs and the set of consumers that are allowed to listen for requests on those URLs. This reservation system provides a mechanism to partition the URL space on a computer. `http.sys` does not actively listen on any reserved ports until an application actually requests to open a port with the system.

As an example, a Windows XP SP3 machine with .NET 3.5 and ActiveSync installed will have the following reservations in `http.sys`:

- URL: http://*:2869/; ACL : NT AUTHORITY\LOCAL SERVICE
- URL : http://+:80/Temporary_Listen_Addresses/; Everyone
- URL : http://+:8731/Design_Time_Addresses/; NT AUTHORITY\ INTERACTIVE
- URL : http://+:10243/WMPNSSv3/; NT AUTHORITY\NETWORK SERVICE
- URL : http://*:26675/Microsoft-Server-ActiveSync/; Everyone

You can retrieve this information by running the command-line tool `HttpCfg.exe`, which you might do from time to time when `http.sys` refuses the connection (you'd check the list to make sure your application was registered). `HttpCfg.exe` ships with the Windows Server 2003 SDK and can be executed with the following command:

```
httpcfg query urlacl
```

`HttpCfg.exe` will emit the user identity in a format called SDDL. You can then use a tool like `SDDLParse.exe` to translate the string into a Windows identity (see http://blogs.microsoft.co.il/files/folders/guyt/entry70399.aspx). Alternatively, `HttpSysCfg.exe` will accomplish both tasks at once (see www.thinktecture.com/resourcearchive/tools-and-software/httpsyscfg). The tool netsh will show the same information on Windows Vista and Windows Server 2008:

```
netsh http show urlacl
```

netsh allows you to make reservations as well. To reserve the path `http://+:80/REST.NET` on a machine named `2K8VM` for myself, I execute this command:

```
netsh http add urlacl url=http://+:80/REST.NET user=2K8VM\sseely
```

These reservations are all stored in the Registry under this key:

```
HKLM\SYSTEM\CurrentControlSet\Services\HTTP\Parameters\UrlAclInfo
```

Given that adding a reservation is possible, when would you want to do this? As a developer, I add this type of reservation for code that I write while testing my own Windows Communication Foundation (WCF) services. I prefer to run my Windows Vista system as a limited user. This means that I cannot create HTTP endpoints at will but have to use a predefined path where I have access to new reservations. To this end, I always have this endpoint reserved for demonstrations: `http://+:80/Demo`. Without this, I would need to run Visual Studio in administrative mode. By reserving a path for my developer account, I can run as a limited user and still get work done.

In production, you want to reserve specific URLs with `http.sys` anytime you write an application that needs to expose an endpoint for data collection or remote control. That remote control endpoint can be a simple Web service. Most often, however, the application will be a long-running Windows Service, typically using WCF.

The IIS Worker Process

Looking back at Figure 5.1, you can see the box labeled "Internet Information Server," and within that the box labeled "/Foo." The information I've presented so far is interesting and often necessary to understand, but when people typically think of working with IIS, they think in terms of their application executing within the IIS "worker process."

The IIS worker process is where your Web application is managed. It's where ASP.NET works. It's where you'll find modules and handlers. And it's where you'll find much (but not all) of the security infrastructure.

The IIS worker process, which is itself an executable application (w3wp.exe), manages request handling for messages sent to IIS for a specific *application pool*. Application pools isolate ASP.NET Web applications, increasing system reliability. If one Web application crashes its worker process, all other worker processes remain unaffected. Application pools are also where you'll find specific user accounts identified to execute the application code. Typically your applications would use the limited-access IIS user account, which was established on your server when you installed IIS. However, you can tailor this and use different accounts through *impersonation*. You should always strive to use accounts with the fewest system privileges so that malicious access is limited in the amount of damage that can be done.

Often you'll find but a single worker process executing on your development computer. In production environments, and perhaps even on your development system, you'll find more than one instance of w3wp.exe executing. If this is the case, it simply means there is more than one application pool active and the server is protected if one of those application pools crashes. Later, you'll learn how to debug managed code by attaching to one of these processes (and I'll even mention how you might decide which process is the correct process to attach to).

Integrating with IIS

Often, you need to expose data to large numbers of clients. In doing so, you wind up encountering a large set of concerns, such as these:

- How do I secure access to the application?
- How do I balance load across a set of servers?
- How do I maintain statistics about what is going on across my applications?
- How do I troubleshoot errors?
- How do I integrate with the rest of my application?

IIS is an ideal host for an application that exposes data and user interface to the outside world. In general, Web applications allow developers to write and deploy an application by simply providing users with the appropriate application URL. We can fix bugs for all users by providing updated software to the servers where the application executes. We get integrated Windows, X.509, and HTTP Basic or Digest Authentication for a price much lower than if we had to develop all those features ourselves. And when creating code that exposes data based on specific endpoints, IIS 7 really shines. IIS 7 provides an updated application model to better integrate with ASP.NET. The IIS 7 model includes the following:

- A processing pipeline that allows for managed code to do things only unmanaged C++ libraries could do in the past.
- Deeper integration with ASP.NET.
- Improvements to manageability and diagnostics.

In this section, we will cover the IIS pipeline and how it works. We will then dive into the classes and mechanisms that actually allow us to integrate with that pipeline to deliver RESTful services.

The IIS Pipeline

When WAS sends an HTTP message to IIS, the message enters the *IIS messaging pipeline*. The pipeline has three primary stages: authentication/ authorization, execution of the message handler, and response return. The pipeline first authenticates the sender of the message to determine who the sender is. The sender might identify herself through Windows authentication, username/password, or some other mechanism. The sender might choose to send no identification and assume the identity of the anonymous user.

In any case, after an identity is determined, the pipeline can authorize the requested URL. After being authorized, the pipeline hands off the request to the actual message processors, who create a response. This is where your application steps in. Finally, the response reaches the end of the pipeline, where it can be compressed or logged before being sent on its way. Figure 5.2 shows the pipeline model.

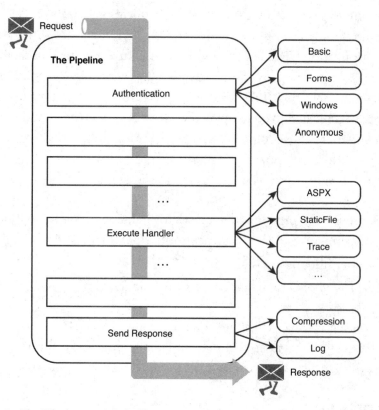

FIGURE 5.2: The IIS 7 integrated pipeline

When integrating with the pipeline, developers can choose to write traditional unmanaged, C++-based IIS extensions, or they can write managed code and use .NET. When using .NET, the developer can write HTTP modules that filter (and perform additional processing on) all incoming requests and outgoing responses by implementing the System.Web.IHttpModule interface, or they can write HTTP handlers to take action for a particular file extension, like `.aspx`, by implementing `System.Web.IHttpHandler`.

> **■■ NOTE**
>
> The code being used in this discussion is in the project named RESTExtensions. If you need to run/deploy the samples from within Visual Studio to your local machine, you will need to run Visual Studio as an administrator.

Implementing HTTP Handlers

As mentioned, ASP.NET HTTP handlers all derive from the `IHttpHandler` interface. As it happens, `IHttpHandler` is a simple interface that defines one read-only property, `IsReusable`, and one method, `ProcessRequest`. `IHttpHandler` is most appropriate for handling a request after it has cleared normal security.

To understand how the interface works, we'll walk through a brief example. To demonstrate an effective use of an ASP.NET handler, we want a resource that is not file-based yet is one that everyone reading this chapter has available with no special setup required. Given this criteria, I decided to expose the list of currently running processes on the computer hosting the handler.

To access the resource (the process list), we need to develop a set of URIs that makes sense when referring to processes. After all, the first thing one does when designing a RESTful Web service is to design the resource URIs. For the list of all processes, let's use `/Process`. For a specific process, we'll use `/Process/{ProcessId}`. Since the service will only be allowed to read the current process list, only HTTP `GET` will be supported.

We need two basic data types to return representational information to our service clients. One data type, `ProcessInfoBasic`, conveys basic process information: process name, process identifier, and a link to the full process information. Full details regarding the process exist in the `ProcessInfo` object. This object contains only those details that an anonymous user could access on the local machine: base priority, handle count, process identifier, machine name, window title, session identifier, and a range of values depicting different aspects of memory usage. Because we want fast, easy serialization, both data types are decorated with appropriate System.Runtime.Serialization attributes for the DataContract and any DataMembers, as shown in Listing 5.1.

LISTING 5.1: ProcessInfoBasic and ProcessInfo

```
[DataContract(Namespace = "http://www.endurasoft.com/REST.NET/")]
public class ProcessInfoBasic
{
    [DataMember]
    public int Id { get; set; }

    [DataMember]
    public string ProcessName { get; set; }

    [DataMember]
    public Uri Link { get; set; }
}

[DataContract(Namespace="http://www.endurasoft.com/REST.NET/")]
public class ProcessInfo
{
    public ProcessInfo() :
        this (Process.GetCurrentProcess().Id)
    {
    }

    public ProcessInfo(int processId)
    {
        Process process = Process.GetProcessById(processId);
        BasePriority = process.BasePriority;
        HandleCount = process.HandleCount;
        Id = process.Id;
        MachineName = process.MachineName.CompareTo(".") == 0 ?
            Environment.MachineName : process.MachineName;
        MainWindowTitle = process.MainWindowTitle;
        NonpagedSystemMemorySize64 = process.NonpagedSystemMemorySize64;
        PagedMemorySize64 = process.PagedMemorySize64;
        PeakPagedMemorySize64 = process.PeakPagedMemorySize64;
        PeakVirtualMemorySize64 = process.PeakVirtualMemorySize64;
        PeakWorkingSet64 = process.PeakWorkingSet64;
        PrivateMemorySize64 = process.PrivateMemorySize64;
        ProcessName = process.ProcessName;
        Responding = process.Responding;
        SessionId = process.SessionId;
        VirtualMemorySize64 = process.VirtualMemorySize64;
        WorkingSet64 = process.WorkingSet64;
    }
```

```
    [DataMember]
    public int BasePriority { get; set; }

    // Remaining members elided.
}
```

With the data types defined, we next need something to process any incoming requests. Here, we implement IHttpHandler in a class aptly named ProcessHandler. First, we do the easy part and allow the handler to be reusable across requests:

```
public class ProcessHandler : IHttpHandler
{
    public bool IsReusable
    {
        get { return true; }
    }
```

This tells ASP.NET that a single instance of our HTTP handler can service multiple concurrent callers. It also allows an instance to be cached (pooled) versus being re-created for each new request.

Next, we need to decide what should happen when IIS hands a request to our handler's ProcessRequest method. At this point, the handler will decide whether it displays a list of ProcessInfoBasic or an individual ProcessInfo. We could perform regular expression matching, use string parsing, or use a mechanism built specifically for this purpose. In this case, we will make use of UriTemplate and friends (see Chapter 2, "The HyperText Transfer Protocol and the Universal Resource Identifier"). After we determine which template is appropriate, we will need to retrieve process information. For this purpose, just as in Chapter 2, a delegate works just fine:

```
delegate void HandleRequest(HttpContext context,
                            UriTemplateMatch template);
```

To provide for this, we'll use an instance of UriTemplateTable, populated with information on demand, as shown in Listing 5.2.

LISTING 5.2: Populating UriTemplateTable

```
UriTemplateTable templateTable = null;
object tableLock = new object();
UriTemplateTable TemplateTable
{
```

continues

LISTING 5.2: Continued

```
get
{
    if (templateTable == null)
    {
        lock (tableLock)
        {
            if (templateTable == null)
            {
                HttpRequest request = HttpContext.Current.Request;
                string fullUrl = request.Url.ToString();
                string baseUrl =
                    fullUrl.Substring(0, fullUrl.IndexOf(
                        request.ApplicationPath));
                templateTable = new UriTemplateTable();
                templateTable.BaseAddress = new Uri(baseUrl);
                templateTable.KeyValuePairs.Add(
                    new KeyValuePair<UriTemplate, object>(
                        new UriTemplate(
                            request.ApplicationPath +
                            "/Process"),
                            new HandleRequest(OutputProcessList)));
                templateTable.KeyValuePairs.Add(
                    new KeyValuePair<UriTemplate, object>(
                        new UriTemplate(request.ApplicationPath +
                            "/Process/{ProcessId}"),
                            new HandleRequest(OutputProcessInfo)));
            }
        }
    }
    return templateTable;
}
```

With a dispatch mechanism in place, we now need to add the code that processes incoming requests. When the request arrives, our code will have full access to the HttpContext and the related HttpRequest and Http Response objects. By looking at the requested URL, the code can figure out whether it knows what is needed and also what action should be taken. If the action is indeterminate, the code knows that the resource request doesn't make sense. In this case the client receives an HTTP 404 (File Not Found) response code. Otherwise, one of the functions assigned in the TemplateTable will handle the request, as shown in Listing 5.3.

Listing 5.3: **The Process Service** ProcessRequest **method**

```
public void ProcessRequest(HttpContext context)
{
    UriTemplateMatch match =
        TemplateTable.MatchSingle(context.Request.Url);
    if (match == null)
    {
        context.Response.StatusCode = 404;
    }
    else
    {
        HandleRequest handleRequest = (HandleRequest)match.Data;
        handleRequest(context, match);
    }
    context.Response.End();
}
```

Assuming that all goes well, we assign the data into the appropriate objects and serialize the information to the output stream using DataContractSerializer. One of the serializers needs to handle the individual ProcessInfo objects for times when someone asks for specific process information. The other serializer has to handle the case in which someone asks for the list of more basic process information. Both cases are shown in Listing 5.4.

LISTING 5.4: **The Process Service** OutputProcessList **and** OutputProcessInfo **methods**

```
DataContractSerializer _processInfoSerializer = new
    DataContractSerializer(typeof(ProcessInfo));
DataContractSerializer _processInfoBasicSerializer = new
    DataContractSerializer(typeof(IEnumerable<ProcessInfoBasic>));

void OutputProcessList(HttpContext context, UriTemplateMatch template)
{
    IEnumerable<ProcessInfoBasic> processInfoList =
        from Process process in Process.GetProcesses()
            select new ProcessInfoBasic()
            {
                Id = process.Id,
                ProcessName = process.ProcessName,
                Link = new Uri(string.Format("{0}/{1}",
                    context.Request.Url.ToString(),
                    process.Id))
            };
```

continues

LISTING 5.4: Continued

```
            // Notify caller that the response resource is in XML.
            context.Response.ContentType = "text/xml";
            _processInfoBasicSerializer.WriteObject(
                context.Response.OutputStream, processInfoList);
        }

        void OutputProcessInfo(HttpContext context, UriTemplateMatch template)
        {
            int processId = 0;
            if (int.TryParse(template.BoundVariables["ProcessId"],
                    out processId))
            {
                try
                {
                    ProcessInfo processInfo = new ProcessInfo(processId);

                    // Notify caller that the response resource is in XML.
                    context.Response.ContentType = "text/xml";
                    _processInfoSerializer.WriteObject(
                        context.Response.OutputStream, processInfo);
                }
                catch (ArgumentException ex)
                {
                    // The message is always appropriate, so just write it out.
                    context.Response.ContentType = "text";
                    context.Response.Write(ex.Message);
                }
            }
            context.Response.Expires = 1;
        }
```

To notify IIS 7 that our handler should handle all traffic coming into the directory, the web.config file needs to declare that all requests go to the one handler. We do this with the following configuration:

```
<?xml version="1.0"?>
<configuration>
    <system.webServer>
        <validation validateIntegratedModeConfiguration="false"/>
        <handlers>
            <add name="RESTResource" verb="GET" path="*"
                type="RESTExtensions.ProcessHandler, RESTExtensions"/>
        </handlers>
    </system.webServer>
    <system.web>
        <compilation debug="true"/>
    </system.web>
</configuration>
```

> ▪ **NOTE**
>
> Note that when I added the handler, I used a path specified to be "*". This is a *wildcard* path, and it has application and performance implications. *All* requests to the given directory will be routed through my handler, which in most cases is not what you typically want. However, in this case it is appropriate.

Figure 5.3 shows the output for a process hosting `notepad.exe`.

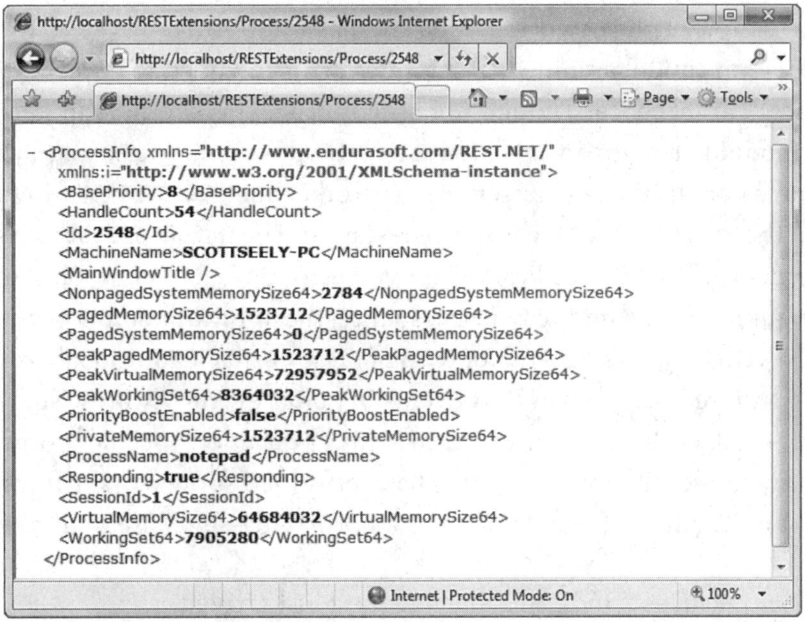

Figure 5.3: Process information for `notepad.exe`

Using the wildcard path is a great way for you to take control of an entire Web folder and display data, but keep in mind you have to worry about dispatch on your own (the functionality provided by `UriTemplateTable`). Using handlers in general does require you to provide some configuration settings, but they're thankfully not too complex.

Everything you have seen here makes it possible to develop RESTful services using things you already know about ASP.NET, and an ASP.NET handler is a very common RESTful service host platform. There are other times, however, when you might like to apply processing to all incoming HTTP packets rather than those destined for a particular URI. In that case, you need an HTTP module.

Implementing HTTP Modules

As you recall, ASP.NET HTTP modules are most appropriate for inspecting and filtering requests passing through the pipeline on their way to or from pipeline HTTP handlers. They are well suited to pipeline tasks such as authentication, authorization, and caching.

HTTP modules are based on the `IHttpModule` interface, which is deceptively simple. It has two methods: `Dispose` and `Init`. Because we see `Dispose`, one might assume that this interface is intended to implement (or replace) `IDisposable`. Though not strictly true, you should still perform any module cleanup in the `Dispose` method, such as releasing system resources or database connections. The other method, `Init`, is invoked when the `HttpApplication` instance is started. The `HttpApplication` is the IIS pipeline. As the application moves through each stage of startup, request processing, and response issuance, the application fires events. In .NET, event handlers register for each of these events if additional processing is required. All the `PostXXX` events fire after event *XXX* fires. They primarily exist to allow you to perform some application-specific processing after another entity in the pipeline has performed some work. Altogether there are 22 different events that, for a normal message, fire in this order:

1. `BeginRequest`: Indicates that a request just arrived.
2. `AuthenticateRequest`: A security module will intercept this event to set the identity of the current user.
3. `PostAuthenticateRequest`: Occurs after the identity of the caller is known.
4. `AuthorizeRequest`: A security module uses this event to decide whether the caller has access to the requested resource.
5. `PostAuthorizeRequest`: Occurs after the caller has been authorized.

6. ResolveRequestCache: Allows a module to respond to the request from a cache. If a cache module does find a suitable response, the response goes back to the caller and the request handler does not get invoked.

7. PostResolveRequestCache: Occurs after ResolveRequestCache.

8. MapRequestHandler: Gives a module a chance to map a specific request handler for the incoming request.

9. PostMapRequestHandler: Occurs after the handler has been mapped.

10. AcquireRequestState: Occurs when ASP.NET grabs the current state. For example, session state gets populated in this stage.

11. PostAcquireRequestState: Occurs after state has been established for the request.

12. PreRequestHandlerExecute: Occurs immediately before the handler gets the request.

13. PostRequestHandlerExecute: Occurs immediately after the handler processes the request.

14. ReleaseRequestState: Any handlers adding state to the request can use this event to remove state from the request.

15. PostReleaseRequestState: Occurs after all state related to the current request has been removed.

16. UpdateRequestCache: At this point, the response is known. Any caching modules have a chance to serialize the data in the response before the response is then sent all the way to the client.

17. PostUpdateRequestCache: Any caching modules have stored their data.

18. LogRequest: Logging modules have a chance to log the request and any data related to the request.

19. PostLogRequest: All loggers are done executing.

20. EndRequest: The response is known and frozen. Modules that handle compression, encryption, or other similar functions can compress the stream or otherwise modify the final response.

21. `PreSendRequestHeaders`: Called before the response headers are returned to the caller. Modules that handled `EndRequest` set other response headers in this stage.

22. `PreSendRequestContent`: Called before the response body is returned to the caller. Modules that handled `EndRequest` can set the final response in this stage.

All of these events allow you to hook into the request or response pipeline processing stream and allow you to perform any aspects of message processing that you might need to handle. If your code needs to examine the request to provide authentication, you can do that (in fact, you'll see this done in Chapter 6, "Building REST Services Using IIS and ASP.NET," where we create a specialized HTTP Basic Authentication module). Or if you have a special need to cache responses for particular scenarios, you can write your own caching mechanism.

Because the goal with this next example is to demonstrate how modules are written, I'll leave the detailed discussion involving security modules to the next chapter, where the details surrounding security could cloud the details involved with creating the module itself. Instead, I'll create a rather simple module that provides for caching operations that are optimized for the Process Service.

> **■. NOTE**
>
> In practice you'd rarely (if ever) need to implement your own cache module as with this example. Instead you'd use the ASP.NET cache directly, which is implemented in a similar fashion to the cache implementation shown here. I chose a cache implementation simply because it's easily understood, but keep in mind that the important points are how modules are developed, how they work, how they are configured, and how they are used within the IIS framework. The fact that this module provides for caching is of secondary importance.

For caches, one of the things a developer needs to do is decide what the cache policy is. Without a well-defined cache policy, a cache can grow out of control, contain stale data, and generally make the application's processing a mess. For process objects, we can assume that processes do not start or change so frequently that a caller needs data accurate to the second. For our purposes, we can assume that items should be no older than 30 seconds.

Another issue we want to tackle is cache depth. How many items should we keep around? Keeping information for all processes is certainly possible. Ideally, we would measure the numbers of which items were most interesting and then tune the cache depth accordingly. Our algorithm will support manual tuning and will have a fixed cache depth of five results. This allows us to demonstrate cache hits and aging of data in a simple manner.

Each cache item will need three pieces of data:

- The URL the cache item represents.
- The byte stream returned from the URL.
- The time the cache item was created so that we know when the cache data needs to be removed.

The CacheItem class is shown in Listing 5.5.

LISTING 5.5: The CacheItem class

```
public class CacheItem
{
    public DateTime Created { get; private set; }
    public byte[] Response { get; private set; }
    public string Url { get; private set; }

    public CacheItem(string url, byte[] response)
    {
        Created = DateTime.UtcNow;
        Response = response;
        Url = url;
    }
}
```

When a cache module is implemented, the module needs a mechanism to intercept the writes to the output stream in order to store that output. The HttpResponse object provided by the HttpContext has a property called Filter of type System.IO.Stream. Filter is used to wrap the response body before transmission. When your code needs to intercept writes to

Filter, you essentially write a Stream that wraps another Stream. By wrapping the response stream instead of replacing it, any code accessing Filter continues to do its work and our code can do whatever it needs to do.

We will use a MemoryStream to collect the output so that we can easily retrieve the bytes and store them in CacheItem. To handle this, the CacheStream class shown in Listing 5.6 works well. CacheStream contains both a MemoryStream and a reference to the original Stream held by Filter. The code delegates most decisions to MemoryStream and repeats a Flush and Write to the wrapped Stream. Note that this is not a general-purpose Stream. This particular implementation is tuned for the behaviors that the sample caching mechanism uses within the context of IIS. If the usage pattern were any different, the CacheStream might not work at all.

LISTING 5.6: The CacheStream class

```
class CacheStream : Stream
{
    public CacheStream(Stream internalStream)
    {
        Cache = new MemoryStream();
        InternalStream = internalStream;
    }

    private Stream InternalStream { get; set; }

    public MemoryStream Cache { get; set; }

    public override bool CanRead { get { return Cache.CanRead; } }

    public override bool CanSeek { get { return Cache.CanSeek; } }

    public override bool CanWrite { get { return Cache.CanWrite; } }

    public override void Close() { InternalStream.Close(); }

    public override void Flush()
    {
        Cache.Flush();
        InternalStream.Flush();
    }

    public override long Length { get { return Cache.Length; } }
```

```
public override long Position
{
    get { return Cache.Position; }
    set { Cache.Position = value; }
}

public override int Read(byte[] buffer, int offset, int count)
{
    return Cache.Read(buffer, offset, count);
}

public override long Seek(long offset, SeekOrigin origin)
{
    return Cache.Seek(offset, origin);
}

public override void SetLength(long value)
{
    Cache.SetLength(value);
}

public override void Write(byte[] buffer, int offset, int count)
{
    InternalStream.Write(buffer, offset, count);
    Cache.Write(buffer, offset, count);
}
```
}

Finally, we have to provide the caching module itself. The caching module registers to receive two HttpApplication events: ResolveRequestCache and UpdateRequestCache. The first event is our opportunity to allow the cache to try to fulfill the request using cached (stored) data. The latter event is issued if the request could not be filled from cache so that the cache module has the opportunity to examine the request, extract the data to be cached, and populate the response. Our caching module makes a couple of simplifying assumptions:

1. The application only handles requests for process information.
2. The ProcessHandler request handler handles all page requests.

If these assumptions were not true, the caching module would have to have some extra rules defining which requests should and should not be served via the cache.

To begin, we derive a class from `IHttpModule`. Let's call it the `Process-CacheModule` since it caches requests from `ProcessHandler` and provides its implementation in Listing 5.7.

LISTING 5.7: The `ProcessCacheModule` ASP.NET module implementation

```
public class ProcessCacheModule : IHttpModule
{
    ReaderWriterLock _cacheLock = new ReaderWriterLock();
    List<CacheItem> _cache = new List<CacheItem>();

    static readonly TimeSpan MaxAge = TimeSpan.FromSeconds(30);
    static readonly TimeSpan ReadLockTimeout = TimeSpan.FromSeconds(1);
    static readonly TimeSpan WriteLockTimeout = TimeSpan.FromSeconds(5);
    const int MaxCacheItems = 5;

    public void Dispose() { }

    public void Init(HttpApplication context)
    {
        context.ResolveRequestCache += ResolveRequestCacheHandler;
        context.UpdateRequestCache += UpdateRequestCacheHandler;
    }

    ...
}
```

The code employs a `ReaderWriterLock` to guard access to `_cache`. When asking for data in `_cache`, the code should be optimized to handle readers since they will not be changing the contents of the `_cache`. Also, note that the cache will be kept small and is being optimized to eliminate old data. As such, lookups will be done by iterating over the cache contents to find the matching URL. Algorithmically speaking, the execution time is O(n), meaning that the time it takes to find the cache element we want depends on the total number of items. If lookup time became an issue, we would use a different data structure (with a faster lookup time, such as a hash table) to hold items.

When resolving the request, we will look through the cache. If we have a response for a request for the same URL and that response is not stale, we serve the request from the cache. Otherwise, we let the handler generate a fresher response. Later, we will remove the stale version and add the fresh version. Finally, we will not wait long to access the cache. If the cache check cannot capture the reader part of the _cacheLock within one second, the code proceeds right to the handler for fresh process information. This approach allows the end user to receive the requested data when the cache cannot be read for whatever reason. This logic is all implemented within the ResolveRequestCacheHandler shown in Listing 5.8.

LISTING 5.8: The ResolveRequestCacheHandler method

```
void ResolveRequestCacheHandler(object sender, EventArgs e)
{
    _cacheLock.AcquireReaderLock(ReadLockTimeout);
    bool responseWritten = false;
    HttpResponse response = HttpContext.Current.Response;
    if (_cacheLock.IsReaderLockHeld)
    {
        try
        {
            string requestUrl =
                HttpContext.Current.Request.Url.ToString();
            var cacheItems = from CacheItem cache in _cache
                where
                    string.Equals(cache.Url, requestUrl,
                    StringComparison.OrdinalIgnoreCase)
                select cache;
            foreach (CacheItem cacheItem in cacheItems)
            {
                if ((cacheItem.Created + MaxAge) >= DateTime.UtcNow)
                {
                    // Only write the response if it is recent.
                    // Otherwise, the slot will be fixed up at the end.
                    // It is possible for two requests for the same URL
                    // to exit through here and hit the handler. This
                    // will be resolved when the cache is updated.
                    response.OutputStream.Write(cacheItem.Response,
                        0, cacheItem.Response.Length);
                    response.ContentType = "text/xml";
                    responseWritten = true;
                    response.End();
                }
                break;
            }
        }
        finally
        {
            _cacheLock.ReleaseReaderLock();
        }
    }
```

continues

LISTING 5.8: Continued

```
    if (!responseWritten)
    {
        // If item was not found in cache, add a filter
        // that can capture the output and put the
        // response into the cache.
        response.Filter = new CacheStream(response.Filter);
    }
}
```

If the request was served from the cache, the act of calling Http
Response.End made sure that the UpdateRequestCache event did not fire.
Using this knowledge, the event handler used to update the cache needs to
remove any stale entries or entries that match the request that are being
served, as shown in Listing 5.9. The cache will not be updated if the cache
module cannot obtain a writer lock within a few seconds. Once again, we
do this so that a caller does not suffer just because our code cannot acquire
a cache lock.

LISTING 5.9: The UpdateRequestCacheHandler method

```
void UpdateRequestCacheHandler(object sender, EventArgs e)
{
    HttpResponse response = HttpContext.Current.Response;
    if (response.StatusCode == (int)HttpStatusCode.OK)
    {
        _cacheLock.AcquireWriterLock(WriteLockTimeout);
        if (_cacheLock.IsWriterLockHeld)
        {
            try
            {
                string requestUrl =
                    HttpContext.Current.Request.Url.ToString();
                for (int i = _cache.Count - 1; i >= 0; −i)
                {
                    CacheItem cacheItem = _cache[i];

                    // Look for an item that is either old or that
                    // matches the current request.
                    if ((
                      (cacheItem.Created + MaxAge) <= DateTime.UtcNow) ||
                      string.Equals(cacheItem.Url, requestUrl,
                          StringComparison.OrdinalIgnoreCase))
                    {
                        _cache.RemoveAt(i);
                    }
                }
```

```
            break;
        }
        while (_cache.Count >= MaxCacheItems)
        {
            _cache.RemoveAt(_cache.Count - 1);
        }
        CacheStream cacheStream = response.Filter as
            CacheStream;
        if (cacheStream != null)
        {
            cacheStream.Cache.Flush();
            byte[] memoryBuffer = cacheStream.Cache.GetBuffer();
            byte[] buffer = new byte[memoryBuffer.Length];
            memoryBuffer.CopyTo(buffer, 0);
            // Insert at the head
            _cache.Insert(0, new CacheItem(requestUrl, buffer));
        }
    }
    catch (Exception ex)
    {
        Debug.WriteLine(ex.ToString());
        throw ex;
    }
    finally
    {
        _cacheLock.ReleaseWriterLock();
    }
}
}
// If the cache could not be acquired, keep on going anyhow.
}
```

To add the module to the IIS pipeline, the web.config file for the application needs to tell IIS7 about the module. When we are done, the complete web.config looks like this (note that I bolded the module configuration element):

```
<configuration>
    <system.webServer>
        <handlers>
            <add name="RESTResource" verb="*" path="*"
                type="RESTExtensions.ProcessHandler, RESTExtensions"/>
        </handlers>
        <modules>
            <add name="RESTCache"
            type="RESTExtensions.ProcessCacheModule, RESTExtensions"/>
        </modules>
    </system.webServer>
```

```
<system.web>
    <compilation debug="true"/>
</system.web>
</configuration>
```

With our cache module in place, when a client asks for our process list 10 times in 10 seconds, the `ProcessHandler` is invoked only once. The remaining nine requests all come from the cache. The cache depth can be changed either by updating the `MaxCacheItems` constant and recompiling or by reading the cache depth information from `web.config` (not shown). That choice is yours.

Diagnostics

Things can go wrong in many ways when you're building and executing applications. The location of the error and the level of debugging you can do are largely dependent on several factors. Knowing the tools and the environment will inform you about which debugging techniques will best help you solve problems. In this section, we look at the tools available and discuss when to use those tools.

Visual Studio

Whenever you are debugging on a development machine or a machine where you can attach a debugger, Visual Studio can be a huge help. When debugging your Web application, you generally want to have some innocuous page that does nothing other than make sure that your application gets loaded. I frequently provide a Web page that displays the current time for this purpose. Doing so tells me two things instantly: that the application loaded and that the response is coming from the application and not from some cache. When you see that test page in your browser, you know that the IIS worker process, `w3wp.exe`, is loaded. At that point, you also have something to debug. From Visual Studio, you then select Debug, Attach to Process. Make sure that Show Processes from All Users and Show Processes in All Sessions are checked, as shown in Figure 5.4. By default, `w3wp.exe` typically runs in session 0 as Network Service, although this is configurable.

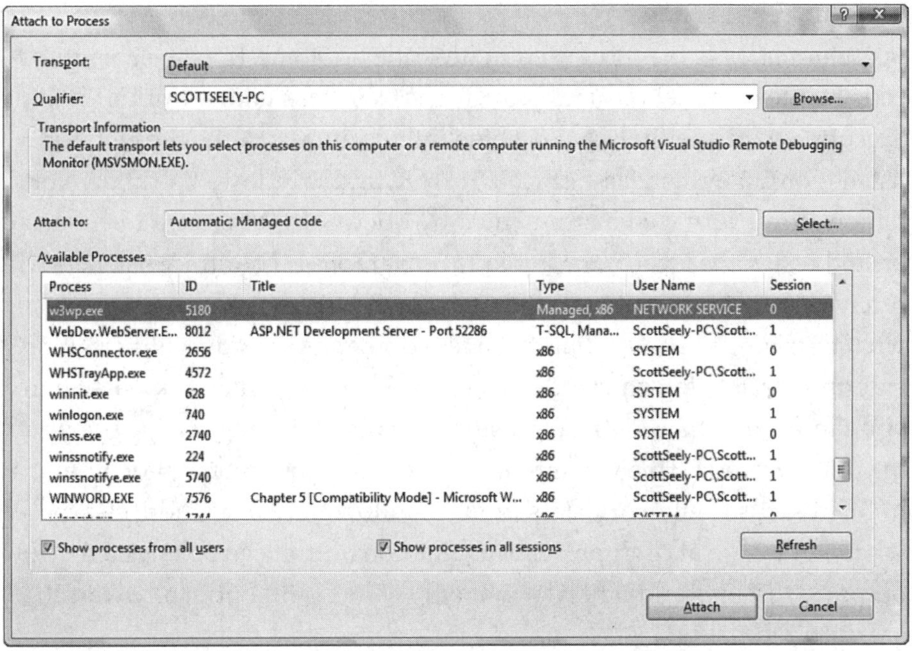

Figure 5.4: Attaching the Visual Studio debugger to a remote process

From here, you click Attach and you can debug your Web application just as you would any other managed code.

> ## ■ NOTE
>
> If you see more than one w3wp.exe process running in this dialog box, you might be tempted to attach the debugger to all of them since you might not know which one is executing your code. Although this can be done, it could dramatically slow down the debugger (because it will be listening to unwanted debuggee events as well). It's better to decide which process is the correct process, and to do that you can execute this command line:
>
> ```
> cscript %windir%\system32\iisapp.vbs
> ```
>
> This enumerates all process identifiers with their respective application pools.

HttpContext.Trace

Instrumentation is the term used to describe applying tracing semantics to code to allow the actions and branches that code is taking during runtime execution to be monitored and potentially written to a file through a trace listener or file writer class. ASP.NET, WCF, and Windows Workflow Foundation are all very well instrumented by Microsoft. When you turn tracing on and assign the level of tracing to Informational, your trace listeners will receive copious amounts of potentially useful diagnostic output regarding what the framework class library code is doing. As threads will be routinely entering and leaving your code and the code of the framework class library, you can augment the Microsoft instrumentation by using tracing semantics in your own code. This will interleave your own instrumentation with that of Microsoft's framework class libraries, allowing you to more clearly see what is going on at runtime. Instrumentation output can be turned to a low output setting in production so that only errors (and optionally warnings) are captured.

Instrumentation and logging are frequently confused. Logging is generally used to capture diagnostic information about errors or critical warnings in your application; logging allows developers to capture information about defects for postmortem repair. Instrumentation, on the other hand, allows developers to observe a program's actual runtime execution flow, thereby allowing the prediction of potential defects and an analysis of environmental assumptions.

You can emit traces correlated by the request being processed by using the HttpContext.Current.Trace property. The Trace property is a TraceContext object. This object allows one to emit what amounts to Informational as well as Warning traces. The TraceContext.Write method supports three overloads:

```
public void Write(string message);
public void Write(string category, string message);
public void Write(string category, string message, Exception errorInfo);
```

The message is the text you want to place in the instrumentation output stream. You can categorize the traces if you want to filter trace information by category. Passing in an exception allows you to record the

`Exception.Message` information in the trace stream. There is also an equivalent set of methods named `Warn` with the same signatures. You can enable tracing through configuration:

```
<configuration>
    <system.web>
        <trace enabled="true"/>
    </system.web>
</configuration>
```

With the configuration and the methods mentioned earlier, this code is possible:

```
HttpContext context = HttpContext.Current;
context.Trace.Write("Writing a simple message");
context.Trace.Write("SomeCategory", "Writing a message with category");
context.Trace.Write("SomeCategory", "Writing a message with category",
    new NotImplementedException());
context.Trace.Warn("Writing a simple warning");
context.Trace.Warn("SomeCategory", "Writing a message with category");
context.Trace.Warn("SomeCategory", "Writing a message with category",
    new NotImplementedException());
```

As a result of calling into the tracing infrastructure, the trace data is dumped to a source that is accessible via an ASP.NET `IHttpHandler` that maps to the URI `[application base]/trace.axd`. The result of the previous traces is shown in Figure 5.5.

Coupled with your trace data, you can see how long the request took between trace items. This can be handy in diagnosing timing issues, especially in long-running requests. Also, you can gain access to this data from machines other than the host machine.

System.Diagnostics

When you need your trace data in some other form, you can always use `System.Diagnostics.TraceSource` and its related `TraceListeners`. An issue you might run into is that file-based `TraceListeners` can potentially wind up writing a lot of data to disk, especially when a denial of service attack causes more diagnostic information than usual to be written. Although it would be unusual to fill a disk with trace information, it's not unheard of, depending on the level of trace information recorded.

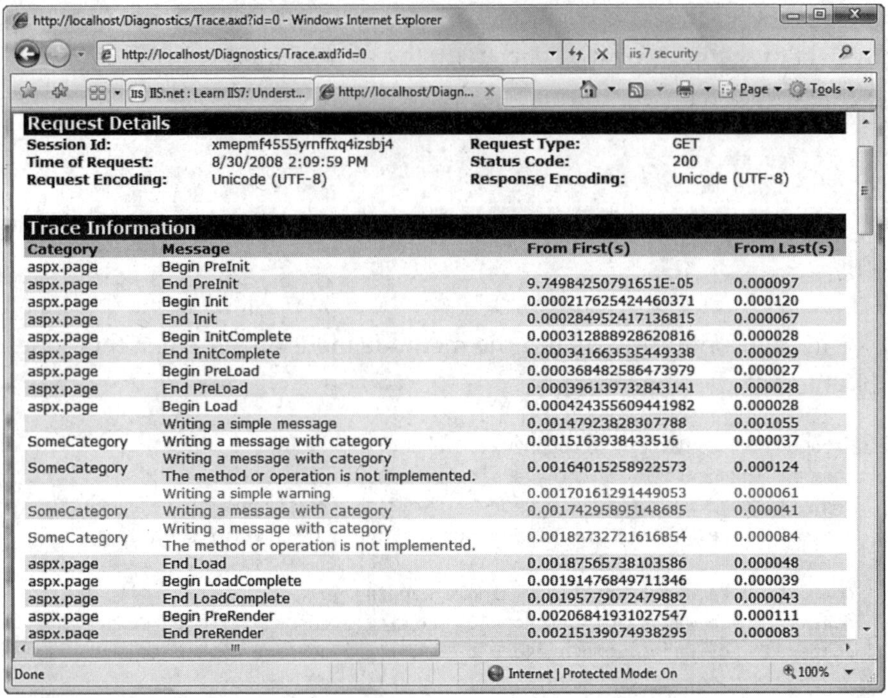

Figure 5.5: Tracing results in Internet Explorer

But another issue you'll face is that `HttpContext.Trace` and `System.Diagnostics.TraceSource` by default write to different places. Since many third-party libraries you might use are likely not Web-specific, you'll find they record instrumentation information using `System.Diagnostics.TraceSource`. Rather than recording this information in two different places, consider sending data to the same trace mechanism as with `HttpContext.Trace`. To do this, use the `System.Web.WebPageTraceListener` in `System.Diagnostics`, which is configured as shown here:

```
<system.diagnostics>
    <trace autoflush="true" indentsize="4">
        <listeners>
            <add name="webListener"
                type="System.Web.WebPageTraceListener, System.Web,
➥Version=2.0.3500.0,Culture=neutral,
➥PublicKeyToken=b03f5f7f11d50a3a"/>
        </listeners>
    </trace>
</system.diagnostics>
<system.web>
```

```
        <trace enabled="true" />
        <compilation debug="true"/>
    </system.web>
```

With this configuration in place, all information routed to System.Diag-
nostics.Trace will instead be routed to the trace.axd file.

Failed Request Tracing

Failed request tracing is a feature that logs information from IIS, ASP.NET,
and other code to show you what happened during times that requests fail.
Failed request tracing is configured on a per-Web-site basis. To configure
the default Web site, open up the Internet Information Services Management Console (shown as Internet Information Services in your system's list
of administrative applications). Next, select a Web site, such as Default Web
Site. The FailedRequestTracing module is included by default. If the module is not present, you need to add the module to the Web site.

With a Web site selected, the right-hand side of your screen should have
an option under Actions that says Configure. Under Configure there is a
link for Failed Request Tracing, as shown in Figure 5.6.

FIGURE 5.6: Failed request tracing in IIS Manager

Click the Failed Request Tracing link and click the Enable check box, as shown in Figure 5.7.

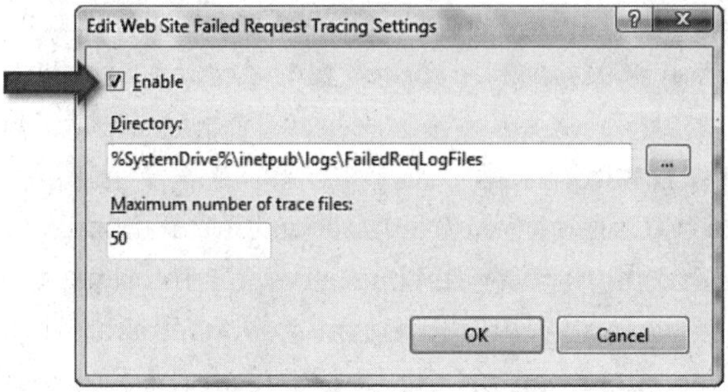

FIGURE 5.7: Enable failed request tracing

Now, create a rule for the types of failures you want to trace. One of the easiest errors to duplicate is a 404 (File Not Found) error. To do this, we will select the default Web site in the Internet Information Services Manager and double-click on the Failed Request Tracing icon. From here, click the Add link under Actions. Select All Content, as shown in Figure 5.8.

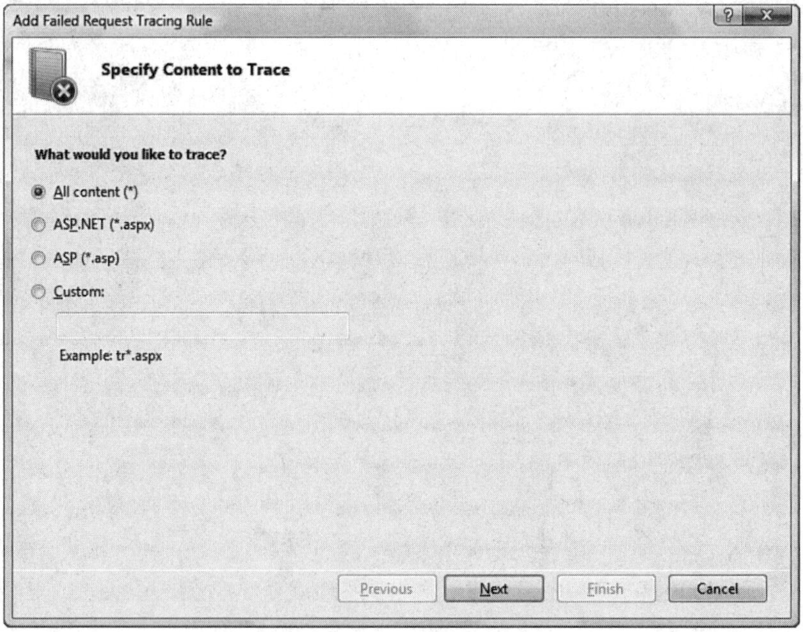

FIGURE 5.8: Trace all content

Click Next. You can now configure tracing for the 404 status code, as shown in Figure 5.9.

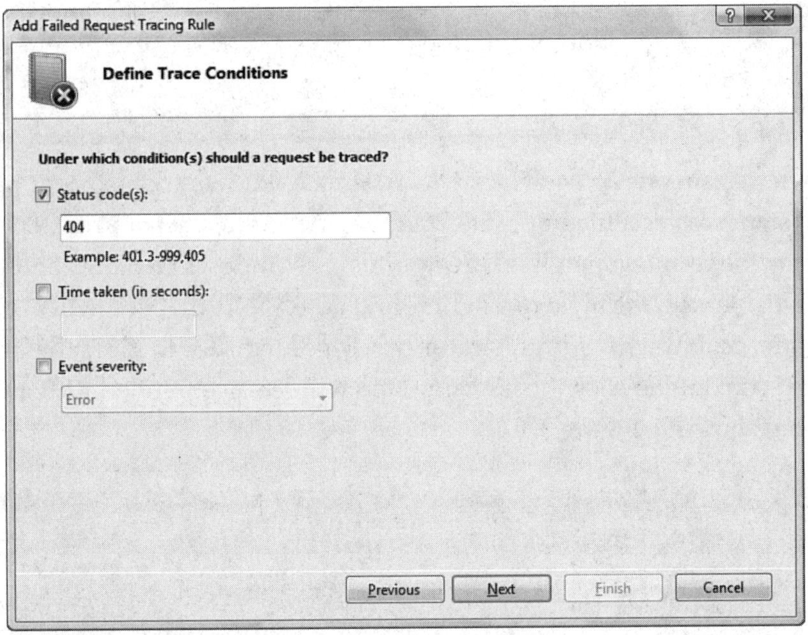

FIGURE 5.9: Trace for file not found (status code 404)

Then click Next and Finish. The new tracing rule is now added.

You can use this to capture data for anything you might need to debug. This feature is particularly useful for catching what is happening when spurious, hard-to-duplicate errors occur. For example, a user might actually be receiving a 404 error every two days, even though he uses a particular Web page frequently. By capturing information surrounding the 404 error, the developers maintaining the Web application are provided with information that should assist them with identification of issues that likely need to be fixed. Any captured data will go to the configured directory (refer to Figure 5.7).

> **⁍ NOTE**
>
> This to me is more "logging" than "tracing" (instrumentation) because it captures errors for post-mortem investigation rather than allowing us to observe any kind of program flow. Even so, it's an exceptionally useful tool.

When I generate a 404 error by requesting a (known) nonexistent page, the system creates a file in `C:\inetpub\logs\FailedReqLogFiles\W3SVC1`. To view the results, open this directory using Windows Explorer and find the XML file with the most recent time and date. (Note that you will need to have an account with administrator privileges in order to view the directory.) If you double-click the filename, you will see nicely styled XML much like that shown in Figure 5.10.

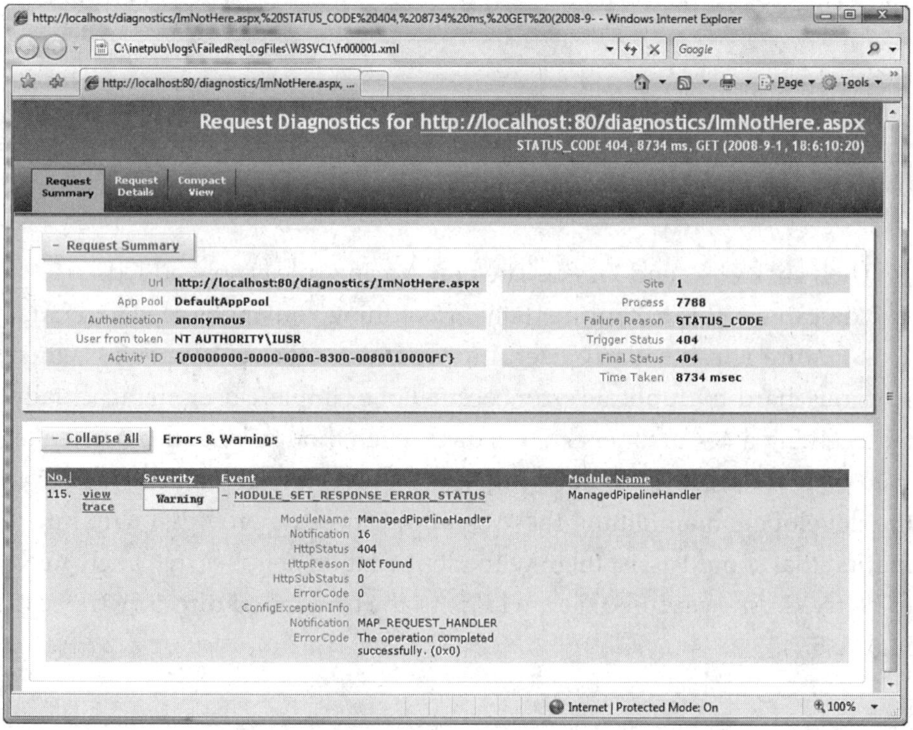

FIGURE 5.10: Failed request tracing output

This log contains data explaining what was happening in the system when the 404 error was generated. By looking through the data, you can discover who was calling, what file was requested, and everything that the system was doing when the error occurred, including how the system reacted to the failure. Having this type of information should make it easier to find and potentially fix those infrequent, hard-to-reproduce bugs.

Security

Finally, let's talk about how IIS and ASP.NET handle security. This section is just an overview of what is available. More complete information is referenced at the end of this section. Security always involves two steps: authentication and authorization. Authentication validates an identity. An identity represents who the user is. For example, on a Windows computer, identity is always *domain name\username*. Authorization, on the other hand, states what that identity can do. Authorization allows your code to make decisions like these:

- Should the user see the contents of that file?
- Can the user change the contents of that Web-based resource?
- Does the user have permission to perform that action?

Authentication happens when the `HttpApplication` instance fires the `AuthenticateRequest` event. By the time the `PostAuthenticateRequest` event has fired, the `System.Security.Principal.IPrincipal`, accessible via the `HttpContext.Current.User` property, will have an identity. This identity will be provided by an authentication module. IIS ships with several authentication modules, many of which have both a managed and an unmanaged version:

- `AnonymousAuthenticationModule`: This module handles authenticating requests that have no credentials.
- `BasicAuthenticationModule`: HTTP Basic Authentication allows the caller to pass the username and password along with the request. This module knows how to handle the case when the HTTP

WWW-Authenticate header is set to Basic realm=*some realm*. Never use this form of authentication without coupling it with transport encryption (HTTPS). The *username:password* value returned by the Authorization header is sent as a Base64-encoded string. Although this encoding preserves the bytes being sent, it does nothing to encrypt them. Anyone can decode these strings.

- CertificateMappingAuthenticationModule: In Active Directory, you can map certificates to identities. When a certificate is used to authenticate a user, the certificate is typically mapped to a Windows Identity. This module converts certificates to Windows identities.

- DigestAuthenticationModule: Digest Authentication uses the concept of a shared secret to overcome the deficiency in basic authentication. Instead of sending the password in the clear, digest authentication uses a combination of the username, a nonce, a secret (the password), and a hash (such as Message Digest 5, otherwise known as MD5) to create a string to be used to authenticate the user. So long as the client and the server both compute the same hash, the server knows that the client knew the password and can authenticate the user. As with HTTP Basic Authentication, you should use transport-level encryption (HTTPS) when using Digest Authentication.

- FormsAuthentication: Implemented in System.Web.Security. FormsAuthenticationModule, this managed authentication module handles information about the forms authentication to keep the proper identity assigned to the caller. The handler understands whether or not a cookie or a portion of the URL was used to maintain the caller's identity.

- IISCertificateMappingAuthenticationModule: You can also map certificates to identities in IIS. This module handles that mapping to generate identities.

- WindowsAuthentication: Implemented by System.Web.Security.WindowsAuthenticationModule, this module grabs the existing user identity and sets the user identity in the current `HttpContext`.

- `WindowsAuthenticationModule`: This module handles the network-based authentication to assign an identity or server variables to the current user.

A smaller set of modules handles authorization:

- `FileAuthorization`: Implemented by `System.Web.FileAuthorizationModule`, this module compares the authorization restrictions of the file against the current user. If the restrictions, aka the access control list (ACL), allow, the user will get the file. Otherwise, the user will be denied access.

- `UrlAuthorization`: Implemented by `System.Web.Security.Url AuthorizationModule`, this module reads the authorization information from configuration in `/system.web/authorization` and allows or denies access to the requested resource.

- `UrlAuthorizationModule`: Instead of requiring a user to set access control for a given resource on the file, the `UrlAuthorizationModule` allows an administrator to administer the file permissions in a Web application outside the file system. This feature is available on IIS 7. One configures this module by selecting the file or folder to be secured. From here, the administrator then selects the authorization rules icon within the IIS administration tool and sets the rights a user must possess in order to access a directory or file.

ASP.NET developers also have access to a rich security model. ASP.NET provides an abstract base class named `System.Web.Security.Membership-Provider`. Whenever you design a site to use Forms Authentication and SQL Server as the user information repository, you use `System.Web.Security.SqlMembershipProvider`, a class derived from `MembershipProvider`. This type handles authentication. Another type, `System.Web.Security.RoleProvider`, handles authorization. Roles that you configure with the

ASP.NET Web Site Administration Tool use this feature. Again, if you're using SQL Server as your user information repository, you will have made use of `System.Web.Security.SqlRoleProvider`. With this tool, you assign various users to various groups. You can then allow or disallow the ability to see various pages by application-level checks to see whether a particular user is in a necessary role. This is done with code like this:

```
if (System.Web.Security.Roles.IsUserInRole("someRole"))
{
    // do something
}
```

When implementing a RESTful Web service, you can include code such as this when authorizing callers. It is even possible that you will write your own authorization provider that will make similar checks, perhaps even using the `SqlRoleProvider`, by handling the `HttpApplication.Authorize Request` event. Whichever option you choose, definitely have a recognized Web security expert review your application to make sure there are no obvious security holes, defects, or hack points.

IIS Resources

The following list provides you with some additional resources you might find helpful when developing IIS modules and handlers.

- *Internet Information Services 7.0 Resource Kit,* ISBN 978-0735624412, Mike Volodarsky, Olga Londer, Brett Hill, Bernard Cheah, Steve Schofield, Carlos Aguillar Mares, Kurt Meyer. Microsoft Press, 2008. Mike Volodarsky wrote a good part of this book. When one is looking for content on IIS 7, his articles frequently come up at the top of most search engine queries.
- *Developing More Secure Microsoft ASP.NET 2.0 Applications,* ISBN 978-0735623316, Dominick Baier. Microsoft Press, 2008. This is an excellent source of security information for ASP.NET.
- *mvolo.com.* This is Mike Volodarsky's home page. (Mike is the former program manager for IIS 7 and blogs extensively on the topic.)
- *iis.net:* This is the IIS team's official Web site, which contains videos, articles, and more regarding how IIS 7 works.

- SDDLParse: http://blogs.microsoft.co.il/files/folders/guyt/ entry70399.aspx. This tool allows one to convert SDDL strings to account IDs.

- HttpSysCfg.exe: www.thinktecture.com/resourcearchive/tools- and-software/httpsyscfg. This tool simplifies setting, removing, and modifying ACLs on URLs for http.sys.

Where Are We?

Much of this chapter is an overview of how http.sys and IIS work together to serve Web content. We took a look at how you can serve custom content from nonexistent Web resources (like the current process list) using an ASP.NET HTTP handler. We also looked at implementing site-wide pro-cessing using an ASP.NET HTTP module, which in our case provided for service-optimized caching. Finally, we took a brief look at security and the built-in modules provided by IIS and ASP.NET. Although IIS and ASP.NET go a long way toward securing your Web application, having an industry expert review your application for possible security holes and hack points is recommended.

In the next chapter you'll take what you learned here and write a major RESTful service using the tools ASP.NET provides. You'll also develop a specialized security module you can use to protect your RESTful service.

6

Building REST Services Using IIS and ASP.NET

I N CHAPTER 5 WE cracked open IIS a little and saw how you can build modules and handlers that work at the lowest levels of the IIS HTTP pipeline. In this chapter we'll look at ASP.NET in a bit more detail, talk about both modules and handlers designed specifically for true RESTful operations, talk more about serialization (bolstering concepts seen in Chapter 3 as well as Chapter 5), and build a secured RESTful service using HTTP Basic Authentication.

Hosting ASP.NET

In Chapter 5, "IIS and ASP.NET Internals and Instrumentation," you saw how IIS 7.0 combines features of ASP.NET, `http.sys`, Windows Process Activation Service (WAS), and some (rather complex) glue code contained in an application named Internet Information Services. In this chapter you'll work more closely with ASP.NET itself as you see how a full-fledged RESTful service is built using the tools you saw in Chapter 5, as well as new tools you'll see here.

Probably the best way to start is to demystify ASP.NET a bit. When you create Web applications using Visual Studio, things seem to happen by magic. Pages are rendered, security "just works" (although my experience is that nothing there ever works quite as easily as the whitepapers say it should), AJAX is baked in, page methods offer significant capabilities, and of course let's not forget the tremendous ASP.NET XML Web Service support.

But at its very core, would you believe that ASP.NET is a collection of classes, not a lot different from any application you have probably written on your own? With all that magic, it's easy to overlook the fact that ASP.NET must run in the same runtime system as any other .NET application. Make no mistake, ASP.NET is a *complex* set of .NET objects, but the components that make up ASP.NET are still objects.

Knowing this, I think, reduces the ASP.NET magic factor a bit, and speaking at least for myself, I find this knowledge liberating. I find myself experimenting and taking risks to deepen my understanding, and I try new things I might not have tried before.

For example, if ASP.NET is a set of classes, it should be possible to write some sort of application of my own to host ASP.NET, just as I might host a set of classes I devised to tackle some business domain problem. And as it happens, this is quite literally possible. Although not quite as simple as creating a single class and calling a method, as you'll, see hosting ASP.NET isn't a lot harder than that.

To kick-start ASP.NET, you need two things: a new AppDomain in which ASP.NET will execute and a worker thread. In fact, if you decide to use the host's application thread just for demonstration purposes, you don't even need to create a new worker thread. I'll use the System.Web. Hosting.ApplicationHost class to create the AppDomain, providing to the AppDomain a small class I'll create that's designed to execute and render a single Web page. Listing 6.1 shows the entire process in action.

LISTING 6.1: Hosting ASP.NET in a console application

```
using System;
using System.Collections.Generic;
using System.Linq;
using System.Text;
using System.IO;
using System.Web;
using System.Web.Hosting;

namespace AspNetHost
{
```

```
class Program
{
    static void Main(string[] args)
    {
        // Validate arg[0]
        if (args.Length > 0)
        {
            if (File.Exists(args[0]))
            {
                // Run the file
                Program pgm = new Program();
                pgm.Run(args[0]);
            }
        }
    }

    void Run(string aspnetFile)
    {
        // Create an AppDomain to host the request processing. Note
        // ApplicationHost requires a copy of the assembly to be
        // located in a "bin" subdirectory, so with the project is
        // a post-build script to create the "bin" directory and
        // copy the .exe file there.
        LocalAspNetHost host =
            ApplicationHost.CreateApplicationHost(
                typeof(LocalAspNetHost),
                "/",
                Directory.GetCurrentDirectory()) as LocalAspNetHost;

        // Process request in new AppDomain
        host.ProcessRequest(aspnetFile);

        // Show the stream
        Console.Write("\n\nPress any key to exit...");
        Console.ReadKey();
    }
}

public class LocalAspNetHost : MarshalByRefObject
{
    public void ProcessRequest(string aspnetFile)
    {
        // Create worker request instance
        HttpWorkerRequest request =
            new SimpleWorkerRequest(aspnetFile, null, Console.Out);

        // Process the request
        HttpRuntime.ProcessRequest(request);
    }
}
```

The Main method simply checks to see that there is at least one argument, the .aspx file to execute. If the file exists, Main hands execution off to the Run method. Run creates an instance of a "hosting" class I created that handles the ASP.NET request (more in a moment) using ApplicationHost. ApplicationHost requires the type of the hosting class, the virtual directory, and the physical directory where the page is located. In this case, I gave it LocalAspNetHost as the hosting type, "/" as the virtual directory (the root of the virtual directory), and the current directory for the physical directory since I created an .aspx page and deploy it with the application executable.

With an instance of my hosting class in hand, I execute its Process Request method (a method I created and named), handing it the specific ASP.NET page to render. In this case, the page file name was provided as an application argument, but any technique you like could have been used.

The page will be processed and rendered, with the resulting HTML output being streamed to a stream of my choosing. Here, I stream it to the console window using Console.Out, but you could use any stream you like, including a memory-based stream, a file-based stream, or most likely a network-based stream. When the .aspx file is completely rendered, I defer application termination while waiting for you to press any key so that you can see the rendered HTML before the console window closes.

ApplicationHost requires the hosting class I mentioned, and for that I created the LocalAspNetHost class shown in Listing 6.1. Since the hosting class will be executed in a new AppDomain, it must derive from Marshal-ByRefObject. For my host object, I designed a single actionable method, ProcessRequest, and within that method I create an instance of HttpWorkerRequest to represent the request made to ASP.NET and then process that request using the HttpRuntime's ProcessRequest method. Yes, *the* HttpRuntime!

There is one small trick to make all of this work, and that's the creation of a bin folder under the application executable directory that contains the hosting class's assembly. In this case, I simply copy the application executable into the bin directory using a post-build script. If I had created a secondary assembly to house LocalAspNetHost, I would have copied that there instead.

The `.aspx` file I created to test this is shown in Listing 6.2, and the console application's output is shown in Figure 6.1.

LISTING 6.2: Sample `.aspx` page

```
<%@ Page Language="C#" %>
<!DOCTYPE HTML PUBLIC "-//W3C//DTD HTML 4.0 Transitional//EN">
<html>
    <head>
        <title>Hosted Test Page</title>
    </head>
    <body>
        <div>The time is:
            <%=DateTime.Now.ToString("MM/dd/yyyy hh:mm:ss tt") %>
        </div>
    </body>
</html>
```

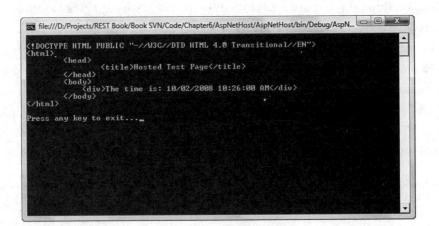

FIGURE 6.1: Hosting ASP.NET in a console application

As I mentioned previously, I think it's important to see that ASP.NET isn't magical—it works just as any .NET-based application would work, even if ASP.NET is a very complex application. If you decide to build RESTful services using raw ASP.NET, as I do in this chapter, you'll find yourself working at levels lower than Web pages. Don't be afraid to experiment and try things. This is good to keep in mind when you dig into ASP.NET security and rip out some of what's there and replace it with a new implementation later in the chapter.

Building a RESTful HttpHandler

A good question when writing RESTful services in ASP.NET at this point is, Where should they be hosted? After all, ASP.NET has a couple of different places you can host XML Web Services: in .asmx files and as page methods in your .aspx pages. So why not try the same with RESTful services?

The approach I'd recommend is to use an HttpHandler. The .asmx service is serviced by an HttpHandler just like .aspx Web pages, so there is a nice symmetry there. The page methods, though cool, require deeper support within the ASP.NET page processing structure. They're also executed farther along (deeper) in the HTTP pipeline, whereas for performance we'd probably rather execute our RESTful code sooner in the HTTP pipeline rather than later if possible.

Something else to consider early in your service design is how you want to secure the service, if it needs to be secured at all. For this chapter, I created a rudimentary blog and a service that allows you to get blog entries, add blog comments, and even modify and delete entries and comments. If some arbitrary Internet user views the blog, they'll use the .aspx page I created that reads the blog information from the database. (A stronger implementation would let users add comments through the .aspx page, but the book would never make it to print if this were a *real* blog implementation.)

■ NOTE

Considering comments for a moment, this service allows clients to add any comment they want. A stronger, perhaps more "real-world" implementation would hold comment insertion pending blog owner review and approval. I'll leave these implementation details to you.

But from a service design perspective, I want service users to be registered with my system before they have access to the underlying representations. Most, if not all, clients would be granted read access. A few clients would be able to add comments and entries, and only one would be able to delete information (that would be me, the blog's owner). To support this, the RESTful service will need to check the request's HTTP method and compare that against roles established for the requesting client. As soon as you even think the thought—*roles associated with your service*—you should be thinking of using the ASP.NET authorization infrastructure. I mention all of this up front because I've found it's always more difficult to go back and add security to existing services than to build in security from the beginning. Although at this point I might not have written the necessary security code (I'll show how this is done later in the chapter), I certainly can add role checks to my code earlier in my implementation process and use a dummy `IPrincipal` and `IIdentity` user to skip those checks temporarily. I'll come back to the topic of security throughout the chapter.

In any case, with the security sermon out of the way, let's look at designing the blog service.

Designing the Blog Service

For this service, the blog consists of *entries* and *comments*, which are tied to specific entries. You can access the service using the following:

- Add a blog entry: `POST` to `[base service address]/Blog`
- Add a blog entry comment: `POST` to `[base service address]/Blog/{BlogID}`
- Update a blog entry: `PUT` to `[base service address]/Blog/{BlogID}`
- Delete a blog entry: `DELETE` to `[base service address]/Blog/{BlogID}`
- Get all blog entries (no comments): `GET` to `[base service address]/Blog`
- Get a single entry with comments: `GET` to `[base service address]/Blog/{BlogID}`
- Get statistics/headers: `HEAD` to a valid service URI

Each blog entry has a unique integer-based blog ID, so an entry representation request URI would look like the following:

```
https://{server}/{virtual directory}/Blog/{blogID}
```

The transport security is, in reality, required because HTTP Basic Authentication will be used to secure access to the RESTful services and

HTTP Basic Authentication transmits credentials in unencrypted form. However, for the purposes of this chapter, I won't enforce the `https://` scheme, but you should be thinking that way when designing your own live services.

The service will provide representations in XML and JavaScript Object Notation (JSON) using `DataContractSerializer` and `DataContractJson-Serializer`. You saw the `DataContractSerializer` in action in the preceding chapter. The JSON version is very similar but formats the data according to the JSON layout (see www.json.org).

■ NOTE

I could also choose to serialize the blog data using an AtomPub representation, but the mechanics for doing so are a bit more oriented toward Windows Communication Foundation (WCF). Although it can be done in pure ASP.NET, it makes sense to leave AtomPub serialization for Chapter 8, "Building REST Services Using WCF." Using what you learn there, you should be able to apply AtomPub to a pure ASP.NET RESTful service implementation. However, AtomPub is *entirely* appropriate here.

I elected to use content negotiation to determine which representation would be returned, if only to show content negotiation in action. In the service you'll then see logic to decide what representation is required, and the appropriate data serializer will be selected. If the HTTP method is PUT or POST, the service will accept either XML or JSON as the representation. The XML representation appears like so:

```
<BlogEntryItem
 xmlns="http://www.endurasoft.com/REST.NET/"
 xmlns:i="http://www.w3.org/2001/XMLSchema-instance">
  <Comments>
    <BlogCommentItem>
      <Comment>I was blown away by how easy it was. Very cool!</Comment>
      <CommentID>1</CommentID>
      <Commentor>CyberJoe</Commentor>
      <EntryID>1</EntryID>
      <PostDate>2008-10-01T13:00:00</PostDate>
    </BlogCommentItem>
    <BlogCommentItem>
```

```
      <Comment>I was too the first time I tried it. Amazing!</Comment>
      <CommentID>2</CommentID>
      <Commentor>Kenn</Commentor>
      <EntryID>1</EntryID>
      <PostDate>2008-10-01T14:00:00</PostDate>
    </BlogCommentItem>
  </Comments>
  <Entry>As it happens, ASP.NET is a terrific platform to use for
    building RESTful services, especially when coupled with IIS 7.0.
    Using an HttpModule for security makes a lot of sense, especially
    when coupled with traditional ASP.NET authorization and provider-
    based database support. HttpHandlers are terrific for implementing
    the service itself as you can handle the request early in the HTTP
    pipeline and avoid the overhead of page generation. It is definitely
    something to look into!
  </Entry>
  <EntryID>1</EntryID>
  <EntryLink>
    http://localhost/AspNetRestService/Default.aspx?BlogID=1
  </EntEntryLink>
  <PostDate>2008-10-01T12:00:00</PostDate>
  <Title>Building RESTful Services using ASP.NET</Title>
</BlogEntryItem>
```

The JSON version appears as follows:

```
{"Comments":
[{"Comment":"I was blown away by how easy it was. Very cool!",
"CommentID":1,
"Commentor":"CyberJoe",
"EntryID":1,
"PostDate":"\/Date(1222880400000-0400)\/"},
{"Comment":"I was too the first time I tried it. Amazing!",
"CommentID":2,
"Commentor":"Kenn","EntryID":1,
"PostDate":"\/Date(1222884000000-0400)\/"}],
"Entry":"As it happens, ASP.NET is a terrific platform to use for
 building RESTful services, especially when coupled with IIS 7.0. Using
 an HttpModule for security makes a lot of sense, especially when
 coupled with traditional ASP.NET authorization and provider-based
 database support. HttpHandlers are terrific for implementing the
 service itself as you can handle the request early in the HTTP pipeline
 and avoid the overhead of page generation. It is definitely something
 to look into!",
"EntryID":1,
"EntryLink":
 "http:\/\/localhost\/AspNetRestService\/Default.aspx?BlogID=1",
"PostDate":"\/Date(1222876800000-0400)\/",
"Title":"Building RESTful Services using ASP.NET"}
```

Something to note is that blog item creation isn't associated with the HTTP PUT method but rather with HTTP POST. This follows RFC 2616 guidance where the URI associated with the creation of the resource isn't dictated by the client but by the service. The client who adds a blog entry item or a comment cannot know beforehand what the identifier for that item will be, so therefore the client cannot know what the final URI will be. When this happens, creation is accomplished by POST and the service returns to the client the inserted representation along with the HTTP 201 (Created) response code (assuming that the service can create the item) and an HTTP Location header with the URI of the new item.

Along with the RESTful service, there is a basic Web page designed to display the blog in a more familiar format. This is shown in Figure 6.2. The text you see in Figure 6.2 should match the textual information you saw in the XML and JSON representations, assuming that the service worked correctly.

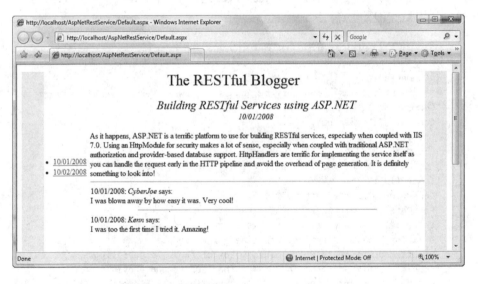

FIGURE 6.2: The RESTful Blogger ASP.NET page

Service Security

Although I'll address the specifics regarding how all of these tasks are accomplished later in the chapter, my goal was to use as much of the

ASP.NET (and IIS) security as I possibly could when developing the service. I did this for a couple of reasons. First, it only makes sense to use as much of the existing infrastructure as possible, and ASP.NET has a good security infrastructure already. But second, I wanted to dig into the details to show how you might use HTTP Basic Authentication with the ASP.NET security infrastructure. As you might already know, IIS handles HTTP Basic Authentication for you, but it does so by validating user credentials against Windows (or domain) accounts. I preferred a more scalable approach and wanted to replace the default IIS HTTP Basic Authentication with a scheme that uses ASP.NET.

I also did this so that I can make use of the ASP.NET role provider rather than creating spurious roles for arbitrary Windows accounts. For this service, the client's role inclusion will dictate their ability to invoke the given RESTful service. Most if not all clients would be granted read access, but a select few might be able to create, update, or delete blog entries or comments. The service will check the authenticated client's set of roles for the one role the service needs in order to allow the request to be processed. On a related note, the service doesn't provide for automatic client registration on the assumption that another process, not shown here, would provide for this since you'd most likely want to collect information about people using your service for something as personal as a blog.

Therefore, when the client makes a service request, the client should include a valid HTTP Authorization header and make requests using the following combinations of HTTP method and role:

Role	HTTP Method
Read	GET
Modify	PUT
Create	POST
Delete	DELETE

If the user has a valid account but tries to access a resource for which he is not authorized, the service returns the HTTP 403 (Forbidden) return code. If the user tries to authenticate but uses the wrong username or password, the service continues to return HTTP 401 (Unauthorized) return codes until the user gains access or is determined to be in a forbidden state (described previously) or locks himself out.

You might imagine the service keeping track of the number of arbitrary client attempts to authenticate and then locking them out if they try and fail too many times. ASP.NET indeed has this capability, but only for users known to the Web application, as stored in the application's security database tables. For client attempts in which the username isn't known to the service, no tracking or filtering is performed. If you're (correctly) concerned about denial of service attacks, you should employ hardware-based solutions as a primary tactic, to filter requests that occur far too often and in great numbers, and apply other typical security measures associated with denial of service prevention, like auditing and other security best practices.

Let's now take a look at the HttpHandler that implements the service.

The BlogService Handler

The blog service is hosted in an HttpHandler called BlogHandler, and like all HttpHandlers, it must implement the IsReusable property and the ProcessRequest method. The BlogService's implementation of these is shown in Listing 6.3. Note that this implementation is synchronous for simplicity. In a production environment you should consider implementing asynchronous handlers to increase scalability.

LISTING 6.3: BlogService primary handler methods

```
public bool IsReusable
{
    get { return true; }
}

public void ProcessRequest(HttpContext context)
{
    UriTemplateMatch match =
      TemplateTable.MatchSingle(context.Request.Url);
    if (match == null)
    {
        context.Response.StatusCode = (Int32)HttpStatusCode.NotFound;
    }
```

```
    else
    {
        HandleRequest handleRequest = (HandleRequest)match.Data;
        handleRequest(context, match);
    }
}
```

The basic logical flow for processing a request is that an incoming URI is matched against the URIs the service expects, and if there is a match, the service request is dispatched. If the incoming URI results in a resource the service can't identify, the request is terminated with an HTTP 404 (NotFound) response status code.

The dispatching mechanism uses .NET delegates, which for this blog service are defined like so:

```
delegate void HandleRequest(HttpContext context,
                            UriTemplateMatch template);
```

Therefore, you would expect to see two methods implemented with the same method signature as the delegate. You expect two because the service design dictates two URI template patterns: /Blog and /Blog/{BlogID}. These patterns are prescribed by the TemplateTable property the service implements.

This service's implementation of the TemplateTable property differs slightly from that of the preceding chapter since the service URIs differ. BlogService's TemplateTable implementation is shown in Listing 6.4. I've bolded the two service URIs in bold to make them easier to find.

LISTING 6.4: BlogService's TemplateTable **property**

```
UriTemplateTable TemplateTable
{
    get
    {
        if (_templateTable == null)
        {
            lock (_tableLock)
            {
                if (_templateTable == null)
                {
                    HttpRequest request = HttpContext.Current.Request;
```

continues

LISTING 6.4: Continued

```
                        string fullUrl = request.Url.ToString();
                        string baseUrl = fullUrl.Substring(0,
                            fullUrl.IndexOf(request.ApplicationPath));
                        _templateTable = new UriTemplateTable();
                        _templateTable.BaseAddress = new Uri(baseUrl);
                        _templateTable.KeyValuePairs.Add(
                            new KeyValuePair<UriTemplate, object>(
                              new UriTemplate(
                                request.ApplicationPath +
                                "/Blog"),
                                new HandleRequest(HandleBlogList)));
                        _templateTable.KeyValuePairs.Add(
                            new KeyValuePair<UriTemplate, object>(
                                new UriTemplate(request.ApplicationPath +
                                  "/Blog/{BlogID}"),
                                  new HandleRequest(HandleBlogItem)));
                    }
                }
            }
            return _templateTable;
        }
    }
```

The handler method for the /Blog URI is shown in Listing 6.5, and the handler for the /Blog/{BlogID} URI is shown in Listing 6.6. Each follows the same pattern: Identify the allowed HTTP methods for the URI (based on the service design), and if the requested HTTP method is allowed, dispatch it. If the HTTP method isn't allowed, the service returns the HTTP 403 status code.

LISTING 6.5: BlogService's /Blog handler method

```
    private void HandleBlogList(HttpContext context,
      UriTemplateMatch template)
    {
        // Check HTTP method and perform appropriate action. For the
        // /Blog URI, we only allow HEAD, GET, and POST.
        switch (context.Request.HttpMethod.ToLower())
        {
            case HttpHeadMethod:
                DispatchGetBlogList(context, false);
                break;

            case HttpGetMethod:
                DispatchGetBlogList(context, true);
                break;
```

```
        case HttpPostMethod:
            DispatchAddBlogItem(context);
            break;

        default:
            DispatchNotAllowed(context);
            break;
    }
}
```

LISTING 6.6: BlogService's /Blog/{BlogID} **handler method**

```
    private void HandleBlogItem(HttpContext context,
      UriTemplateMatch template)
    {
        // Interpret the blog ID
        Int32 blogID = 0;
        if (!Int32.TryParse(template.BoundVariables["BlogID"], out blogID))
        {
            // Invalid blog ID, so return error
            DispatchBadRequest(context);
            return;
        }

        // Assign the blog ID to the Items collection in the context
        // so we don't have to pass it around as a separate value.
        context.Items.Add("BlogID", blogID);

        // Check HTTP method and perform appropriate action. For the
        // /Blog/{BlogID} URI, we allow HEAD, GET, POST, PUT, and DELETE.
        switch (context.Request.HttpMethod.ToLower())
        {
            case HttpHeadMethod:
                DispatchGetBlogItem(context, false);
                break;

            case HttpGetMethod:
                DispatchGetBlogItem(context, true);
                break;

            case HttpPutMethod:
                DispatchUpdateBlogItem(context);
                break;

            case HttpPostMethod:
                DispatchAddBlogComment(context);
                break;
```

continues

LISTING 6.6: Continued

```
        case HttpDeleteMethod:
            DispatchDeleteBlogItem(context);
            break;

        default:
            DispatchNotAllowed(context);
            break;
    }
}
```

As you can see from Listings 6.3 and 6.4, the URI handler methods implement what amounts to a dispatch table, where the method to be invoked is based on the HTTP method present in the request. The individual dispatch methods do the actual work. I won't show all of them, but two interesting cases do merit some discussion. The GET handler can also serve as the HEAD handler if the method simply forgoes issuing the representation to the client, so I'll show the GET handler for a blog entry item in Listing 6.7. Creating new entries is interesting because of content negotiation. For content negotiation to work when updating a resource, the incoming representation must be interpreted based on the HTTP Content-Type header. I'll show this in action in Listing 6.8.

LISTING 6.7: BlogService's DispatchGetBlogList **method**

```
private void DispatchGetBlogList(HttpContext context, bool issueContent)
{
    // Test the user's credentials
    if (context.User.IsInRole("Read"))
    {
        // Retrieve all blog entries
        IEnumerable<BlogEntryItem> blogItems = _model.QueryBlog();

        // Determine stream to write to. If we're issuing content,
        // we'll write to the output stream. If a HEAD request,
        // we'll write to a temporary stream so we can determine the
        // content length.
        Stream outputStream = context.Response.OutputStream;
        if (!issueContent)
        {
            // Create a temporary stream
            outputStream = new MemoryStream();
        }
```

```
    if (context.Request.Headers["Accept"].ToLower() ==
        "application/json")
    {
        // Notify caller that the response resource is in JSON.
        context.Response.ContentType = "application/json";
        _blogJsonListSerializer.WriteObject(
            outputStream, blogItems);
    }
    else
    {
        // Notify caller that the response resource is in XML.
        context.Response.ContentType = "text/xml";
        _blogXmlListSerializer.WriteObject(
            outputStream, blogItems);
    }

    // If we're not issuing content, we'll need to set
    // the content length header ourselves...
    if (!issueContent)
    {
        // Set the content length header
        context.Response.Headers["Content-Length"] =
            outputStream.Length.ToString();
    }
    }
    else
    {
        // Return forbidden
        context.Response.StatusCode = (Int32)HttpStatusCode.Forbidden;
    }
}
```

When it comes to returning simple query information, the Dispatch GetBlogList method shown in Listing 6.7 creates a temporary variable for storing a reference to a stream. If the query is a GET, the temporary stream reference is assigned a reference to the response's output stream and the representation is conveyed to the client using this stream. On the other hand, if the query is a HEAD request, a throwaway MemoryStream is used to hold the contents of the response so that the method can ascertain the size of the response, to be returned in the Content-Length header. Later the throwaway stream is destroyed along with its contents.

The stream is filled with the serialized representation, the type for which is based on the HTTP Accept header. If the desired content type is application/json, the DataContractJsonSerializer is used. Any other value is assumed to be `text/xml`, and the `DataContractSerializer` is used to convert the in-memory query result into an XML value. If that can't be deserialized as an XML stream, the client receives an error.

This is all predicated on the user's inclusion into the Read role. If the client doesn't enjoy read privileges, the service returns the HTTP 403 (`Forbidden`) response code. This type of role determination isn't unusual in ASP.NET programming. You, the programmer, must add the appropriate logic to make the role determination and decide what to do if the client request fails through inadequate authorization. Returning the HTTP 403 response code is normally the best practice.

If there is an exception, the service allows the default ASP.NET unhandled exception infrastructure to handle the exception as it normally would.

> **■ NOTE**
>
> It's also not always necessary to catch and handle every exception. ASP.NET, for example, will return an error to the service client if an unhandled exception occurs. By allowing unhandled exceptions to traverse the ASP.NET infrastructure, you gain the benefits of configurable health monitoring and client error reporting. Another thing you can do is handle the `Error` event in your `global.asax` file and take whatever action is required at that time.

The `DispatchAddBlogItem` method shown in Listing 6.8 performs some of the same functions as the `DispatchGetBlogList` method in the sense that it checks the client's role, in this case against the `Create` role, and it manages errors and forbidden responses. It differs, of course, by its function, which is to insert a blog entry into the blog entry table.

LISTING 6.8: BlogService's `DispatchAddBlogItem` method

```
private void DispatchAddBlogItem (HttpContext context)
{
    // Test the user's credentials
    if (context.User.IsInRole("Create"))
    {
        // Extract the representation from the request stream.
        // Note we check the Content-Type header for the type of
        // information we're to deserialize (we accept XML and
        // JSON).
```

```
BlogEntryItem item = null;
if (context.Request.Headers["Content-Type"].ToLower() ==
    "application/json")
{
    // Deserialize the incoming JSON stream
    item = _blogJsonItemSerializer.ReadObject(
        context.Request.InputStream) as BlogEntryItem;
}
else
{
    // Deserialize the incoming XML stream
    item = _blogXmlItemSerializer.ReadObject(
        context.Request.InputStream) as BlogEntryItem;
}

// If the object was deserialized, insert it into
// the database.
BlogEntry entry = _model.InsertBlogItem(item);

// We now have several tasks we need to perform:
//
// 1) Serialize the object to be returned in the
//    response stream, which represents the object
//    as inserted into the database.
// 2) Return 201 (Created)
// 3) Create a Location header and fill it with the
//    URI that will access the blog entry.
if (context.Request.Headers["Accept"].ToLower() ==
    "application/json")
{
    // Serialize the new object for return
    item = new BlogEntryItem(entry, null);
    _blogJsonItemSerializer.WriteObject(
        context.Response.OutputStream, item);

    // Set the return type
    context.Response.ContentType = "application/json";
}
else
{
    // Serialize the new object for return
    item = new BlogEntryItem(entry, null);
    _blogXmlItemSerializer.WriteObject(
        context.Response.OutputStream, item);

    // Set the return type
    context.Response.ContentType = "text/xml";
}
```

continues

LISTING 6.8: Continued

```
        // Return created status
        context.Response.StatusCode = (Int32)HttpStatusCode.Created;

        // Create the URI that would access the new item
        string fullUrl = context.Request.Url.ToString();
        string baseUrl = fullUrl.Substring(0, fullUrl.IndexOf(
            context.Request.ApplicationPath));
        string locationValue =
            String.Format("{0}{1}/Default.aspx?BlogID={2}",
              baseUrl,
              context.Request.ApplicationPath,
              entry.EntryID);
        context.Response.AddHeader("Location", locationValue);
    }
    else
    {
        // Return forbidden
        context.Response.StatusCode = (Int32)HttpStatusCode.Forbidden;
    }
}
```

Like the `DispatchGetBlogList` method, the `DispatchAddBlogItem` method needs to determine what type of entity is to be dealt with. However, in this case the method is provided a representation in the request stream, so the entity type is determined using the `Content-Type` header. The incoming blog entry is then deserialized and inserted into the database using the service's `Model` class, which serves as a simplistic data access layer.

Here is the interesting part, though. As you read in Chapter 2, "The HyperText Transfer Protocol and the Universal Resource Identifier," when inserting information using HTTP `POST`, you are bound by RFC 2616 to finish things off by returning three key pieces of information:

1. Return the created entity representation in the response stream.
2. Return the HTTP `201` (`Created`) response code.
3. Create a `Location` header and add it to the response header list, with the value of the header being the URI of the newly created resource.

So the code in Listing 6.8 also performs these actions before returning to the client.

The remaining dispatch methods, both for blog entry items and for comments, are similar. The Model class, which implements the simple data access layer for the service, wraps methods that use LINQ to SQL. For completeness, Listing 6.9 shows the Model class's QueryBlog method.

LISTING 6.9: The Model **class's** QueryBlog **method**

```
public IEnumerable<BlogEntryItem> QueryBlog()
{
    // Retrieve all blog entries
    BlogDataClassesDataContext context =
      new BlogDataClassesDataContext();
    var blogQuery = from b in context.BlogEntries
                             orderby b.PostDate
                             select b;
    List<BlogEntryItem> entries = new List<BlogEntryItem>();
    foreach (var entry in blogQuery)
    {
        // Create the new comment item
        BlogEntryItem entrytItem = new BlogEntryItem(entry, null);
        entries.Add(entrytItem);
    }
    return entries;
}
```

The BlogEntryItem object mentioned in Listing 6.9 is a simple data transfer object (DTO) used to convey information out of the service. For the most part it consists of properties that match the table columns in the database table that supports blog entries, but I did create some specialized constructors to make life easier, as shown in Listing 6.10.

LISTING 6.10: The BlogEntryItem **class**

```
using System;
using System.Diagnostics;
using System.Runtime.Serialization;
using System.Web;

namespace AspNetRestService
{
    [DataContract(Namespace = "http://www.endurasoft.com/REST.NET/")]
    public sealed class BlogEntryItem
    {
        public BlogEntryItem()
        {
        }
```

continues

LISTING 6.10: Continued

```csharp
        public BlogEntryItem(Int32 entryID, string title,
                             string entry, DateTime postDate,
                             BlogCommentItem[] comments)
        {
            // Store the basic information
            this.EntryID = entryID;
            this.Title = title;
            this.Entry = entry;
            this.PostDate = postDate;
            this.Comments = comments;

            // Generate the link (remember HATEOAS)
            HttpRequest request = HttpContext.Current.Request;
            string fullUrl = request.Url.ToString();
            string baseUrl = fullUrl.Substring(0, fullUrl.IndexOf(
                request.ApplicationPath));
            this.EntryLink =
              String.Format("{0}{1}/Default.aspx?BlogID={2}", baseUrl,
                request.ApplicationPath, entryID);
        }

        public BlogEntryItem(BlogEntry entry,
                             BlogCommentItem[] comments) :
            this(entry.EntryID, entry.Title, entry.Entry,
                entry.PostDate, comments)
        {
        }

        [DataMember()]
        public Int32 EntryID { get; set; }

        [DataMember()]
        public string Title { get; set; }

        [DataMember()]
        public string Entry { get; set; }

        [DataMember(IsRequired = false)]
        public string EntryLink { get; set; }

        [DataMember()]
        public DateTime PostDate { get; set; }

        [DataMember(IsRequired = false)]
        public BlogCommentItem[] Comments { get; set; }
    }
}
```

Since the EntryLink property is calculated, I've marked it as not required for serialization, or more precisely, for deserialization. The same is true for the comment collection. The reason for this is that when clients create a representation to be inserted, they won't have the associated link, and semantically it's unlikely they would be creating comments to their own blog entry. With the IsRequired setting set to false, these values can be null coming into the service, and the data contract serializers will still deserialize them properly. Without IsRequired set to false, the null value properties cause an exception during deserialization.

A reasonable question at this point is how to create client-side representations. Having the unfair advantage of having created the service, I felt I couldn't just copy the classes into the Windows Presentation Foundation (WPF) client application I created to demonstrate the service. If you find you can do this based on your own implementation, that's great. But the reality is that most clients won't have access to the code that implements the service, so you have to do the next best thing.

The "next best thing" is to request an XML representation from the service and save it as an XML file. Then you use the xsd.exe tool that comes with Visual Studio to first create a schema, and from the schema generate a C# (or Visual Basic .NET) source file you can include into your client application code. In my case, I did modify the resulting source code in two primary areas:

- I removed the XML Serializer attributes in favor of the data contract attributes.
- I modified the date properties to use DateTime versus a string representation of the date.

The first tactic simply allowed me to create both XML-based and JSON-based representations for demonstration purposes. All that's truly required is the capability to create one accepted representation on the client side, but in this case I opted for both. The second tactic came about when I tried to create a serialized version of a JSON-based date. Even when the date string I created matched what the JSON data contract serializer would create on its own, I found it wouldn't deserialize the string directly on the server.

So by modifying the date to become a `DateTime` object, the data contract serializer on the client was able to serialize the JSON value in a form acceptable to its server-based counterpart. If I ever needed to re-create this class using `xsd.exe`, I would have to reapply these changes, but I felt the risk was small that I'd actually need to do so.

Looking at `Web.config`

Even though I've yet to talk about the security module, I'll show the modifications I made to the `Web.config` file that cause the service handler (and the security module) to be brought into the IIS 7.0 operating environment. If you look at Listing 6.11, you'll see two primary sections. The first section, denoted by the `<location>` element, identifies the "folder" that will require ASP.NET authentication and authorization. I placed *folder* in quotes in the preceding sentence because the folder that's mentioned isn't an actual folder but rather the virtual URI that represents the RESTful service endpoint. This virtual URI originally came from the `UriTemplateTable` code you saw in Listing 6.4. As it happens, ASP.NET doesn't actually care whether the URI identified by the `<location>` element is real or virtual, which is perfect for securing the service just as if it were another ASP.NET Web application folder. Here you see I deny all users except those belonging to one of the four identified roles.

The other main section is, of course, the section devoted to IIS 7.0, `<system.webServer>`. This section contains several child elements, many of which I removed in Listing 6.11 for clarity. The two sections I do show are used to identify the modules and handlers to be added, or, in this case, also removed. I added both this chapter's custom security module, `BasicAuth-Module`, and the RESTful service handler, `BlogHandler`. But note that I also had to remove the `UrlAuthorization` module. If I didn't, my own security module might allow me to access the secured service URIs, but the built-in ASP.NET URL authorization module would not. Any service URI I used failed with an HTTP `403` (`Forbidden`) response code until I removed the built-in handler and implemented similar code in my own security handler. Another small ASP.NET security-related change to `Web.config` was that I set the authentication mode to `None` versus the default `Windows` mode, and

I checked to make sure that I turned off all cookies, such as for security and for roles.

LISTING 6.11: `BlogService` Web.config **handler/module settings**

```
<location path="Blog">
  <system.web>
    <authorization>
      <deny users="*" />
      <allow roles="Read, Create, Modify, Delete" />
    </authorization>
  </system.web>
</location>
...
<system.webServer>
  <modules runAllManagedModulesForAllRequests="true">
    <remove name="UrlAuthorization" />
    ...
    <add name="BasicAuthModule" preCondition="managedHandler"
      type="AspNetRestService.AuthModule, AspNetRestService" />
  </modules>
  <handlers>
    ...
    <add name="BlogHandler" path="Blog" verb="*"
      type="AspNetRestService.BlogService, AspNetRestService"
      resourceType="Unspecified" requireAccess="Script"
      preCondition="integratedMode" />
  </handlers>
</system.webServer>
```

A RESTful Client

I won't spend a lot of time discussing the client application for the blog service, but I will show the user interface and discuss the implementation briefly. In the basic user interface, shown in Figure 6.3, you can provide the service URI to call and select the content type (XML or JSON) and the HTTP method. The results are shown in the text box to the left of the buttons.

The application uses `HttpWebRequest` to issue requests and return responses from the service URI you provide to the application. Since the service will request credentials, the application will display the credential request dialog box shown in Figure 6.4.

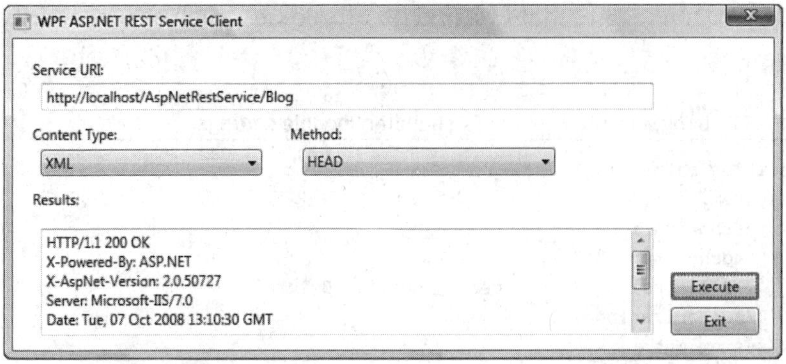

FIGURE 6.3: The WPF ASP.NET REST client application

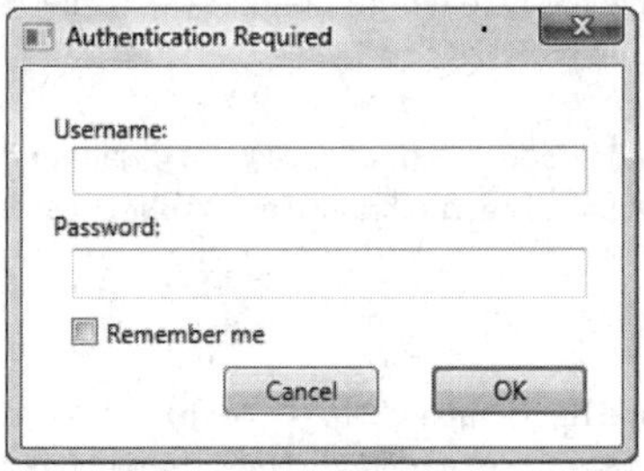

Figure 6.4: The WPF client credentials dialog box

Checking the Remember Me check box merely caches the credentials in the application for later use, precluding the necessity of retyping them for each service call. Unlike the other settings (service URI, HTTP method, and so on), the credentials aren't stored in the application Settings repository, so each execution of the application will require reauthentication.

If you want to create a new blog entry or comment, or perhaps update an existing blog entry, you select either the PUT or POST HTTP method and provide an appropriate URI. The application determines your actions based on URI and selected HTTP method and displays the dialog box shown in Figure 6.5.

Using this client application, you can exercise all the service functionality. If you execute the service in the debugger (press F5 with the AspNet-RestService project loaded into Visual Studio) and then execute this client from a Windows Explorer window, you can even single-step into the service code and see things in action one line at a time. That's exactly how I debugged the service myself.

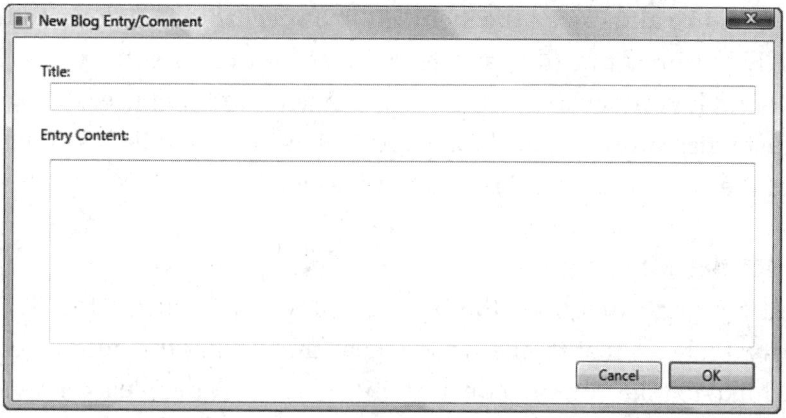

FIGURE 6.5: The WPF client blog entry dialog box

Securing the Service

In Chapter 1, "RESTful Systems: Back to the Future," I made a very strong statement, which was that RESTful services are secured using HTTP Basic Authentication each time the service is accessed. I made the case for this statement in that chapter, but it's a hollow statement if I don't have a means for actually doing this.

As I mentioned previously in the chapter, since its inception IIS has provided support for HTTP Basic Authentication, and you could indeed use the off-the-shelf implementation. But keep in mind this major restriction: All service clients must also have Windows or domain accounts on your system, and if you elect to use roles, you'll need to create and administer those roles as Windows roles as well.

This is very handy and quite secure, but it also is limiting and not very scalable. What I wanted was a way to use HTTP Basic Authentication without being saddled with creating Windows accounts for any Internet client that comes along. After all, the service is hosted by ASP.NET, so one would think there should be a way to create a new security module to replace the default module IIS provides.

And indeed this is the case. Moreover, the module I'll show you also handles ASP.NET authorization, so forcing a client to both authenticate (log in) and be authorized (be included in a specific role) follows the same ASP.NET security practices and techniques you've used for years. I also didn't find it very satisfying to force the general Internet user to authenticate just when browsing the blog page itself, so the module takes the location of the secured resource into account as well.

ASP.NET Security Internals

Actually, I don't dive into the blow-by-blow mechanisms for ASP.NET security. I'll leave that to another book, as that's what it would take. But I would like to take you on a deeper dive than most people experience, as you'll need a fundamental understanding of ASP.NET security to work with the authentication module I've created if you want to make changes on your own.

The ASP.NET Provider Model

ASP.NET bases much of its internal workings on the strategy pattern, which as implemented it calls the *provider model*. The providers are strategized in `Web.config` and used for all manner of things, from security to roles to personalization. The role provider for the `BlogService` is configured as such:

```
<roleManager enabled="true"
  cacheRolesInCookie="false"
  createPersistentCookie="false">
    <providers>
        <clear />
        <add connectionStringName="MyLocalSQLServer"
            applicationName="AspNetRestService"
            name="AspNetSqlRoleProvider"
            type="System.Web.Security.SqlRoleProvider, System.Web, ... "
    </providers>
</roleManager>
```

Here you see the various provider properties established (note that cookies are disabled), but arguably the most important property, the database connection string, is also dictated here. The connection string is configured in the usual ASP.NET location. Note *connectionStringName* and *name* in both bits of code match (I've placed the name in bold for emphasis):

```
<connectionStrings>
  <add name="MyLocalSQLServer" connectionString="..." />
</connectionStrings>
```

The connection string provides ASP.NET a way to access a custom database that sports tables specific to ASP.NET security. Happily, you don't need to create these tables yourself in SQL Server Management Studio. Instead, you can use a tool named `aspnet_regsql.exe` that creates these tables for you. If you simply execute the tool, follow the steps the resulting wizard offers, and complete the configuration, the database you select will be updated with the necessary tables, stored procedures, and schemas the various ASP.NET providers will require.

ASP.NET has but a single ASP.NET-specific security module, that being the `FormsAuthenticationModule`. The other modules you might come across, such as `WindowsAuthenticationModule`, `PassportAuthentication-Module`, or `AnonymousIdentificationModule`, all defer most of their internal execution to external agents, such as the Windows NT LAN Manager (NTLM) or IIS. But the goal of all the security modules is the same: Authenticate the user and provide access to the roles whose membership includes the user. Which module is used is dictated by the following:

```
<!--
      The <authentication> section enables configuration
      of the security authentication mode used by
      ASP.NET to identify an incoming user.
  -->
<authentication mode="None" />
```

If you set the mode to `Windows`, the Windows NTLM system will be used, assuming that you disable anonymous authentication in IIS. Similarly, if you set the mode to `Forms`, the ASP.NET Forms Authentication system kicks in. Since you'll be using a custom security module, simply set the mode to `None`.

> **■ NOTE**
>
> The security module implementation shown here is fine for IIS 6.0, but it is lacking a bit for a true IIS 7.0 implementation. Functionally it's fine, but because IIS 7.0 provides tighter integration with ASP.NET, the module has more responsibility with respect to configuration. For example, a well-implemented module provides a user interface for easier configuration and management. IIS 7.0 uses standard invocation mechanisms for displaying this user interface and recording the settings in `Web.config`. In addition, the module should be written to be asynchronous (whereas what's shown here is synchronous). Given time, I'll try to provide a more complete example at the book's Web site, www.endurasoft.com/rest.aspx. However, from a security perspective, the security module shown here is fully capable.

Each of these security modules has the responsibility of authenticating the user, caching the roles, and creating an `IPrincipal`-based object that represents the authenticated user. Some, such as the `FormsAuthenticationModule`, go even further and create a cookie that is returned for each request, alleviating the need to reauthenticate for each associated request. Regarding `IPrincipal`, after it is created, it's assigned to the `HttpContext.Current.User` property so that it is carried with the context for the duration of the request.

You can imagine the `IPrincipal` interface defined like so:

```
interface IPrincipal
{
    bool IsInRole(string role);
    IIdentity Identity { get; }
}
```

`IsInRole` accepts a role, as a string, and returns a Boolean value indicating that the user is, or is not, a member of that role. The `Identity` property is based on the `IIdentity` interface:

```
interface IIdentity
{
    string AuthenticationType { get; }
    bool IsAuthenticated { get; }
    string Name { get; }
}
```

Starting at the bottom of the IIdentity property list and working up, the Name property is simply the username associated with the user. IsAuthenticated is probably obvious—it returns the authenticated status of the user. The AuthenticationType is the most unusual property. It is a string-based property that identifies the type of authentication that was used to authenticate the user. This property might return various values, but for my security module it will return the string Basic since the user was subjected to HTTP Basic Authentication.

The .NET Framework provides you with the GenericPrincipal and GenericIdentity types that implement these security interfaces, but I wanted to assign my own AuthenticationType value as well as cache the user's role set for quick role verification. Therefore, I created my own principal and identity classes. ServiceUser, my principal class, is shown in Listing 6.12; ServiceIdentity, my identity class, is shown in Listing 6.13. Having these custom classes for my service is nice because I can tinker with the implementation should I need to do so.

LISTING 6.12: The ServiceUser **class**

```
[Serializable]
public sealed class ServiceUser : IPrincipal
{
    IIdentity _identity = null;
    string[] _roles = new string[0];

    internal ServiceUser(string username, bool isAuthenticated)
    {
        // Store the identity
        _identity =
          new ServiceIdentity(username, isAuthenticated) as IIdentity;

        // Get the roles for the user
        if (isAuthenticated)
        {
            _roles = Roles.GetRolesForUser(username);
        }
    }

    public bool IsInRole(string role)
    {
        // Look up role
        foreach (string testRole in _roles)
```

continues

LISTING 6.12: Continued

```
        {
            // Compare
            if (role.ToLowerInvariant() == testRole.ToLowerInvariant())
            {
                // Found it...
                return true;
            }
        }

        // Role not found
        return false;
    }

    public IIdentity Identity
    {
        get {return _identity; }
    }
}
```

Most of the implementation for ServiceUser is pretty straightforward, with the possible exception of the following:

```
// Get the roles for the user
if (isAuthenticated)
{
    _roles = Roles.GetRolesForUser(username);
}
```

Here I gather the roles assigned to the user as stored in the ASP.NET security tables in my database, and I do so using the ASP.NET role manager, Roles. The roles are cached as an array of strings, and when the user's role is challenged, the code merely iterates over the array of valid roles and looks for a positive comparison.

The ServiceIdentity class is simple as well, with its implementation shown in Listing 6.13. The only thing to really note here is that the authentication type is coded to be Basic, as previously mentioned.

LISTING 6.13: The ServiceIdentity class

```
[Serializable]
public sealed class ServiceIdentity : IIdentity
{
```

```
    private const string AuthenticationTypeString = "Basic";
    private string _username = String.Empty;
    private bool _isAuthenticated = false;

    internal ServiceIdentity(string username, bool isAuthenticated)
    {
        _username = username;
        _isAuthenticated = isAuthenticated;
    }

    public string AuthenticationType
    {
        get { return AuthenticationTypeString; }
    }

    public bool IsAuthenticated
    {
        get { return _isAuthenticated; }
    }

    public string Name
    {
        get { return _username; }
    }
}
```

Kicking Things Off

So how does all of this get started? The ASP.NET HTTP pipeline on a per-application basis is managed by the HttpApplication class, and the HttpApplication class monitors the state of the request processing and fires events at the appropriate time to move things along. There are events for application startup, shutdown, and more, but the event the security module is interested in is the AuthenticateRequest event. When this event fires, the HttpApplication is indicating that an incoming request requires authentication, and at that point the security module springs to life.

Listing 6.14 shows you the basic methods any HttpModule must implement, and though there isn't a lot there, what's there is important. This is where the security module hooks the AuthenticateRequest event, and each time that event fires, the security module will be called on to process an incoming client request authentication action.

LISTING 6.14: BlogService AuthModule **basic** HttpModule **implementation**

```
public void Dispose()
{
}

public void Init(HttpApplication context)
{
    // Hook the authentication request event
    context.AuthenticateRequest +=
      new EventHandler(OnAuthenticateRequest);
}
```

The delegate OnAuthenticateRequest handles the authentication request, and this is where the meat of the job is accomplished. Listing 6.15 shows you OnAuthenticateRequest in action. Following Listing 6.15, I'll break things down line by line.

LISTING 6.15: OnAuthenticateRequest **method implementation**

```
void OnAuthenticateRequest(object sender, EventArgs e)
{
    // Pull the current context
    HttpContext context = HttpContext.Current;

    // Pull the authorization information for this URI
    string url = context.Request.Url.LocalPath;
    AuthorizationManager authMgr =
      AuthorizationManager.CreateAuthorizationManager(url);

    // Check to see if we need authentication
    if (authMgr.RequiresAuthorization)
    {
        // Look for the authorization header
        bool isAuthorized = false;
        string authHeader = context.Request.Headers["Authorization"];
        if (!String.IsNullOrEmpty(authHeader) &&
            authHeader.ToLower().StartsWith(BasicAuthProtocol))
        {
            // Pull the credentials
            string[] credentials = stripCredentials(authHeader);

            // Authenticate
            if (credentials.Length == 2 &&
                Membership.ValidateUser(credentials[0], credentials[1]))
            {
                // Set the caller's credentials...note we may rescind
                // this depending upon the authorization check from the
```

```
            // configuration file.
            context.User = new ServiceUser(credentials[0], true);

            // Verify the configuration file supports this user
            if (authMgr.VerifyAuthorization(context.User))
            {
                // Mark as authorized
                isAuthorized = true;
            }
            else
            {
                // Rescind temporary authorization and indicate that
                // the resource is forbidden.
                context.Response.StatusCode =
                  (Int32)HttpStatusCode.Forbidden;

                // End the request
                context.Response.End();
                return;
            }
        }
    }

    // Check for authentication and return HTTP 401 if none
    if (!isAuthorized)
    {
        // Assign the status code
        context.Response.StatusCode =
          (Int32)HttpStatusCode.Unauthorized;

        // Calculate the realm
        string realm = String.Format("Basic realm=\"{0}\"",
            context.Request.Url.GetLeftPart(UriPartial.Path));

        // Add the authentication header
        context.Response.AddHeader("WWW-Authenticate", realm);

        // End the request
        context.Response.End();
    }
  }
}
```

The security module actually needs to accomplish two things: authenticate the user and filter the user based on applied roles for the location as specified in Web.config. If the user provides an incorrect username/password pair, that's one issue. But if an otherwise authenticated user tries to access the service without the appropriate role membership at a high level, the user is also forbidden. (The individual service methods filter to an even finer degree, as you've seen.)

The first thing the module does is access Web.config to see if the URI is secured using either the <authorization> element or the <location> element. ASP.NET provides a built-in tool to read the authorization components of the configuration file, AuthorizationManager:

```
// Pull the authorization information for this URI
string url = context.Request.Url.LocalPath;
AuthorizationManager authMgr =
  AuthorizationManager.CreateAuthorizationManager(url);
if (authMgr.RequiresAuthorization)
{
    ...
}
```

AuthorizationManager reads and interprets the configuration file, and if the incoming URL is identified as requiring authentication and authorization, the security module moves forward with that. If not, the request proceeds without authentication. I felt this was a required feature of the security module since this sample supports a simple .aspx page to display the blog, and the intention there was to leave that page unsecured.

Assuming that the URI is secured, the security module looks for the HTTP Authorization header:

```
// Look for the authorization header
bool isAuthorized = false;
string authHeader = context.Request.Headers["Authorization"];
if (!String.IsNullOrEmpty(authHeader) &&
    authHeader.ToLower().StartsWith(BasicAuthProtocol))
{
    ...
}
```

If there is no Authorization header, the security module requests one using the WWW-Authenticate header:

```
// Check for authentication and return HTTP 401 if none
if (!isAuthorized)
{
    // Assign the status code
    context.Response.StatusCode =
```

```
    (Int32)HttpStatusCode.Unauthorized;

    // Calculate the realm
    string realm = String.Format("Basic realm=\"{0}\"",
        context.Request.Url.GetLeftPart(UriPartial.Path));

    // Add the authentication header
    context.Response.AddHeader("WWW-Authenticate", realm);

    // End the request
    context.Response.End();
}
```

Now, assuming that there is an `Authorization` header, the security module interprets the username and password according to the usual HTTP Basic Authentication rules using a small helper method named `strip Credentials`. If the credentials are syntactically valid, which is to say there are both username and password values, then the security module uses the ASP.NET `Membership` provider to validate (authenticate) the user.

```
// Pull the credentials
string[] credentials = stripCredentials(authHeader);

// Authenticate
if (credentials.Length == 2 &&
    Membership.ValidateUser(credentials[0], credentials[1]))
{
    ...
}
```

If the credentials aren't syntactically valid, or if the client provided an invalid username, password, or both, then the `WWW-Authenticate` header is issued. But if the client did pass authentication, the security module creates an instance of `ServiceUser`, assigns it to the current `HttpContext`, and again turns to the `AuthorizationManager` and asks it to verify the role inclusion specified for both the client and the secured URI.

```
// Set the caller's credentials...note we may rescind
// this depending upon the authorization check from the
// configuration file.
context.User = new ServiceUser(credentials[0], true);

// Verify the configuration file supports this user
if (authMgr.VerifyAuthorization(context.User))
{
```

```
            // Mark as authorized
            isAuthorized = true;
    }
    else
    {
            // Rescind temporary authorization and indicate that
            // the resource is forbidden.
            context.Response.StatusCode =
              (Int32)HttpStatusCode.Forbidden;

            // End the request
            context.Response.End();
            return;
    }
```

If the client also is authorized to access the secured URI, the request proceeds normally. If the user isn't included in the necessary set of roles, the security module returns the HTTP 403 (Forbidden) return code.

You'll find this security module used throughout the rest of the book, so taking a moment to understand how it's designed and how it operates is important. The chapter's sample service is accompanied by a Visual Studio database project that contains scripts for creating sample users and roles, as well as initial blog entry and comment tables.

Where Are We?

This chapter introduced you to the lowest level of professional-grade RESTful service development, that being using ASP.NET directly. You saw how to create an HttpHandler that implements a full-fledged RESTful service, and you saw how to create a robust security module, based on HttpModule, to replace the default HTTP Basic Authentication module included with ASP.NET and IIS 7.0. As a reminder, keep in mind that the credentials are Base64 encoded, not encrypted, so you would need to ensure transport security by using some form of transport layer security (such as HTTPS) to ensure their confidentiality. Using HTTP Basic Authentication in your production application without the protection of SSL is not recommended.

The following few chapters build in the basic ASP.NET model and allow you to take RESTful service development to higher levels of abstraction. As you see how the ASP.NET model-view-controller (MVC) framework operates in the next chapter, you'll notice a great many similarities to the code you saw here, at least in spirit if not also in function. The ASP.NET MVC framework will hopefully not be too mysterious because of the experience you gained here. Of course, then you'll graduate to a full-fledged WCF implementation, in which many aspects of RESTful development are handled for you, reducing the amount of code you need to write and maintain.

7

Building REST Services Using ASP.NET MVC Framework

I N CHAPTER 6 we created a basic RESTful service using bare-bones ASP.NET techniques such as implementing an HTTP handler that represents our service. Interestingly, this isn't far from what happens with the ASP.NET MVC framework, but we don't look at it quite that way. Moreover, we gain some niceties revolving around URL routing and controller action invocations.

The ASP.NET MVC Framework

In mid-2007 or so, Microsoft introduced a new way to build ASP.NET applications that is based on the classic model-view-controller (MVC) design pattern. Although we could argue whether it fits the true MVC pattern or the more contemporary front controller pattern, the idea is that the traditional Web Forms method of creating Web pages is replaced by a framework that is actually based on RESTful principles. If you've not tried the ASP.NET MVC framework, it is available for download from this URL: http://www.asp.net/mvc

Traditional Web pages are rooted in disk files, and the representation they offer is the rendered HTML that comes from either the HTML stored in the file or, in the case of ASP.NET, the page offered up by the ASP.NET PageHandlerFactory. Consider what happens when you enter a URI such as the following:

```
http://www.contoso.com/Default.aspx
```

Here, ASP.NET receives the incoming request and shuttles it to the PageHandlerFactory. PageHandlerFactory's job is to locate the compiled code that represents the requested page. This code, based on IHttpHandler, then passes through a series of what amounts to workflow steps to render the HTML that is ultimately returned to the client. In the end, though, whether the client requests an HTML page or an ASP.NET page, the URI they use targets a resource that (typically) resides in a specific file on disk. And if you're using PageHandlerFactory, the representation the client will receive is HTML or some dialect of HTML, like XHTML.

The ASP.NET Web Forms model uses two files most of the time. The first file is a markup file that contains basic HTML and ASP.NET-specific markup that indicates which controls the page handler will instantiate and otherwise manipulate. The second file is called the "code-behind" file (or sometimes "code-beside"), and it contains programming logic in your choice of .NET language. As far as it goes, this page mechanism is fine and it works. But there is a tight coupling that exists between the markup and the logic that drives the page since the markup and code-behind pages are closely related. This doesn't separate the view from the logic behind the view, which causes difficulties when considering such things as automated unit testing or test-driven design, or even when trying to inject standard practices like separation of concerns. Although much can be done by developers to mitigate this tight coupling, in practice most development teams don't (or can't) make the investment because it is not self-evident, and it requires planning, training, and code review to ensure consistent implementation. Ironically, these techniques involve separating the data, the user interface, and the manipulation of that user interface—which in itself is a form of MVC.

Moreover, ASP.NET had received negative comments from time to time from some in the developer community due to the way the Web Forms page is rendered. These developers consider the Web Forms page rendering process to be "heavy," meaning it takes too long and requires too much server resource to render a simple page. Authoring and rendering ASP.NET controls isn't a simple process either, and at times scalability can be impacted. In addition, the Web Forms model is inherently stateful, using information caches such as view state, control state, and even the easy-to-access session state. It's entirely too easy to get yourself into trouble when implementing a Web site with more complexity than simple content pages.

■ NOTE

It isn't my intention to argue the merits or demerits of either ASP.NET platform here. In my opinion both Web Forms and ASP.NET MVC are good and have beneficial uses. To me it's more a matter of selecting the proper tool for the job. Web Forms are more resource-centric whereas ASP.NET MVC is more action-centric. Web Forms give you some programming niceties, because view state isn't necessarily a bad thing at times, whereas ASP.NET MVC allows you to program "closer to the metal."

I also found the MVC framework to be a wonderfully RESTful platform, but I understand Microsoft doesn't necessarily agree with this sentiment, preferring for developers to instead use Windows Communication Foundation services. The ASP.NET MVC framework is a terrific platform on which to build RESTful solutions using the very constructs the framework itself provides, but I also understand Microsoft's position. In practice, I think you should decide for yourself based on your application's requirements. I wouldn't hesitate to create a RESTful solution based on ASP.NET MVC if that best fit my application's needs.

The ASP.NET MVC framework was created to address these issues, and you can download the framework as well as learn much more about it at http://asp.net/mvc. The ASP.NET MVC framework is built using a modified version of the venerable model-view-controller pattern, the original concept for which is shown in Figure 7.1. Although you won't find this figure in the original source material, the idea Figure 7.1 embodies comes from

the original source, which you can find at http://heim.ifi.uio.no/
~trygver/1979/mvc-1/1979-05-MVC.pdf. I used the word "modified" only
because when creating a new ASP.NET MVC project, you're given sample
views and controllers. However, any model creation is up to you, so implementing the feedback to the view is therefore also up to you to implement
should you choose to do so.

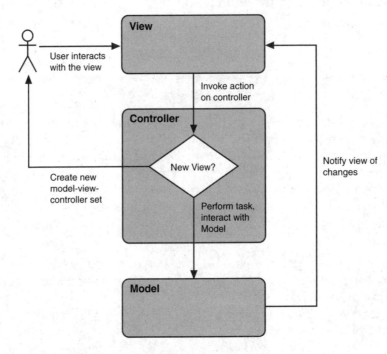

FIGURE 7.1: Original model-view-controller pattern

■ NOTE

If you're wondering about the feedback line on the right side of the
diagram (as I was for a long time), it comes from the definition of the
view in the aforementioned reference. Other patterns, like the model-
view-presenter (and more contemporary patterns based on MVC, like
the front controller pattern of which the ASP.NET MVC framework is
built around) often seek to address things such as this direct model-
view feedback or provide for other pattern optimizations.

The model-view-controller pattern was revolutionary in the sense that it clearly separated the user interface–specific rendering (the view) from the logic that drives what is shown. User actions, such as button clicks, are passed from the view to the controller, which will either create a new model-view-controller set (such as when redirecting to a different Web page) or interact with the model, which is where both the application logic and the data access reside.

The ASP.NET MVC framework relies on the `UrlRoutingModule` to shuttle Web server requests to the `MvcHttpHandler`, which then interprets the requested URL and activates the appropriate controller. Controller activation is therefore ultimately based on the URI, and a controller action (method) is activated instead of directly targeting a disk-based resource. At its very core, the ASP.NET MVC framework is based on RESTful principles!

In fact, think back to the preceding chapter. Remember the virtual nature of the service I created? The `BlogService` didn't actually exist as a `.aspx` or `.ashx` file but rather was created and registered through the use of `UriTemplateTable`. By adding items to the `UriTemplateTable` and then later checking the incoming URI against the preregistered URIs the service would accept, the service could discern valid URIs, at least from the service's point of view. It could then also dispatch the processing of those URIs along with matched information, such as the parsed `blogID`.

This is very similar to the mechanisms I just described when looking at the ASP.NET MVC framework. The framework provides a more programmer-friendly and standardized way to execute your own code (the `BlogService` is fully custom, after all), but the process for accessing resources is very, very similar in both cases. Let's now look at some MVC framework details.

URL Routing

The URL routing module is driven by "mapped routes," which are URIs you specify and couple to a specific controller. This process is much like setting up the `UriTemplateTable` in the preceding chapter. Here is the route map for the default route when you create a brand-new MVC Web application:

```
routes.MapRoute(
    "Default",
    "{controller}/{action}/{id}",
    new { controller = "Home", action = "Index", id = "" }
);
```

Default is the name of the route, and you can imagine that this is used as a key in a route table (undoubtedly a dictionary object). The value {controller}/{action}/{id} is the "designed" URI, which essentially says this mapped URL will be activated like so:

http://servername/virtualdirectory/controller/action/id

If no controller is specified, it will default to HomeController. The MVC framework will take the value placed in the route map, Home, and automatically concatenate the word Controller to look up the appropriate controller class in the Controllers folder, which in this case is HomeController. If no action is specified, the MVC framework will examine the HomeController class for a method named Index. However, if the URI

http://servername/virtualdirectory/Home/About

is used, then the MVC framework will invoke the About method contained within the HomeController.

In both sample URLs there was no id value. None was specified in the URL, and the Index and About methods contained within the HomeController have no parameters to deal with it since none is expected for those actions. However, if you created a blog and provided an action that listed pages in your blog, the id value could become the page number:

```
public ActionResult Page(Int32 id)
{
    ...
}
```

In this case, the URL for page 3 of your blog would be this:

http://*servername*/*virtualdirectory*/Home/Page/3

The HomeController's Page method would be invoked and passed the value 3 as the id parameter. You'd then process the page number using whatever logic makes sense for locating and displaying the desired view.

There is a special case this chapter's service takes advantage of when it registers the RESTful service URI with the URL routing framework, and that is the parameter wildcard. If your application has the specific pattern the default route maps for you, which is controller, action, and then ID, the default route works fine. But if your application might have a URI that varies, you could map your route using the wildcard and decide what to do when your controller is invoked. Here's an example:

```
routes.MapRoute(
    "VariableURI",
    "{MyController}/{*contentUri}",
    new { controller = "MyController", action = "ServiceRequest" }
);
```

This URI is registered using the `VariableURI` name, but it can be activated using an infinite number of URIs, all of which map to `MyController`'s `ServiceRequest` action method. The remainder of the URI is provided to the `ServiceRequest` method as a string parameter. You'd use this if you simply can't define the URI for all possible client invocations or your URI will vary. Later in the chapter I'll show you how to register a new route in the route map.

Controller Actions

Note that the `Page` method shown previously returns something known as an `ActionResult`. You might imagine an `ActionResult` returning some rendered HTML value, but in fact an `ActionResult` is simply an abstract class defined as such:

```
public abstract class ActionResult
{
    protected ActionResult();

    public abstract void ExecuteResult(ControllerContext context);
}
```

Several concrete `ActionResult` classes are shipped with the ASP.NET MVC framework, including `ViewResult`, which is returned from the controller's `View` method (I'll discuss this in a bit more detail in a following section), `RedirectToRouteResult`, and `PartialViewResult`. Of course, nothing says you can't create your own, and I did exactly that when creating the RESTful service for this chapter. (And of the six cases the service handles, only one of those cases returns HTML to the client.)

As I alluded to earlier in the chapter, URIs are mapped to controller actions (not disk files as with traditional ASP.NET). Controller actions are implemented by methods hosted by your controller classes that return `ActionResult` values. The behavior of the controller action in most cases would be to spin up a `.aspx` page (the view), but though this is common, it isn't required. Your controller can take other actions, depending on your application's needs.

Accepting HTTP Methods

A nice feature of the ASP.NET MVC framework is the capability to separate controller actions based on HTTP method. That is, you can specify one controller action for HTTP `GET` and another for `POST`, `PUT`, `DELETE`, or whatever. Coupled with this concept is the capability to overload the naming of the methods from the framework's point of view. This is a great feature for RESTful services in which you generally support more than HTTP `GET`.

Let's look at an example. Here is a valid URI for this chapter's sample service, `CodeXRC`:

```
https://servername/virtualdirectory/CodeXRC
```

You can imagine `CodeXRC` as a simple-minded source code repository. If a client accessed this URI, to determine what to do, you would need to examine the HTTP method. If it was `HEAD`, you would do one thing. If it was `GET` or `POST`, you would do another. To accomplish this, you would probably write code that used a switch statement using the HTTP Method to decide what to do:

```
public ActionResult Index()
{
    switch (this.HttpContext.Request.HttpMethod.ToLower())
    {
        case "head":
            // Do HTTP HEAD
            return DispatchHead();

        case "get":
            // Do HTTP GET
            return DispatchGet();

        case "put":
            // Do HTTP PUT
            return DispatchPut();
```

```
        case "post":
            // Do HTTP POST
            return DispatchPost();

        case "delete":
            // Do HTTP Delete
            return DispatchDelete();

        default:
            // Unknown method, process error
            break;
    }

    // Process error
    DispatchErrorMethodNotAllowed();
}
```

In fact, this is precisely what you saw in the preceding chapter. It's another example of a dispatch table in which the appropriate service handler is invoked based on HTTP method. It's also very much "boilerplate" code that could be rolled into a framework, and that's exactly what was done in ASP.NET MVC.

But then we have an issue. We can't have identically named methods with identical method signatures. If the framework can route actions to a controller based on HTTP method, then there has to be some way to overload the name of the method so that we don't have syntactical errors. That is, we can't have this situation:

```
// HTTP HEAD?
public ActionResult Index()
{
    ...
}

// HTTP GET?
public ActionResult Index()
{
    ...
}
...
// HTTP DELETE?
public ActionResult Index()
{
    ...
}
```

Clearly this won't compile, but this is exactly the situation we would have since a single URI serves all HTTP methods (keeping the original service URL in mind: https://servername/virtualdirectory/CodeXRC).

It's for this reason the ASP.NET MVC framework coupled the ability to handle different HTTP methods with different controller actions using an aliased name. The `AcceptVerbs` and `ActionName` attributes cleanly disambiguate the HTTP method and aliased name:

```
// HTTP HEAD
[AcceptVerbs("HEAD")]
[ActionName("Index")]
public ActionResult ProcessHead()
{
    ...
}

// HTTP GET
[AcceptVerbs("GET")]
[ActionName("Index")]
public ActionResult ProcessGet()
{
    ...
}
...
// HTTP DELETE
[AcceptVerbs("DELETE")]
[ActionName("Index")]
public ActionResult ProcessDelete()
{
    ...
}
```

In this case I've rewritten the previous example to show the proper technique. From a URI perspective, the controller action is always `Index`. But the true controller action to be invoked will depend on the HTTP method used to invoke the action. If the HTTP `GET` method is used, the `ProcessGet` action is invoked, and so forth.

This chapter's sample RESTful service makes heavy use of this new feature, and I'd expect that many services will do so over time as well.

Views

Although this book isn't about building Web sites using ASP.NET MVC, I thought a paragraph or two that describes how the views are handled is appropriate since I'm introducing the framework.

> ■ **NOTE**
>
> You'll find that I didn't make use of the view capability in the chapter's sample application. Perhaps I should have. I certainly could have. I just found it more convenient to take the notion of a controller "action" literally and have the controller address the service request. The point was not to render a "view" but to respond to a call for action, even if that action results in rendered HTML. Had I been building Web pages, I would have done things differently. (If you disagree with my implementation, that's fine. When you build your own services, by all means follow your own interpretation of the pattern.)

The ASP.NET MVC framework uses a folder (conventionally) named Views to contain all the views, with views associated with a particular controller in a subfolder named after the controller. Views associated with the HomeController, for example, are found in the Home folder, which is a child folder of Views in the main application directory. If all you ever do is invoke the view associated with the action, the MVC framework will automatically select the view named for the action. For example, the default HomeController has an About action that invokes the About view in the Home folder of the Views Web application directory. This code does that job, with the MVC framework's help:

```
public class HomeController : Controller
{
    ...
    public ActionResult About()
    {
        ViewData["Title"] = "About Page";

        return View();
    }
}
```

The About action returns a ViewResult from the controller's base View method, which implements the algorithm I mentioned for locating the default view for the action. And as you recall, ViewResult is derived from ActionResult.

However, you might want to use another view, and as it happens the controller's base View method is overloaded, allowing you to select other views based on name. One I find myself using a lot is this overloaded version:

```
protected internal ViewResult View(string viewName, object model);
```

With this overloaded version, you provide the name of the view you would rather invoke as well as some page-specific data the view can access through its ViewData property (specifically ViewData.Model). Perhaps you have one view that's based on a data grid and another based on a chart. Using this overloaded View method, you can select the most appropriate view based on your application's needs.

You also can redirect to another page entirely. The simplest way is to use the controller's Redirect method, which returns a RedirectAction object. But other redirect methods exist, such as RedirectToAction and Redirect-ToRoute. Of course, these allow you to redirect to a different controller action or mapped route.

The Model

In MVC terms, the model is where you place your data access layer and any application-specific business logic. When you create a brand-new ASP.NET MVC Web application, the project wizard creates controllers and views for you as starter code. But no model is created—only a subdirectory is created for you within which you place model code. Nearly all the CodeXRC service functionality is implemented in classes that are housed in the model folder, and you'll find this is typical for MVC-style applications.

ASP.NET MVC Security

ASP.NET MVC incorporates the notion of an Authorize attribute and the AccountController class. Imagine a controller that looks something like this:

```
public class MyController : Controller
{
    ...
    [Authorize]
    public ActionResult DoSomething()
    {
        ...
    }
}
```

The `Authorize` attribute causes the ASP.NET MVC handler to look for a controller named `AccountController` and invokes its `Login` action. The `Login` action, and the `AccountController` for that matter, are designed to work with the ASP.NET Forms Authentication module. Therefore, `Login` and `Register` generate an authentication cookie, `Logout` destroys the cookie, and everything else the account controller does favors the Forms authentication process in ASP.NET.

After seeing the additional work ASP.NET MVC offered, which was to wrap access to the Forms authentication services (or at least a couple of them) behind a custom interface, I thought it would be useful to try to work the HTTP Basic Authentication module from the preceding chapter into the MVC framework. But the simple truth is that given the module from the preceding chapter, the entire concept behind the `AccountController`, or at least the Forms authentication parts of it, aren't needed.

With Forms authentication, navigating between secured pages is accomplished using the ASP.NET security cookie. The Forms Authentication module looks for the cookie, and if it's present and valid when accessing secured resources, the Forms Authentication module allows the secured page to render. The `Authorize` attribute controls which actions are secured.

HTTP Basic Authentication, however, doesn't use a cookie. In fact, this is what makes it so appealing to RESTful services. The client needs to cache the credentials and offer them to the Web server each time access to a secured resource is desired. Modern Web browsers all do this for you, and most (if not all) of the sample desktop applications in this book will also cache the credentials for you if you choose so that each service access doesn't force reauthentication.

In the end, I simply copied the module from the preceding chapter into this chapter's sample application, changed the namespaces involved, and made the necessary adjustments to the `web.config` file, and the HTTP Basic Authentication worked tremendously well. Since I didn't require the `AccountController`, I deleted it and the views associated with it, knowing that the browser itself would query me for my credentials—I don't need a "login" page for that. True, I also then dismissed the registration and password change request pages, but there is some merit for brevity when producing chapter samples.

> **■ NOTE**
>
> I also can't use the spectacular `Authorize` attribute, but I found I didn't need it with the custom authentication module. If I were producing a traditional MVC Web application, one based on views, I'd embrace these new ASP.NET MVC tools—the account controller and security attribute—but for a truly RESTful service that requires HTTP Basic Authentication, I discovered they're just not the right tools for the job.

Building an MVC RESTful Service—CodeXRC

With this understanding of the basic ASP.NET MVC framework, it's time to actually build a RESTful service that relies on the framework for basic operations. This service, unlike the blog service in the preceding chapter, won't create an `HttpHandler` to service the RESTful requests but will instead be based on controller actions that are activated by the specific service URI mapped in the URL routing table.

To show a service that did more than produce "Hello, World!" I decided to implement the basis of a source code vault, or perhaps a cloud-based file system. The idea behind this is that you select files on your local hard drive and store them in this secured service. This is an aggressive service for the schedule I had to work with, but though it was becoming more complex the further I got into development, I was more convinced it made for a great chapter sample because it addresses many interesting RESTful concepts. These will be evident when I discuss the URI design.

> **■ NOTE**
>
> Although not provided with this chapter's sample application, the ASP.NET MVC framework is perfectly suited for creating test-driven design (TDD) applications. Creating applications using test-driven techniques tends to reduce the number of latent bugs and increases code maintainability.

I named the service CodeXRC, the "XRC" part having no particular meaning except it isn't copyrighted as far as I could tell. (I don't want to upset the publisher's legal staff.) The URIs for the service are designed like so:

- Add/update a project: PUT to /CodeXRC
- Add/update a project (alternate): PUT to /CodeXRC/{project}
- Add/update a project folder: PUT to /CodeXRC/{project}/{folder}
- Add/update a file: PUT to /CodeXRC/{project}/{folder}/{ext}/{file}
- Delete all projects: DELETE to /CodeXRC
- Delete a project: DELETE to /CodeXRC/{project}
- Delete a folder: DELETE to /CodeXRC/{project}/{folder}
- Delete files by extension: DELETE to /CodeXRC/{project}/{folder}/{ext}
- Delete a file: DELETE to /CodeXRC/{project}/{folder}/{ext}/{file}
- Get all projects (high level): GET to /CodeXRC
- Get a project (all folders/files): GET to /CodeXRC/{project}
- Get a folder: GET to /CodeXRC/{project}/{folder}
- Get files by extension: GET to /CodeXRC/{project}/{folder}/{ext}
- Get a file: GET to /CodeXRC/{project}/{folder}/{ext}/{file}
- Get statistics/headers: HEAD to a valid service URI

This complex-looking set of URIs really amounts to simulating a file system using REST (see Figure 7.2).

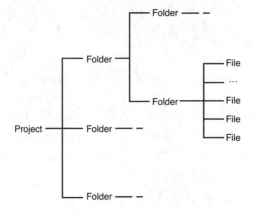

FIGURE 7.2: CodeXRC **project storage**

The files are stored on the server's file system in the hierarchy shown in Figure 7.2, but there is also a database associated with the service to maintain ownership of the projects and files as well as foreign key relationships for searching and deletion. Users are registered using a process not provided with the service, but when they're registered their account information is stored in the typical ASP.NET tables contained within the database. Projects are owned by the registered users and are identified by their user ID, which is a Guid. Roles are also maintained: View, Insert, and Delete. At present the service allows you to access only your own projects, but it would be a relatively easy extension to add View capabilities to projects not your own.

Creating the URL Mapping

With the URI set defined for the service, the place to start is with the URL routing table and mapping. To do this, you open the Global.asax.cs file and look for the RegisterRoutes method. There, you'll see the default route mapped into the route table (this is created for you by the Visual Studio MVC application wizard). Add this code just before the default route:

```
// Register the RESTful service URIs...note this *MUST*
// come before the default URI mapping or you'll sustain
// 404 errors if the URI doesn't match the default
// mapping.
routes.MapRoute(
    "CodeXRC",
    "CodeXRC/{*contentUri}",
    new { controller = "CodeXRC", action = "ServiceRequest" }
);
```

Of course, this looks a lot like the mapping I discussed previously in the chapter, and given the variable nature of the URI set, you can probably see why I opted for the wildcard approach.

> ■ **NOTE**
>
> You could individually map each URL segment and apply a default, as is done with the Default URL route map, but I chose to simplify the action signatures and parse the URI manually.

When requests come into the server designated for the CodeXRC service, the CodeXRCController will be called on to take the appropriate action. As is proper for the ASP.NET MVC framework, the CodeXRCController is located in the Web application Controllers folder.

The CodeXRCController

The CodeXRCController contains four actions, one for each HTTP method the service handles: HTTP HEAD, GET, PUT, and DELETE. Each action is adorned with the appropriate AcceptVerbs and ActionName attributes. The HEAD action is shown in Listing 7.1.

LISTING 7.1: The CodeXRCController HTTP HEAD action

```
[AcceptVerbs("HEAD")]
[ActionName("ServiceRequest")]
public ActionResult HeadRequest(string contentUri)
{
    // Filter the query string and remove any trailing '/' so
    // we don't have an extra array element.
    contentUri = FilterUri(contentUri);
```

continues

LISTING 7.1: Continued

```
    // Save the URI parameters
    string[] directives = null;
    if (!String.IsNullOrEmpty(contentUri))
    {
        directives = contentUri.Split('/');
    }

    // Output to a temporary stream
    MemoryStream strm = new MemoryStream();
    this.HttpContext.Items.Add("OutputStream", strm);

    // Handle the request
    CodeXRCGetService result = new CodeXRCGetService(directives, true);
    return result;
}
```

In Listing 7.1 you can see that the controller action is named Head-
Request, but because I applied the ActionName attribute, the ASP.NET MVC
framework will route the action as if it were named ServiceRequest, which
matches the name of the action I registered in Global.asax.cs. And since
the AcceptVerbs attribute lists only HTTP HEAD as the accepted HTTP
method, this action is called only for HEAD requests.

The parameter contentUri will contain anything on the query string
past the controller name. That is, if the client issued a request to the URI
http://*servername*/AspNetMvcRestService/CodeXRC/Project1/Folder2/
cs/CodeFile3
the contentUri parameter would contain the string Project1/Folder2/cs/
CodeFile3.

To decide what parameters are present, the contentUri string is split
using the slash as the delimiter. However, I filter the string first to remove
a trailing slash. This prevents a phantom entry in the resulting string array.
That is, this URI would result in three parameters after the string split:
http://*servername*/AspNetMvcRestService/CodeXRC/Project1/Folder2/
In reality, though, only two parameters are present: Project1 and Folder2.
The third entry in the string array would be an empty string, present only
because of the trailing slash. By removing the slash, the service doesn't
need to check for empty parameter elements in the parameters string array.

In the case of HTTP HEAD, the service will perform all the normal GET
processing. However, the stream the information is written to will differ for

the other HTTP methods. For example, GET will use the actual output stream, thus sending a response to the client. HEAD will use a temporary stream, allowing the service to determine the size of the stream so that the appropriate Content-Length header can be returned to the client. The output stream to use is assigned a slot in the HttpContent Items collection so that it won't need to be passed around as a separate method parameter in all the internal processing methods.

The request is handled by a class that derives from ActionRequest: CodeXRCGetService. As you might imagine, there are corresponding service classes for PUT and DELETE as well. Since GET and HEAD are closely related, a single service class handles both HTTP methods. Something to keep in mind is that the response output stream is not seekable, meaning we can't query its length. It would have been nice to simply write to the appropriate stream and just query the stream length, but unfortunately the response output stream throws an exception when you access its Length property. This means you have to ask the question "Is this a HEAD request?" If so, then (and only then) should you access the stream's Length property and create the Content-Length header. I use the stream's CanSeek property for that.

In contrast, the HTTP PUT method service controller action is shown in Listing 7.2.

LISTING 7.2: The CodeXRCController HTTP PUT action

```
[AcceptVerbs("PUT")]
[ActionName("ServiceRequest")]
public ActionResult PutRequest(string contentUri)
{
    // Filter the query string and remove any trailing '/' so
    // we don't have an extra array element.
    contentUri = FilterUri(contentUri);

    // Save the URI parameters
    string[] directives = null;
    if (!String.IsNullOrEmpty(contentUri))
    {
        directives = contentUri.Split('/');
    }

    // Output to the true response stream
    this.HttpContext.Items.Add("OutputStream",
                this.HttpContext.Response.OutputStream);
```

continues

LISTING 7.2: Continued

```
    // Handle the request
    CodeXRCPutService result = new CodeXRCPutService(directives);
    return result;
}
```

I've included the PutRequest method here only to highlight the differences: the HTTP method it accepts is PUT, the controller action is actually ServiceRequest even though the controller method is called PutRequest, the stream to be used for the response is the true output stream (versus a temporary one), and the PUT behavior is exhibited by the CodeXRCPut Service class. Otherwise, the request handling for each HTTP method is similar at the controller level.

CodeXRC Service Classes

All the CodeXRC service classes use ActionResult as their base class. In fact, there is a single CodeXRC service base class, CodeXRCServiceBase, that is used to maintain instances of the URI parameters (which I called "directives" because they direct the service), the data access component, and an auxiliary component that sports helper methods for supporting error responses and such. This base class is shown in Listing 7.3.

LISTING 7.3: The CodeXRCServiceBase class

```
public class CodeXRCServiceBase : ActionResult
{
    protected CodeXRCAuxServices _aux = new CodeXRCAuxServices();
    protected CodeXRCDataAccess _dal = new CodeXRCDataAccess();
    protected string[] _directives = new string[0];

    public CodeXRCServiceBase()
    {
    }

    public CodeXRCServiceBase(string[] directives)
    {
        // Later logic depends on this not being
        // null even if it has no elements.
        if (directives != null)
        {
            // Assign value
            _directives = directives;
        }
```

```
    }

    public abstract void ExecuteResult(ControllerContext context);
    {
        // Disallow base implementation...note you can't make
        // this abstract since this class is itself derived and
        // this method overridden.
        throw new NotImplementedException(
            "You must override the base ExecuteResult implementation.");
    }
}
```

Since all the derived classes need to use the data access component, the auxiliary helper method component, and the directives, it made sense to collect that in a base class.

Returning HTML, XML, and JSON

The services themselves are broken out into "get," "put," and "delete" versions, each handling the respective HTTP method. Each service method handler also overrides the `ActionResult ExecuteResult` method. The `CodeXRCGetService` implementation is shown in Listing 7.4. The other implementations are similar.

LISTING 7.4: CodeXRCGetService ExecuteResult **method**

```
public override void ExecuteResult(ControllerContext context)
{
    // Test the user's credentials
    if (context.HttpContext.User.IsInRole("View"))
    {
        try
        {
            if (context.HttpContext.Request.AcceptTypes.Count() > 0)
            {
                // Loop through the collection of accepted types.
                // The first one we hit we understand, take it...
                foreach (string type in
                        context.HttpContext.Request.AcceptTypes)
                {
                    switch (type.ToLower())
                    {
                        case "text/html":
                        case "*/*":
                            RenderHtml(context);
                            return;
```

continues

```
                            case "text/xml":
                                RenderXml(context);
                                return;

                            case "application/json":
                                RenderJson(context);
                                return;

                            default:
                                // Try next one...
                                break;
                        }
                    }

                    // Couldn't accept any requested type
                    _aux.RenderErrorNotAcceptableGet(context);
                }
                else
                {
                    // Couldn't accept any requested type
                    _aux.RenderErrorNotAcceptableGet(context);
                }
            }
            catch (Exception ex)
            {
                // Couldn't accept any requested type
                _aux.RenderErrorInternalError(context, ex.ToString());
            }
        }
        else
        {
            // User forbidden
            _aux.RenderErrorForbidden(context);
        }
    }
```

NOTE

I am a fervent believer in application tracing, and for any Web application I write, I put as much tracing into the code as possible. However, for demonstration purposes here, I've omitted such code to focus instead on the functional nature of the service itself. Tracing is critical to debugging deployed Web applications and I heartily recommend using it.

In Listing 7.4 you can see that the code begins by checking the client's role (the client was authenticated or this method wouldn't be executing). If the client has the appropriate role credentials, the method then checks the desired return type: HTML, XML, or JSON. The default content type, */*, will return HTML. This allows browsers to view the contents of a project, as shown in Figure 7.3. The chapter's sample client will always provide the service with an `Accept` header containing just one accepted content type, but because browsers often include many requested content types, the loop allows the service to check the list of content types for the first one the service has the capability of supporting.

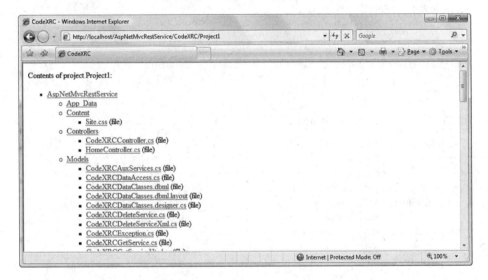

FIGURE 7.3: Browser REST service access

If you use the chapter's Windows Forms sample client, you can interact with the service in a greater variety of ways, including asking for the project contents as XML, as shown in Figure 7.4.

After the desired return content type is determined, the code in Listing 7.4 then invokes the appropriate rendering method. Listing 7.5 shows you how XML is rendered. I won't show all the supporting methods because there are many, and they often are recursive (and therefore complex) since the methods often need to traverse directory structures. They're also not important to demonstrate how to create RESTful services using the

ASP.NET MVC framework, so I'll leave spelunking their inner workings to you. They're just business logic, so to speak, and as such you'll find them all in the Models folder of the AspNetMvcRestService Web application.

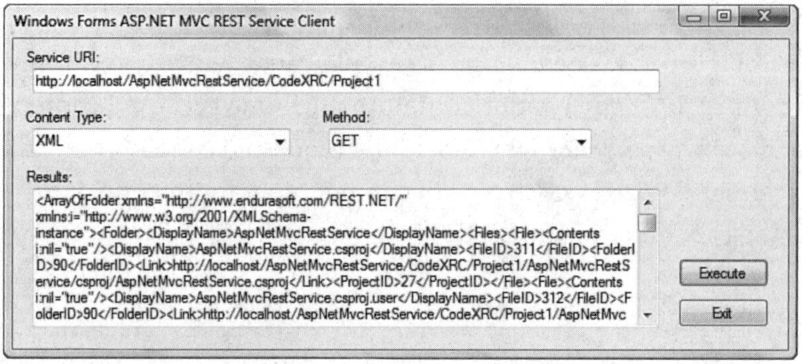

FIGURE 7.4: CodeXRC project contents as XML

LISTING 7.5: The RenderXML method

```
private void RenderXml(ControllerContext context)
{
    // Pull the user's ID. This works here since we're using the
    // SQL-based membership provider.
    MembershipUser user =
      Membership.GetUser(context.HttpContext.User.Identity.Name);
    Guid ownerID = (Guid)user.ProviderUserKey;

    context.HttpContext.Response.ContentType = "text/xml";
    switch (_directives.Count())
    {
        case 0:
        default:
            // List all projects for user:
            // http://{host}/{vdir}/CodeXRC
            RenderXmlProjectList(context, ownerID);
            break;

        case 1:
            // List specific project for user:
            // http://{host}/{vdir}/CodeXRC/{project}
            RenderXmlProject(context, ownerID, _directives[0]);
            break;
```

```
       case 2:
           // List specific folder for user:
           // http://{host}/{vdir}/CodeXRC/{project}/{folder}
           RenderXmlFolder(context, ownerID, _directives[0],
             _directives[1]);
           break;

       case 3:
           // List files by extension for user:
           // http://{host}/{vdir}/CodeXRC/{project}/{folder}/{ext}
           RenderXmlFilesByType(context, ownerID, _directives[0],
             _directives[1], _directives[2]);
           break;

       case 4:
           // Return specific file to user:
           // http://{host}/{vdir}/CodeXRC/{proj}/{folder}/{ext}/{file}
           RenderXmlFileByName(context, ownerID, _directives[0],
             _directives[1], _directives[2], _directives[3]);
           break;
   }

   // Assign the content length, but only if HEAD.
   Stream stream = context.HttpContext.Items["OutputStream"] as Stream;
   if (stream != null && stream.CanSeek)
   {
       context.HttpContext.Response.Headers["Content-Length"] =
         GetContentLength(context).ToString();
   }
}
```

The methods to render HTML and JSON are similar. Actually, rendering XML and JSON is easy using the `DataContractSerializer` and `DataContractJsonSerializer` objects, respectively. But the HTML is rendered by hand (again, one could perhaps use a view for this or augment the XML output with an XSLT reference, but I chose to keep the service logically contained, for right or wrong). After the content is rendered, the stream is examined for its length if the HTTP method was HEAD.

An important aspect of returning a resource representation is creating the links (remember hypermedia as the engine of application state). When representations are created, a special class is used to generate the appropriate links, which are shown in Listing 7.6.

LISTING 7.6: The CodeXRC link builder class

```
public static class CodeXRCLinkBuilder
{
    public static string BuildProjectLink(ControllerContext context,
                                          string projectName)
    {
        // Generate the link (remember HATEOAS)
        string fullUrl = context.HttpContext.Request.Url.ToString();
        string baseUrl = fullUrl.Substring(0, fullUrl.IndexOf(
          context.HttpContext.Request.ApplicationPath));
        return String.Format("{0}{1}/CodeXRC/{2}", baseUrl,
          context.HttpContext.Request.ApplicationPath, projectName);
    }

    public static string BuildFolderLink(ControllerContext context,
                                         string projectName,
                                         string folderName)
    {
        // Generate the link (remember HATEOAS)
        string fullUrl = context.HttpContext.Request.Url.ToString();
        string baseUrl = fullUrl.Substring(0, fullUrl.IndexOf(
          context.HttpContext.Request.ApplicationPath));
        return String.Format("{0}{1}/CodeXRC/{2}/{3}", baseUrl,
          context.HttpContext.Request.ApplicationPath,
          projectName, folderName);
    }

    public static string BuildFileLink(ControllerContext context,
                                       string projectName,
                                       string folderName,
                                       string fileExtension,
                                       string fileName)
    {
        // Generate the link (remember HATEOAS)
        string fullUrl = context.HttpContext.Request.Url.ToString();
        string baseUrl = fullUrl.Substring(0, fullUrl.IndexOf(
            context.HttpContext.Request.ApplicationPath));
        return String.Format("{0}{1}/CodeXRC/{2}/{3}/{4}/{5}", baseUrl,
          context.HttpContext.Request.ApplicationPath, projectName,
          folderName, fileExtension, fileName);
    }
}
```

The link builder class simply encapsulates the logic in a single place that's necessary to build valid URIs for the various resources.

Creating Resources with XML

The only representation the CodeXRC service accepts for creating new resources is XML, and the CodeXRCPutService ExecuteResult method code is shown in Listing 7.7.

LISTING 7.7: CodeXRCPutService ExecuteResult **method**

```
public override void ExecuteResult(ControllerContext context)
{
    // Test the user's credentials
    if (context.HttpContext.User.IsInRole("Insert"))
    {
        // We'll accept only XML for creating/updating a
        // resource. We could accept JSON easily, but this
        // is how you'd limit inputs to a specific type.
        if (context.HttpContext.Request.ContentType.ToLower() ==
            "text/xml")
        {
            // Create the indicated resource
            CreateResource(context);
        }
        else
        {
            // Wasn't XML...
            _aux.RenderErrorNotAcceptablePut(context);
        }
    }
    else
    {
        // User forbidden
        _aux.RenderErrorForbidden(context);
    }
}
```

The ExecuteResult in this case checks for the appropriate role as well as XML as the content type, but only to return an error if the indicated type isn't appropriate. Therefore, there is only one "create resource" method, which is shown in Listing 7.8.

LISTING 7.8: CodeXRCPutService CreateResource **method**

```
private void CreateResource(ControllerContext context)
{
    // Pull the user's ID. This works here since we're using
    // the SQL-based membership provider.
    MembershipUser user =
```

continues

LISTING 7.8: Continued

```
        Membership.GetUser(context.HttpContext.User.Identity.Name);
    Guid ownerID = (Guid)user.ProviderUserKey;

    context.HttpContext.Response.ContentType = "text/html";
    switch (_directives.Count())
    {
        case 0:
        default:
            // Create a project for user (will be a specific project):
            // http://{host}/{vdir}/CodeXRC
            CreateProject(context, ownerID);
            break;

        case 1:
            // Create specific project for user (all child folders
            // and files):
            // http://{host}/{vdir}/CodeXRC/{project}
            CreateProject(context, ownerID, _directives[0]);
            break;

        case 2:
            // Delete specific folder (all child folders and files):
            // http://{host}/{vdir}/CodeXRC/{project}/{folder}
            CreateFolder(context, ownerID, _directives[0],
              _directives[1]);
            break;

        case 3:
            // Delete files by extension in specified folder:
            // http://{host}/{vdir}/CodeXRC/{project}/{folder}/{ext}
            CreateFileByType(context, ownerID, _directives[0],
              _directives[1], _directives[2]);
            break;

        case 4:
            // Delete specific file:
            // http://{host}/{vdir}/CodeXRC/{proj}/{folder}/{ext}/{file}
            CreateFile(context, ownerID, _directives[0], _directives[1],
              _directives[3] + "." + _directives[2]);
            break;
    }
}
```

The code in Listing 7.8 is somewhat similar to the code for retrieving a resource representation in Listing 7.5. The URI is examined and the appropriate resource is created. Of course, there is no need to return a content length, so that code is missing from Listing 7.8. The code to handle HTTP DELETE is similar to the code shown in Listing 7.8, so I won't show that here either.

Returning Error Information

In the preceding chapter, error information was returned according to the application's error handling configuration. For this service, I chose to return explicit error information as HTML I create at the point where the exception is caught. The CodeXRCAuxServices class provides several error response methods, with an example being the HTTP 403 (Forbidden) response shown in Listing 7.9.

LISTING 7.9: The CodeXRCAuxServices RenderErrorForbidden method

```
public void RenderErrorForbidden(ControllerContext context)
{
    context.HttpContext.Response.StatusCode =
      (Int32)HttpStatusCode.Forbidden;
    context.HttpContext.Response.ContentType = "text/html";
    using (StreamWriter wtr =
    new StreamWriter((Stream)context.HttpContext.Items["OutputStream"]))
    {
        StringBuilder sb = new StringBuilder();
        sb.Append("<html><head><title>CodeXRC</title></head><body>");
        sb.Append("You are not authorized to access the resource you ");
        sb.Append("requested.<br/></body><html>");
        wtr.WriteLine(sb.ToString());
        wtr.Flush();
        wtr.Close();
    }
}
```

Other errors are handled in a similar manner.

The CodeXRC Data Access Layer

The service's data access is provided by the CodeXRCDataAccess class. I personally generally prefer to provide data access service through an interface and use a strategy pattern to load the appropriate data access component, but here I keep the example simple and just deal with data access directly.

Listing 7.10 contains the data access code used to read the database and return all the user's projects.

LISTING 7.10: The CodeXRCDataAccess ListProjects **method**

```
public List<ProjectDTO>
  ListProjects(ControllerContext context, Guid ownerID)
{
    // Retrieve all projects
    CodeXRCDataClassesDataContext dataContext =
      new CodeXRCDataClassesDataContext();
    var projectQuery = from p in dataContext.Projects
        orderby p.ProjectID
        where p.OwnerID == ownerID
        select p;
    List<ProjectDTO> projects = new List<ProjectDTO>();
    foreach (var project in projectQuery)
    {
        // Create the new project item
        ProjectDTO projectItem = new ProjectDTO(project);
        projectItem.Link = CodeXRCLinkBuilder.BuildProjectLink(
          context, project.DisplayName);
        projects.Add(projectItem);
    }
    return projects;
}
```

As you can see from Listing 7.10, I make heavy use of LINQ to SQL, and you'll find this throughout the data access code. The LINQ to SQL context is shown in Figure 7.5.

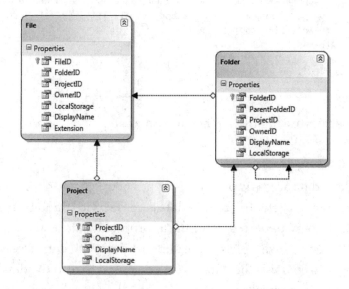

FIGURE 7.5: The CodeXRC **LINQ data context**

The foreign keys shown in Figure 7.5 make it easier to query for specific entities. The data access code also creates the folders and files, and when it does, it stores the local directory or file paths in the LocalStorage column for later recall. The service stores all folders and files within the App_Data sub-directory, but you could easily change this if you prefer. I selected it simply because the service didn't require any changes to file system permissions to read, write, and delete files in that location.

The data is conveyed to the client using data transfer objects (DTO). I've shown the ProjectDTO in Listing 7.11, but the other DTOs are similar.

LISTING 7.11: The project data transfer object

```
[DataContract(Namespace = "http://www.endurasoft.com/REST.NET/",
➡ Name="Project")]
public class ProjectDTO
{
    public ProjectDTO()
    {
    }

    public ProjectDTO(Project dbProject) :
        this()
    {
        // Copy properties
        this.ProjectID = dbProject.ProjectID;
        this.DisplayName = dbProject.DisplayName;
    }

    public ProjectDTO(Project dbProject, FolderDTO[] folders) :
        this(dbProject)
    {
        // Copy folders
        this.Folders = folders;
    }

    [DataMember]
    public Int32 ProjectID { get; set; }

    [DataMember]
    public string DisplayName { get; set; }

    [DataMember(IsRequired = false)]
    public string Link { get; set; }

    [DataMember(IsRequired = false)]
    public FolderDTO[] Folders { get; set; }
}
```

Each DTO provides several constructors, including a copy constructor that accepts the corresponding LINQ entity. (Note that another way to approach this is to create extension methods and keep the DTOs in a separate assembly, which has advantages from a code-separation standpoint, and the DTOs wouldn't have to reference LINQ.) The client has similar DTOs I created using the same technique described in the preceding chapter—I queried the service for the appropriate XML and used `xsd.exe` to create a corresponding C# class. I then removed the `XmlSerializer` attributes and replaced them with `DataContractSerializer` attributes. This is cheating a little since I had unfair knowledge as to how the XML was generated, but you could use either serializer as long as you faithfully re-create the XML the service requires.

The CodeXRC Service Client

Even though this service will return HTML, to demonstrate creation and deletion of projects, folders, and files, I created a Windows Forms client you can use to experiment with the various aspects of the service. The client won't exercise all aspects of the service. It only adds projects, whereas the service will accept folders and files as well (but keep in mind you'll need to provide correct foreign keys, which is typical of many RESTful services when updating resources).

The basic user interface you've already seen in Figure 7.4. The client also uses a similar authentication dialog box as the preceding chapter's client, so I won't repeat that as well. However, adding a new project does merit some description. The dialog box for this is shown in Figure 7.6.

The Create Project dialog box appears only when XML is selected as the content type, PUT is selected as the HTTP method, and you click the Execute button. Other content types for PUT display an error dialog box; and other HTTP methods don't involve resource creation, so no error is necessary.

After you provide a project name, you can select folders or files. If you choose to add folders, you'll be presented with the dialog box shown in Figure 7.7.

After you select a folder, the child folders and files will be added to the tree view control shown in the Create Project dialog box. From this tree control you can remove files and folders simply by selecting them and pressing the Delete key.

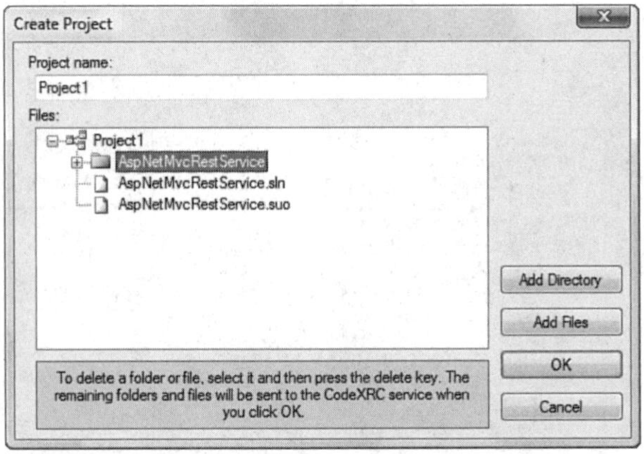

FIGURE 7.6: The CodeXRC client **Create Project dialog box**

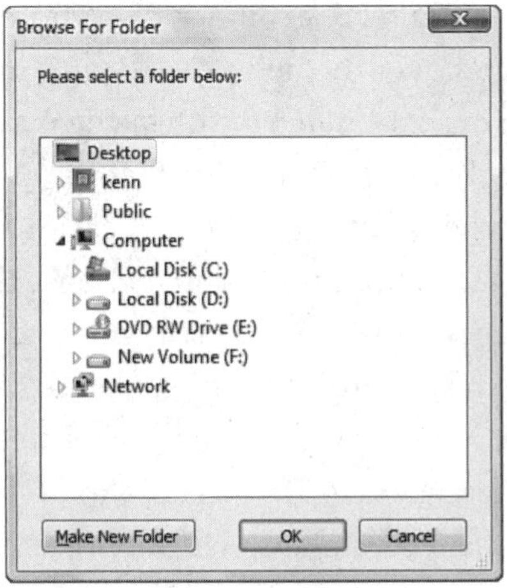

Figure 7.7: The CodeXRC client **folder browser dialog box**

If you instead decide to add files directly to the project, the client creates a virtual folder, with the same name as the project, and adds the files to that. The service doesn't add files directly to a project, but this is simply an implementation detail you could change fairly easily if you wanted. I kept this as a business rule simply to have the rule in play. My reasoning was that projects and folders aren't the same in the service I implemented even though a project is implemented as a folder on disk. Figure 7.8 shows the Create Project dialog box when files are added to the project directly.

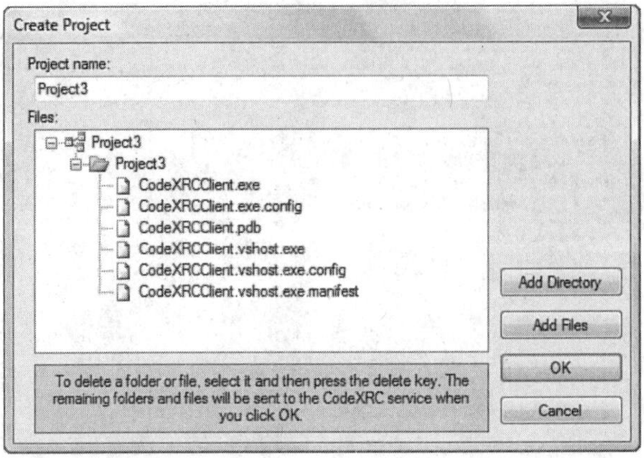

FIGURE 7.8: Adding files directly to a project

In all cases the files are read as binary files and converted into Base64 strings for transmission over the network. Base64, on average, introduces a 30% (or so) increase in size, but it's the only safe way to send binary information over a network using XML. The client will convert the files into Base64 and the service will convert them back into their original binary form for storage; but the client is limited in the sense that it cannot recall the files. I'll leave the implementation of that to you to complete, but the basic conversion logic is already present in the service itself. The service will return to the client the XML representation of a created project, but this is so you could cache the foreign keys if you chose to do so. The contents of the files are wiped from the representation to conserve bandwidth.

Where Are We?

This chapter introduced the ASP.NET MVC framework and how you could create classes based on `ActionResult` to handle RESTful actions and responses. The ASP.NET MVC framework is based on the model-view-controller design pattern, or more accurately on the contemporary front controller pattern. The actions you create are directly mapped to URIs you design and provide to the URL routing subsystem the framework provides. This is a bit different from traditional ASP.NET, in which URLs are mapped directly to disk-based files.

The MVC framework has the capability to differentiate controller actions based on HTTP method by judicious application of the `AcceptVerbs` attribute, and you can disambiguate the action method names using the `ActionName` attribute.

The service logic itself is considered model code. The model in MVC terms is where the data access and business logic for your Web application is properly placed. I elected not to use a view to generate the HTML the service returned, but you certainly could if you chose to do so.

It's at this point you might notice a pattern emerging. When working with pure ASP.NET, you need to provide quite a bit of infrastructure and "glue" logic. With the MVC framework, quite a bit of the infrastructure is provided for you. It's more a matter of understanding what the framework provides and how to best fit your service into that framework.

The next chapter, however, shows you how to use the Windows Communication Foundation (WCF) to implement RESTful services, and by using WCF you implement even less boilerplate infrastructure, allowing you to concentrate nearly entirely on the core service functionality. WCF is also very much more configurable, allowing you to tailor your service's behavior even after it has been deployed.

■8■

Building REST Services Using WCF

I F YOU HAVE EVER read any of the introductory material for Windows Communication Foundation (WCF), you know that a big reason for its existence is to facilitate convergence of messaging architectures. REST is a messaging architecture, so we should be able to use the WCF knowledge that we have been accumulating since .NET 3.0 shipped in November 2006 to build RESTful services. This chapter looks at the classes within WCF 3.5, SP1 and later, that allow us to build XML, JSON, RSS, ATOM, and ADO.NET Data Services endpoints.

WCF: The Swiss Army Knife of Messaging

Windows Communication Foundation really is the "Swiss Army Knife" of messaging. It works with an unlimited number of transports, encoding formats, and protocols. WCF supports different messaging styles, such as one way, simplex, and duplex. Out of the box, WCF handles a wide array of transports, including TCP/IP, Microsoft Message Queue (MSMQ), HTTP/S, Microsoft Exchange, PeerNet, and named pipes. WCF supports all other transports via extensibility mechanisms built into the class library, allowing you to add support for your favorite transport if not already present.

WCF unifies the programming model to consume messages sent over all of these different mechanisms through a common set of abstractions known as "ABC": address, binding, and contract. You will need to have a moderate understanding of the overall model and architecture to understand how WCF supports RESTful applications. And to help with that, in this chapter we will cover a range of topics pertinent to WCF and how to use it to build REST applications. This chapter begins by covering the basics common to any application that uses WCF by showing how to build the Photo Service originally presented in Chapter 3, "Desktop Client Operations," and Chapter 4, "Web Client Operations." We will then move to the REST-specific features in WCF. We'll finish the chapter by examining ADO.NET Data Services—a specific application of WCF REST.

WCF is capable of communications using various messaging patterns as opposed to strictly conventional request/response messaging. It also supports a number of WS-* protocols to ensure reliability and security of messaging in a platform-agonistic manner. WCF comes with a number of security mechanisms baked in as well. Encryption, nonrepudiation, integration with transport-level security, certificates, and Windows authentication are all available.

If you need to know intimate details of WCF inner workings or all the ways you might use it, you need to buy several books on WCF (not a single one tells the whole story, but several do a good job with the topics they do cover). The library is vast and complex. This chapter takes a myopic view, looking only at those parts that are needed to build RESTful applications. As a result, the chapter contains reduced detail and even intentionally omits some important subjects, simply due to space. Juval Lowy, Michelle Bustamante, and Justin Smith have all written great books covering different aspects of WCF. If you need to know what was left out here, add these books to your bookshelf.

WCF: The Basics

Everyone who teaches WCF starts out with an explanation of "ABC": address, binding, and contract. These three concepts are important to WCF because they are important to all messaging systems. Anytime an application needs to send data to another computer, that application needs to know where to send the data, how to send the data, and how to format that data. For example, let's take a look at the combination of things you need to do in order to access the Web page coming from http://www.scottseely.com.

From the address, we know that we send the message to the server identified as www.scottseely.com. The http:// portion, called the *scheme*, informs us that we will use the TCP/IP transmission protocol combined with the HTTP application protocol. Finally, the choice of HTTP declares a contract (or expectations and commitments) of sorts. HTTP compliance means that the message will contain a verb in the set {DELETE, GET, HEAD, POST, PUT}, and some set of headers. If the Content-Length header is set, that means that the request message contains some information beyond the HTTP headers. We also know that the response will come back over the TCP/IP, and have similar HTTP headers, and the Content-Length will indicate the size of any information contained in the response. The following shows the headers from the sample request as captured and formatted by Firebug:

```
Host: www.scottseely.com
User-Agent: Mozilla/5.0 (Windows; U; Windows NT 6.0; en-US; rv:1.9.0.3)
➥Gecko/2008092417 Firefox/3.0.3 (.NET CLR 3.5.30729)
Accept: text/html,application/xhtml+xml,application/xml;q=0.9,*/*;q=0.8
Accept-Language: en-us,en;q=0.5
Accept-Encoding: gzip,deflate
Accept-Charset: ISO-8859-1,utf-8;q=0.7,*;q=0.7
Keep-Alive: 300
Connection: keep-alive
Cache-Control: max-age=0
```

HTTP is an application-level protocol, as are some of the other protocols, such as Microsoft Message Queue (MSMQ), that are supported by WCF. WCF tries to work around a set of issues that developers have whenever they deploy an application that communicates with other applications. Those other applications can be on the same machine, on an intranet, or on the Internet. Prior to WCF, each of those applications would require developers to use a different set of skills depending on how messages came into the system. For example, a developer accepting messages over bare TCP/IP sockets has to know how to accept a connection, read the information in the message, interpret/process the information, and then return a proper response. If the application needs to also use MSMQ for other messages, the developer uses an entirely different set of programming interfaces to receive and process messages from the queue. Having this broad set of skills greatly limits the number of people who can build multiprotocol distributed applications. WCF opens this door much wider to application developers by significantly abstracting away much of the complexity.

Microsoft made a number of interesting choices to allow the multiprotocol vision to come together. First, many of the .NET messaging stacks are now united under one group. Until .NET 2.0 shipped, the COM+/ Enterprise Services, MSMQ, RPC, System.Net, Transactions, ASMX, and .NET Remoting teams all worked together to produce early forms of WCF (remember *Indigo*?). Today these teams work together with a unified vision, which is to enable developers to learn a single methodology to send and receive messages. This allows the application to specify the set of protocols to be used based on the required messaging patterns and protocols. For example, internal partners could use TCP/IP to enable connectivity. External partners would get HTTP-based connection options. But the WCF developers would write code in a standardized way to use both communication technologies.

With the WCF's ABC abstraction, address and binding can be defined outside of the service implementation. The developer only needs to think about C, the contract. The developer begins by defining an interface that indicates the information they expect to receive as well as the responses, if any, that go back out.

A WCF Service

We will explore how WCF can be used to develop a RESTful Web service by building the `ImageManager` service, consumed by the clients in Chapters 3 ("Desktop Client Operations") and 4 ("Web Client Operations"). For your reference, the `ImageItem`, used to represent the pictures from the service, is repeated in Listing 8.1. If you need a refresher on the meaning of the attributes contained here, refer to Chapter 3, where I discuss the `DataContract-Serializer`.

LISTING 8.1: The `ImageItem` class

```
[DataContract(Namespace = "http://www.scottseely.com/RESTBook/2008")]
public class ImageItem
{
    public ImageItem() { }

    [DataMember]
    public string ImageUrl { get; set; }

    [DataMember]
    public Guid ImageId { get; set; }

    [DataMember]
    public string Description { get; set; }

    [DataMember]
    public string Caption { get; set; }

    [DataMember]
    public bool PublicImage { get; set; }

    [DataMember]
    public string UserName { get; set; }

    [DataMember]
    public byte[] ImageBytes { get; set; }
}
```

At this point we need to think about the set of operations that the `Image-Manager` service needs to support. We want a mechanism to provide a list of `ImageItem` objects by user, to retrieve a single `ImageItem` by its identifier, and mechanisms to create, update, and delete `ImageItem` resources. Listing 8.2 provides you with an interface that supports these mechanisms.

LISTING 8.2: `IImageService` interface

```
public interface IImageManager
{
    Guid AddImage(ImageItem item);

    ImageItem GetImage(string imageId);

    ImageItem[] GetImagesForUser(string username);

    void UpdateImage(ImageItem item, string imageId);

    void DeleteImage(string imageId);
}
```

From here, it is a simple matter to create a class implementing the IImageManager interface. Using this interface definition, code within your application can manipulate any object that implements the IImageManager interface. So what does WCF add to the mix to create a service?

WCF adds a declarative model that uses classes and interfaces as contract declarations. WCF then uses reflection to determine what you, the developer, declared about how a given implementation class will look when it plays the role of WCF service. When a class is exposed as a WCF service, code living outside the application and outside the computer can instantiate and invoke methods on that class. Using System.ServiceModel. ServiceContractAttribute, a developer declares which interfaces represent WCF contracts. The developer then declares which methods on that interface can be called when an address and binding are associated with the interface by applying the System.ServiceModel.OperationContract-Attribute. This collection of methods then forms the contract for the interface. The interpretation and representation of that contract depends on how the service is exposed—the binding presents the contract as appropriate.

ServiceContractAttribute allows the developer to declare some contract items:

- ConfigurationName: This allows for the contract to be identified in the app.config or web.config file using a name identified by the developer. By default, the ConfigurationName is set to the Type.FullName.
- Namespace: This allows for the developer to specify the namespace used when the contract appears in a Web Services Description Language (WSDL) document. This namespace also sets the default namespace for any incoming messages. When JavaScript Object Notation (JSON) is used in conjunction with a RESTful service, it will represent part of the proxy class name when the proxy JavaScript is issued to the client.

The OperationContractAttribute also has various settings. Because none of these other settings is actually useful for someone developing

RESTful Web services, I will skip presenting them here. With these attributes, we can mark up the `IImageService` interface so that WCF knows exactly how to expose the contract as a service. Listing 8.3 shows the updated interface.

LISTING 8.3: `IImageManager` with `ServiceContract` and `OperationContract`

```
[ServiceContract(Namespace = "http://www.scottseely.com/RESTBook/2008")]
public interface IImageManager
{
    [OperationContract]
    Guid AddImage(ImageItem item);

    [OperationContract]
    ImageItem GetImage(string imageId);

    [OperationContract]
    ImageItem[] GetImagesForUser(string username);

    [OperationContract]
    void UpdateImage(ImageItem item, string imageId);

    [OperationContract]
    void DeleteImage(string imageId);
}
```

At this point, we have a generic interface that describes how you send and receive messages to a class that implements the `IImageManager` interface. So far, I have not shown you anything that helps or hinders you from making the interface RESTful. We'll look at the components that help REST services work next.

WCF Takes a REST

The contract definition tells WCF which set of methods have been exposed to external callers. This contract definition has a natural transformation to WS-* style messaging without any extra adornment. This is to be expected because WCF focuses on WS-* messaging first. Don't believe me? Well, consider this: The entire WCF framework focuses around one unit of communication, `System.ServiceModel.Channels.Message`. This object has a property, Version, of type System.ServiceModel.Channels.Message-Version, that communicates the version of the message being processed by the WCF infrastructure and any related developer code. MessageVersion has one value that means *not* WS-*, None, and six values indicating the permutation of SOAP envelope and WS-Addressing in use by the message.

To communicate using REST, an application uses a MessageVersion of None to get the job done. To invoke a method on the interface using the WS-* mechanisms, one passes an HTTP header or WS-Addressing SOAP header. WCF then reads this information to decide which OperationContract to call. REST services do not have SOAP headers. Instead, they have HTTP methods and URLs. What we need is some mechanism to match an HTTP method and a URL to a method on the class implementing the service. With .NET 3.5 and later, the WCF team added a bunch of code to make this simple for us and packaged that functionality in an assembly named System.ServiceModel.Web. This section is about those classes and how they are used. But in this section we will also look at how to integrate these features with ASP.NET security, and we'll close by showing how to hide the fact that part of the service endpoint is a WCF service.

Putting Together a WCF REST Stack

We talked earlier about these things called *bindings*. In WCF, System.ServiceModel.Channels.Binding represents the objects that receive a message. Each Binding creates a stack of System.ServiceModel.Channels.Channel. At a minimum, the Binding must contain a System.ServiceModel.Channels.TransportBindingElement. Normally, a Binding will also contain a piece that knows how to read, write, and transform a Message between an array of bytes and a Message object: a System.ServiceModel.Channels.MessageEncodingBindingElement. If no encoding is configured, a protocol-specific default encoding will be used. The TransportBindingElement creates something capable of sending or receiving a Message.

For RESTful services, WCF provides a binding named System.ServiceModel.WebHttpBinding. This binding includes pieces that know how to read and write information using the HTTP and HTTPS transports, as well as encode messages suitable for use with HTTP. We have seen previously in the book that two serialization formats are especially important:

XML and JSON. Our service will also need to process large messages, which means we need to customize the WebHttpBinding binding and behavior. The following configuration file snippet accomplishes this task for us:

```
<system.serviceModel>
    <serviceHostingEnvironment aspNetCompatibilityEnabled="true" />
    <bindings>
        <webHttpBinding>
            <binding name="PhotoBinding" maxReceivedMessageSize="655360">
                <readerQuotas maxArrayLength="655360" />
                <security mode="None">
                    <transport clientCredentialType="None" />
                </security>
            </binding>
        </webHttpBinding>
    </bindings>
    <behaviors>
        <endpointBehaviors>
            <behavior name="httpBehavior">
                <webHttp />
            </behavior>
        </endpointBehaviors>
    </behaviors>
    <services>
        <service name="PhotoWeb.ImageManager">
            <endpoint address="" behaviorConfiguration="httpBehavior"
            binding="webHttpBinding" bindingConfiguration="PhotoBinding"
            contract="PhotoWeb.IImageManager" />
        </service>
    </services>
</system.serviceModel>
```

WebHttpBinding and its related components need a few more pieces of information in order to properly dispatch HTTP requests to the right methods of your service. Specifically, WebHttpBinding needs to know the HTTP verb and service path to use when dispatching an incoming HTTP request to a specific method. Two attributes provide this functionality: System. ServiceModel.Web.WebGetAttribute and System.ServiceModel.Web.Web InvokeAttribute. The WebGetAttribute handles the common case of providing data in response to an HTTP GET. Typical Web page requests are more than 99% GET requests (based on an informal survey of sites I regularly visit and the results shown in Firebug). To a user of these attributes, the only difference between the two is that WebInvokeAttribute has an extra property: System.String Method. This string lets you specify which HTTP method, DELETE, GET, HEAD, POST, or PUT, to use when dispatching an incoming HTTP request to code. Being able to dispatch based on HTTP method and URL allows REST to work. These two attributes share the following properties:

- System.ServiceModel.Web.WebMessageBodyStyle BodyStyle: By default, XML responses are BodyStyle.Wrapped. That means that the request and response will have a root XML element that maps to the name of the method being called. Other options are

  - BodyStyle.WrappedRequest: The extra element appears only on the request.

  - BodyStyle.WrappedResponse: The extra element appears only on the response.

  - BodyStyle.Bare: No extra element appears on the request or response, which is what you'll use for RESTful implementations most of the time.

- System.ServiceModel.Web.WebMessageFormat RequestFormat: This allows the developer to state whether the request will be formatted as XML or JSON. The WebMessageFormat enumeration has two self-explanatory values: Xml and Json. By default, this property is set to WebMessageFormat.Xml.

- System.ServiceModel.Web.WebMessageFormat ResponseFormat: Take the previous bullet and replace *request* with *response.*

- System.String UriTemplate: This is the URI to use and parse when mapping a request to a method. This also allows simple parameters to be passed via the HTTP URL. For example, a method signature of public System.String GetData(System.Int someNum, System.String someString) would use a UriTemplate of /getData/ {someNum}/{someString}. Data types that do not have a simple string representation, such as a row in a database table, must be passed as an entity body in an HTTP request using an HTTP PUT or HTTP POST.

When creating a Web service that supports a RESTful representation, you can put the REST information directly on the interface definition or on the implementation. I prefer to keep the REST information away from the service definition. The setup of the REST endpoint tends to be tightly coupled to the implementation, and normally I would prefer to place the REST information directly on the implementation. However, we also need to handle a couple of specialized issues such as honoring HEAD requests, which is very HTTP-specific. Looking back at the interface we need to implement, then, how should we attribute the IImageManager interface on a RESTful endpoint? Whenever we retrieve, update, or delete an existing resource, we access one URL using a different HTTP method: GET for retrieve, PUT for update, and DELETE for a delete. When we're retrieving the list of images, the list is a new resource, unique per user. With this thought in mind, we know that we need to declare two URLs:

1. /Images/{userId}: Lists of ImageItems for a specific user. At this URL, we get the list of images and upload new images. This tells us that this URL accepts a GET, HEAD, and POST method.

2. /Image/{imageId}: The URL identifying an individual ImageItem resource. The actual identifier for an image is decided after the upload occurs. This URL allows code to access only existing resources, meaning we need to support only GET, POST, DELETE, and HEAD.

To handle the HEAD methods, the IImageManager interface requires two new methods: GetImageHead and GetImagesForUserHead. For both of these, we will want identical UriTemplates and identical argument lists. Listing 8.4 shows the updated interface.

LISTING 8.4: IImageManager with RESTful attributes

```
[ServiceContract(Namespace = "http://www.scottseely.com/RESTBook/2008")]
public interface IImageManager
{
    [OperationContract]
    [WebInvoke(Method = "POST",
        BodyStyle = WebMessageBodyStyle.Bare,
```

continues

```
        UriTemplate = "/Images/")]
    Guid AddImage(ImageItem item);

    [OperationContract]
    [WebInvoke(Method = "DELETE",
        BodyStyle = WebMessageBodyStyle.Bare,
        UriTemplate = "/Image/{imageId}")]
    void DeleteImage(string imageId);

    [OperationContract]
    [WebGet(BodyStyle = WebMessageBodyStyle.Bare,
        UriTemplate = "/Image/{imageId}")]
    ImageItem GetImage(string imageId);

    [OperationContract]
    [WebInvoke(Method = "HEAD",
        BodyStyle = WebMessageBodyStyle.Bare,
        UriTemplate = "/Image/{imageId}")]
    ImageItem GetImageHead(string imageId);

    [OperationContract]
    [WebGet(BodyStyle = WebMessageBodyStyle.Bare,
        UriTemplate = "/Images/{username}")]
    ImageItem[] GetImagesForUser(string username);

    [OperationContract]
    [WebInvoke(Method = "HEAD",
        BodyStyle = WebMessageBodyStyle.Bare,
        UriTemplate = "/Images/{username}")]
    ImageItem[] GetImagesForUserHead(string username);

    [OperationContract]
    [WebInvoke(Method = "PUT",
        BodyStyle = WebMessageBodyStyle.Bare,
        UriTemplate = "/Image/{imageId}")]
    void UpdateImage(ImageItem item, string imageId);
}
```

Listing 8.5 demonstrates a typical HEAD request. In it the code calls the actual method that would be executed via a GET. In the example, we are looking at the HEAD request for /Image/{imageId}. The code writes the response to a stream, checks the length of the stream, and updates the response. We have to set the HTTP Content-Length header on the HttpContext.Current.Response.Headers, and to help with this, WebOperationContext.Current.OutgoingResponse has a ContentLength property.

If you assign this value but leave the response stream empty, the infrastructure will override any values set with zero. You must explicitly set the `StatusCode` on the `WebOperationContext.Current.OutgoingResponse` when implementing a method with a void return type.

LISTING 8.5: `GetImageHead` **implementation**

```
public ImageItem[] GetImagesForUserHead(string username)
{
    ImageItem[] imageToReturn = GetImagesForUser(username);
    if (imageToReturn == null)
    {
        WebOperationContext.Current.OutgoingResponse.StatusCode =
            HttpStatusCode.NotFound;
    }
    else
    {
        WebOperationContext.Current.OutgoingResponse.SuppressEntityBody
            = false;
    }

    return imageToReturn;
}
```

The `WebOperationContext` class is new and deserves a bit more explanation. The type has a `Current` property that retrieves the `WebOperationContext` with all members configured. It integrates with the `System.SeviceModel.OperationContext` available from all `OperationContract` methods. The `WebOperationContext` acknowledges that the exchange will happen over HTTP and provides easy access to all the HTTP information you might need in your code. In a sense, it's the WCF counterpart to ASP.NET's `HttpContext`. Finally, to do hard things like handle a HEAD request, you let the infrastructure do all the work for you by returning something, then setting the `OutgoingResponse.SuppressEntityBody` property to `true` to prevent the entity body information from actually being returned to the caller. The headers will remain just as if the response entity body contained information.

Emitting a JavaScript File

At times, you will want to create something with client-side JavaScript by automatically creating all the `XMLHttpRequest` (XHR) and JSON-related code for your service's client. As a general rule, the easiest way to do this is to map all the ServiceContract-related methods to respond to XHR via the following:

```
[WebInvoke(Method = "POST")]
```

Isn't forcing all REST calls to use HTTP POST a bit Draconian? Perhaps. Is this REST? No. But it's done this way to prevent cross-site scripting attacks, as covered in Chapter 4. It's a small price to pay for more secure Asynchronous JavaScript and XML (AJAX) operations.

After your ServiceContract is attributed to properly respond to POST messages everywhere, you need to host the service so that all the JSON operations can happen. Here, you can choose to either configure your service's bindings and behaviors by hand or force WCF to do it for you. Since your goal is to provide your service clients with the JavaScript proxy file with a minimal amount of work, let WCF handle the configuration for you. In the .svc file exposing your service endpoint, edit the markup so that the Factory attribute points to the WebScriptServiceHostFactory, like so (shown in bold font for emphasis):

```
<%@ ServiceHost Language="C#" Service="PhotoWeb.JsonImageManager"
    Factory="System.ServiceModel.Activation.WebScriptServiceHostFactory"
    CodeBehind="JsonImageManager.svc.cs" %>
```

The Factory attribute is available in every .svc file. By default, it points to System.ServiceModel.Activation.ServiceHostFactory. ServiceHostFactory follows the normal WCF configuration process using web.config. WebScriptServiceHostFactory is a bit different: No configuration is needed and it adds the correct information automatically. All endpoints accept JSON encoded data and, when accessing [service address].svc/js or jsdebug, the service endpoint will generate a JavaScript proxy file for your clients. As you might recall, we examined the output and interaction in Chapter 4, in the section "Moving Up a Level: WCF Provided JavaScript/AJAX."

> **■ NOTE**
>
> It's easy to confuse `WebScriptServiceHostFactory` with the similarly-named `WebServiceHostFactory`. Both are designed for creating REST-ful WCF endpoints. However, only `WebScriptServiceHostFactory` enables JavaScript clients to request the proxy and work with your service in an AJAX fashion. `WebServiceHostFactory`, while RESTful and configuration-free (unless you need to tailor the default configuration), is not designed to create the JavaScript proxy. Aside from this, both service factories are functionally equivalent.

Integrating with ASP.NET and ASP.NET Security

In Chapter 6, "Building REST Services Using IIS and ASP.NET," we covered ASP.NET security and introduced some code to integrate the ASP.NET model with any request. If you need a refresher, take a look at the section "Securing the Service." For WCF to take advantage of access to `HttpContext.User` as well as the membership services, we need to apply an explicit dependency on ASP.NET. Making a dependency on ASP.NET requires two steps:

1. Declare a dependency to ASP.NET in your code. We do this by applying the `AspNetCompatibilityRequirementsAttribute` from the `System.ServiceModel.Activation` namespace and setting the `RequirementsMode` property to `AspNetCompatibilityRequirements-Mode.Required`.

2. Instruct the runtime to make the `System.Web.HttpContext` available to WCF services and run all requests through the HTTP pipeline. This is done through configuration. Be sure to set the `/system.serviceModel/serviceHostingEnvironment` properly:

```
<serviceHostingEnvironment aspNetCompatibilityEnabled="true" />
```

> **■ NOTE**
>
> In Chapter 5, "IIS and ASP.NET Internals and Instrumentation," you saw how the IIS application pipeline processed HTTP requests. However, WCF in its native form has nothing to do with ASP.NET request processing. They're two completely separate processes. Therefore, it probably isn't surprising to find you can't just access ASP.NET-based objects like `HttpContext` from your WCF service. When the ASP.NET compatibility attribute and configuration file setting are applied, the WCF service is routed through ASP.NET, at which time intrinsic ASP.NET objects are available for use.

Our service, `ImageManager`, implements `IImageManager`. The class definition declares its dependency on ASP.NET like so:

```
[AspNetCompatibilityRequirements(RequirementsMode =
    AspNetCompatibilityRequirementsMode.Required)]
public class ImageManager : IImageManager
```

With that, we can reuse the authentication code and ASP.NET principles discussed in Chapter 6. The `ImageManager` has a very simple security model. Only authenticated users may retrieve information. If the current user is requesting her own images, the user can see and change everything associated with her identity. If the user is asking for the pictures from another identity, only public images are returned. Listing 8.6 shows how this simple mechanism works in `GetImagesForUser`.

LISTING 8.6: `ImageManager.GetImagesForUser` **method implementation**

```
public ImageItem[] GetImagesForUser(string username)
{
    List<ImageItem> retval = new List<ImageItem>();
    IEnumerable<Image> images = null;
    using (PhotoWebDbDataContext dataContext =
        new PhotoWebDbDataContext())
    {
        if (string.Equals(HttpContext.Current.User.Identity.Name,
            username, StringComparison.Ordinal))
        {
            // Return all images for the user.
            images = from image in dataContext.Images
                        where
                            image.UserName == username
```

```
                    select image;
        }
        else
        {
            // Only return public images for the user.
            images = from image in dataContext.Images
                        where
                            image.UserName == username &&
                            image.PublicImage
                        select image;
        }
        // Format the image URL to be relative to the current
        // application.
        string baseUrl = string.Format("http://{0}{1}/{2}",
            HttpContext.Current.Request.Url.Authority,
            HttpContext.Current.Request.ApplicationPath,
            "ImageHandler.ashx");
        foreach (var image in images)
        {
            ImageItem imageItem = Utility.ConvertImage(image);
            imageItem.ImageUrl = string.Format("{0}/{1}", baseUrl,
                image.ImageId.ToString("D"));
            retval.Add(imageItem);
        }
    }
    if (retval.Count == 0)
    {
        WebOperationContext.Current.OutgoingResponse.StatusCode =
            System.Net.HttpStatusCode.NotFound;
    }

    return retval.ToArray();
}
```

I had a specific reason for using HttpContext to discover request information instead of using WCF's WebOperationContext. The HttpContext
will tell you exactly how the Web application was accessed. A machine on
a network is typically accessed using one of three machine names: the
actual machine name (requires mapping to an IP address), the machine's IP
address, and localhost, which is self-referencing. The WebOperationContext normalizes all requests to the local machine name. This can have interesting side effects. In my case, the difference in the normalized machine
identity delivered by WebOperationContext versus the value the user provided as reported by HttpContext created photo URIs that weren't quite
what I'd intended. (In fact, the resulting IP address lookup necessary for

each photo caused a noticeably slow response.) When creating URLs that link resources on the same machine, as is done here, I was able to create the proper URI only by using the `HttpContext`.

Adding A URL Rewriter

Some WCF developers dislike the fact that the WCF characteristics are present for all to see. They really dislike the embedded `.svc` extension present in WCF-based service URIs. For example, to obtain all images for the user named `sseely1`, the URI would appear like this:

```
http://localhost/PhotoWebCh8/ImageManager.svc/Images/sseely1
```

Ideally, we would rather provide the service client with something like this:

```
http://localhost/PhotoWebCh8/Images/sseely1
```

To do this, we need to add a *URL rewriter*. A URL rewriter is software that intercepts incoming requests and then formats them in a way that is understandable by the internal infrastructure. Externally, you might want nicely structured URLs. Internally, the Web application might understand only URLs containing ugly query strings. Rewrite modules bridge those two worlds—from memorable URLs to URLs acceptable to your application code.

As it happens, the IIS team released a URL Rewriter for IIS 7 after IIS 7 shipped. You can download this module from www.iis.net/extensions/URLRewrite. After it has been installed, your Web applications can each take advantage of the techniques I'm about to show you.

I've selected the site for this chapter, PhotoWebCh8, within the IIS Management Studio, as shown in Figure 8.1.

When you double-click on the URL Rewrite icon, you are presented with a window that shows existing rules and allows you to add new ones, as shown in Figure 8.2.

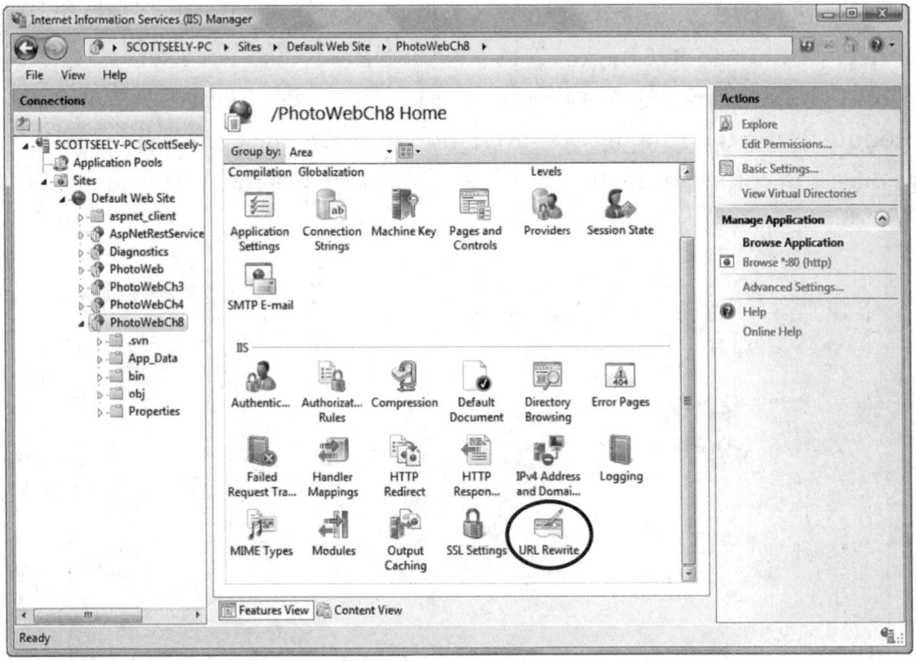

FIGURE 8.1: The IIS URL Rewrite configuration module

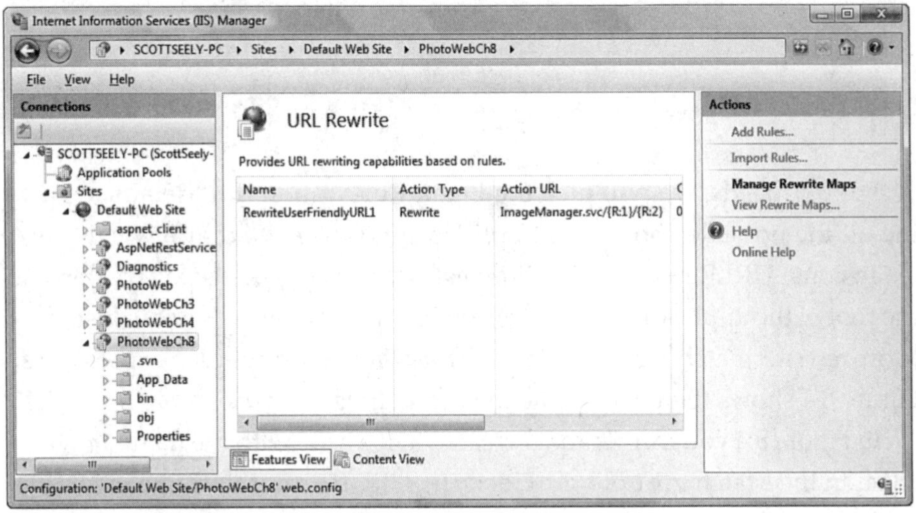

FIGURE 8.2: URL Rewrite rules

To map a URL your application might expect, typically one of the ugly variety mentioned in Chapter 2, to a clean URL, which your service client would probably prefer, you'll need to add a new rule to the URL rewriter module. From the rule view shown in Figure 8.2, click Add Rules in the upper-right corner to create a new rule. This activates the Add Rules selection dialog box, shown in Figure 8.3.

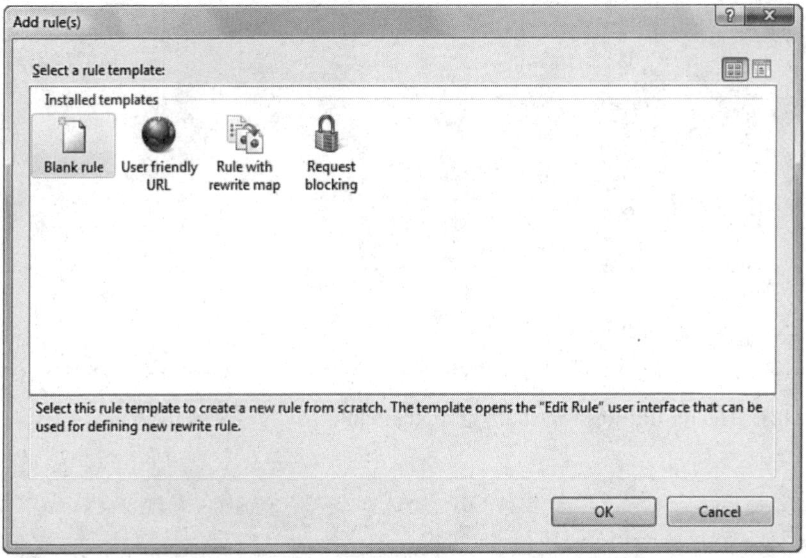

FIGURE 8.3: Rule type selection

For our needs, we will pick the Blank Rule option (full details regarding all the possible choices and options are documented at www.iis.net/extensions/URLRewrite). The simplest rewrite rule matches a pattern at the root of the application as well as wildcard parameters. You can also perform rewrite matching using JavaScript-compatible regular expressions. Figure 8.4 shows the rewrite rule to handle Images queries.

In Figure 8.4 you can see that I created a new rule with the name Images-Rule. In the Match group, I provided the URL rewriter with the incoming URL pattern I expect to see, or in other words, the nicely formatted URL my service clients will prefer. Any incoming URL that now matches the pattern {host}/Images/* will be mapped to the URL you see in the Action group, which is {host}/ImageManager.svc/Images/{R:1}. The {R:1} simply provides my application with anything following `Images` in the nicely formatted URL (anything mapped to *).With this modification to the application, we now support URLs of the form http://localhost/PhotoWebCh8/Images/sseely1.

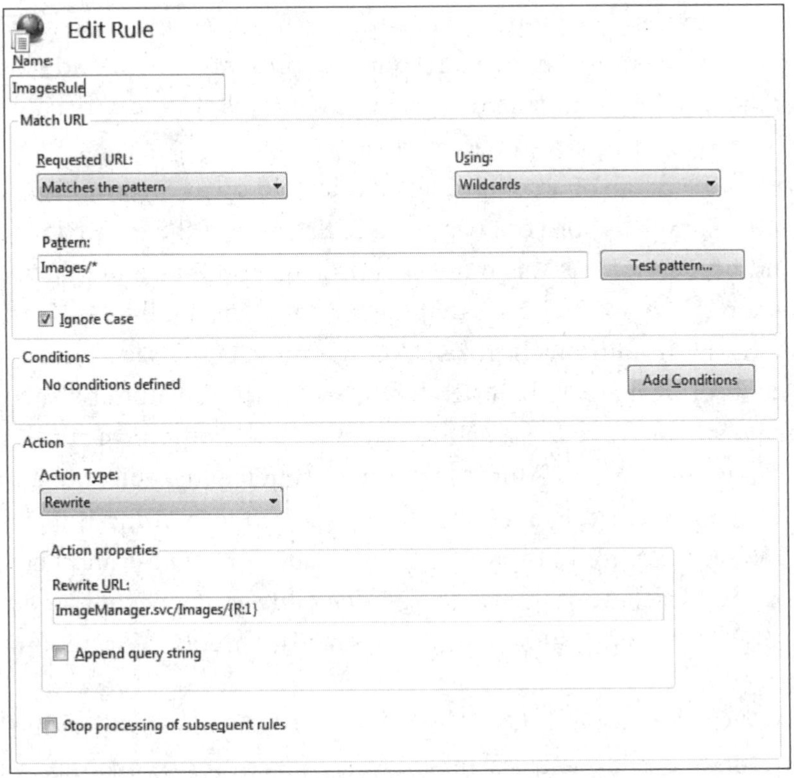

FIGURE 8.4: URL rewrite rule edit/creation

Feeding on WCF: Atom, AtomPub, and RSS Support

Every day, people all over the world share information and thoughts over the Internet. They do this via blog posts, posting information on wikis, publishing reports, and updating collections of images. Because these activities are so popular, the developer community has standard mechanisms for broadcasting information and for other computers to consume those broadcasts. A stream of updates is consumed via a *feed*—essentially a resource representation containing metadata regarding the information being published. To publish and consume feeds, two formats have gained the most popularity. The oldest is RDF Site Summary (RSS), which started life in March 1999 and evolved from there. RSS is also known as Really Simple Syndication as of version 2.0. With RSS, channels as well as items available in those channels convey resource representation metadata. The format itself is very simple and is primarily intended to support a public diary or feed of easily consumed media.

Atom is the name of a competing standard to do everything RSS does and more. Atom was born out of a need to fix some of the shortcomings of RSS, and because of this it is more descriptive as well as more flexible. A major shortcoming of RSS 2.0 is that the format is copyrighted by Harvard University and is fairly well frozen. Atom is an IETF standard and enjoys the benefits of working with the IETF processes, including the ability to easily update and improve the specification over time. For typical application usage, however, RSS and Atom are relatively interchangeable. Most of the time you will be creating a generic feed and then formatting it in RSS or Atom format as appropriate based on the request. *AtomPub* is another specification, building on Atom, which handles more sophisticated layouts of information including categorization, media definition information, and more.

The WCF Atom and RSS formatting classes all exist within the `System.ServiceModel.Web` assembly in the `System.ServiceModel.Syndication` namespace. The namespace has classes to fully support all the features of Atom and RSS and makes your job of providing formatted information to your service consumers much easier.

When working with feeds, you will typically work with an abstracted view of the Atom and RSS feeds. Then, your code will ask WCF to produce the feed format as requested by the client. Typically, services will produce Atom or RSS depending on a parameter named `format` or based on the last few characters of the URL. For example, Atom will usually be requested via a URL such as `example.com/SomeFeed.svc/[id]?format=atom` or `example.com/SomeFeed.svc/[id].atom`. RSS will follow a similar model—simply replace `atom` in the preceding example with `rss`.

When developing feeds, you typically use just a few simple types from the System.ServiceModel.Syndication namespace:

- SyndicationFeed: Represents a collection of items and categories. Within a feed, you can find lists of authors and contributors. Basic information about the feed, such as a title, description, and copyright, are also available to be set.

- SyndicationItem: Represents a feed item (blog post, media, and so forth). You can set the author and contributors for the item as well as a description, the content, and any links to view more details.

- SyndicationFeedFormatter: Takes a SyndicationFeed and formats the feed as appropriate. For us, this means formatting for RSS 1.0, RSS 2.0, or Atom 1.0.

To see how these classes work, let's add a new feature to our service. For each owner of a set of photos, let's allow them to publish their public photos as either an RSS 2.0 or an Atom 1.0 feed. We start by defining the ServiceContract as shown in Listing 8.7.

LISTING 8.7: IPhotoFeed interface definition

```
[ServiceContract]
[ServiceKnownType(typeof(Atom10FeedFormatter))]
[ServiceKnownType(typeof(Rss20FeedFormatter))]
public interface IPhotoFeed
{
    [OperationContract()]
    [WebGet(UriTemplate = "*", BodyStyle = WebMessageBodyStyle.Bare)]
    SyndicationFeedFormatter CreateFeed();
}
```

The UriTemplate associated with the CreateFeed method says that all messages coming to this service are processed by one (and only one) method. The method returns a SyndicationFeedFormatter to write any feed information into the response to be returned to the caller. You will also notice the use of the ServiceKnownType attribute. This informs the internal WCF mechanisms controlling serialization that they can expect to format the method output using one of two formatters: Atom10FeedFormatter or

Rss20FeedFormatter. You rarely interact with a SyndicationFeedFormatter other than to return one as a result of an OperationContract.

The implementation of CreateFeed has distinct stages. First, the method needs to determine the user and which flavor of feed to return. Some initialization also needs to happen such that metadata about the feed is available when requested. Next, the method needs to gather applicable data and add those items to the feed. Finally, the feed needs to be serialized and returned to the user. Listing 8.8 gives you a feel for how to extract and return the feed to a user of the service.

LISTING 8.8: PhotoFeed.CreateFeed service method implementation

```
public SyndicationFeedFormatter CreateFeed()
{
    Uri requestUri = HttpContext.Current.Request.Url;

    // Look at the URL to figure out which user and the response format
    // (Atom | RSS).
    string fileName = requestUri.Segments[
        requestUri.Segments.Length - 1];
    string username = Path.GetFileNameWithoutExtension(fileName);
    string feedType= Path.GetExtension(fileName.ToUpper());
    SyndicationFeedFormatter formatter = null;
    SyndicationFeed feed = new SyndicationFeed(
        string.Format("Photo feed for user {0}",
            username), "A Photo Feed", HttpContext.Current.Request.Url);

    // Allow an image to show up for this feed once someone subscribes.
    feed.ImageUrl =new Uri(string.Format("http://{0}{1}/FeedImage.jpg",
        HttpContext.Current.Request.Url.Authority,
        HttpContext.Current.Request.ApplicationPath));

    // Pick the feed.
    if (feedType.Equals(".ATOM"))
    {
        formatter = feed.GetAtom10Formatter();
    }
    else if (feedType.Equals(".RSS"))
    {
        formatter = feed.GetRss20Formatter();
    }
    else
    {
        // We don't understand the request type, so
        // tell the caller that the resource they want can't
```

```
        // be found.
        WebOperationContext.Current.OutgoingResponse.StatusCode =
            System.Net.HttpStatusCode.NotFound;
        return null;
    }

    using (PhotoWebDbDataContext dataContext =
        new PhotoWebDbDataContext())
    {
        // Get all the public images for the user in question
        var images = from image in dataContext.Images
                        where
                            image.UserName == username &&
                            image.PublicImage
                        select image;

    •   // No public images means no resource to return.
        // Maybe the user doesn't exist?
        if (images.Count() == 0)
        {
            WebOperationContext.Current.OutgoingResponse.StatusCode =
                System.Net.HttpStatusCode.NotFound;
            return null;
        }

        List<SyndicationItem> items = new List<SyndicationItem>();
        foreach (var image in images)
        {
            // Create and add the SyndicationItem to the feed
            SyndicationItem si = new SyndicationItem(image.Caption,
                image.Description,
                  new Uri(string.Format(
                  "http://{0}{1}/ImageHandler.ashx/{2}",
                  HttpContext.Current.Request.Url.Authority,
                  HttpContext.Current.Request.ApplicationPath,
                  image.ImageId.ToString("D"))),
                  image.ImageId.ToString(),
                  new DateTimeOffset(image.Updated.Value));
            items.Add(si);
        }
        feed.Items = items;
    }
    return formatter;
}
```

When the service executes, it returns a viable feed. Figure 8.5 shows the view of the feed from Internet Explorer (*note:* the image is available only after you subscribe to the feed).

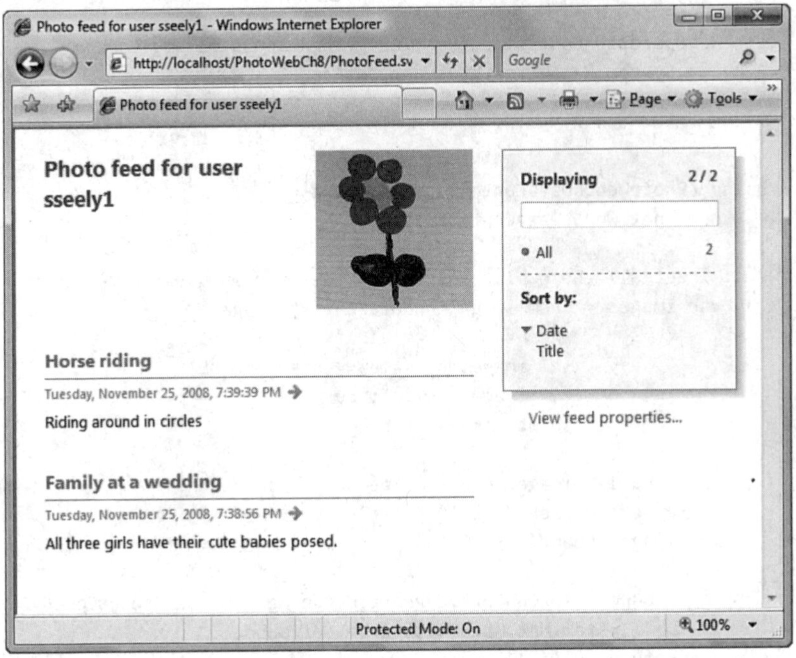

FIGURE 8.5: Viewing the feed in Internet Explorer

Listing 8.9 shows the feed as RSS, and Listing 8.10 shows the same data, as Atom, for comparison. I deliberately made the number of items small so that you can more easily compare the way the same information is presented.

LISTING 8.9: Photo service RSS 2.0 feed

```xml
<?xml version="1.0" encoding="utf-8"?>
<rss version="2.0" xmlns:atom="http://www.w3.org/2005/Atom"
    xmlns:cf="http://www.microsoft.com/schemas/rss/core/2005"
    xmlns:a10="http://www.w3.org/2005/Atom">
    <channel xmlns:cfi=
        "http://www.microsoft.com/schemas/rss/core/2005/internal"
        cfi:lastdownloaderror="None">
        <title cf:type="text">Photo feed for user sseely1</title>
        <link>
            http://localhost/PhotoWebCh8/PhotoFeed.svc/sseely1.rss
        </link>
        <description cf:type="text">A Photo Feed</description>
        <image>
            <url>http://localhost/PhotoWebCh8/FeedImage.jpg</url>
            <title>Photo feed for user sseely1</title>
            <link>
                http://localhost/PhotoWebCh8/PhotoFeed.svc/sseely1.rss
```

```
            </link>
        </image>
        <item>
            <guid isPermaLink="false">
                7dc8773c-9040-4c75-b79b-34d23062ebad
            </guid>
<link>http://localhost/PhotoWebCh8/ImageHandler.ashx/7dc8773c-9040-4c75-
➥b79b-34d23062ebad</link>
            <title
                xmlns:cf="http://www.microsoft.com/schemas/rss/core/2005"
                cf:type="text">Horse riding</title>
            <description
                xmlns:cf="http://www.microsoft.com/schemas/rss/core/2005"
                cf:type="html">Riding around in circles</description>
            <atom:updated xmlns:atom="http://www.w3.org/2005/Atom">
                2008-11-26T01:39:39Z</atom:updated>
            <cfi:id>1</cfi:id>
            <cfi:read>true</cfi:read>
            <cfi:downloadurl>
                http://localhost/PhotoWebCh8/PhotoFeed.svc/sseely1.rss
            </cfi:downloadurl>
            <cfi:lastdownloadtime>
                2008-11-26T03:37:07.991Z</cfi:lastdownloadtime>
        </item>
        <item>
            <guid isPermaLink="false">
                086e4248-5bb5-4007-acdd-a7e244e0e579</guid>
            <link>
http://localhost/PhotoWebCh8/ImageHandler.ashx/086e4248-5bb5-4007-acdd-
➥a7e244e0e579</link>
            <title
                xmlns:cf="http://www.microsoft.com/schemas/rss/core/2005"
                cf:type="text">Family at a wedding</title>
            <description
                xmlns:cf="http://www.microsoft.com/schemas/rss/core/2005"
                cf:type="html">
                All three moms have their cute babies posed.
            </description>
            <atom:updated
                xmlns:atom="http://www.w3.org/2005/Atom">
                2008-11-26T01:38:56Z</atom:updated>
            <cfi:id>0</cfi:id>
            <cfi:read>true</cfi:read>
            <cfi:downloadurl>
                http://localhost/PhotoWebCh8/PhotoFeed.svc/sseely1.rss
            </cfi:downloadurl>
            <cfi:lastdownloadtime>
                2008-11-26T03:37:07.991Z</cfi:lastdownloadtime>
        </item>
    </channel>
</rss>
```

LISTING 8.10: Photo service Atom feed

```
<feed xmlns="http://www.w3.org/2005/Atom">
    <title type="text">Photo feed for user sseely1</title>
    <subtitle type="text">A Photo Feed</subtitle>
    <id>uuid:011e8f07-ebba-4e5b-9437-f1b04e604677;id=1</id>
    <updated>2008-11-29T20:29:20Z</updated>
    <logo>http://localhost/PhotoWebCh8/FeedImage.jpg</logo>
    <link rel="alternate"
        href="http://localhost/PhotoWebCh8/PhotoFeed.svc/sseely1.atom"/>
    <entry>
        <id>7dc8773c-9040-4c75-b79b-34d23062ebad</id>
        <title type="text">Horse riding</title>
        <updated>2008-11-25T19:39:39-06:00</updated>
        <link rel="alternate" href="http://localhost/PhotoWebCh8/
➥ImageHandler.ashx/7dc8773c-9040-4c75-b79b-34d23062ebad"/>
        <content type="text">Riding around in circles</content>
    </entry>
    <entry>
        <id>086e4248-5bb5-4007-acdd-a7e244e0e579</id>
        <title type="text">Family at a wedding</title>
        <updated>2008-11-25T19:38:56-06:00</updated>
        <link rel="alternate" href="http://localhost/PhotoWebCh8/
➥ImageHandler.ashx/086e4248-5bb5-4007-acdd-a7e244e0e579"/>
        <content type="text">
            All three moms have their cute babies posed.
        </content>
    </entry>
</feed>
```

Interestingly, the formatters not only create feed information but also can consume it. RSS and Atom feeds can then be consumed from a number of places and used in all sorts of ways. They are a popular mechanism for creating dashboards, news pages, and other items. On the home page of scottseely.com, I consume my own blog feed to display the most recent posts to my occasionally active blog. I have had this code in production for over a year with few issues. The display is managed by a custom ASP.NET server control I wrote, ScottSeely.Web.FeedSummary, which consumes a feed and displays the items as received. Figure 8.6 shows the control output.

FIGURE 8.6: FeedSummary control pointing to my personal blog

The control handles three different display styles:

1. Title only: In case the RSS feed is chatty.
2. Title and short description: To encourage readers to click through.
3. Title and full description: To provide readers with all their news on one page.

The control itself supports full data binding and toolbox support. But the interesting part to us is how it handles consuming feeds. To retrieve a feed from some location and parse that feed, regardless of whether it is Atom or RSS, requires just one line of code:

```
SyndicationFeed feed = SyndicationFeed.Load(
    new XmlTextReader(feedUri.ToString()));
```

From there, it is a simple step to loop over the feed items and display them however you like, using the ASP.NET skills you already have:

```
foreach (SyndicationItem feedItem in feed.Items){ /* do something */}
```

The complete server control that I wrote to do this is available in this chapter's sample code (available for download from the book's Web site) for you to review. I have found the syndication support in WCF 3.5 to be very well thought out and designed, and I'm sure you'll find working with syndication to be easy as well.

ADO.NET Data Services

No discussion of WCF and REST would be complete without talking about the technology that allows you to create a completely RESTful view of your data with amazingly minimal effort: ADO.NET Data Services (which I'll abbreviate to ANDS in this discussion). WCF provides the service portion of this feature (hosting, channels, dispatch, and so on).

Many of the demonstrations of ANDS show how to combine an Entity Data Model with `System.Data.Services.DataService<T>` to create a service that allows you to query the data model using RESTful HTTP calls with very little coding on your part. Typically, the demonstration shows how you can query some database table, navigate to a specific row in that table, and maybe navigate to a relationship, and then closes by selecting a single row element. The whole demonstration works from any Web browser.

> **■ NOTE**
>
> After the excitement dies down, however, think about it. When would someone actually want to expose their entire database to the world? After seeing this typical ANDS demonstration, most developers realize they won't be exposing their databases any time soon through ANDS, and they write off the technology. From my point of view, writing off the technology based on this observation is a huge mistake. In this section, I will show you how to take advantage of the technology using features that are not well publicized but are, ultimately, more applicable to real-world REST applications.

The question is, then, when should you use ANDS? Ultimately, you should use it when you have data that can be easily collected via some sort of LINQ expression. When you want to support some sort of data query capability, having the ability to select elements by their identifiers, or the ability to select individual elements within the data, you should think about using ANDS. This choice can save you days of development time. This also provides a way to make your data model RESTful in the extreme: every collection, element in the collection, and data member of an element can have a URI. To demonstrate this, I will take the existing list of images and create an ANDS service to sit alongside the other WCF service I've created. Along the way, I will introduce the technologies that make this effort easy. I will build the service in several steps:

1. Define the data service.
2. Add metadata to our objects to expose them over ANDS.
3. Add an ANDS/WCF service endpoint to listen for messages.

Define the Data Service

Although you can link to an existing Entity Data Model and easily publish a service, I do not believe that this is the path most developers will take when it comes time to actually expose a data service to the world. Instead, they will have existing data that needs to be exposed, and it's quite likely that they cannot redesign their data store to make the information friendlier for ANDS.

That's when you start by deciding what information you will expose as collections. If an item being exposed happens to contain collections, you need to add those collections to the list you are creating. In our case, we want to expose a collection of ImageUser items, as shown in Listing 8.11. An ImageUser consists of two pieces of information: a username and a collection of ImageItem objects. Each ImageItem is a leaf node and has no child collections to expose.

LISTING 8.11: ImageUser, **before prepping for ANDS**

```
public class ImageUser
{
    public string Username { get; set; }

    public List<ImageItem> Images
    {
        get
        {
            ImageManager imgMgr = new ImageManager();
            return new List<ImageItem>(
                imgMgr.GetImagesForUser(this.Username));
        }
    }
}
```

Each collection exposed by the service needs to support the System. Linq.IQueryable interface. This requirement exists to allow a standard set of ANDS query strings to exist:

- $expand: Indicates which collections within the target should be expanded when returned. For example, when fetching ImageUser instances, one could pass along $expand=Images in the query string to also return the set of ImageItems associated with each ImageUser.

- $filter: Returns only the elements that match a specific set of criteria, such as all ImageUser.Usernames equal to sseely1.

- $orderby: Tells how to order the elements and explains the order for the sort.

- $skip: Skips a set of elements in the target. When used with $top, this value can be used to page through the return values, returning *n* elements at a time.

- $top: Returns at most the number of elements indicated by the positive number passed in.

Because ImageUser contains a collection of ImageItem objects, our interface also needs to return a collection of ImageItems. If you fail to provide this, you will receive an InvalidOperationException while processing the collection of `ImageUser` objects. The exception will have a message similar to this: `The property 'Images' on type 'PhotoWeb.ImageUser' is not a valid property. Properties whose types are collection of primitives or complex types are not supported.` Figure 8.7 shows the Graph view of the SvcTraceViewer tool and what you can expect to see when this issue arises on a service. (I'll address WCF service tracing and logging later in the chapter.) The issue manifests itself by failing to include the `Images` definition shown in Listing 8.12. `Images` must also be based on `IQueryable`, or any service method returning `Images` will fail.

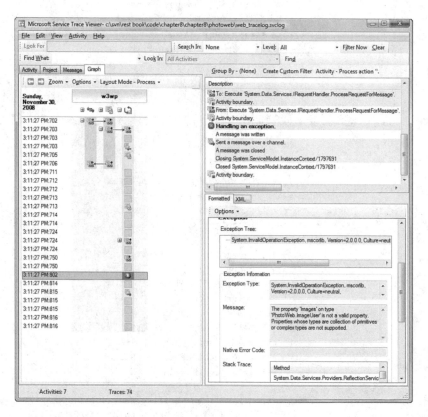

FIGURE 8.7: Service Trace Viewer output showing missing `IQueryable` on the base service

Knowing this, we create a simple class to define our data service. Listing 8.12 shows the `UserDataService`.

LISTING 8.12: UserDataService implementation

```
public class UserDataService
{
    public IQueryable<ImageUser> Users
    {
        get
        {
            using (PhotoWebDbDataContext dataContext =
                new PhotoWebDbDataContext())
            {
                var users = (from Image image in dataContext.Images
                        select new ImageUser() {
                            Username = image.UserName }
                        ). Distinct().OrderBy(n => n.Username);
                List<ImageUser> retval = new List<ImageUser>(users);
                return retval.AsQueryable<ImageUser>();
            }
        }
    }

    public IQueryable<ImageItem> Images
    {
        get
        {
            List<ImageItem> retval = new List<ImageItem>();
            IEnumerable<Image> images = null;
            using (PhotoWebDbDataContext dataContext =
                new PhotoWebDbDataContext())
            {
                images = from image in dataContext.Images
                            where
                                image.PublicImage
                            select image;
                string baseUrl = string.Format(
                    "http://{0}{1}/ImageHandler.ashx",
                    HttpContext.Current.Request.Url.Authority,
                    HttpContext.Current.Request.ApplicationPath);
                foreach (var image in images)
                {
                    ImageItem imageItem = Utility.ConvertImage(image);
                    imageItem.ImageUrl = string.Format("{0}/{1}",
                        baseUrl, image.ImageId.ToString("D"));
                    retval.Add(imageItem);
                }
            }
            return retval.AsQueryable<ImageItem>();
        }
    }
}
```

We now have a definition for a service that should be capable of exposing data to the outside world using ANDS. Next, we have to modify the data objects to prepare them for use with ANDS. To do that, we will add some metadata to the definitions of the types returned by the public IQueryable members.

Add Metadata

When you return a data type via ANDS, you need to define which property can be treated as a key when the data type appears in a collection. Failure to do so results in another InvalidOperationException:

```
On data context type 'UserDataService', there is a top IQueryable property
'Users' whose element type is not an entity type. Make sure that the
IQueryable property is of entity type or specify the IgnoreProperties
attribute on the data context type to ignore this property.
```

I point out this exception only so that you can fix the problem quickly and easily. There are two reasons the exception appears: No key has been defined, or you have a public property that needs to be ignored. For ImageUser, the problem is a missing key. The System.Data.Services.Common.DataServiceKeyAttribute has a constructor that takes one or more property names (as a params string[] argument) that you can use to define a key composed of one or more properties. In the case of ImageUser, the Username property is the key. All public fields on the object are accessible via a custom URL. Listing 8.13 shows the completed ImageUser class.

LISTING 8.13: ImageUser class with DataServiceKey applied

```
[DataServiceKey("Username")]
public class ImageUser
{
    public string Username { get; set; }

    public List<ImageItem> Images
    {
        get
        {
            ImageManager imgMgr = new ImageManager();
            return new List<ImageItem>(
                imgMgr.GetImagesForUser(this.Username));
        }
    }
}
```

The venerable `ImageItem` class from Listing 8.1 also requires a bit of an update. The key is the `ImageId` field. If you think about it, the `Image` property (of type `System.Drawing.Image`) should not be a part of the queryable interface—it isn't part of the `DataContract`. We remove the property from consideration by applying the `System.Data.Services.IgnoreProperties-Attribute`. This means that the class definition requires this small update, shown in bold:

```
[DataContract(Namespace = "http://www.scottseely.com/RESTBook/2008")]
[DataServiceKey("ImageId")]
[IgnoreProperties("Image")]
public class ImageItem {...}
```

We now have our classes and our data service properly defined. It is time to add an ANDS service endpoint.

Add a Service Endpoint

Here, we will use the Visual Studio wizards to add an ANDS endpoint. Right-click on the Web project and select Add New Item. Select ADO.NET Data Service from the list of templates, name the service file something appropriate, and click Add. For this example, I named the class `ImageUser Service`. This generates a `.svc` file and an associated C# class file. The `.svc` file uses a custom `ServiceHostFactory`, meaning that the class itself can still use standard WCF configuration but can also exist without configuration. The `.svc` file has the following markup:

```
<%@ ServiceHost Language="C#"
    Factory="System.Data.Services.DataServiceHostFactory,
➥System.Data.Services, Version=3.5.0.0, Culture=neutral,
➥PublicKeyToken=b77a5c561934e089"
    Service="PhotoWeb.ImageUserService" %>
```

At this point, we have an endpoint that is very much locked down. The service itself will not expose any information until we tell the service what to expose. To begin, we need to tell the generated class about `User-DataService`. The service defined by the wizard inherits from `System.Data.Services.DataService<T>`. A quick edit and the class definition reads like this:

```
public class ImageUserService : DataService<UserDataService>
```

Next, we need to tell the service that it is allowable to expose information about the Images and Users collections through UserDataService. The wizard created for us a static method named InitializeService. In InitializeService, we establish the ability to read and write different collections of information. For our service, that means we write the following code:

```
public static void InitializeService(IDataServiceConfiguration config)
{
    config.SetEntitySetAccessRule("Images", EntitySetRights.AllRead);
    config.SetEntitySetAccessRule("Users", EntitySetRights.AllRead);
}
```

You can also set rules that allow for writing values back to the collections. For the Images collection, the service will want to make sure that none of the outgoing responses contains nonpublic images unless the request is made by the collection owner. ANDS supports reviews of the collections returned by an HTTP GET request using a special attribute: System.Data. Services.QueryInterceptorAttribute. You can apply one of these interceptors per entity set. The return value is a function that takes an item of the entity set and returns a Boolean value. Here is an example of filtering out private images. You could use something similar based on other business rules for data your own service returns.

```
[QueryInterceptor("Images")]
public Expression<Func<ImageItem, bool>> OnQueryImages()
{
    return o => o.PublicImage ||
                o.UserName == HttpContext.Current.User.Identity.Name;
}
```

To handle inserts, updates, and deletes, we use the System.Data. Services.ChangeInterceptorAttribute. This attribute also identifies an entity set name, but it has a different signature: an entity and a System. Data.Services.UpdateOperations enumerated value, set to None, Add, Change, or Delete. If the operation is not allowed, the method throws an exception and the caller is blocked from updating the entity. In this case we don't need one of these—we are not allowing changes over the ANDS service endpoint. However, if we were, we would create a method that looked something like this:

```
[ChangeInterceptor("Images")]
public void OnChangeImages(ImageItem imageItem,
                          UpdateOperations updateOperation)
{
    // Check security/access for item.
}
```

Because ANDS builds on WCF, you could also inject your own security handlers into the message stack via a custom security binding or service/endpoint behavior. The end result of this work is that you can actually query the service for data. When navigating to the root of the service, you get the response shown in Listing 8.14.

LISTING 8.14: ANDS service definition (AtomPub service)

```
<service xml:base="http://localhost/PhotoWebCh8/ImageUserService.svc/"
    xmlns:atom="http://www.w3.org/2005/Atom"
    xmlns:app="http://www.w3.org/2007/app"
    xmlns="http://www.w3.org/2007/app">
  <workspace>
    <atom:title>Default</atom:title>
    <collection href="Users">
      <atom:title>Users</atom:title>
    </collection>
    <collection href="Images">
      <atom:title>Images</atom:title>
    </collection>
  </workspace>
</service>
```

This Atom document tells us a few things. First, it tells us that the base URL for items in the document is http://localhost/PhotoWebCh8/Image UserService.svc/. It also tells us that two collections exist at the relative URLs Users and Images. By accessing http://localhost/PhotoWeb Ch8/ImageUserService.svc/Users or http://localhost/PhotoWebCh8/ ImageUserService.svc/Images, a service client should be able to look at the contents of these two collections.

We can also see a description of the data the service shares. The description for any ANDS can be found at the relative URL /$metadata. For our service, http://localhost/PhotoWebCh8/ImageUserService.svc/$meta-data provides the data shown in Listing 8.15. This listing describes the layout of the entities as well as the relationships between the entities.

LISTING 8.15: **ANDS** `ImageUserService` **metadata**

```
<edmx:Edmx Version="1.0"
    xmlns:edmx="http://schemas.microsoft.com/ado/2007/06/edmx">
  <edmx:DataServices>
    <Schema Namespace="PhotoShared"
        xmlns:d="http://schemas.microsoft.com/ado/2007/08/dataservices"
xmlns:m="http://schemas.microsoft.com/ado/2007/08/dataservices/metadata"
        xmlns="http://schemas.microsoft.com/ado/2006/04/edm">
      <EntityType Name="ImageItem">
        <Key>
          <PropertyRef Name="ImageId" />
        </Key>
        <Property Name="ImageUrl" Type="Edm.String" Nullable="true" />
        <Property Name="ImageId" Type="Edm.Guid" Nullable="false" />

        <Property Name="Description" Type="Edm.String"
            Nullable="true" />
        <Property Name="Caption" Type="Edm.String" Nullable="true" />
        <Property Name="PublicImage" Type="Edm.Boolean"
            Nullable="false" />
        <Property Name="UserName" Type="Edm.String" Nullable="true" />
        <Property Name="ImageBytes" Type="Edm.Binary" Nullable="true" />
      </EntityType>
    </Schema>
    <Schema Namespace="PhotoWeb"
        xmlns:d="http://schemas.microsoft.com/ado/2007/08/dataservices"
xmlns:m="http://schemas.microsoft.com/ado/2007/08/dataservices/metadata"
        xmlns="http://schemas.microsoft.com/ado/2006/04/edm">
      <EntityType Name="ImageUser">
        <Key>
          <PropertyRef Name="Username" />
        </Key>
        <Property Name="Username" Type="Edm.String" Nullable="false" />
        <NavigationProperty Name="Images"
            Relationship="PhotoWeb.ImageUser_Images" FromRole="ImageUser"
            ToRole="Images" />
      </EntityType>
      <Association Name="ImageUser_Images">
        <End Role="Images" Type="PhotoShared.ImageItem"
            Multiplicity="*" />
        <End Role="ImageUser" Type="PhotoWeb.ImageUser"
            Multiplicity="*" />
      </Association>
      <EntityContainer Name="UserDataService"
          m:IsDefaultEntityContainer="true">
        <EntitySet Name="Users" EntityType="PhotoWeb.ImageUser" />
        <EntitySet Name="Images" EntityType="PhotoShared.ImageItem" />
```

continues

LISTING 8.15: Continued

```
        <AssociationSet Name="ImageUser_Images"
          Association="PhotoWeb.ImageUser_Images">
            <End Role="Images" EntitySet="Images" />
            <End Role="ImageUser" EntitySet="Users" />
        </AssociationSet>
      </EntityContainer>
    </Schema>
  </edmx:DataServices>
</edmx:Edmx>
```

Finally, you can query the Atom endpoint using simple URLs. For example, let's start by looking at the list of users at http://localhost/PhotoWeb Ch8/ImageUserService.svc/Users. Listing 8.16 shows the Atom response.

LISTING 8.16: Response from http://localhost/PhotoWebCh8/ImageUserService.svc/Users

```
<?xml version="1.0" encoding="utf-8" standalone="yes"?>
<feed xml:base="http://localhost/PhotoWebCh8/ImageUserService.svc/"
    xmlns:d="http://schemas.microsoft.com/ado/2007/08/dataservices"
    xmlns:m=
        "http://schemas.microsoft.com/ado/2007/08/dataservices/metadata"
    xmlns="http://www.w3.org/2005/Atom">  <title type="text">Users</title>
  <id>http://localhost/PhotoWebCh8/ImageUserService.svc/Users</id>
  <updated>2008-11-30T23:19:58Z</updated>
  <link rel="self" title="Users" href="Users" />
  <entry>
    <id>
      http://localhost/PhotoWebCh8/ImageUserService.svc/Users('sseely')
    </id>
    <title type="text"></title>
    <updated>2008-11-30T23:19:58Z</updated>
    <author>
      <name />
    </author>
    <link rel="edit" title="ImageUser" href="Users('sseely')" />
    <link rel=
"http://schemas.microsoft.com/ado/2007/08/dataservices/related/Images"
        type="application/atom+xml;type=feed" title="Images"
        href="Users('sseely')/Images" />
    <category term="PhotoWeb.ImageUser" scheme=
        "http://schemas.microsoft.com/ado/2007/08/dataservices/scheme" />
    <content type="application/xml">
      <m:properties>
        <d:Username>sseely</d:Username>
      </m:properties>
    </content>
  </entry>
```

```
    <entry>
    <id>http://localhost/PhotoWebCh8/ImageUserService.svc/Users('sseely1')
    </id>
        <title type="text"></title>
        <updated>2008-11-30T23:19:58Z</updated>
        <author>
          <name />
        </author>
        <link rel="edit" title="ImageUser" href="Users('sseely1')" />
        <link rel=
    "http://schemas.microsoft.com/ado/2007/08/dataservices/related/Images"
          type="application/atom+xml;type=feed" title="Images"
          href="Users('sseely1')/Images" />
        <category term="PhotoWeb.ImageUser" scheme=
          "http://schemas.microsoft.com/ado/2007/08/dataservices/scheme" />
        <content type="application/xml">
          <m:properties>
            <d:Username>sseely1</d:Username>
          </m:properties>
        </content>
    </entry>
</feed>
```

Again we see that there is a base URL associated with the service. We can access the user, sseely1, by referencing http://localhost/PhotoWeb Ch8/ImageUserService.svc/Users('sseely1'). That URL just points to the individual Atom entry. If we want that entry to be returned along with the Images, in an expanded fashion, we browse to http://localhost/PhotoWeb Ch8/ImageUserService.svc/Users('sseely1')?$expand=Images.   Listing 8.17 shows the results of accessing that expanded image URL.

LISTING 8.17: http://localhost/PhotoWebCh8/ImageUserService.svc/
Users('sseely1')?$expand=Images

```
    <?xml version="1.0" encoding="utf-8" standalone="yes"?>
    <entry xml:base="http://localhost/PhotoWebCh8/ImageUserService.svc/"
        xmlns:d="http://schemas.microsoft.com/ado/2007/08/dataservices"
        xmlns:m=
          "http://schemas.microsoft.com/ado/2007/08/dataservices/metadata"
        xmlns="http://www.w3.org/2005/Atom">
    <id>
    http://localhost/PhotoWebCh8/ImageUserService.svc/Users('sseely1')</id>
        <title type="text"></title>
        <updated>2008-12-01T00:07:44Z</updated>
        <author>
```

continues

LISTING 8.17: Continued

```xml
      <name />
    </author>
    <link rel="edit" title="ImageUser" href="Users('sseely1')" />
    <link rel=
"http://schemas.microsoft.com/ado/2007/08/dataservices/related/Images"
      type="application/atom+xml;type=feed" title="Images"
      href="Users('sseely1')/Images">
      <m:inline>
        <feed>
          <title type="text">Images</title>
          <id>
http://localhost/PhotoWebCh8/ImageUserService.svc/Users('sseely1')/
➡Images</id>
          <updated>2008-12-01T00:07:44Z</updated>
          <link rel="self" title="Images"
            href="Users('sseely1')/Images" />
          <entry>
            <id>
http://localhost/PhotoWebCh8/ImageUserService.svc/Images(guid'7dc8773c-
➡9040-4c75-b79b-34d23062ebad')</id>
            <title type="text"></title>
            <updated>2008-12-01T00:07:44Z</updated>
            <author>
              <name />
            </author>
            <link rel="edit" title="ImageItem"
              href="Images(guid'7dc8773c-9040-4c75-b79b-34d23062ebad')" />
            <category term="PhotoShared.ImageItem" scheme=
        "http://schemas.microsoft.com/ado/2007/08/dataservices/scheme" />
            <content type="application/xml">
              <m:properties>
                <d:ImageUrl>
http://localhost/PhotoWebCh8/ImageHandler.ashx/7dc8773c-9040-4c75-b79b-
➡34d23062ebad</d:ImageUrl>
                <d:ImageId m:type="Edm.Guid">
                    7dc8773c-9040-4c75-b79b-34d23062ebad</d:ImageId>
                <d:Description>Riding around in circles</d:Description>
                <d:Caption>Horse riding</d:Caption>
                <d:PublicImage m:type="Edm.Boolean">true</d:PublicImage>
                <d:UserName>sseely1</d:UserName>
                <d:ImageBytes m:type="Edm.Binary" m:null="true" />
              </m:properties>
            </content>
          </entry>
          <entry>
            <id>
http://localhost/PhotoWebCh8/ImageUserService.svc/Images(guid'086e4248-
➡5bb5-4007-acdd-a7e244e0e579')</id>
```

```
            <title type="text"></title>
            <updated>2008-12-01T00:07:44Z</updated>
            <author>
              <name />
            </author>
            <link rel="edit" title="ImageItem"
              href="Images(guid'086e4248-5bb5-4007-acdd-a7e244e0e579')" />
            <category term="PhotoShared.ImageItem" scheme=
        "http://schemas.microsoft.com/ado/2007/08/dataservices/scheme" />
            <content type="application/xml">
              <m:properties>
                <d:ImageUrl>
http://localhost/PhotoWebCh8/ImageHandler.ashx/086e4248-5bb5-4007-acdd-
➡a7e244e0e579</d:ImageUrl>
                <d:ImageId m:type="Edm.Guid">
                    086e4248-5bb5-4007-acdd-a7e244e0e579</d:ImageId>
                <d:Description>
                    All three moms have their cute babies posed.
                </d:Description>
                <d:Caption>Family at a wedding</d:Caption>
                <d:PublicImage m:type="Edm.Boolean">true</d:PublicImage>
                <d:UserName>sseely1</d:UserName>
                <d:ImageBytes m:type="Edm.Binary" m:null="true" />
              </m:properties>
            </content>
          </entry>
        </feed>
      </m:inline>
    </link>
    <category term="PhotoWeb.ImageUser" scheme=
        "http://schemas.microsoft.com/ado/2007/08/dataservices/scheme" />
    <content type="application/xml">
      <m:properties>
        <d:Username>sseely1</d:Username>
      </m:properties>
    </content>
  </entry>
```

Finally, I can even retrieve just the caption from a specific image and a specific user. The URL http://localhost/PhotoWebCh8/ImageUserService. svc/Users('sseely1')/Images(guid'7dc8773c-9040-4c75-b79b-34d23062ebad')/Caption returns the following:

```
<?xml version="1.0" encoding="utf-8" standalone="yes" ?>

<Caption xmlns="http://schemas.microsoft.com/ado/2007/08/dataservices">
  Horse riding
</Caption>
```

Because of this capability to filter collections of information that are IQueryable, ANDS is a powerful tool in your toolbox. With it, you can support query interfaces over collections, paging for your data, and direct access to fields within your data. All the data appears using Atom and can be modified using AtomPub. When designing solutions that use ANDS and custom return values, you have to check each collection for a few things.

1. How big can an individual collection get? Because you might be querying a database and using custom filtering on the returned data set to return data, you need to be wary of how large the data set can be. For example, 50,000 might be classified as a "big" number in your system. In that system, it might be fine to perform in-memory filtering of collections under 5,000 elements, but not so good to do filtering after grabbing 50,000 (10 times more) elements. Based on your needs, you might need to aggressively partition the data and guard against direct access to complete collections.

2. Do you need updates? If so, you might be better off securing an endpoint that uses the Entity Framework to query the database instead of using the custom solution presented here. Then again, you might want to go with a mechanism presented earlier in this chapter to handle updates to data. AtomPub is nice, but it might not handle your business rules adequately.

3. Do you need AtomPub compatibility? ANDS generates Atom feeds. This is handy for a lot of design scenarios and many tools support Atom. If this is not a project requirement, you might be better off supporting GET, POST, PUT, and DELETE operations on your own instead of using ANDS.

Be sure to use ANDS when it makes sense. It is a niche tool, but it fills that niche extremely well. If you need to implement a search/query/paging access mechanism for a data set, use ANDS. Otherwise, make sure it is the right tool for the job at hand.

> **■ NOTE**
>
> If you happen to know that your client application will be working with ANDS, Microsoft has provided you with a tool you can use that accepts the metadata from the ANDS service and creates entity classes for service interaction for you. This tool, `DataSvcUtil.exe`, is found in the directory \WINDOWS\Microsoft.NET\Framework\v3.5\. If you provide it with the URI of the ANDS service, and output filename, and (optionally) the source language (C# or Visual Basic), it will access the service and produce source files for your client application to use. I didn't mention this in Chapter 3 since `DataSvcUtil.exe` is specific to ANDS services and therefore quite specialized. However, when you can use it, it's a powerful tool.

Now that we have covered many WCF technologies and how to use them, we should spend some time looking at how to debug applications that use WCF.

WCF Diagnostics

I would be remiss if did not introduce you to my favorite feature in WCF, diagnostics. WCF diagnostics features allow developers and administrators to see what is happening right now in the form of performance counters and Windows Management Instrumentation (WMI). You can also view what just happened through tracing. While developing any WCF solution, I use many of the features presented here to figure out what is going on within my application.

Performance Counters

WCF comes ready to roll with a large set of performance counters. Counters are scoped to four levels: AppDomain, ServiceHost, Endpoint, and Operation. In this section, we will cover what is available and how to apply each set of counters.

All the operation performance counters allow you to monitor the following types of information:

- Calls per second
- Calls duration
- Security behavior of the function
- Transaction behavior

Operation performance counters are found within the `ServiceModel-Operation 3.0.0.0` performance object. Each operation will have an individual instance. That is, if a given contract has ten operations, then ten operation counter instances will be associated with that contract. The object instances are named according to the following pattern:

```
(ServiceName).(ContractName).(OperationName)@(first endpoint listener
address)
```

Portions of the name will be mangled to permit the entire name to fit within 64 characters. Like all instance names in WCF performance counters, the mangling algorithm is consistent across time on a given machine. This allows users to save performance counter sessions from `PerfMon.exe` or set up trace profiles with `LogMan.exe` and use those sessions to monitor a service over time and across restarts. These numbers let you know how the call is being used and how well the operation is performing.

The endpoint performance counters, provided by the `ServiceModel-Endpoint 3.0.0.0` performance object, allow you to look at the data based on which endpoint is accepting information. The instances are named using this pattern:

```
(ServiceName).(ContractName)@(endpoint listener address)
```

The data is similar to what is collected for individual operations, but it is aggregated across the service endpoint. For example, let's take a look at how total calls would look on a method exposed by one contract with one method on one service over two endpoints. Endpoint one listens at `net.tcp://localhost/Service`. Endpoint two listens at `net.pipe://localhost/Service`. Imagine that the counters indicate that the `net.tcp` endpoint processes roughly two times more traffic than the `net.pipe` end-point processes. If the service sustains 99 calls to its solitary method, we would see that the `net.tcp` endpoint instance would report 66 total calls and that the `net.pipe` endpoint would report 33 total calls.

The service-based counters, supported by the `ServiceModelService 3.0.0.0` performance object, look at the service behavior as a whole. Service instances help diagnose the health of the whole service. Applications enable performance counters through configuration. The configuration required to enable performance counters is this:

```
<configuration>
    <system.serviceModel>
        <diagnostics performanceCounters="All" />
    </system.serviceModel>
</configuration>
```

If you want performance counters active for all WCF applications, you will want to place the configuration settings in `machine.config`. In testing, we have seen that applications exposing many endpoints will run out of space to store extra performance counters. `System.ServiceModel` allocates performance counters for each `ServiceHost`, `EndpointListener`, and `Operation`. These are instance counters. All performance counters are written using a memory mapped file, and you need to know how big to make this file ahead of time. As the number of counters increases, the space in this memory mapped file is consumed. If you find that you cannot see all the counters in `PerfMon`, you will need to increase the size of the memory mapped file. The default size of this file is 524,288 bytes, and of course any number you select should be larger than this. To increase the size of the memory mapped file to a megabyte, add the following to `app.config`:

```
<configuration>
    <system.diagnostics>
        <performanceCounters fileMappingSize="1048576" />
    </system.diagnostics>
</configuration>
```

You will need to restart the application for these settings to take effect. `System.ServiceModel` will also place traces in the Event Log to let you know when performance counters for a service or endpoint could not be loaded.

Event Log

WCF will write to the Event Log in a number of cases. The Application Event Log contains most of the events. Most of the entries indicate that a particular feature failed to start for an application. Examples include these:

- Message logging/tracing: If the `System.Diagnostics.TraceSource` construction has a failure and traces will not appear, an event is logged. WCF will also log an event when periodic traces do not appear. Rules exist in WCF to make sure that the Event Log does not get flooded with traces when the `TraceSource` gets created but the `System.Diagnostics.TraceListener` writing the traces has many failures.
- Shared Listener: The WCF TCP Port Sharing Service logs an event when it fails to start.
- Security: This logs some security audit events to the Security Event Log.
- InfoCard: This logs events when the service fails to start.

Basically, if you expect to see a feature work and it doesn't, go look in the Event Log's Application log. If you see an entry from any of the following sources, you will have a place to start looking into why things are not working right:

- `Microsoft.InfoCard.Diagnostics`
- `Microsoft.TransactionBridge.Dtc`
- `System.Runtime.Authorization`
- `System.ServiceModel`

Windows Management Instrumentation

`System.ServiceModel` exposes information about active services through Windows Management Instrumentation, or WMI. Through WMI, you can find out information about `System.ServiceModel` settings at the App Domain level as well as about the makeup of all active services. Using tools like WMI CIM Studio, available free (download it from www.microsoft.com/downloads/details.aspx?familyid=6430F853-1120-48DB-8CC5-F2ABDC3ED314&displaylang=en), you can navigate the `ServiceDescription` of running services. Figure 8.8 shows the main objects you can query.

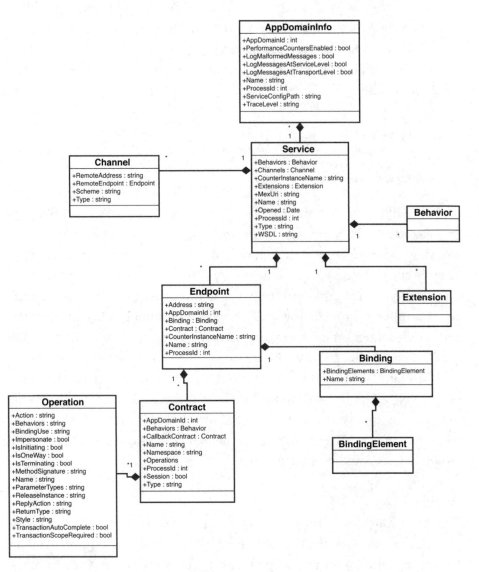

FIGURE 8.8: `root\ServiceModel` **WMI object model (not shown: detail for** `BindingElement`, `Extension`, **or** `Behavior`**)**

Using WMI, administrators can now answer various questions regarding the state of currently executing Web services. The administrator can determine which protocols are in use, whether an endpoint requires impersonation, or whether transactions are required. The settings on every behavior or binding are completely visible at runtime. Because of these capabilities, an administrator for an enterprise application should always make sure that WMI is enabled for all WCF applications. Applications enable WMI information through configuration. The configuration required to enable performance counters is this:

```
<configuration>
    <system.serviceModel>
        <diagnostics wmiProviderEnabled="true" />
    </system.serviceModel>
</configuration>
```

You will notice that many of the objects exposed via WMI include the process identifier. Knowing the process identifier allows administrators and developers to write code that periodically polls the system to find out what is currently running. For example, your organization might prohibit anonymous access to Web services and might require that all requests require authentication. If any WCF services are running using an expressly forbidden configuration, a WMI script can use the process identifier to kill the process hosting the insecure service.

WMI can also be used to just figure out what the services are doing. Find out which endpoints are open. Look at the contracts these endpoints expose. Anytime you want to see what the system is doing right now, the combination of WMI and WCF performance counters can provide you with a tremendous amount of information.

Tracing

The WCF team spent a lot of time focusing on tracing. For about two years, one of your authors, Scott Seely, spent all his time working on WCF at Microsoft, thinking of and implementing diagnostics scenarios to make sure that the right information would be available to fix various problems. If you understand how to view the various tracing sources, levels, and settings, you should be able to figure out what is going wrong with the system.

WCF uses several trace sources. Most of the trace sources emit information only when throwing an exception. Some also emit more information. For the first release of WCF, we spent most of our time focusing on messaging scenarios, but today WCF ships with several different `TraceSources`. Unless otherwise noted, the `TraceSource` emits data only when an exception is thrown.

- `Microsoft.TransactionsBridge.Dtc`: Use this `TraceSource` on `msdtc.exe.config` when you are diagnosing issues with `WS-Atomic-Transaction` across distributed transaction coordinators.
- `System.Runtime.Serialization`: This `TraceSource` logs when objects are serialized and deserialized.
- `System.ServiceModel`: This `TraceSource` logs at all stages of message processing, whenever configuration is read, and for various points in the lifetime of any `System.ServiceModel.Channels.CommunicationObject` derived class.

Each `TraceSource` can appear in configuration using the XML shown in Listing 8.18.

LISTING 8.18: Trace source configuration

```
<configuration>
    <system.diagnostics>
        <sources>
            <source name="Microsoft.InfoCards.Diagnostics">
                <listeners>
                    <add name="xml" />
                </listeners>
            </source>
            <source name="Microsoft.TransactionsBridge.Dtc">
                <listeners>
                    <add name="xml" />
                </listeners>
            </source>
            <source name="System.IO.Log">
                <listeners>
                    <add name="xml" />
                </listeners>
            </source>
```

continues

LISTING 8.18: Continued

```xml
            <source name="System.Runtime.Serialization">
                <listeners>
                    <add name="xml" />
                </listeners>
            </source>
            <source name="System.Security.Authorization">
                <listeners>
                    <add name="xml" />
                </listeners>
            </source>
            <source name="System.ServiceModel"
                    switchValue="Information, ActivityTracing"
                    propagateActivity="true">
                <listeners>
                    <add name="xml" />
                </listeners>
            </source>
        </sources>

        <sharedListeners>
            <add name="xml"
                type="System.Diagnostics.XmlWriterTraceListener"
                initializeData="Traces.e2e" />
        </sharedListeners>

    </system.diagnostics>
</configuration>
```

Several different values can be set for the switchValue item. Here is how to think about the different levels.

Critical traces typically indicate that the WCF has found itself in a state it should not be in. WCF is going to execute a System.Environment.FailFast call, which will typically shut down the AppDomain. If you discover that a FailFast occurred, you should report the event to Microsoft. Any FailFast is considered to be a product bug.

Error traces are used to indicate that an exception is being thrown.

Warning traces indicate that something might be wrong but is not quite bad yet. For example, if all possible TCP connections are consumed, a warning will be emitted to let you know that the service might start refusing client connections. Refusing client connections is normal behavior. If warnings continually appear indicating that client connections are all filled, that might be an indication that the particular endpoint needs to be reconfigured to support more clients.

Information level traces indicate that normal behavior is working. At this level, you see activity start/stop events. Start events give names to activities. When a message is sent or received, an event is traced. When configuration is read, an event is traced. At this level, lots of traces appear. At the more critical levels, you should be able to use tracing all the time without any noticeable impact on message throughput. At an Information level, however, you begin to see an impact on message throughput if you have used up nearly all available resources on the machine. Otherwise, most scenarios will be impacted by 75% or less.

Finally, there is the Verbose level. Developers are meant to use this level as a "white box" view into what their WCF code is doing. No guarantees are made as to how many messages you can send through per second and still trace at a Verbose level.

The System.ServiceModel TraceSource indicates a couple of things that might not look familiar to you. First is the ActivityTracing flag. System.Diagnostics uses this flag to indicate that the producer of traces should do something to aggregate related traces. In WCF, the following things constitute an activity:

- ChannelFactory construction: Use this activity to ascertain what settings are read from configuration and to see whether any issues exist in creating the System.ServiceModel.Design.ContractDescription for the ChannelFactory.
- ServiceHost construction: Use this activity to determine what settings are read from configuration and to see whether any issues exist in creating the System.ServiceModel.Design.ServiceDescription for the ServiceHost.
- ChannelFactory open: Look in this activity to solve problems when sending the initial message from a proxy/client.
- ServiceHost open: Look in this activity to understand problems when creating the EndpointListeners.
- Message processing: Consult this for information about what happened during processing of a WCF message.

You can view the activities and their utility in the `SvcTraceViewer.exe` tool. This tool takes the traces and sorts them based on `Activity`. With `ActivityTracing` enabled, you will also see *trace transfers*. A trace transfer indicates how different activities are related to each other. You can see that a particular activity caused another to start. For example, you could see that a message request started a security handshake to get a Secure Conversation Token.

The other new setting is `propagateActivity`. This Boolean valued property applies only to the `System.ServiceModel TraceSource`. This setting indicates whether the `Activity` should be propagated to other endpoints participating in the message exchange. By setting this value to `true`, you can take trace files generated by any two endpoints and correlate a set of traces associated with one endpoint to a set of traces associated with another endpoint.

For any of the traces to work, you need to use a `TraceListener` that emits the E2E ("end to end") trace format. As of this writing, the only capable listener was the `System.Diagnostics.XmlWriterTraceListener`. The `SvcTraceViewer` can also read Event Tracing for Windows (ETW) logs and convert those logs to E2E schema if the associated ETW provider has registered a Managed Object Format (MOF) file. Tracing will work with other `TraceListeners`, but the other listeners will not provide the write output for consumption by the `SvcTraceViewer` tool.

Finally, the `System.ServiceModel TraceSource` also supports changing the trace level at runtime via WMI. The `AppDomainInfo` exposes a `TraceLevel`. If the level is set to `Disabled`, no listeners are available. If the level is anything else, including `Off`, one can change the level, and all future traces from `System.ServiceModel` will be emitted at the new level.

Message Logging

The first generation of messaging stacks all used a common mechanism to log messages: using a "man in the middle" that intercepts the message, writes the message to some repository, and then forwards the message to another recipient. This approach requires users to change the topology of the endpoints in order to store messages. This changed topology can also cause changes to security behavior, messaging behavior, and latencies associated with the system. This particular approach was frequently implemented in the first generation of Web service toolkits. An example of a widely used man-in-the-middle tool is the WS-I.org Monitor Tool, as described by the WS-I Monitor Tool Specification, available at www.ws-i.org/Testing/Specs/MonitorFunctionalSpecification_1.02.pdf. The biggest benefit of the man-in-the-middle choice is that you do not have to depend on the organization that creates the SOAP stack to also implement diagnostic tools.

While I was editing the Monitor Tool Specification, I participated in discussions with several organizations. During this time, we all recognized that monitoring messages by changing the messaging pattern could introduce new behavior to the system. We also recognized that this form of diagnostics frequently introduced the problem of diagnosing the diagnostic system and remembering to restore things when the man in the middle was removed. Keith Stobie, also from Microsoft, suggested that the optimal approach is to place the message interceptor within the messaging stack. If you read section A1.3 of the Monitor Tool Specification, you will see the idea that the Tool Working group sketched out is based on Keith's initial design.

For WCF, we took the idea of an in-stack message logger and implemented it. For messaging diagnostics on a secure system to be useful, the messages need to be capable of being logged at two points: as the messages are received over the transport and sometime after the messages have been processed for security. Logging the message as it was received allows you to diagnose malformed messages as well as to see how the message arrived. You can see things such as the security tokens used, what parts were encrypted, what parts were signed, and what parts were left alone.

WCF also logs messages just before they are dispatched to the application. Logging these messages at this point in processing allows you to see what the message looked like as well as what the message body looked like. This type of logging is particularly helpful when you're determining what arguments were passed in and how the receiving endpoint saw the arguments expressed as XML.

The message logging feature can be used to only log a subset of all messages. To handle this, the feature also allows for filtering of the messages using one or more XPath expressions. All message logging is enabled through configuration. To enable tracing, you need to make entries in `<system.serviceModel>` and you need to configure a `TraceSource` in `<system.diagnostics>`. To capture all messages, including malformed messages, at the transport and prior to/after dispatch, the configuration appears as shown in Listing 8.19.

LISTING 8.19: Message logging configuration

```
<configuration>
    <system.serviceModel>
        <diagnostics>
            <messageLogging logEntireMessage="true"
                logMessagesAtServiceLevel="true"
                logMessagesAtTransportLevel="true"
                logMalformedMessages="true"
                maxMessagesToLog="1000"/>
        </diagnostics>
    </system.serviceModel>

    <system.diagnostics>
        <sources>
            <source name="System.ServiceModel.MessageLogging">
                <listeners>
                    <add name="xml"
                        type="System.Diagnostics.XmlWriterTraceListener"
                        initializeData="Messages.Log"/>
                </listeners>
            </source>
        </sources>
    </system.diagnostics>
</configuration>
```

Where Are We?

We have reviewed how WCF can be used to create RESTful Web services. We saw how to respond to HEAD, GET, PUT, POST, and DELETE methods. We also took a look at how to use WCF to create services that are consumable from pages on the same Web site using WCF-generated JavaScript. RSS and Atom showed us how we can create syndicated content. Blogs and other types of feeds can be created through WCF and the System.Service-Model.Syndication namespace. We then looked at a framework that builds on WCF: ADO.NET Data Services. ANDS enables us to query collections and has some interesting capabilities beyond its obvious database-related use cases. Finally, we spent some time looking at how to debug the applications built atop WCF.

In the next chapter, you'll combine what you learned about WCF and syndication to create a RESTful service that is hosted in Microsoft Azure. Azure is a "cloud"-based operating system you can use to host your WCF services from anywhere, even your home computer.

▛9 ▪

Building REST Services Using Azure and .NET Services

T HE PREVIOUS CHAPTERS have focused on how RESTful services are built using .NET technologies. This chapter takes a different approach, which is to introduce RESTful services hosted through Azure, Microsoft's "cloud computing" platform. .NET Services, a part of the Azure cloud-computing platform, is capable of RESTful operations but at present requires some special steps for client access. Nonetheless, you can "tunnel" RESTful services into .NET Services, interact with its own services in a RESTful manner, and enjoy many of the benefits of cloud computing, including centralized authentication, location transparency, and superior peer-to-peer support.

Azure and .NET Services

You've probably heard about amazing-sounding Internet-based services from Amazon and Google that allow you to do all sorts of interesting things, such as searching, out-of-box storage, and geospatial referencing and mapping. Although it would be interesting to discuss each of those in a book on REST, the fact is that any of them could nearly fill a book of their own. Instead, I'll focus on Microsoft's entry into Internet-based service hosting, which is known as *Azure*, and specifically on a subset of Azure known as *.NET Services*. This is, after all, a book that focuses on implementing RESTful services using .NET technologies.

This chapter's goal is to give you an introduction to .NET Services and explain how you can create RESTful services that publish information to the *fabric*, as the Microsoft engineers like to call it, or subscribe to services that come from the fabric. These services might be provided by Microsoft, but it's more likely many more will be provided by third parties. Some might involve fees, whereas others might not. Some might have special requirements for use. Others, anyone can use. One thing to keep in mind, however, is that .NET Services is continuously evolving—it is considered a Community Technology Preview (CTP) as I write this. Be sure to visit the .NET Services page regularly for updates and new information:

```
www.microsoft.com/azure/netservices.mspx
```

Also visit the Azure portal itself for information about other services you might find useful:

```
www.microsoft.com/azure/default.mspx
```

Azure and .NET Services that fit into Azure represent a relatively new classification of services known as "cloud services." The idea is that somewhere on the Internet there exists a huge computing resource you can access to perform work or perhaps store information. Figure 9.1 shows you the basic architecture, and I've highlighted .NET Services so you can see where those fit into the bigger picture.

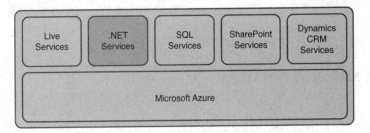

FIGURE 9.1: Basic Azure architecture

Figure 9.1 simply regurgitates some of the more recent marketing materials you might have seen from Microsoft. But don't let the simplicity of the illustration fool you. The capabilities .NET Services bring to the table are significant, as are the applications and solutions you can now create.

■ NOTE

.NET Services and Azure in general are works in progress. The sample I've included for this chapter is based on a specific release and might be completely inoperable by the time you read this book. Typically, to make any Azure service work, you download the latest software development kit (SDK), install it, re-reference the basic assemblies (at present only Microsoft.ServiceBus), and recompile. The latest SDK is available here:

http://go.microsoft.com/fwlink/?LinkID=129448

If you consider for a moment where things have gone over the past 15 years or so, Azure represents a new style of operating system. And in fact that's probably the best way to envision it, according to Ray Ozzie, Microsoft's Chief Software Architect. You have your local computer's operating system, of course, and if you're working in a corporate environment, you have your enterprise services to rely on for performing your daily work-related tasks. Azure acts as a new Internet-scale operating system.

■ NOTE

Of course, this assumes you accept the architectural premise that an operating system provides services…it's just that some services are at a very low level.

.NET Services represent extensions of things you can do locally on your own computer—Workflow, for example. Using Windows Workflow Foundation (WF), you can create and execute workflow-based applications. .NET Services provides you with a similar workflow service that allows you to put a workflow in the cloud for general client use. I won't say a lot more about workflow in this chapter, but I will talk in some detail about the other two foundational services included in .NET Services in a following section.

The Need for .NET Services

You might rightly ask, "Why the need for cloud-based services?" Aren't traditional services we write on a daily basis enough? They're available over the Internet, just like .NET Services. What's the difference?

If you confine your thinking to today's applications, I understand the confusion. However, there are two primary driving factors from an application development perspective: Applications are demanding two-way connectivity, and there are no more IPv4 addresses to hand out.

> ■ **NOTE**
>
> Another driving aspect is financial. Purchasing and maintaining security-hardened yet highly scalable servers to run your RESTful service is expensive and requires an experienced staff. Using Azure, you gain all of this in a cost-effective manner. It's true you can host your service at a third-party host provider's site, but you still don't gain two-way connectivity and have no way to deal with client addressing. Let's just look at connectivity, though, and leave the financial argument to the corporate executives.

Typical (traditional) Web applications involve a client making a request of a server and the server providing a response. The client always initiates this process, however. Servers sit idle until there is a client request to be handled. Of course, some aren't idle for long or very often, but the point is that the servers do not initiate the contact.

There is a desire for this to change, however. Server applications are starting to seek solutions for contacting clients, such as with a notification or an event. Today, those applications might send an e-mail, send a text message, or initiate a pager communiqué, but they don't tickle an application running on your computer and communicate directly.

And even if they could, how would they find your computer? My computer sits behind a router and two firewalls. Moreover, my interface with the Internet is with a Dynamic Host Configuration Protocol (DHCP) connection, not a static network (IP) address. Client access to my computer via the Internet is much more problematic—my computer's address changes as DHCP assigns a new IP address to my connection. Non-DHCP addresses, or static IP addresses, are harder to come by simply because the address itself has an upper bound on the number of unique computers that can be addressed using the old-style IPv4 address, which looks like this:

```
192.0.0.107
```

Each value between the dots ranges from 0 to 255, for a total of 256^4 possible addresses (4,294,967,296). That seems like a big number, but when you consider the huge number of network-enabled devices available—printers, test equipment, networking gear, and so forth, in addition to computers you and I use—it's not a very large number at all. The simple truth is we've run out of IPv4 addresses. IPv6 is on the horizon, but it will be many years before IPv6 provides a total solution. When you throw in network address translation (NAT), routers, and all sorts of security-related stuff, asking a server to communicate with a client without the client initiating the conversation is one of those classical "hard" problems.

Then consider the way the Internet looks up names, via DNS. DNS, or Domain Name Service, allows you to type in "www.microsoft.com" and actually start communicating with the Microsoft servers. The problem is that in order to physically communicate over the network, you need the IP address of a server, not the domain name. DNS marries the domain name to the server's IP address, and this "yellow pages" process has worked for many years.

The issue here is that Microsoft exports a large number of services, to use them as an example. Your company might also as well. DNS won't provide your potential clients with a list of services you provide, however. DNS merely provides the IP address of a server (or set of servers if load balanced) regardless of how many services that server provides.

.NET Services provides solutions to all of these problems. When your application connects with .NET Services, the information about the connection is examined and maintained. As clients log in to the service, a service application now can access the clients through .NET Services simply because the connection information is known. It's more complex than that, of course, but that's the idea. And there is only one domain name for .NET Services, which is currently http://servicebus.windows.net/services/ using the December 2008 Azure CTP SDK release, but note that this might change as new SDK versions are released. To address the varying number of possible services, .NET Services breaks apart the URI and individually determines the appropriate endpoint routing through its own naming tables.

Of course, Microsoft wrote this, and therefore so could you. But the usual trade-offs apply. If you write it, you have to maintain it. If you write it, it's likely customized to your needs, making interoperability questionable. If you write it, you incur the expense. And so forth. So, assuming that I've convinced you to look at .NET Services a little more closely, let's start with the services that .NET Services provides.

The Many Faces of .NET Services

.NET Services is today broken into three main parts: the .NET Access Control Service, the .NET Service Bus, and the .NET Workflow Service. However, it's easy to imagine future services, so don't be surprised if by the time you read this more exist.

The .NET Access Control Service

The .NET Access Control Service is the central security service for .NET Services. This is the service you use when authenticating with .NET Services, and it's responsible for managing both authentication and claims. *Claims* are statements about the client and are validated by an independent but trusted source known as the *Secure Token Service*, or STS. When receiving a token that is confirmed by the STS, the service accepts the claims as valid and proceeds with processing. Invalid claims, or more precisely requests for an authentication token that don't support the proper set of claims, cause the service to deny the activity. Therefore, the service places a certain amount of trust in the validity of the authentication token and the STS that provided it. To your service, this essentially means you don't check user requests for role inclusion or permissions but instead verify that specific claims are present in the authentication token. If the claim your service needs to proceed isn't present, the service request fails.

> ### ■■ NOTE
>
> It's possible to skip this federated type of security and work directly with protocol-level security schemes, like HTTP Basic Authentication. But there are many issues with this approach. For one, you open your service to the Internet but route requests through .NET Services. .NET Services, of course, limits connections to your service for resource management reasons. But it is possible, even if not necessarily recommended. The recommended approach is to use the federated security inherent with the .NET Access Control Service, and you'll see how this is done in a RESTful fashion later in the chapter.

The "authentication token" I'm referring to is a Security Assertion Markup Language (SAML) token, and you can find more information about SAML here:

www.oasis-open.org/committees/tc_home.php?wg_abbrev=security

The SAML token contains a number of things, one of which is a set of claims in digitally signed and encrypted form to be tamper-proof. The SAML token and its interaction with the client, the service, and the secure token service, STS, are dictated by the WS-Trust specification found here:

http://docs.oasis-open.org/ws-sx/ws-trust/200512/ws-trust-1.3-os.html

How this all works is quite complex—the sample service in this chapter will make use of it, but only indirectly (as is normal for RESTful service access). However, I very much recommend reviewing this video to gain a deeper understanding:

http://channel9.msdn.com/shows/Going+Deep/Vittorio-Bertocci-WS-Trust-Under-the-Hood/

As I alluded to, when you're working with RESTful Azure services, the rules are bent a little. There will still be authentication checks and claim verification, but as you'll see later in the chapter, you won't receive a SAML token when invoking a RESTful Azure service. SAML tokens are best left in SOAP headers. Instead, you'll receive (for lack of a better term) a "cookie." It won't be a true HTTP cookie but rather another token that will identify your authentication information as held (temporarily) by the Access Control Service. The reason for this secondary token is that a true SAML token is far too lengthy to fit into an HTTP header. This secondary token serves as a key to index a true SAML token held on your behalf within the Access Control Service.

> ### ■ NOTE
>
> I should also mention that Azure doesn't speak in terms of "username" but rather "solution name." In this chapter I tend toward "username," but only because the term is more familiar and developers consider it one word, which works well in code. Although the terms are interchangeable in this chapter, they don't really imply the same thing to Azure. Azure provides a service framework, and you use what is essentially a "solution account" rather than a personal identity when you authenticate since your services provide solutions.

The .NET Service Bus

The .NET Service Bus provides basic connectivity between the client and the service provider. Connectivity revolves around the concept of *relay*. When you provide a service and expose that service through .NET Services, there are many benefits to doing so. First, your service is given a single endpoint your clients can access. If you later change your service's host location, your clients aren't exposed to that change. This gives your service a level of location transparency.

You also can utilize the access control mentioned in the preceding section. Now instead of your service maintaining the list of authorized users as well as their respective roles, permissions, or claims, the .NET Access Control Service can do that for you. If many services agree to use the .NET Access Control Service to *federate,* or in other words, to offer services that can be easily combined into an integrated application (basically *Software as a Service,* or SaaS), then even more interesting and useful applications are possible than are possible today without a central security service.

But one of the most fascinating aspects of the .NET Service Bus, in my opinion, is the ability to create publishers and subscribers, and what's more, have multiples of each. You could have a single publisher and a single subscriber, a single publisher and multiple subscribers, or even multiple publishers and multiple subscribers. This allows for some interesting possibilities for remote control, collaboration, and Internet-based notifications. The service can work in various ways, including peer-to-peer, as a relayed connection (the connection from client to service goes through the cloud), or as a direct connection (the client talks directly to the service after access has been established).

The .NET Workflow Service

The final service provided by .NET Services is the .NET Workflow Service. This service essentially provides you with an out-of-box workflow runtime you can use to execute Windows Workflow Foundation workflows.

The .NET Services Programming Model

You program for .NET Services using the familiar Windows Communication Foundation (WCF) programming model. The biggest difference involves the channel bindings. Whereas a traditional WCF application might open a socket directly with a service, the bindings used with .NET Services connect the channel to the cloud and relay information or provide an alternative means for direct connection (such as when circumventing NAT).

> ■ **NOTE**
>
> When I say "circumventing," I don't mean .NET Services opens holes in firewalls or actually bypasses the security aspects of NAT. The way to view this is more like .NET Services creates a wide demilitarized zone (DMZ) that includes your service and your service clients. NAT and firewalls are in no way affected unless you choose to open specific sockets and such. As for NAT specifically, .NET Services uses an internal algorithm for determining which socket to use, which happens to be the same algorithm used by Windows Live Messenger.

When you install the .NET Services SDK, you are provided with a new WCF channel, the *RelayChannel*. Channels in terms of WCF are a lot like handlers in ASP.NET, which is to say you can add and remove channels easily, and each channel is responsible for part of the overall messaging pipeline. Channels are formed into a stack. Messages flow into and out of the channel stack and are processed as required by each channel along the way. The RelayChannel "knows" how to communicate with Azure and sets up the details for you. All you need to do is to establish the proper channel configuration, starting with the bindings.

Associated with the RelayChannel are the relay bindings. Several relay bindings exist for WCF in general, as well as for Azure specifically. The one binding we're most interested in, however, is the `WebHttpRelayBinding`. This binding, which is a lot like the `WebHttpBinding` in Chapter 8, "Building REST Services Using WCF," is used to create RESTful WCF-based services that are accessed in the cloud. Your service clients can access your RESTful Azure service using pure HTTP access, but they will require Azure accounts to do so unless you open your service to the world as mentioned previously (which is *not* recommended, also mentioned previously).

Along with the channel and its bindings, you'll need something to actually run the service. .NET Services provides for security and connectivity, but it won't execute your service for you. For that, you'll need to use WCF's `WebServiceHost`. `WebServiceHost` is a derivative of `ServiceHost` that provides easier configuration and use. But `WebServiceHost` merely establishes the WCF mechanics for you...you'll still need an application surrounding the instance of `WebServiceHost` you're using. In a production environment this would likely be a Windows Service, IIS, or perhaps even "Dublin," the new Windows application server. But for this chapter's example it will be a simple console application to reduce the amount of code you'll need to wade through to find the useful parts.

The good news is that using Azure isn't that different from using pure WCF. The binding is specific to Azure, and as you'll see, you'll need to understand and work with Azure's security models. But for the most part working with Azure is as easy as working with a simple RESTful WCF service.

> **■ NOTE**
>
> You'll probably tire of reading that Azure is ever-changing and that by the time you read this and try the sample, Azure might have changed to the point that the sample no longer works. This is true, and you should be aware of it. Azure is a preview at the moment and not ready for production-level work. However, the changes to Azure that are coming are to add more services and to specifically make accessing Azure by RESTful techniques easier, so the changes should be welcome ones. As Azure changes, I'll try to post the changes on the book's Web page (noted in the introduction). Even if specific mechanical things change, the concepts introduced here will still be valid.

Service Initiation

I mentioned that using Azure involves an STS and the issuance of a SAML token containing claims. This doesn't sound very RESTful, and in fact it's not. The SAML token is designed to be placed in a SOAP header, and as you know, SOAP isn't RESTful. So how are services secured?

There are two aspects to this: authorizing the execution of the service in the first place and client access. I'll discuss client access in the next section, but as for starting the service, Azure has several authentication schemes you can use: username/password, X509 certificates, and CardSpace. If you do nothing, your service will be started using CardSpace to request your Azure account credentials. I'll show you how to write your service such that you can use a username and password when I describe the sample service for this chapter.

> **■ NOTE**
>
> For many user-interface-based applications, CardSpace is a great way to provide credentials to Azure. But the services themselves often are hosted in Windows Services or IIS, and asking for credential information isn't appropriate in those cases. Instead, you'd store the authentication information in a secured location and access it when the service is initiated.

Client Access

I mentioned that using CardSpace to request your service client's authentication information is a great way to have them authenticate, but that falls short in the specific case of RESTful service access. The reason again relates to the SAML token the STS provides. If you're not using SOAP, and the SAML token is too large to fit into an HTTP header (trust me, it is), how do you authenticate your RESTful service clients?

If your client is a Web browser that supports CardSpace, the browser will automatically request the user's CardSpace card and provide that to the service. Assuming that a valid card was selected and provided, your service will execute the client's request normally.

The difficulty arises when your RESTful service client is a nonbrowser application. In this case, you have no mechanism for requesting and providing CardSpace credentials. You simply have an HTTP request object. You could try using *NetworkCredentials* and assigning your Azure credentials to that, but that approach will fail since you're not providing the service with a SAML token. You're just handing the service your Azure username and password. The service itself has no way to validate those credentials, so access to the service will be denied.

■ ■ NOTE

This is not to say that someday you couldn't access an Azure-based service this way. This is an area that is under the closest scrutiny with the Azure development team, and what its final form might be isn't clear at this time. Currently, however, you must follow the algorithm outlined following this note.

The current Azure CTP provides a mechanism for this task, but this is one area that will definitely change. The algorithm is simple: Using a second HTTP request, access the .NET Services Access Control Service to create a SAML token and retrieve a "cookie" that identifies that token within Azure services. This value, which is called a cookie but is really a string, is then assigned to a custom HTTP header: X-MS-Identity-Token. For each RESTful service request, you insert this header and the cookie value, and

Azure will allow your RESTful service client's request to proceed. I'll show you the details when I describe a Windows Presentation Foundation (WPF) client I created to access the chapter's sample service.

Introducing the Azure Comments Service

For this chapter's sample service, I elected to create a service you could use to provide comments and suggestions directly to the authors. (Hopefully the comments would pertain to the book!) What is interesting is that the service would run directly on my computer, and if you have an Azure account, you could access my service from anywhere, even from a mobile client.

> ### ■ NOTE
>
> My intention was to actually build and run this service, but after I began writing it, I realized that a "correct" implementation would use workflow to support an approval process. This approval process would be to filter out inappropriate comments, such as those containing foul language or pharmaceutical advertisements...the usual garbage you find on some blog sites that don't filter comments. Given that the service you see here doesn't implement this workflow, you won't actually find it running in the cloud. If I miraculously find some time, I'll implement a workflow-based approval process and place a note to that effect on the book's Web page.

The service, which is of course based on WCF, allows you to perform the following operations:

- Get a comment: GET to /Comments/{CommentID}
- Get all comments: GET to /Comments}
- Add a comment: POST to /Comments}

The service returns comment representations using the Atom Syndication Format, version 1.0. Posting a new comment, however, is done using plain old XML. And as you might expect, you POST a comment instead of using PUT because the comment identifier, and hence its final URI, isn't known at the time you add the new comment. The service doesn't allow you to update or modify comments, so there is no PUT requirement; you can't delete them either, so DELETE is out.

Implementing the Service

The beginning of any WCF-based service is the design of the contract definition, and the WCF channel definition that supports the Comments service is shown in Listing 9.1. Here you see relatively standard RESTful WCF attributes, including identified reply actions for the outgoing messages, a "bare" message body style, and, for posting new comments, code that identifies the request and response as containing XML.

LISTING 9.1: The Azure Comment service channel definition

```
[ServiceContract]
public interface ICommentService
{
    [OperationContract(ReplyAction = "GETALLRESPONSE")]
    [WebGet(UriTemplate = "/Comments",
        BodyStyle = WebMessageBodyStyle.Bare)]
    Message GetAllComments();

    [OperationContract(ReplyAction = "GETRESPONSE")]
    [WebGet(UriTemplate = "/Comments/{CommentID}",
        BodyStyle = WebMessageBodyStyle.Bare)]
    Message GetComment(string commentID);

    [OperationContract(ReplyAction = "POSTRESPONSE")]
    [WebInvoke(Method = "POST", UriTemplate = "/Comments",
        BodyStyle = WebMessageBodyStyle.Bare,
        RequestFormat = WebMessageFormat.Xml,
        ResponseFormat = WebMessageFormat.Xml)]
    Message SaveComment(CommentDTO item);
}
```

The XML posted to the service for new comment insertion is a serialized form of a comment object, which is shown in Listing 9.2. Comments consist of a comment ID, which is the primary key in the comment database; the comment text itself; the name of the person making the comment; and the person's e-mail address. The name and e-mail address may be null. There is also a link for application state purposes, but this isn't stored in the database. Instead, it's generated on the fly as required since the URI of the Azure service might change.

LISTING 9.2: The Comment data transfer object

```
[DataContract(Namespace = "http://www.endurasoft.com/REST.NET/",
              Name = "Contact")]
public sealed class CommentDTO
{
    public CommentDTO()
    {
    }

    public CommentDTO(Int32 commentID, string name,
                      string email, string comment)
    {
        // Store the basic information
        this.CommentID = commentID;
        this.Name = name;
        this.EMail = email;
        this.Comment = comment;
    }

    public CommentDTO(Comment comment) :
        this(comment.CommentID, comment.Name,
             comment.EMail, comment.CommentText)
    {
    }

    [DataMember()]
    public Int32 CommentID { get; set; }

    [DataMember(IsRequired = false)]
    public string Name { get; set; }

    [DataMember(IsRequired = false)]
    public string EMail { get; set; }

    [DataMember(IsRequired = false)]
    public string Link { get; set; }

    [DataMember()]
    public string Comment { get; set; }
}
```

Because `ICommentService` identifies three methods, the service must implement those same three methods. The simplest of the three, `GetAll-Comments`, is shown in Listing 9.3. The method begins by making sure the URI ends with a slash so that individual comment links can be easily generated by concatenating their comment IDs to the end of the base URI. It then calls a helper method, `GetAllCommentsFormatter` (shown in Listing

9.4), to create a suitable Atom feed formatter. With the formatter created, the method then creates the response message and assigns the content type to be Atom (application/atom+xml).

LISTING 9.3: GetAllComments implementation

```
public Message GetAllComments()
{
    // Tweak the URI if necessary...we need for it to end with '/'
    // so we can generate proper item URIs.
    Uri baseUri =
      OperationContext.Current.IncomingMessageProperties.Via;
    if (!baseUri.AbsoluteUri.EndsWith("/"))
    {
        baseUri = new Uri(baseUri.AbsoluteUri + "/");
    }

    // Retrieve the formatter
    Atom10FeedFormatter formatter = GetAllCommentsFormatter(baseUri);

    // Create the response message
    Message response = Message.CreateMessage(
      OperationContext.Current.IncomingMessageVersion,
      "GETALLRESPONSE", formatter);

    // Return the Atom feed
    WebOperationContext.Current.OutgoingResponse.ContentType =
      AtomContentType;
    return response;
}
```

GetAllCommentsFormatter is also used in the method for returning a single comment. There, if the comment ID cannot be parsed into an integer or the integer represents a nonexistent comment, all comments will be returned rather than an error.

LISTING 9.4: The GetAllCommentsFormatter helper method

```
private Atom10FeedFormatter GetAllCommentsFormatter(Uri itemUri)
{
    // Retrieve all comments
    CommentModel model = new CommentModel();
    CommentDTO[] items = model.GetComments();

    // Generate the feed
    List<SyndicationItem> list = new List<SyndicationItem>();
    foreach (CommentDTO item in items)
    {
```

```
        // Generate the link
        item.Link = String.Format("{0}{1}", itemUri.AbsoluteUri,
                                    item.CommentID);

        // Add the comment
        list.Add(GetSyndicatedComment(item));
    }
    SyndicationFeed feed = new SyndicationFeed(itemUri.ToString(),
                            FeedTitle, itemUri, list);
    Atom10FeedFormatter formatter = new Atom10FeedFormatter(feed);

    // Return the formatter
    return formatter;
}
```

Creating an Atom syndicated feed is a simple matter with WCF.
The desired comments are first retrieved using a custom model object,
CommentModel. Assuming that there are comments, each comment is
assigned its link and then converted into a syndication item using another
helper method, GetSyndicatedComment, which is shown in Listing 9.5. With
all the comments converted into feed items, the feed itself is created and the
associated formatter is returned.

LISTING 9.5: The GetSyndicatedComment helper method

```
private SyndicationItem GetSyndicatedComment(CommentDTO comment)
{
    // Sanitize the name and e-mail, as these could
    // be null...
    string name = String.IsNullOrEmpty(comment.Name) ?
                    DefaultFeedItemName : comment.Name;
    string email = String.IsNullOrEmpty(comment.EMail) ?
                    String.Empty : comment.EMail;

    // Create a syndication item using the information contained
    // in the comment.
    SyndicationItem item = new SyndicationItem(DefaultFeedItemTitle,
        comment.Comment, new Uri(comment.Link));
    item.Authors.Add(new SyndicationPerson(email, name,
                                        DefaultFeedItemUri));
    item.Summary = new TextSyndicationContent(
                    String.Format(DefaultFeedItemSummaryFormat, name));

    // Return the item
    return item;
}
```

The comments database is accessed using LINQ to SQL, and the database context for this is encapsulated in the `CommentModel` class. The implementation of the query methods is relatively straightforward. The insertion method also isn't terribly revolutionary, but I've shown it in Listing 9.6 anyway to show the assignment of the comment ID to the data transfer object so that the object can be returned to the client in its inserted form. The client can then keep track of the new comment ID should it need to do so.

LISTING 9.6: The `CommentModel` `InsertComment` **method implementation**

```
public void InsertComment(CommentDTO item)
{
    // Quick check...
    if (item == null) return;

    try
    {
        // Create the data context
        CommentDataClassesDataContext context =
          new CommentDataClassesDataContext();

        // Create the comment into the blog comment table
        Comment comment = new Comment();
        comment.CommentText = item.Comment;
        comment.Name = item.Name;
        comment.EMail = item.EMail;

        // Schedule the new comment for insertion
        context.Comments.InsertOnSubmit(comment);

        // Transact the comment into the database
        using (TransactionScope ts = new TransactionScope())
        {
            // Submit the entry
            context.SubmitChanges();

            // Commit the insert
            ts.Complete();
        }

        // The comment ID is updated on insert, so we'll return
        // the updated object so that we can create the response
        // to the caller.
        item.CommentID = comment.CommentID;
    }
```

```
    catch
    {
        // Some error...just return
    }
}
```

Of course, the comment model's `InsertComment` method is used by the service's `SaveComment` method, which is shown in Listing 9.7. The service first saves the comment in the database and then returns to the client an Atom representation of the newly inserted item. The reason I'm showing this is to reinforce the notion that you should set the HTTP `Location` header to the item's link upon creation, and if you plan on returning HTTP `201` (Created), you should provide the new object in the response's entity body. You see this toward the end of Listing 9.7.

LISTING 9.7: The Comment service `SaveComment` **method implementation**

```
public Message SaveComment(CommentDTO item)
{
    // NOTE: This method assumes the content of the comment has been
    // reviewed and approved through some workflow process not shown
    // here. It is not advisable to simply post comments without
    // reviewing them first. Also consider SQL Injection attacks and
    // preventive measures.
    //
    // Make sure we have a DTO
    Message response = null;
    if (item != null)
    {
        // Save the comment
        _model.InsertComment(item);

        // Tweak the URI if necessary...we need for it to end with '/'
        // so we can generate proper item URIs.
        Uri baseUri =
          OperationContext.Current.IncomingMessageProperties.Via;
        if (!baseUri.AbsoluteUri.EndsWith("/"))
        {
            baseUri = new Uri(baseUri.AbsoluteUri + "/");
        }

        // Generate the link
        item.Link = String.Format("{0}{1}", baseUri.AbsoluteUri,
                                item.CommentID);
```

continues

LISTING 9.7: Continued

```
        // Generate the feed
        List<SyndicationItem> list = new List<SyndicationItem>();
        list.Add(GetSyndicatedComment(item));
        SyndicationFeed feed = new SyndicationFeed(FeedTitle,
          FeedDescription, new Uri(item.Link), list);
        Atom10FeedFormatter formatter = new Atom10FeedFormatter(feed);

        // Create the response message
        response = Message.CreateMessage(
          OperationContext.Current.IncomingMessageVersion,
          "POSTRESPONSE", formatter);

        // Assign the usual headers
        WebOperationContext.Current.OutgoingResponse.Location =
          item.Link;
        WebOperationContext.Current.OutgoingResponse.StatusCode =
          System.Net.HttpStatusCode.Created;
        WebOperationContext.Current.OutgoingResponse.StatusDescription =
          "Created";

        // Assign the content type
        WebOperationContext.Current.OutgoingResponse.ContentType =
          AtomContentType;
    }
    else
    {
        // Problem deserializing...
        WebOperationContext.Current.OutgoingResponse.StatusCode =
          System.Net.HttpStatusCode.BadRequest;
        WebOperationContext.Current.OutgoingResponse.StatusDescription =
          "Bad Request";

        // Create the response message
        response = Message.CreateMessage(
          OperationContext.Current.IncomingMessageVersion,
          "POSTRESPONSE", (object)DeserializationFault);

        // Assign the content type...WCF will place this in an
        // XML format for us.
        WebOperationContext.Current.OutgoingResponse.ContentType =
          XmlContentType;
    }

    // Return the Atom feed with the newly inserted item or the
    // error message
    return response;
}
```

Two things remain as far as digging into the service itself: hosting the service and configuring the service.

Hosting the Service

Earlier in the chapter, I mentioned using WebServiceHost to house the executing service. For this service, I'm running WebServiceHost in a console application, but production-quality services would likely use a Windows Service or perhaps use IIS. I've chosen a console application simply because it's the easiest to use for this example.

The code for the console application's Main method is shown in Listing 9.8. If the service isn't using CardSpace for authentication, it must provide for some other means to request Azure credentials. Probably the easiest and most common way to do this is to simply provide a username and password. For this service, I chose to request those each time you execute the service host rather than storing them in some persistent location, like the configuration file. If this service is hosted using a Windows Service or IIS, you'll need to securely record the username and password somewhere rather than requesting them dynamically.

LISTING 9.8: The host console application's Main method

```
static void Main(string[] args)
{
    // Request credentials
    LoginForm dlg = new LoginForm();
    if (dlg.ShowDialog() != DialogResult.OK) return;

    // Create the Azure URI for the service
    Uri address = new
      Uri(String.Format("http://{0}/services/{1}/CommentService/",
          ServiceBusEnvironment.DefaultRelayHostName, dlg.Username));

    // Establish the endpoing credentials using the username
    // and password provided (we could use CardSpace by omitting
    // this behavior entirely).
    TransportClientEndpointBehavior behavior =
      new TransportClientEndpointBehavior();
    behavior.CredentialType =
      TransportClientCredentialType.UserNamePassword;
    behavior.Credentials.UserName.UserName = dlg.Username;
    behavior.Credentials.UserName.Password = dlg.Password;
```

continues

LISTING 9.8: Continued

```
        // Create the host and apply the endpoint behavior
        WebServiceHost host =
          new WebServiceHost(typeof(CommentService), address);
        host.Description.Endpoints[0].Behaviors.Add(behavior);
        host.Open();

        // Print a banner
        Console.WriteLine("Copy the following address into a browser to" +
                          " see the response: ");
        Console.WriteLine("{0}Comments", address);
        Console.WriteLine();
        Console.WriteLine("Press any key to exit...");
        Console.ReadKey();

        // Close the connection
        host.Close();
    }
```

Looking at Listing 9.8, you'll notice that the first thing the service host does is pop up a small Windows Forms dialog box to allow you to provide your credentials (shown in Figure 9.2). After you provide your Azure account information and click Login, the service host takes the information and provides it to `TransportClientEndpointBehavior`. With the URI and endpoint behavior specified, the service host application then creates an instance of `WebServiceHost`, applies the username/password endpoint behavior, and then opens the channel.

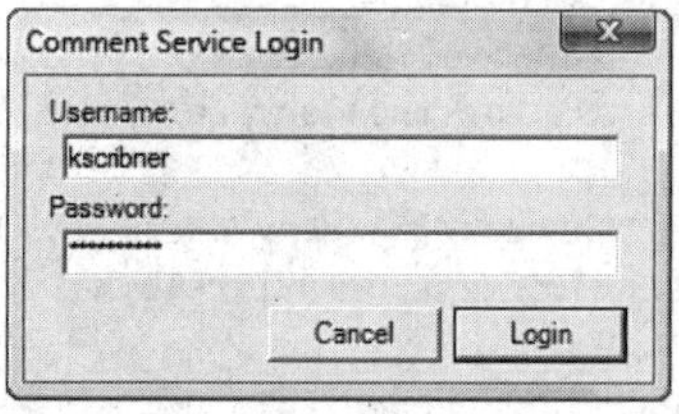

FIGURE 9.2: The Comment service login form

At this point Azure is consulted and your credentials are validated. Assuming that you provided accurate information, the console appears (see Figure 9.3). The service will execute until you press any key, at which time the channel is closed and the application terminates.

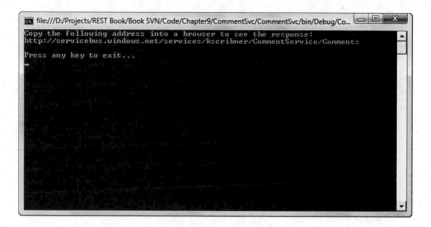

FIGURE 9.3: The Comment service host console application

Configuring the Service

The magic that makes all of this work is rolled into Microsoft.ServiceBus, which is installed when you install the Azure software development kit. Microsoft.ServiceBus reads your application's configuration information and configures the channel stack accordingly. For this sample service, the application's WCF-related configuration information is as shown in Listing 9.9.

LISTING 9.9: The Comment service host application configuration file

```
<system.serviceModel>
  <bindings>
    <webHttpRelayBinding>
      <binding name="default">
        <security relayClientAuthenticationType="RelayAccessToken"/>
      </binding>
    </webHttpRelayBinding>
  </bindings>

  <services>
    <service name="CommentSvc.CommentService"
             behaviorConfiguration="default">
      <endpoint name="RelayEndpoint"
                contract="CommentSvc.ICommentService"
                binding="webHttpRelayBinding"
                bindingConfiguration="default"
                address="" />
```

continues

LISTING 9.9: Continued

```
        </service>
    </services>

    <behaviors>
      <serviceBehaviors>
        <behavior name="default">
          <serviceDebug httpHelpPageEnabled="false"
                        httpsHelpPageEnabled="false" />
        </behavior>
      </serviceBehaviors>
    </behaviors>
  </system.serviceModel>
```

Looking first at the bindings element, notice that `WebHttpRelayBinding` is used, which is precisely the binding I mentioned earlier in the chapter. The only real configuration here is the application of the `RelayAccessToken` for the client authentication type (and in fact this could be omitted because this is the default configuration…your other option is `None`, which is how you disable authentication to your service entirely). `WebHttpRelayBinding` is the binding that causes this service to execute within the bounds of Azure.

> **■ NOTE**
>
> Interestingly, changing the binding is all you must do to take a traditional WCF service and turn it into an Azure-based service. This is one of the strengths of WCF.

The remaining configuration sections identify the contract definition the service will use, the endpoint configuration, and specific Web-related behaviors. The endpoint address is left empty here because the main application will configure it imperatively (refer to Listing 9.8). Otherwise, these are typical WCF configuration elements—nothing special.

Now that you've seen the service, it's time to look at the client side of the RESTful conversation. There isn't much of a trick to using a browser, but as you'll see, you'll need to code some special behavior into your applications if they're to communicate with an Azure REST service.

The Service Client

Throughout the book the clients you've used have authenticated using HTTP Basic Authentication. And although other authentication schemes could be used, in the specific case of Azure, HTTP Basic Authentication can't be used in conjunction with the .NET Services Access Control Service, or at least not at the time this was written.

> **▪ NOTE**
>
> You could disable Azure security entirely and use whichever scheme you like, but this is not recommended by the Azure team for reasons mentioned earlier in the chapter.

Therefore, the client code you write will differ slightly if your client is a Windows application. Browsers should be able to access RESTful services, at least if they can render the given representation they obtain, and Azure does support this with little effort on your part. Let's look at the simpler case first, the browser, and then look at the C# code that's required to access the RESTful service from a Windows application.

Browser-Based Clients

To access a RESTful service in the Azure cloud, you begin by typing in the URI for the service. The URI shown here results in an Atom feed when accessing the Comments service hosted using my personal Azure account:

```
http://servicebus.windows.net/services/kscribner/CommentService/Comments
```

> **▪ NOTE**
>
> If you access the previous URI, you'll probably receive a generic (empty) ATOM feed listing "publicly available services" instead of the Comments service results I show here. The reason for this is simple: The service isn't running on my local computer. Another alternative is for you to host the service on your local computer and substitute my Azure username in the URI ("kscribner") for your own.

As soon as you type in this URI, or perhaps a valid URI for the service when you're running it using your Azure account since I'm probably not running it, an HTTP request like this is issued:

```
GET /services/kscribner/CommentService/Comments HTTP/1.1
Accept: image/gif, ... , */*
Accept-Language: en-us
UA-CPU: x86
Accept-Encoding: gzip, deflate
User-Agent: Mozilla/4.0 (compatible; MSIE 7.0; ...; .NET CLR 3.0.30618)
Host: servicebus.windows.net
Connection: Keep-Alive
```

This HTTP request is nothing special—just another typical browser request. However, Azure responds with a redirect since you're not (yet) authenticated:

```
HTTP/1.1 302 Found
Transfer-Encoding: chunked
Content-Type: text/html
Location: http://accesscontrol.windows.net/IPSelector.aspx?sv=http://
➥servicebus.windows.net/services/kscribner/CommentService/Comments
Server: Microsoft-HTTPAPI/2.0
Date: Fri, 07 Nov 2008 21:04:35 GMT

<html><head><title>Object moved</title></head><body><h2>Object moved to
➥<a href="http://accesscontrol.windows.net/IPSelector.aspx?sv=
➥http://servicebus.windows.net/services/kscribner/CommentService/
➥Comments">here</a>.</h2></body></html>
```

The browser accepts the redirect and issues this request:

```
GET /IPSelector.aspx?sv=http://accesscontrol.../Comments HTTP/1.1
Accept: image/gif, ... , */*
Accept-Language: en-us
UA-CPU: x86
Accept-Encoding: gzip, deflate
User-Agent: Mozilla/4.0 (compatible; MSIE 7.0; ...; .NET CLR 3.0.30618)
Cookie: ANON=A=C5F8...fA&W=4
Connection: Keep-Alive
Host: accesscontrol.windows.net
```

This request redirects you to a login page, the response for which is here (I abbreviated the HTML content, however):

```
HTTP/1.1 200 OK
Cache-Control: private
Content-Length: 6126
```

```
Content-Type: text/html; charset=utf-8
Server: Microsoft-IIS/7.0
X-AspNet-Version: 2.0.50727
Set-Cookie: ASP.NET_SessionId=cy3g...yo; path=/; HttpOnly
X-Powered-By: ASP.NET
Date: Fri, 07 Nov 2008 21:04:36 GMT

<!DOCTYPE html PUBLIC "-//W3C//DTD XHTML 1.0 Transitional//EN"
➥"http://www.w3.org/TR/xhtml1/DTD/xhtml1-transitional.dtd">

<html xmlns="http://www.w3.org/1999/xhtml">
<head id="Head1"><meta http-equiv="X-UA-Compatible" content=
➥"IE=EmulateIE7" /><title>
   Microsoft .NET Services Access Control
</title>
...
</html>
```

You were redirected because Azure sensed that you didn't provide evidence of a successful login, and it requires you to do so. (You'll see how it knew momentarily.) The HTML I abbreviated appears in rendered form in Figure 9.4.

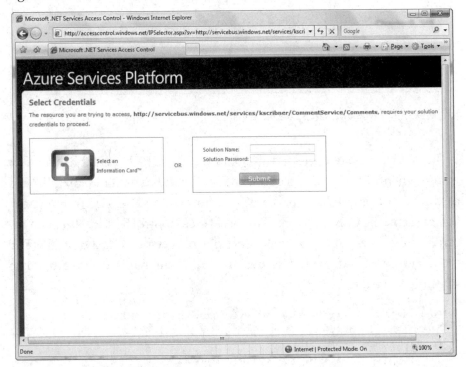

FIGURE 9.4: Azure credential request

The Web page shown in Figure 9.4 allows you to provide either a username and password or a CardSpace card to validate your access request. If you select the CardSpace option, the CardSpace manager appears, as shown in Figure 9.5.

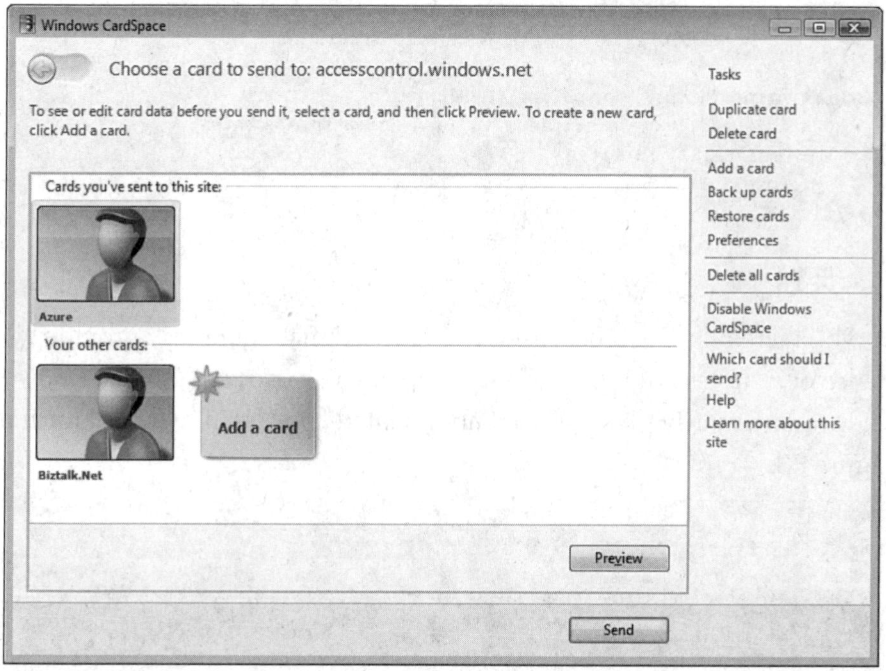

FIGURE 9.5: The Windows CardSpace manager

In this case I have selected my Azure card, which I established with Azure when I created my account (notice I still have an old Biztalk.NET card, which was used with Azure's precursor cloud service framework). When I send the CardSpace card to the Access Control Service, the data the card represents is issued to the Access Control Service using a typical HTTP POST. Here is the request that issues my card (note that I've elided the data since it's a live card!):

```
POST /services/kscribner/CommentService/Comments HTTP/1.1
Accept: image/gif, ... , */*
Accept-Language: en-us
Content-Type: application/x-www-form-urlencoded
UA-CPU: x86
Accept-Encoding: gzip, deflate
```

```
User-Agent: Mozilla/4.0 (compatible; MSIE 7.0; ...; .NET CLR 3.0.30618)
Host: servicebus.windows.net
Content-Length: 52
Connection: Keep-Alive
Pragma: no-cache

token=sDjO...3Q%3D%3D
```

The information represented by my CardSpace card is rolled up into the *token* parameter and sent to Azure's Access Control Service. The Access Control Service then responds with this:

```
HTTP/1.1 200 OK
Transfer-Encoding: chunked
Content-Type: application/atom+xml
Server: Microsoft-HTTPAPI/2.0
Set-Cookie: HashToken=sDjO...3Q==;path=/
Date: Fri, 07 Nov 2008 21:04:47 GMT

<feed xmlns="http://www.w3.org/2005/Atom"><title type="text">
➥http://servicebus.windows.net/services/kscribner/CommentService/
➥CommentC/</title>
...
</feed>
```

The returned content is the feed shown in Figure 9.6 (I once again abbreviated the response because of its length). But notice that a cookie (marked as bold) has been added to the response. The browser will cache this cookie, which represents the CardSpace card I presented to the Access Control Service earlier. Future requests will include this cookie so that I'm asked for the CardSpace card only once for this session.

Application-Based Clients

Nonbrowser applications need to handle Azure authentication a little differently, primarily because they likely don't handle redirects in the same way. The Azure team recognized this limitation and implemented the algorithm I mentioned earlier in the chapter. The algorithm is described by the Microsoft team in an article at this URI:

http://msdn.microsoft.com/en-us/library/dd129877.aspx#Web-Style_REST)_Authentication

This reference makes no bones about it—this algorithm is living on borrowed time; so don't implement mission-critical applications using this authentication technique, and check with the Azure portal or the book's Web page for updated information.

> **NOTE**
>
> This is important enough that I'll follow that statement with this note. The Microsoft article specifically says the following: "Along with the interactive credentials mechanism explained above, this is a temporary implementation for the .NET Services November 2008 CTP and will be superseded in a release in the near future." Caveat emptor (it still works for the December release).

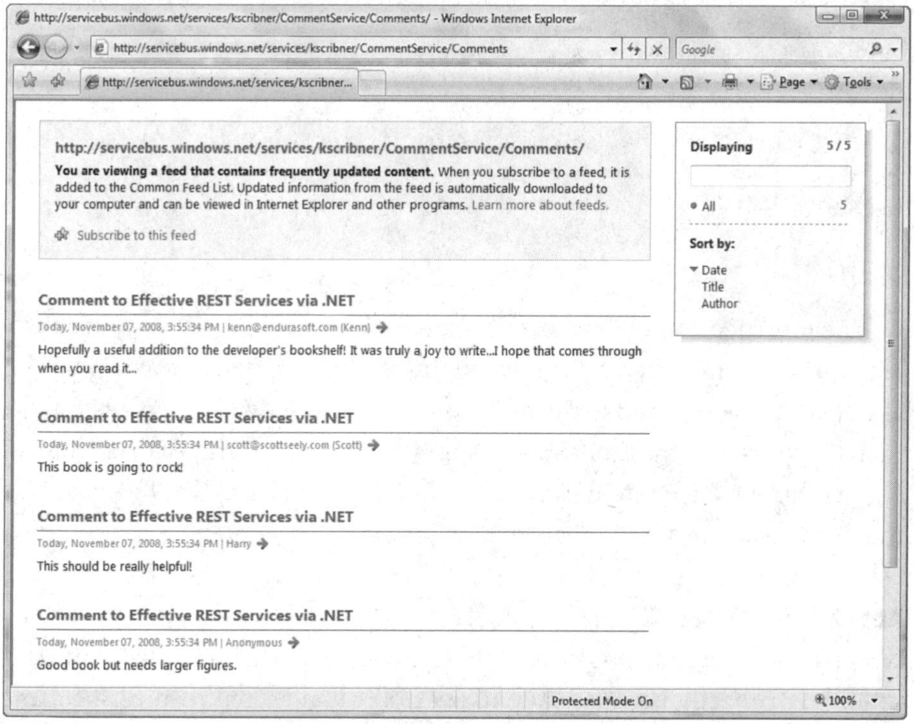

FIGURE 9.6: The Azure Comment service atom feed

The "interactive credentials mechanism" that the Microsoft reference refers to is the algorithm you need to follow to authenticate your application with Azure:

1. Issue an HTTP request to the .NET Services Access Control Service using the following URI:

   https://accesscontrol.windows.net/issuetoken.aspx?u={username}&p={password}

2. Assuming that the token request was successful, read the response into a string and cache it.

3. Access the Azure service using the cached string as assigned to a custom HTTP header, X-MS-Identity-Token.

As a side note, if you look at the third step of the algorithm, you'll notice the custom HTTP header X-MS-Identity-Token, which breaks the RESTful notion of self-description. The members of the Azure team are very aware of this (because they're exceptionally strong REST developers), which is probably the reason for the "temporary implementation." Interestingly, the term the Azure team uses for this is "REST Tunneling."

The Sample Application User Interface

To demonstrate the Comments service, as well as to demonstrate posting information to an Azure RESTful service, I created a WPF application you can use to test service interaction. The basic user interface looks like most of the applications I created for this book (sorry), and it's shown in Figure 9.7.

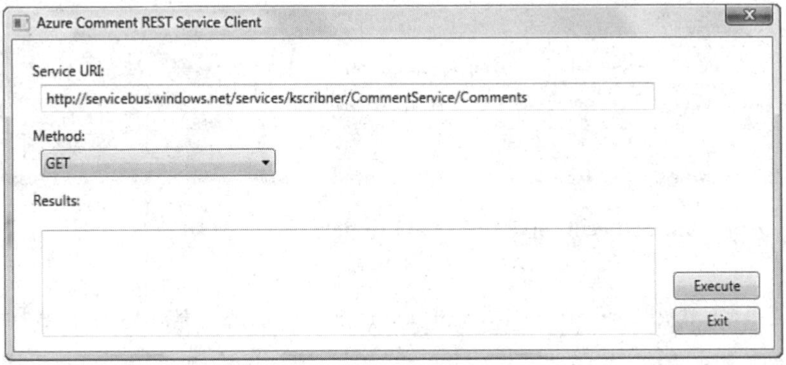

FIGURE 9.7: The Azure Comment REST service WPF client

The client allows you to issue both an HTTP GET and a POST. If you issue a GET, you'll receive and view the Atom-based XML in the results text box. Clicking the Execute button brings up the usual dialog box to request your username and password, as shown in Figure 9.8.

FIGURE 9.8: Azure client authentication dialog box

The application follows the algorithm I mentioned, and if the authentication request is successful, you should see an Atom response much like what is shown in Figure 9.9.

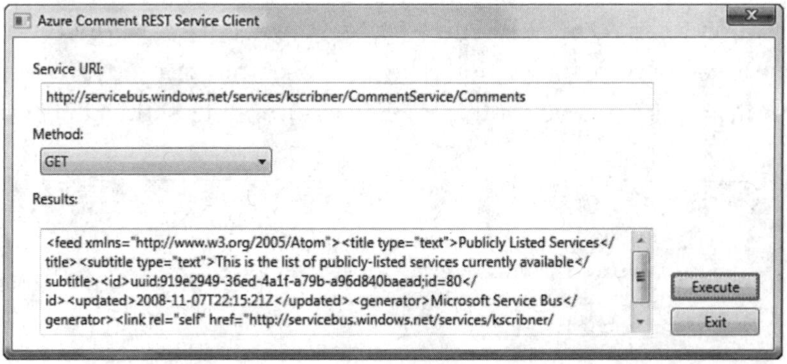

FIGURE 9.9: Azure Comment service HTTP GET response

Adding a new comment involves an HTTP POST, but you also have to provide the comment itself. The sample application allows for this by implementing a comment dialog box, shown in Figure 9.10.

FIGURE 9.10: Azure client New Comment dialog box

The information contained in the New Comment dialog box is rolled into an object, serialized, and issued to the Azure Comments service using typical HTTP means. (The custom HTTP header must still be applied, of course.)

Client Application Code

If you open the WPF client application and look inside the main window's code, you'll find code that looks a lot like the other client applications you've seen throughout the book. The major difference is the authentication scheme. Instead of allowing three tries using HTTP Basic Authentication, the application asks for your credentials once. If your credentials are valid, the application caches the token issued by the Access Control Service. You'll find this code in Listing 9.10.

LISTING 9.10: The client application QueryAuthenticationToken method

```
private bool QueryAuthenticationToken()
{
    // Assume not authenticated
    bool authenticated = false;

    // First request username/password
    ClientAuthenticationWindow authWindow =
```

continues

LISTING 9.10: Continued

```
        new ClientAuthenticationWindow();
authWindow.Owner = this;
bool? dialogResult = authWindow.ShowDialog();
if (dialogResult == true)
{
    try
    {
        // Next, query the Azure identity service for
        // a valid authentication token.
        Uri uri = new Uri(String.Format(AzureIdentityUriFormat,
          authWindow.Username,
          Uri.EscapeDataString(authWindow.Password)));
        HttpWebRequest request =
          WebRequest.Create(uri) as HttpWebRequest;
        request.Method = "GET";

        // Call for the response
        HttpWebResponse response =
          request.GetResponse() as HttpWebResponse;

        // Read the response
        using (StreamReader rdr = new
                StreamReader(response.GetResponseStream()))
        {
            // Scrape the token cookie
            _xIdentityToken = rdr.ReadToEnd();

            // HACK: Remove extraneous content noted at times from
            // Access Control Service. Sometimes we obtain a valid
            // token, and other times we obtain the token with some
            // HTML attached telling us there was a server-side
            // error. Since we have a token, slice off the HTML
            // and ignore it. Note the token is a Base64 string,
            // so we can safely parse the '>'
            Int32 htmlStart = _xIdentityToken.IndexOf('<');
            if (htmlStart > 0)
                _xIdentityToken = _xIdentityToken.Substring(0,
                              _xIdentityToken.IndexOf('<'));
        }

        // With the cookie in hand, indicate we authenticated
        authenticated = true;
    }
    catch (Exception ex)
    {
        // Some error...show user
        MessageBox.Show(String.Format(
```

```
        "Error accessing Azure identity service: {0}",
        ex.ToString()),"Authentication Error",
        MessageBoxButton.OK, MessageBoxImage.Error);
    }
}

    return authenticated;
}
```

An interesting side effect is indicated by the "hack" comment. At the time this was written, there existed a known bug that would concatenate HTML to the returned token. You would receive a valid token, but you would also receive an HTML-based error message…of course, there was no error, so the code following the "hack" comment simply removes the HTML and carries the token forward. If in the near future the bug is corrected, this code will never execute, so it's harmless to leave it in this sample.

QueryAuthenticationToken is called when you click the Execute button, the handler code for which is shown in Listing 9.11. (Some of the code lines were a bit lengthy, so I scooted the interior code over by removing the first level of indentation.)

LISTING 9.11: The client application Execute button event handler

```
private void Execute_Click(object sender, RoutedEventArgs e)
{
// Check for a URI...we can't let the user progress without
// one...
if (String.IsNullOrEmpty(tbServiceUri.Text))
{
    // No URI...
    MessageBox.Show(
      "You must provide a URI before executing the service call.",
      "URI Required", MessageBoxButton.OK, MessageBoxImage.Error);
    return;
}

// Check for a username and password. We'll only need to
// perform this once...
if (String.IsNullOrEmpty(_xIdentityToken))
{
    // Request user's username and password, then query
    // Azure's identity service for a valid authentication
    // token.
```

continues

```
            if (!QueryAuthenticationToken())
            {
                // Exception or user cancelled...
                return;
            }
        }

        CommentItem newCommentItem = null;
        if (cmbMethod.SelectedIndex == 1)
        {
            // We're executing a POST, so we need a representation
            // to send to the service. We'll ask for the information
            // before communicating with the server.
            NewCommentWindow newCommentDlg = new NewCommentWindow();

            // Show the dialog
            bool? result = newCommentDlg.ShowDialog();
            if (result == true)
            {
                // Pull comment item...
                newCommentItem = newCommentDlg.CommentItem;
            }
            else
            {
                // User canceled, so exit method
                return;
            }
        }

        try
        {
            // Create the request
            Uri uri = new Uri(tbServiceUri.Text);
            HttpWebRequest request = WebRequest.Create(uri) as HttpWebRequest;
            request.Method =
((ComboBoxItem)cmbMethod.Items[cmbMethod.SelectedIndex]).Tag.ToString();
            request.Headers.Add(IdentityHeader, _xIdentityToken);

            // Send any data
            if (cmbMethod.SelectedIndex == 1)
            {
                // Insert a new comment
                PushCommentItem(request, newCommentItem);
            }

            // Call for the response
            HttpWebResponse response = request.GetResponse() as HttpWebResponse;
```

```
    // Retrieve content
    string responseContent = String.Empty;
    using (StreamReader rdr =
      new StreamReader(response.GetResponseStream()))
    {
        responseContent = rdr.ReadToEnd();
    }
    tbResults.Text = responseContent;
}
catch (Exception ex)
{
    // Pop up a messagebox showing the error...
    MessageBox.Show(ex.Message, "Error Invoking Azure Comments Service",
      MessageBoxButton.OK, MessageBoxImage.Error);
    tbResults.Text = ex.ToString();
}
}
```

The Execute button handler begins by making sure there is a URI to interact with. If there is a URI, it then checks to see whether the user has authenticated with .NET Services' Access Control Service. If the user authenticated, the field containing the token to be placed in the custom HTTP X-MS-Identity-Token header will have a value and the service invocation continues. If not, the user is queried for the Azure username and password and the Access Control Service is accessed for authentication.

After the user is authenticated, the application looks to see whether the user's request is a GET or a POST. If it's a POST invocation, the user is asked for the comment information to send to the service. The comment information is placed into a local class I created that's compatible with the CommentDTO class on the server for serialization purposes.

> ■ **NOTE**
>
> Unlike most of the previous services you've seen in this book, the representation you receive from the service and the representation you use to create new resources differ. In this case the service returns XML using the Atom Syndication Format, but you'll need to add comments using a custom XML vocabulary that is arbitrarily based on a server-side object. There is nothing wrong with this approach, but in a production setting you'll want to provide your service users with some guidance as to what the XML for adding a comment should look like.

The remainder of the Execute button handler is typical C# code for calling a RESTful service, with the exception of the creation of the custom header:

```
private const string IdentityHeader = "X-MS-Identity-Token";
...
request.Headers.Add(IdentityHeader, _xIdentityToken);
```

Here the value returned from .NET Services' Access Control Service is provided to the Comments service to provide proof that the user is authenticated and able to access the service.

The final bit of code I'll show is the code that actually serializes the local application comment object and issues it to the Comments service. From Listing 9.12 you can see that I use the DataContractSerializer to both serialize the comment and forward it through the request stream to the service. Finally, I set the content type to be XML, which the WCF service expects because I dictated the service SaveComment method's RequestFormat to be WebMessageFormat.Xml.

LISTING 9.12: The client application PushCommentItem method

```
private void PushCommentItem(HttpWebRequest request, CommentItem item)
{
    Stream requestStream = request.GetRequestStream();
    try
    {
        DataContractSerializer serializer =
            new DataContractSerializer(typeof(CommentItem));
        serializer.WriteObject(
            requestStream, item);
    }
    finally
    {
        // Clear the stream;
        requestStream.Flush();
        requestStream.Close();
    }

    // Set the content type
    request.ContentType = "text/xml";
}
```

You've now seen how to create a RESTful service of your own that lives harmoniously in the cloud as well as access it using a browser and a custom

Windows application. But there is one more area I'll briefly describe where you can work with Azure in a RESTful fashion, and that is for managing your own account information.

Azure RESTful Account Management

I won't go into great detail here since accessing your account information requires you to have a good understanding of certain Azure concepts I haven't described in this chapter. I intended to use this chapter to highlight how to work with Azure in a RESTful way rather than spending a lot of time describing how Azure itself works, which could easily fill a book. (Like you, I'd love to own a good Azure book to fill in the details.)

However, I should at least mention the services Azure provides that allow you to manage your account information in a RESTful way. I won't provide any code for this because you'll find a nice sample provided with the Azure .NET Services SDK that covers everything I'll discuss here.

Claims, Rules, and Scope

I discussed claims earlier in the chapter. Claims are just statements: "I am over 21 years of age." "My e-mail address is.…" Claims-based authentication allows your service to examine truths about the client rather than fit the client into a specific role or grant a certain set of permissions. If the client's claims don't match the needs of your service, simply fail the client access.

But how do you do that? Nothing in the Comments service I presented dealt with examining claims and failing the service invocation. It turns out that Azure handles this job for you, and it does so by querying a set of access rules you establish for your solution account. You can log in to your Azure account and set up various access rules, including which users can access your service and which claims are required, and if a client attempts to access your service without meeting the rules you established, the client will automatically be disallowed access to your service. If your service executes at all, you can be confident that the client met your access requirements.

But establishing one set of rules for your entire solution account is very limiting. If you wrote a second service that had a different set of rules, you would need to establish a second Azure account. Clearly this isn't optimal, so Azure has the concept of *scope*. You can access your Azure account information and create any number of scopes, and access rules can then be applied to individual scopes rather than to your solution account as a whole.

Working with Azure Access Control Manager

If you prefer working with claims, rules, and scope using an application, you can simply log in to Azure with your Web browser and make any changes there. However, the functionality you find at the Azure portal is also available to RESTful clients. The representations you work with for claims, rules, and scope are XML-based and issued to the Azure Access Control Manager in the same way the comment XML was presented to the Comments service in this chapter. For a full-fledged working sample, download and install the Azure .NET Services SDK and look for the sample titled "RESTSample."

Where Are We?

In this chapter you explored Azure, Microsoft's cloud-based operating system. Clients from across the Internet can access a RESTful service running on your local computer no matter how your computer is connected to the Internet. The only requirements are that you have an Azure account and your computer is capable of running .NET 3.5 and WCF.

You learned a bit about how Azure secures accounts, and what services are currently offered by .NET Services: Access Control Service, Service Bus, and Workflow Service. Access Control Service deals with authenticating clients and understands claims, rules, and scope. Service Bus connects your RESTful service to the cloud, and hence to the world. And Workflow Service can run your workflows in the cloud so that you don't have to host them yourself.

Then you saw how to create a RESTful WCF-based service designed to work in the cloud. The service itself was no different than any other WCF RESTful service with the exception of the channel binding, which was `Web-HttpRelayBinding`. This binding provides the plumbing that connects your service to the cloud and grants you all the benefits of cloud computing.

Finally, you looked at accessing RESTful services hosted in the cloud using both a browser and a custom Windows application. Browser access uses CardSpace to authenticate, assuming that you didn't disable service authentication. Custom Windows applications need to perform a little extra work to authenticate by requesting a token from the Access Control Service. This technique worked at the time this was written, but you can anticipate this changing in the future, perhaps even by the time you read this text. Be sure to check out the Azure portal for more recent information, and the authors will do their best to keep the information on the book's Web page (www.endurasoft.com/rest.aspx) accurate and up-to-date.

A.

.NET REST Architectural Considerations and Decisions

DESIGN AND ENGINEERING is arguably about making decisions and evaluating trade-offs. It's a rare case where an option presents itself that is perfectly suited to each and every requirement you have to fulfill. In software, for example, you often trade increased speed for increased memory consumption. Or with server-based services, you trade increased call latency for enhanced functionality you can't provide locally.

Because of this, architects and developers often ask questions like "Should I use IIS directly or go with WCF?" Or "Which is faster, WCF or ASP.NET?"

Clearly these are important questions to address, but unfortunately the answer is usually "It depends." It depends on your application's requirements. It depends on your development staff's skill set. It depends on your anticipated deployment environment. It depends on a lot of things.

Then there is what I like to call "lifestyle" decisions. If you are one of the die-hard ASP.NET MVC fans who likes to generate mocks and test cases for breakfast, I'd be hard-pressed to recommend switching back to using an HttpHandler without good reason. You live the MVC lifestyle, and there are good reasons for doing so. Even so, there are sometimes good reasons for using an HttpHandler even when your primary application framework is

ASP.NET MVC. But that doesn't mean that building a service using the controller-model pattern you saw in Chapter 7, "Building REST Services Using ASP.NET MVC Framework," won't work or won't support your application's requirements. It depends.

In the end, deciding which .NET technology to use is a personal decision, and although I'll provide some guidance here, you should evaluate what you see here against your particular application needs. If you can find a technological fit that's better than other options, select that option. If you're convinced one approach is better than all the rest, by all means use that approach. This appendix isn't here to convince you to implement your services using one technology over another. It's simply a compilation of author experience and generalizations. One way to enhance an "it depends" answer is to also say "in general, do this...."

■. NOTE

I can't imagine receiving not a single negative response to the graph I'm about to present. Surely someone will be upset and argue that their favorite technology isn't fairly or properly placed. To all of you I apologize, but I maintain that this is a real-world graph based on author experience. I know and use each of these technologies and firmly believe all have their place in my distributed systems toolbox. The graph is not meant to shortchange any technology or make one technology "look good" or "look bad" when compared to the others. I'm just trying to help architects and developers decide which technology to use given their needs, based on experience and intuition.

To shed some light on my own architectural and developmental decision-making process, I've drawn the graph shown in Figure A.1, based on primarily subjective inputs but with some inputs backed by numbers. In particular, I found this article helpful:

http://msdn.microsoft.com/en-us/library/bb310550.aspx

This article objectively tests WCF performance against ASP.NET XML Web Services as well as other distributed processing technologies. Although REST-based services don't use the SOAP protocol, in which case a direct comparison of WCF performance in the referenced article and WCF performance here isn't necessarily exceptionally accurate, I believe it's indicative of the performance you can expect. WCF will be slightly slower from a performance standpoint, but it might be faster to implement and much faster to dynamically reconfigure than a pure IIS/ASP.NET approach. But also keep in mind that "slightly slower" could be mere handfuls of milliseconds. The importance of this depends on whether a handful of milliseconds per invocation matters to your application. Sometimes yes, sometimes no.

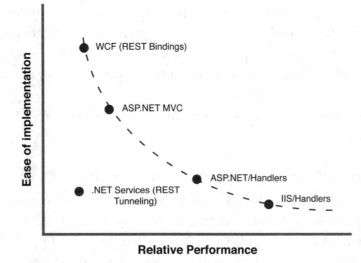

FIGURE A.1: .NET technology implementation versus performance

The graph shown in Figure A.1 merely says that, in general, you'll find that WCF is one of the easier .NET technologies you can use to implement RESTful services, but in terms of relative performance, you'll find that WCF throughput will slightly lag other implementations. Keep in mind the graph shows *relative* ease of implementation and *relative* performance. Your mileage may vary, and your own experience may differ. That's fine. Again, it depends. WCF is also configurable after deployment, and with minor changes you can shift from a SOAP-based service to REST and back again. That's much harder to do with the other technologies.

The slowest and arguably most difficult RESTful .NET technology to work with is the cloud services you find with .NET Services, if today you can even consider this technology RESTful. But as Chapter 9, "Building REST Services Using Azure and .NET Services," points out, if you need your services to run on your computer from your local network, .NET Services is the only option you really have. Again, it depends on your application requirements. And you can expect that future iterations of .NET Services will be easier to develop for and more capable as it moves from community preview to beta to a full-fledged and released technology.

You should find, however, that the highest service throughput will be gained by using IIS with custom `HttpHandlers`. The reason for this is simple: The less framework you place between yourself and the network interface card, the less processing the server must do to prepare a response. All the other .NET technologies are frameworks and impose some performance penalty/overhead, even if slight.

Putting the graph aside, here are some common questions and responses.

I'm creating a RESTful service from scratch. What should I use?

It depends. If you want to implement something in a day or two and you are comfortable with WCF, consider WCF until objective performance measurements dictate that WCF isn't handling the load. If you know and love the ASP.NET MVC framework, it's hard to beat using a service-based controller because it fits into the MVC framework so well. If later performance measurements tell you the controller isn't meeting performance needs, you can back out most of your code into an `HttpHandler` relatively easily. If you're more comfortable working with ASP.NET than the other technologies, by all means write an `HttpHandler` to support your service needs. If you're convinced you will need speed from the start, work directly with IIS.

I have an existing Web application and want to add a RESTful service. Should I (or do I need to) switch frameworks?

You might wonder why someone would ask that type of question, but in fact it comes up a lot. But don't take the decision to drop existing code to work with a new framework lightly. You have a lot invested in the existing application's code base, so keeping with the current framework is probably the best first step.

You have options as well, though, if you need them. If you're currently using pure ASP.NET, most of the RESTful services you've seen in this book were based on `HttpHandlers`, so adding a handler to your application is probably a great alternative anyway. But if you're using the ASP.NET MVC framework, keep in mind that the MVC framework is still based on ASP.NET, so adding an `HttpHandler` in that case isn't necessarily an inappropriate thing to do, especially if performance numbers dictate that stepping outside the controller-model architecture is necessary.

I hear arguments for and against using SOAP, or for and against using REST. Which is correct?

Both authors have been using SOAP since its inception and have written extensively on the topic. We know and love SOAP and the capabilities WS-* and the Web Service Definition Language (WSDL) bring to the party. But we see SOAP (and remote procedure call–based services in general) as a tool ideally suited for a specific range of tasks, and merely suitable for others. REST is similarly positioned, but the range of tasks differs. In the broadest sense, both technologies offer remote service-based functionality. But choosing one or the other depends on the specific requirements the service must fulfill and the architecture in which the service will operate. We don't see the argument as one being better than the other, but instead one will likely be more suited for the specific task at hand than the other, depending on the needs of the application.

Figure A.2 isn't meant to be all-inclusive of features each service model offers, but it hopefully portrays our thoughts regarding remote procedure–based services, especially those based on SOAP and WS-*, versus RESTful services.

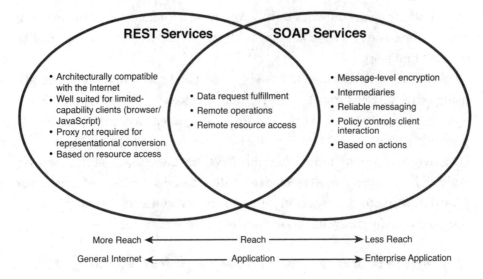

FIGURE A.2: REST/SOAP comparison

Both technologies will provide for remote operations and resource access. But if your application requires capabilities specific to WS-*, such as reliable messaging, message-level encryption, or intermediaries (the message is shuttled to several different services before being returned to you), then a RESTful solution probably isn't the best alternative. Opponents to REST argue that this is a limitation, but we say it's no more than a difference in architecture and applied use.

REST is architecturally compatible with the Internet itself, and any client application capable of making Web requests and interpreting the results is suitable for use with REST. You don't need fancy proxies, unless you want to encapsulate the Web request processing mechanics. No proxy is required to extract the response from a protocol-specific framing structure (like the SOAP envelope). Opponents to SOAP argue that the architectural complexities associated with SOAP are its limitation, but again we see the two types of service architectures as suitable for tasks in different task spaces.

REST, because it is suitable for any client that is capable of accessing the Internet, has the longest *reach*, or in other words, there are very few clients that cannot consume a RESTful resource (those that can't accept RESTful responses typically can't because of content type). SOAP-based services require specialized software on the client to fabricate the SOAP request and interpret the SOAP response. This limits the types of clients that can be used because processing SOAP queries can be complex, depending on the serialized data structures. For this reason SOAP-based services have less reach.

Considering the types of applications we might use remote services for, our experience has been that applications for general Internet consumption tend to be more suited for REST, whereas applications designed to be used within an enterprise tend to be more suited to SOAP and WS-*. This isn't a hard-and-fast rule but rather a generalization based on years of experience and hundreds of applications written. You should evaluate your own application's requirements and select the technology most appropriate for your application's needs.

The ASP.NET MVC framework has recently released and .NET Services hasn't been released. Should I be using them?

At the time this was written, the ASP.NET MVC framework was just released as a shipping product. After a well-executed period as a community preview, beta, and release candidate, I'm sure it has a robust feature set and the worst bugs have been ironed out. I'd personally feel very comfortable building live Web applications using the ASP.NET MVC framework.

As for .NET Services, I anticipate that changes will continue to roll out with each new preview release. Microsoft recommends not releasing production-level applications that are based on .NET Services technology, and given the changes I've seen in the past few preview release cycles, I believe that advice to be good advice. Instead, my recommendation is to keep your eye on the technology if it solves an application need or a requirement you anticipate coming about in the moderately near future. How soon "moderately near" might be is anyone's guess, but the technology is too compelling to drop sight of entirely.

As a parting thought, keep good design principles in mind. Loose coupling, high cohesion, and well-designed interfaces make shifting from RESTful framework to RESTful framework less painful should you need to do so. Also keep in mind efficiency and work to write performance-minded code. Even the fastest technology can become bogged down with poorly implemented logic and code. Keep your services simple, but not too simple (to paraphrase Mr. Einstein). Manipulate data as much as necessary, but no more than necessary. Drive responses to the client as quickly as possible with the fewest lines of code necessary to do the job.

■ B ■
HTTP Response Codes

THE INTERNET ENGINEERING Task Force (IETF) is in charge of many of the documents that govern how the Internet behaves. They call these documents RFCs, Request for Comments. You can find all existing RFCs at www.ietf.org/rfc/rfc####.txt where "####" is replaced by a four-digit, zero-padded representation of the RFC you want to look up. There are RFCs that define things you use every day. For example, RFC 2696 defines how to establish URI/URL/URN. RFCs 821 and 1939 define how to send e-mail using SMTP and POP3, respectively. In this appendix, we look at RFC 2616, www.ietf.org/rfc/rfc2616.txt, which defines HTTP. When you read this RFC, you will recognize the first name in the author list: R. Fielding from UC-Irvine. Yes, the person behind the REST ideas also defined how that architecture should be implemented. In this appendix, we primarily focus on section 10, which defines the set of status codes to return with any response to an HTTP request.

HTTP status codes have five defined ranges:

1. **1xx**: Informational HTTP codes. The request was received and is being processed.
2. **2xx**: Success codes. The request was received, understood, and accepted.
3. **3xx**: Redirection codes. The client needs to do something more in order to finish fulfilling the request.

4. **4xx**: Client errors. These are caused when the request contains a syntax error or cannot be fulfilled for another reason.

5. **5xx**: Server error. In this case, the request appeared to be valid but the server could not fulfill the request.

The HTTP specification has a list of specific values you can return and describes when a service should use any of the codes. This appendix looks at all the codes in RFC 2616. Before looking at what the codes are, let us examine how to view the status codes in a .NET application.

Some of the codes interact with entity-tags, also known as ETags. ETags are strings used to represent a resource. RFC 2616 defines two types of ETags: weak and strong. A weak ETag can belong to one or more entities. A strong ETag belongs to only one entity. You can spot the difference by looking at the ETag string. All weak ETags begin with the characters W/. All strong ETags start with any string other than W/.

Setting the Status Code

When returning an error, your code needs to get its hands on the `System.Web.HttpResponse` object. Typically, you will find the current instance hanging off of `System.Web.HttpContext.Current.Response`. Response has a member named `StatusCode` of type `System.Int32`. The value is an integer because it is possible to set the returned status code to something other than the set of approved, predefined values that section 10 of RFC 2616 suggests. For example, you can set the response with this line of code:

```
HttpContext.Current.Response.StatusCode = 200; //OK
```

Great, right? Maybe, but now you have some code that is a little harder to read or perform a code review on. You can make the code a bit more self-documenting by using the `System.Net.HttpStatusCode` enumeration instead. The `StatusCode` property still needs to support an integer for custom enhancements. When you use the `HttpStatusCode` enumeration whenever possible, code becomes easier to read. For example, the previous line can also read this way:

```
HttpContext.Current.Response.StatusCode = (int)HttpStatusCode.OK;
```

When status codes are used, there is a small set that every developer must understand:

- `200` OK, `HttpStatusCode.OK`: The request was received and everything worked fine. No errors at all.
- `400` Bad request, `HttpStatusCode.BadRequest`: The request that was sent over was just wrong. Don't send it again; it won't work then either.
- `404` Not found, `HttpStatusCode.NotFound`: The resource you asked for is not present.
- `409` Conflict, `HttpStatusCode.Conflict`: The client request could not be completed because the request conflicts with the current state of the resource.
- `410` Gone, `HttpStatusCode.Gone`: The resource used to be here, but it has left.
- `500` Internal server error, `HttpStatusCode.InternalServerError`: Something is wrong on the server. Ask the server owner to fix the problem and let you know when all is well again.

The following sections provide details about all HTTP status codes, the `System.Net.HttpStatusCode` value, and when the status code is appropriate in a RESTful service.

1xx **Informational Codes**

`100` **Continue,** `HttpStatusCode.Continue`

This response indicates that the client should continue with its request. Typically, the client sends a request with an empty body and the HTTP Expect header contains `100-continue`. When the response is received, the client sends the body of the message. Because your system will handle this transparently, you only need to understand this header in order to understand your transfer logs.

101 **Switching Protocols,** `HttpStatusCode.SwitchingProtocols`

The client will send an HTTP `Upgrade` header indicating the preferred protocol to use. If the server agrees, the response comes back and the HTTP connection gets closed. This might happen when the client supports moving from HTTP to HTTPS. If the server agrees, a `101` response will be returned. Again, this scenario is commonly handled by .NET and IIS.

2xx **Success Codes**

200 **OK,** `HttpStatusCode.OK`

This is a catchall code that indicates everything went fine. When the client sends a `GET` for a resource that can be found, return `OK`. By default, IIS 7 will return a `200` if everything appears to be successful.

201 **Created,** `HttpStatusCode.Created`

When your service creates a new resource as a result of a request, you should return a `201`. Because the resource ID is usually managed by the server instead of the client, the response should contain a link to the newly created resource. Place that link in the HTTP `Location` header within the response.

202 **Accepted,** `HttpStatusCode.Accepted`

In some cases, the client request cannot be processed immediately. By returning the code `Accepted`, the server tells the client that the request appeared to be fine. When returning this code, you should return an HTTP `Location` header indicating a resource that the client can retrieve to find out the status of the request as it proceeds through your system. If your Web service knows the location right away, return `HttpStatusCode.SeeOther` (`303`) instead of `Accepted`.

203 **Non-authoritative Information,** `HttpStatusCode.NonAuthoritativeInformation`

This status code indicates that the actual response headers did not come from the server that owns the resource. In this case, the response might have come from a cache between the client and the final server. You should not be using this response code in your RESTful Web services.

204 **No content,** `HttpStatusCode.NoContent`

Think of this code as void return code. The request succeeded, everything is okay, but the server is declining to return any more information. Return this code whenever your RESTful service succeeds and you have nothing more to say to the caller. This return value also means that whatever action happened, the client and server have the same view of the existing data.

205 **Reset content,** `HttpStatusCode.ResetContent`

This is another void return code. Like the 204, it means that PUT, POST, or DELETE succeeded and no other data is returned to the caller. Unlike a 204, this also means that the resource changed. The caller should GET the original resource again before showing or manipulating that resource any further.

206 **Partial content,** `HttpStatusCode.PartialContent`

Many services allow you to get part of a resource. For example, when a search is executed on any search engine, each page typically shows you a part of the list of results. When subsets of data are being returned, either through using the HTTP Content-Range header or through a protocol like OpenSearch, a PartialContent return code makes sense when the data being returned is a subset of the data contained by the resource.

3xx **Redirection Codes**

300 **Multiple choices,**
`HttpStatusCode.MultipleChoices/HttpStatusCode.Ambiguous`

HttpStatusCode defines two codes, Ambiguous and MultipleChoices, to 300. They mean the same thing to callers. It is possible to differentiate the representation of a resource depending on the set of values in the HTTP Accept headers. For example, many REST services can provide both a JSON and a generic XML version of a resource. If you choose to not serve a default version of the resource, return `HttpStatusCode.MultipleChoices`. In the body of the response, return a list of links with information about the representations that are available.

301 **Moved permanently,** `HttpStatusCode.MovedPermanently/HttpStatusCode.Moved`

`HttpStatusCode` defines two codes, `MovedPermanently` and `Moved`, to 301. They mean the same thing to callers. When a resource moves, the maintainer of that resource can either let calls to the old URI fail or forward the caller to the new home of the resource. If the maintainer knows the forwarding address, return `Moved`. The HTTP `Location` header in the response tells the caller where the resource lives. The body of the response can also contain a document with a link to the new home.

302 **Found,** `HttpStatusCode.Found/HttpStatusCode.Redirect`

`HttpStatusCode` defines two codes, `Found` and `Redirect`, to 302. They mean the same thing to callers. As a client, if you get this response, read the HTTP `Location` tag in the response and try the request again at the new location. With HTTP 1.1, issues around redirects were handled by creating codes `SeeOther` (303) and `TemporaryRedirect` (307), which have much more specific semantics. In general, do not return `Found` when implementing the server side of a RESTful service. Instead, use `SeeOther` (303) or `TemporaryRedirect` (307) as appropriate.

303 **See other,** `HttpStatusCode.SeeOther/HttpStatusCode.RedirectMethod`

`HttpStatusCode` defines two codes, `SeeOther` and `RedirectMethod`, to 303. They mean the same thing to callers. You use `SeeOther` when a resource has many representations but only one canonical URI. For example, a file-based resource can have two URIs that point to the same thing. The latest version of a file might be known by the URIs http://www.example.com/document/softwaredesign/latest.docx and http://www.example.com/document/softwaredesign/v3.5.2.docx. The v3.5.2.docx represents the canonical URI; latest.docx redirects to the canonical form. The HTTP `Location` header contains the canonical URI in the request response.

304 **Not modified,** `HttpStatusCode.NotModified`

Often, a client might already have a cached copy of a resource. The client knows when it retrieved the resource, so it knows how up-to-date the copy of that resource is. When requesting a new copy, the request can contain the HTTP `If-Modified-Since` header and set the header to the date the client last requested a copy. If the resource has not changed, the server should return `HttpStatusCode.NotModified`. Doing so uses minimal bandwidth for both the client and the server. This response can also be returned if the client set the HTTP `If-None-Match` header to an ETag that does have a match.

305 **Use proxy,** `HttpStatusCode.UseProxy`

Depending on the amount of volume a given resource or set of resources sees, it might make sense to spread the load across many proxies. The main data store will know who the proxies are and can filter out any requests from machines not on that list of proxies. The server must put the proper proxy to use in the HTTP Location header within the response. The location might be something that is geographically close to the caller or just a location representing a Web farm.

306 **Unused,** `HttpStatusCode.Unused`

Clients and servers do not use this code. Originally, the code was meant to be used by a proxy server to send the equivalent of `UseProxy` (305) from a proxy server. Do not use this code.

307 **Temporary redirect,** `HttpStatusCode.TemporaryRedirect/` `HttpStatusCode.RedirectKeepVerb`

`HttpStatusCode` defines two codes, `TemporaryRedirect` and `RedirectKeepVerb`, to 307. They mean the same thing to callers. This code is unlike `SeeOther` (303), in which the request is processed but the response is waiting at another URL. In the case of receiving or sending `TemporaryRedirect`, the server is telling the client two things: (1) the request was not processed at all, and (2) try the same request, including verbs, at the URL set in the HTTP `Location` header of the response.

4xx Client Errors

When receiving a 4xx-level status code from IIS and other Web servers, you frequently need to interrogate two levels of detail: `HttpResponse.Status-Code` and `HttpResponse.SubStatusCode`. The `StatusCode` property indicates the main reason something bad happened. The `SubStatusCode` property offers more specificity about why the client request is being refused.

400 Bad request, `HttpStatusCode.BadRequest`

Like other x00 status codes, BadRequest is the catchall status for the 4xx level. When none of the other codes applies, return `BadRequest` to tell the caller that the request cannot be processed.

401 Unauthorized, `HttpStatusCode.Unauthorized`

You receive this status code only when incorrect credentials, including *no* credentials, were used to access a secured resource. If your RESTful service happens to handle security, you will need to send this HTTP status code when the user is unauthorized. When responding with this error code, be sure to set the HTTP `WWW-Authenticate` response header, indicating the type(s) of authentication the server accepts. When you implement client code, you need to handle the cases in which the credentials passed in cannot be used to authenticate the client. Client code needs to grab the right set of credentials based on the `WWW-Authenticate` header. Typically, this involves properly populating the `System.Net.CredentialCache` that the client code uses. On IIS, an `Unauthorized` status code can offer additional levels of detail in the `HttpResponse.SubStatusCode` field:

- 1: The user credentials passed in are invalid.
- 2: The server and the client could not agree on an authentication mechanism. As a result, the caller cannot access the resource.
- 3: The user was successfully authenticated, but the resource's access control list (ACL) prevents the user from seeing the resource.
- 4: A filter handling authorization denied the request.
- 5: An application denied access to the resource.

402 **Payment required,** HttpStatusCode.PaymentRequired

This code does not have a defined meaning in the HTTP RFC. RFC 2616 states, "This code is reserved for future use." If you were to use this code, it might have meaning under the following context:

- Your Web service uses micro-payments to earn revenue. Users have a credit account that they draw from, pulling sums each time they make a call.
- The user authenticates properly against a resource they are authorized to use.
- The user does not have enough credit on account to execute the request.

Many Web services simply allow an end user to set up an account and then bill the user on a monthly basis against their usage. If your goal is to develop a service that doesn't surprise the user with new billing commitments, you should make the PaymentRequired status code part of your notification system. Otherwise, you should not use this status code.

403 **Forbidden,** HttpStatusCode.Forbidden

This status code indicates that the request was properly formed but the server refuses to do any work. A server can have many reasons for doing this, such as that only particular machines can carry out the work or for other policy reasons. This is distinct from ServiceUnavailable (503) status. If the service can be accessed only during a predefined schedule, use ServiceUnavailable (503). On IIS, a Forbidden status code can offer additional levels of detail in the HttpResponse.SubStatusCode field:

- 1: The user does not have permission to execute the requested page. For example, you might be trying to retrieve an ASP page or execute a CGI application.
- 2: The user does not have access to read the resource.
- 3: The user does not have access to write to the resource.
- 4: The page requires SSL (https) for any access.
- 5: Only 128-bit SSL can be used to access the resource.

- 6: The client is coming from an untrusted IP address.
- 7: The client must provide a client certificate.
- 8: The client cannot view any pages on the Web site.
- 12: The entity that maps the client certificate to a Windows account has denied access to the client.
- 13: The provided client certificate has been revoked.
- 14: The client requested some folder URL, like http://www.contoso.com/folder/. If the folder does not have a default document to show and the client does not have permission to list the contents of the folder, the client will be told that directory listing is denied.
- 16: The client certificate is not trusted or is invalid. For example, the certificate might be signed by an authority that the server does not trust.
- 17: The client certificate has a date range during which it is valid. `404.17` means that the current date is not within the date range in the certificate.
- 18: The requested URL cannot be executed in the application pool.
- 19: The server cannot execute CGI applications for the client in this application pool.

404 Not found, `HttpStatusCode.NotFound`

Whenever a resource request does not map to a known resource, return `NotFound`. It is possible that the resource did exist and was deleted. If the server does know that the resource URI used to be valid and the resource has been removed, return `Gone` instead of `NotFound`. If the resource has moved and the new location is known, return `Redirect` (302). On IIS, a `NotFound` status code can offer additional levels of detail in the `Http Response.SubStatusCode` field:

- 0: The resource does not exist.
- 2: An ISAPI or CGI restriction caused IIS to give up. Typically, this means that the service trying to be accessed, such as an ISAPI or other IIS extension is disabled.

- 3: The requested MIME type is restricted. Note that this does not mean that the file does not exist. A 3 means that the Web server did not even look because of the requested MIME type.

- 4: No handler is configured for the file type the client requested. With IIS 7, a file named `foo.bar` does not need to exist so long as some `IHttpHandler` or `IHttpModule` can see that URL and craft a response for `foo.bar`.

- 5: The request filter denied the response. The response never got anywhere thanks to the filter.

- 6: The verb in the request is not supported for the requested URL. If a URL only supports `GET` via its handler, then a `PUT` will generate a `404.6` response.

- 7: The file extension being requested is being denied. For example, requesting `global.asax` will generate a `404.7` response from an IIS Web server.

- 8: The namespace is hidden. Request a file like `web.config`, and you will see `404.8` returned from your IIS Web server.

- 9: The file exists but is currently marked as hidden on the file system.

- 10: The request header itself is too long. Processing stops and `404.10` gets returned to the caller.

- 11: URLs are frequently escaped. For example, a space becomes `%20`. When a URL is normalized to its unescaped form once, it goes to a normal form. If the normalized form runs through the process a second time, IIS expects the second iteration to be unchanged from the first. If there is a change, IIS responds with `404.11`: request contains a double escape sequence.

- 12: If the request contains an International Resource Identifier (IRI, RFC 3987) and part of the IRI contains non-ASCII characters, the server will return `404.12`.

- 13: The server read the `Content-Length` field. Because the client claims it will send an excessively large request, the server immediately gives up and responds with a `404.13`.

- 14: While processing the request URL, the server read too many bytes and is giving up now. It immediately sends `404.14` to the client. If your service runs into this scenario, a more appropriate response is `RequestUriTooLong` (414).

- 15: The query string is too long.

405 **Method not allowed,** `HttpStatusCode.MethodNotAllowed`

A server should return this code whenever the resource exists but the resource does not support the HTTP method the client used. For example, if a resource is read-only, any verb other than `GET` should return `Method NotAllowed`. This status code is distinct from `NotImplemented` (501). `Not-Implemented` signals that a standard or some other specification indicates that implementing the method could be a good idea but this particular resource chose not to implement the method. At some future time, the implementation might evolve to implement more features. `MethodNot-Allowed` tells a client that the reason the request is bad is that the HTTP method is explicitly being blocked.

406 **Not acceptable,** `HttpStatusCode.NotAcceptable`

A server returns this code when the client puts a set of restrictions in the HTTP `Accept` request header and the server cannot send a response that fits. Some servers choose to ignore the client's `Accept` header and instead send the preferred representation with an `OK` (200) response.

407 **Proxy authentication required,**
`HttpStatusCode.ProxyAuthenticationRequired`

A server never generates this code. As a client, you need to worry about this one. This is a proxy's version of `Unauthorized` (401). In this case, make sure that the client code has proper credentials for both the proxy and the server. You will run into this status code when deploying code on many corporate networks.

408 **Request timeout,** `HttpStatusCode.RequestTimeout`

When the client opens a connection to the server and then does not complete sending its request before some server-defined timeout, the server will send a `RequestTimeout` response and close the connection.

409 **Conflict,** `HttpStatusCode.Conflict`

Send out `Conflict` whenever executing the request would cause the caller to put a resource into a bad or inconsistent state. For example, a policy might be that `PUT/DELETE` changes are valid only if the caller has some token that shows that the caller knows about the latest version of the resource. A common database technique in SQL Server involves using a timestamp field. If the caller has a timestamp value that matches the value in the database, we know with reasonable certainty that the caller's modifications are against the most recent copy of the resource. If the value is different, the caller has an old copy and the change will likely cause a conflict. Another common example occurs when the client tries to put a resource in a place where an identically keyed resource already exists.

410 **Gone,** `HttpStatusCode.Gone`

This code is similar to `NotFound` (404). In this case, the service knows about the resource and knows that the resource has been removed. Do not return this code in response to a `DELETE` request. If a user tries to `DELETE` a resource once or a hundred times, the correct execution of a `DELETE` is OK (200). According to section 9.1.2 of RFC 2616, `GET`, `HEAD`, `PUT`, and `DELETE` are supposed to be idempotent.

411 **Length required,** `HttpStatusCode.LengthRequired`

For clients, your underlying .NET libraries will fill in the HTTP `Content-Length` request header. In the event that this header is not filled in, the server will reject the request, telling the client that the `Content-Length` header is required in order to process the message.

412 **Precondition failed,** `HttpStatusCode.PreconditionFailed`

Clients can pass preconditions to an HTTP server in a request. Only a subset of the precondition HTTP headers can return `PreconditionFailed`. These preconditions interact with `PreconditionFailed` as detailed here:

- `If-Match`: This parameter is intended to be used by `PUT` operations. If the value * is passed, the client states that the request should be performed only if the resource already exists. If any other value is passed, the value passed must be a valid entity-tag (ETag) representation of the resource. If the resource fails a match, the server returns `PreconditionFailed`.

- `If-None-Match`: When the client issues anything other than a `GET` or `HEAD` method, any matches will cause `PreconditionFailed` to be returned. When passing *, the client is asking to execute the method only if the resource in the URI does not exist. Any other value means to execute the method only if the ETag passed along does not exist.

- `If-Unmodified-Since`: This states that the URI plus method should perform work only if the resource has not been modified since the time specified by the client. If the resource has been modified, the server returns `PreconditionFailed`.

413 **Request entity too large,** `HttpStatusCode.RequestEntityTooLarge`

When the client tries to send data to the server, it fills in the HTTP `Content-Length` header. If the value in this header exceeds the server's maximum request size, the server sends `RequestEntityTooLarge` back to the client. A server will normally close the connection after sending this status code to prevent receiving the data the client wants to send.

414 **Request URI too long,** `HttpStatusCode.RequestUriTooLong`

Many servers assume that sensible URIs will be only a particular length. If a server receives a URL that exceeds this length, it will stop processing the request, respond with `RequestUriTooLong`, and close the connection. On IIS 7, the URL cannot exceed 4,096 characters.

415 **Unsupported media type,**
`HttpStatusCode.UnsupportedMediaType`

A server should respond with `UnsupportedMediaType` when the content of the request is in a format that the server does not understand or support for the current URI. This is different from sending in a request that identifies a supported media type, such as XML, but sends a different format, such as JSON. When the claimed media type and the actual media type do not match, respond with `BadRequest` (`400`).

416 **Requested range not satisfiable,**
`HttpStatusCode.RequestedRangeNotSatisfiable`

In this case, the client has set the `Content-Range` HTTP header to specify a range that is not available at the resource. When the server responds with `RequestedRangeNotSatisfiable`, the server should set the `Content-Range` HTTP header to the actual size of the representation.

417 **Expectation failed,** `HttpStatusCode.ExpectationFailed`

You can issue requests where you expect `Continue` (`100`) as a response. If all is well, then `Continue` will show up. When IIS wants you to give up, it returns `ExpectationFailed`.

5*xx* **Server Errors**

When a server returns a server error status code, it tells any clients that there is a problem at the server end. When possible, the server should set the HTTP `Retry-After` response header, indicating when things should be good again. In general, do not return too much information in a 5*xx* status response. With server-side errors, your focus should be on logging information on the server. You cannot depend on callers to send error pages back to you. A downside to giving debugging information to a caller is that the debugging information can also be used to figure out how to harm the server.

As with the 4*xx*-level status codes, your client code might need to interrogate two levels of detail: `HttpResponse.StatusCode` and `Http Response.SubStatusCode`. The `StatusCode` property indicates the main reason something bad happened. The SubStatusCode property offers more specificity about why the client request is being refused.

500 **Internal server error,** HttpStatusCode.InternalServerError

Many times, something went bad at the server, you know why, and telling the client will not make things any better. In this case, just tell the client that "things went wrong" and, if possible, fill in the HTTP Retry-After response header. On IIS, an InternalServerError status code can offer additional levels of detail in the HttpResponse.SubStatusCode field:

- 0: An error occurred while processing a module or ISAPI extension.
- 11: The application is being shut down and is not accepting connections at the moment.
- 12: The application is restarting and cannot accept connections yet.
- 13: The Web server is too busy and cannot process your request.
- 15: You tried to access Global.asax. This is a bad practice but is something that IIS does do. For your own Web services, you should return HttpStatusCode.Forbidden for a resource that someone is not allowed to access or HttpStatusCode.BadRequest if you do not want to tell the caller that the requested resource exists.
- 19: The resource you tried to access is incorrectly configured.
- 21: A module that was configured to process the request is not recognized. The module might not exist or it might be invalid in some other way.
- 100: ASP experienced an internal error.

501 **Not implemented,** HttpStatusCode.NotImplemented

When a RESTful standard is implemented, such as OpenSocial (www.opensocial.org), a complete implementation might have chosen to not implement parts of the standard marked as SHOULD, MAY, or OPTIONAL. According to RFC 2119, www.ietf.org/rfc/rfc2119.txt, an implementation can claim to support the standard without implementing the parts of the standard marked with these words. Return this code only if your endpoint received a valid request based on the endpoint and HTTP verb but your implementation has chosen to not implement the feature.

502 **Bad gateway,** HttpStatusCode.BadGateway

As a client, you get this value only from an HTTP proxy. This status indicates that there is a problem either at the proxy or between the proxy and the destination server. A RESTful Web service should never return this status code. On IIS, a BadGateway status code can offer additional levels of detail in the HttpResponse.SubStatusCode field:

- 1: A common gateway interface (CGI) application timed out. In this case, the problem is at the destination server.
- 2: The problem appears to be at the gateway.

503 **Service unavailable,** HttpStatusCode.ServiceUnavailable

This return value means that the service could not process the request due to "other issues." Those other issues include such things as too many requests or system maintenance. Set the HTTP Retry-After header if an estimated restore time is known. On IIS, a ServiceUnavailable status code can offer additional levels of detail in the HttpResponse.SubStatusCode field:

- 0: The application pool is unavailable.
- 2: The application has already exceeded the number of allowed concurrent requests. This is caused by a feature called request throttling. When developing an application, you might discover that having 100 concurrent users allows things to work just fine, but 101 users causes things to go into some sort of performance abyss where everyone has a horrible user experience. Throttling allows you to maintain a good user experience for the number of users the application can support.

504 **Gateway timeout,** `HttpStatusCode.GatewayTimeout`

As a client, you get this value only from an HTTP proxy. This status indicates that the proxy cannot contact the upstream server. A RESTful Web service should never return this status code.

505 **Http version not supported,**
`HttpStatusCode.HttpVersionNotSupported`

On IIS, this status code is supported by the Web server. A Web service should never send this response. Most HTTP clients know how to handle the status code as well. Just in case you find yourself needing to handle this status code, you need to be able to either try a different HTTP version or know how to give up. If you can change versions, the normal implementation pattern is to start with the highest version you understand and continue to downgrade versions until you reach a match or give up. Frequently, the Web server will return information in the response body indicating which versions of HTTP are supported. This information should be standardized based on the Web server software (Apache, IIS, and so on).

C.

REST Best Practices

M OST OF THIS APPENDIX is actually derived from RFC 2616, but some of it does come from Dr. Roy Fielding's dissertation (see Chapter 1, "RESTful Systems: Back to the Future," and Chapter 2, "The Hyper-Text Transfer Protocol and the Universal Resource Identifier"). My goal for producing this appendix was to provide a quick lookup for common situations when you're developing RESTful solutions.

Read RFC 2616 end to end at least once.

It is simply amazing how many Web developers have never read RFC 2616. Having done so several times while writing this book, I can say that even as I read it, I learn something new or see things in a new light each time I go through it.

But more important than simple knowledge is the understanding you gain in terms of REST and how HTTP supports REST at a transport level. The mechanics of REST are based on the capabilities of the HTTP protocol. To create truly RESTful services using .NET technologies, you must understand HTTP. So for homework, read RFC 2616 at least once, end to end. You might be surprised what you'll learn.

Know and understand what "safe" and "idempotent" mean, and make absolutely sure your services follow the guidelines for safety and idempotency set forth in RFC 2616.

Client HEAD and GET requests should in *no way* change the state of the resource. These HTTP methods should be safe, meaning accessing the RESTful service using these HTTP methods will in no way change the resource. HEAD and GET are joined by PUT and DELETE in supporting idempotency, which means that invoking the RESTful service using one of these HTTP methods once or a thousand times has the same effect. It's not an error to create the resource more than once, nor is it an error to delete it more than once. HTTP POST, of course, is neither safe nor idempotent.

Resources are "things," and the URIs that represent them should be based on nouns, not verbs.

When you use SOAP or XML-RPC, you are invoking a remote method, which is an action. Actions are verbs, and when you design remote methods, they're often designed according to the action they will take on your behalf.

REST, however, is based on returning representations of resources. Resources are "things," and "things" are nouns. Imagine the URI almost as the name of the resource, and any action you want to take with the resource is dictated by the HTTP method you provide to the service.

Every resource has at least one unique URI, and if you prefer not to use content negotiation, then each representation will have at least one unique URI.

Resources clearly must have a URI to be accessed via the Internet, but make sure that you don't employ tricky logic to support more than one resource (or representation) per URI. You can, however, use more than one URI per resource (or representation).

Service versioning is accomplished via URI, but resource versioning can be accomplished using the HTTP ETag header.

SOAP-based services are usually versioned by changing the URI, generally to include some sort of version number somewhere in the URI. But it's not unlikely that you'll want to version the resource, and to do that you would use the HTTP ETag header. ETag's meaning is resource-specific, but it can be handy for concurrency management purposes.

RESTful services do not maintain traditional ASP.NET application or session state.

They don't do so because maintaining such state means that two invocations cannot logically be idempotent. State should be maintained by the client. Application state, moreover, is to be provided through the use of links that are embedded in your service's responses. This is the concept of Hypermedia as the Engine of Application State, or HATEOAS. These links allow clients to maneuver through the Internet and choose their own path (which represents application state).

RESTful services should interpret and honor the Accept* family of request HTTP headers.

The client is communicating their desired response encoding through this family of headers. The HTTP Accept header is the most obvious, but Accept-Encoding and Accept-Language should also be considered. Many of the samples in this book took only the Accept header into consideration, but this was to provide meaningful services in a condensed form. Full-fledged services would also return their responses using the appropriate encoding and language.

RESTful services should return newly created resource representations in the HTTP entity body as well as a link to the new representation using the HTTP Location header, assuming that the resource is created immediately.

The client might have provided your service with enough information to create a resource, but your service should return the created representation to the client for that client's use. Often representations include some form of foreign key the client will need to cache for later use. Returning the newly created representation to the client removes the need for a second HTTP GET request to retrieve the representation. Assuming that you do create the new resource, be sure to include a link using the HTTP Location header and return the HTTP 201 (Created) return code. If you can't create the resource right away, you should return 202 (Accepted). If you return HTTP 202, you should include some status indication in the response entity body.

If your RESTful service is to be used by cross-domain clients, such as Rich Internet Applications (RIAs) based on Silverlight, be sure to provide the necessary cross-domain permission files.

As noted in Chapter 4, "Desktop Client Operations," Silverlight (or Flash) clients making RESTful calls to domains other than the domain that generated the client markup (called "cross-domain" calls) will require cross-domain permission files on the service's server. These files reside at "well-known" URI's and come in two flavors: Flash and Silverlight-specific. Flash clients will respond only to the Flash variety of policy file, but Silverlight clients can access either type.

The files are XML-based and signify what cross-domain clients the service can and cannot work with. For example, here is a Flash policy file:

```
<?xml version="1.0"?>
<cross-domain-policy xmlns:xsi=http://www.w3.org/2001/XMLSchema-instance
➥xsi:noNamespaceSchemaLocation="http://www.adobe.com/xml/schemas/
➥PolicyFile.xsd">
  <allow-access-from domain="*" />
</cross-domain-policy>
```

A corresponding Silverlight file looks like this:

```
<?xml version="1.0" encoding="utf-8"?>
<access-policy>
  <cross-domain-access>
    <policy>
      <allow-from http-request-headers="*">
        <domain uri="http://*"/>
        <domain uri="https://*"/>
      </allow-from>
      <grant-to>
        <resource path="/" include-subpaths="true"/>
      </grant-to>
    </policy>
  </cross-domain-access>
</access-policy>
```

Both of the files shown open access to all domains, but it's possible to limit access to specific domains. This URI provides a bit more information: http://msdn.microsoft.com/en-us/library/cc197955(VS.95).aspx.

The files have specific names and typically reside at the root of the domain (e.g.: `http://www.endurasoft.com/Clientaccesspolicy.xml`). The Flash file would be named `Crossdomain.xml`, while the Silverlight file would have the name `Clientaccesspolicy.xml`. Silverlight clients will request these files by name. When you use Silverlight to make a cross-domain call, Silverlight first submits a request to the RESTful service's server for `Clientaccesspolicy.xml`. If that returns a 404 (Not Found) response code, Silverlight then asks for `Crossdomain.xml`. If that request also returns a 404, Silverlight throws an exception and prevents the cross-domain RESTful service request from being issued. Note also that Silverlight honors Flash cross-domain policy files only if those files provide calling permission to "*" as shown here. If the domains are limited, Silverlight will refuse to make the service call.

Index

Symbols

A

X-Y-Z

Addison
Wesley

REGISTER

THIS PRODUCT

informit.com/register

Register the Addison-Wesley, Exam Cram, Prentice Hall, Que, and Sams products you own to unlock great benefits.

To begin the registration process, simply go to **informit.com/register** to sign in or create an account. You will then be prompted to enter the 10- or 13-digit ISBN that appears on the back cover of your product.

Registering your products can unlock the following benefits:

- Access to supplemental content, including bonus chapters, source code, or project files.
- A coupon to be used on your next purchase.

Registration benefits vary by product. Benefits will be listed on your Account page under Registered Products.

About InformIT — **THE TRUSTED TECHNOLOGY LEARNING SOURCE**

INFORMIT IS HOME TO THE LEADING TECHNOLOGY PUBLISHING IMPRINTS Addison-Wesley Professional, Cisco Press, Exam Cram, IBM Press, Prentice Hall Professional, Que, and Sams. Here you will gain access to quality and trusted content and resources from the authors, creators, innovators, and leaders of technology. Whether you're looking for a book on a new technology, a helpful article, timely newsletters, or access to the Safari Books Online digital library, InformIT has a solution for you.

THE TRUSTED TECHNOLOGY LEARNING SOURCE

Addison-Wesley | Cisco Press | Exam Cram
IBM Press | Que | Prentice Hall | Sams

SAFARI BOOKS ONLINE

Microsoft .NET Development Series

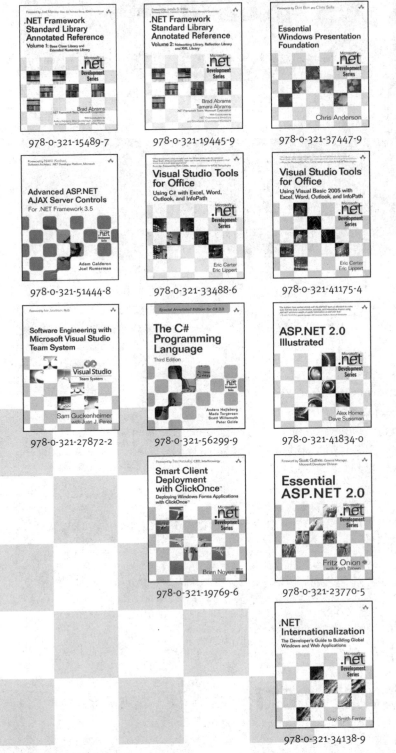

.NET Framework Standard Library Annotated Reference
Volume 1: Base Class Library and Extended Numerics Library
Brad Abrams
978-0-321-15489-7

.NET Framework Standard Library Annotated Reference
Volume 2: Networking Library, Reflection Library and XML Library
Brad Abrams, Tamara Abrams
978-0-321-19445-9

Essential Windows Presentation Foundation
Chris Anderson
978-0-321-37447-9

A Developer's Guide to SQL Server 2005
Bob Beauchemin, Dan Sullivan
978-0-321-38218-4

Advanced ASP.NET AJAX Server Controls
For .NET Framework 3.5
Adam Calderon, Joel Rumerman
978-0-321-51444-8

Visual Studio Tools for Office
Using C# with Excel, Word, Outlook, and InfoPath
Eric Carter, Eric Lippert
978-0-321-33488-6

Visual Studio Tools for Office
Using Visual Basic 2005 with Excel, Word, Outlook, and InfoPath
Eric Carter, Eric Lippert
978-0-321-41175-4

Domain-Specific Development
with Visual Studio DSL Tools
Steve Cook, Gareth Jones, Stuart Kent, Alan Cameron Wills
978-0-321-39820-8

Software Engineering with Microsoft Visual Studio Team System
Sam Guckenheimer with Juan J. Perez
978-0-321-27872-2

The C# Programming Language
Third Edition
Anders Hejlsberg, Mads Torgersen, Scott Wiltamuth, Peter Golde
978-0-321-56299-9

ASP.NET 2.0 Illustrated
Alex Homer, Dave Sussman
978-0-321-41834-0

The .NET Developer's Guide to Directory Services Programming
Joe Kaplan, Ryan Dunn
978-0-321-35017-6

Smart Client Deployment with ClickOnce
Deploying Windows Forms Applications with ClickOnce
Brian Noyes
978-0-321-19769-6

Essential ASP.NET 2.0
Fritz Onion with Keith Brown
978-0-321-23770-5

Essential Windows Communication Foundation
For .NET Framework 3.5
Steve Resnick, Richard Crane, Chris Bowen
978-0-321-44006-8

.NET Internationalization
The Developer's Guide to Building Global Windows and Web Applications
Guy Smith-Ferrier
978-0-321-34138-9

Visual Studio Team System
Better Software Development for Agile Teams
Will Stott, James Newkirk
978-0-321-41850-0

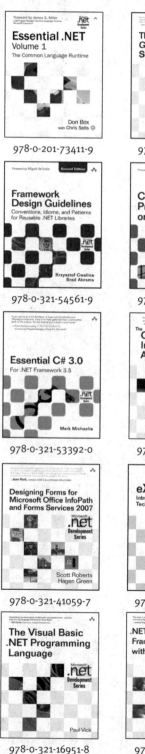

Essential .NET
Volume 1
The Common Language Runtime

Don Box
with Chris Sells

978-0-201-73411-9

The .NET Developer's Guide to Windows Security

Keith Brown

978-0-321-22835-2

Framework Design Guidelines
Conventions, Idioms, and Patterns for Reusable .NET Libraries

Krzysztof Cwalina
Brad Abrams

978-0-321-54561-9

Concurrent Programming on Windows

Joe Duffy

978-0-321-43482-1

Effective Use of Microsoft Enterprise Library
Building Blocks for Creating Enterprise Applications and Services

Len Fenster

978-0-321-33421-3

Essential C# 3.0
For .NET Framework 3.5

Mark Michaelis

978-0-321-53392-0

The Common Language Infrastructure Annotated Standard

James S. Miller
Susann Ragsdale

978-0-321-15493-4

Enterprise Services with the .NET Framework
Developing Distributed Business Solutions with .NET Enterprise Services

Christian Nagel

978-0-321-24673-8

Data Binding with Windows Forms 2.0
Programming Smart Client Data Applications with .NET

Brian Noyes

978-0-321-26892-1

Designing Forms for Microsoft Office InfoPath and Forms Services 2007

Scott Roberts
Hagen Green

978-0-321-41059-7

eXtreme .NET
Introducing eXtreme Programming Techniques to .NET Developers

Dr. Neil Roodyn

978-0-321-30363-9

Windows Forms 2.0 Programming

Chris Sells
Michael Weinhardt

978-0-321-26796-2

Essential Windows Workflow Foundation

Dharma Shukla
Bob Schmidt

978-0-321-39983-0

The Visual Basic .NET Programming Language

Paul Vick

978-0-321-16951-8

.NET Compact Framework Programming with C#

Paul Yao
David Durant

978-0-321-17403-1

.NET Compact Framework Programming with Visual Basic .NET

Paul Yao
David Durant

978-0-321-17404-8

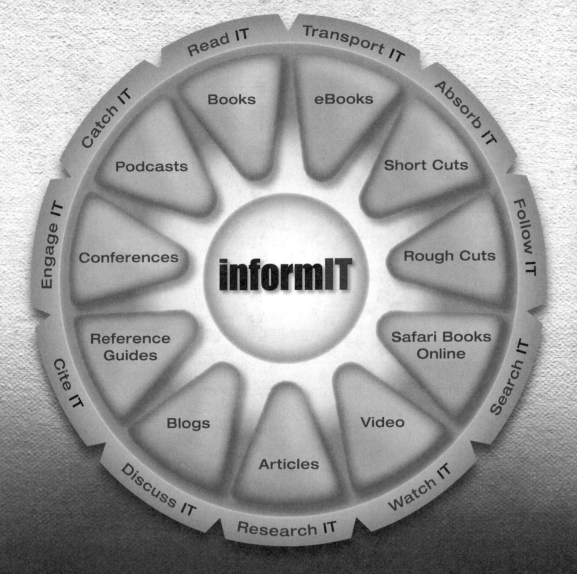

LearnIT at InformIT

Go Beyond the Book

inform**IT**

Read IT — Books
Transport IT — eBooks
Catch IT
Absorb IT — Short Cuts
Podcasts
Follow IT — Rough Cuts
Engage IT
Conferences
Cite IT
Reference Guides
Search IT — Safari Books Online
Blogs
Video
Articles
Discuss IT
Watch IT
Research IT

11 WAYS TO LEARN IT at **www.informIT.com/learn**

The online portal of the information technology
publishing imprints of Pearson Education